Economics and Sociology

Richard Swedberg

ECONOMICS AND SOCIOLOGY

REDEFINING
THEIR BOUNDARIES:
CONVERSATIONS
WITH ECONOMISTS
AND SOCIOLOGISTS

Princeton
University Press

Copyright © 1990 by Princeton University Press

Published by Princeton University Press, 41 William Street,
Princeton, New Jersey 08540

In the United Kingdom: Princeton University Press, Oxford

All Rights Reserved

Library of Congress Cataloging-in-Publication Data

Swedberg, Richard.
Economics and Sociology : redefining their boundaries :
conversations with economists and sociologists / Richard Swedberg.
p. cm.
Includes bibliographical references.
ISBN 0-691-04248-9 (alk. paper)
ISBN 0-691-00376-9 (pbk. : alk. paper)
1. Economics—Sociological aspects. 2. Sociology. 3. Economists—
Interviews. 4. Sociologists—Interviews. I. Title.
HM35.S93 1990   300—dc20   89-10964

This book has been composed in Adobe Laser Garamond

Princeton University Press books are printed on acid-free paper, and meet the guidelines
for permanence and durability of the Committee on Production Guidelines for
Book Longevity of the Council on Library Resources

Printed in the United States of America by Princeton University Press,
Princeton, New Jersey

     10 9 8 7 6 5 4 3 2 1
(Pbk.) 10 9 8 7 6 5 4 3 2 1

Designed by Laury A. Egan

Contents

Acknowledgments

THIS BOOK was conceived and written mostly during the academic year of 1987–1988, which I had the pleasure of spending at the department of sociology at Harvard University. In many ways it was the best year of my life, and I hope that some of the joy of being in Cambridge during those months is reflected in the book. I spent most of my days reading, buying books, talking to people, and slowly working my way through Joseph Schumpeter's work in the Pusey Archives. I originally envisioned this work as a book about Schumpeter and his views on economics and sociology. However, after reflecting for some time on *Capitalism, Socialism and Democracy* and similar works, I decided that the issues I really wanted to explore could be expressed much better in the present format.

My gratitude to the people who agreed to be interviewed is great. They very graciously allotted me time, sometimes during the weekends or in the middle of a busy week. Many other people were also quite helpful. My interviews with many of Schumpeter's students and colleagues, for example, often generated very profitable insights into the relationship between economics and sociology. I had several long and interesting discussions with Amitai Etzioni about "socio-economics." I also made an effort to look up and talk with the economists and sociologists who during the 1950s had tried to open a dialogue between economics and sociology. And finally, my friends and colleagues were extremely supportive. So special thanks go to many people for their patience and the friendliness with which they answered questions or were in some other way of assistance: Howard Brick (University of Oregon), James Buchanan (George Mason University), William Buxton (University of New Brunswick), Gösta Carlsson (University of Stockholm), Tom Colbjørnsen (The Norwegian Business School), James Duesenberry (Harvard University), Karl Eschbach (Harvard University), Peter Hedström (University of Chicago), Ulf Himmelstrand (Uppsala University), Barbara Hobson (University of Chicago), Irving Louis Horowitz (Rutgers University), Rosabeth Moss Kanter (Harvard Business School), Carl Kaysen (MIT), Arjo Klamer (University of Iowa), David Samuel Krusé (Boston College), Robert Merton (Columbia University), Lee Mintz (Harvard University), Trond Petersen (Berkeley Business School), Charles Perrow (Yale University), Paul Samuelson

(MIT), Edward Shils (University of Chicago), Hege Skjeie (The Institute for Social Research, Oslo), George Stigler (University of Chicago), Francis X. Sutton, and James Tobin (Yale University). For financial assistance during the project I am especially grateful to the American Council of Learned Societies, and especially to Steven C. Wheatley. I also thank Humanistisk-Samhällsvetenskapliga Forskningsrådet (HSFR) in Stockholm, Sweden, for all of its assistance. The economics editor at Princeton University Press, Jack Repcheck, has been of great help with his insight, support, and enthusiasm. Karen M. Verde saw to it that a lot of errors were avoided and that my language was improved. I should also mention that while working on this book, I met my wife—to whom it is dedicated. So if a tone of happiness is apparent in these pages, it has a very natural cause.

Stockholm
January 1989

Economics and Sociology

Introduction

> It is hardly possible to overrate the value, in the present low state of human improvement, of placing human beings in contact with persons dissimilar to themselves, and with modes of thought and action unlike those with which they are familiar. . . . Such communication has always been, and is peculiarly in the present age, one of the primary sources of progress.
>
> —**John Stuart Mill,** *Principles of Political Economy*

THIS BOOK has two main themes. The first is the need for more interaction and communication between economists and sociologists. These two groups have been estranged from each other for far too long, to the detriment of both. The second theme concerns the opportunity that now exists to break with old habits and to redraw the boundaries between economics and sociology. To redefine these boundaries is not an easy task nor a particularly rewarding one. The whole enterprise may seem peculiarly abstract and may appear, as do many methodological questions, to be something that can only divert attention from the real task of science, namely to solve substantial problems. In reality, of course, the issues are more complicated than that. The solution to a host of problems may be dependent first of all on whether the topic in question is classified as "sociological," "economic," or both; or, alternatively, whether the decision is made to apply a sociological perspective, an economic perspective, or a combination of both. It is also clear that if there is no effective communication between economists and sociologists, social problems will be analyzed as if they had no economic dimension, and economic problems will be analyzed as if they had no social dimension. This dissociation will lead to many difficulties, since most real problems are not as easily categorized under the rubrics of "economics" or "sociology" as are academic disciplines.

Still, it is difficult to find a way to talk about the kind of problems that one typically encounters in the interactions between two neighboring social sciences like economics and sociology. In addition, not very much is known about the relationship between economists and sociologists. It is relatively easy to find literature on economics and psychology, economics and history, economics and philosophy, and so on, but no equivalent literature exists about economics and sociology (see Hahn and Hollis 1975;

Hogarth and Reder 1986; Parker 1986). To some extent this situation reflects the fact that for a long time—more precisely from the 1920s to the 1960s—economists and sociologists have completely ignored each other and have gone about their research as if the other science simply did not exist. It is, for example, symptomatic that when James Buchanan published an article in the mid-1960s on "economics and its scientific neighbors" (Buchanan 1966; see also Leontief 1966; Olson 1969c), he discussed *nine* such "neighbors" and their possible contributions to economics ("spillins") as well as their incorporations of economics ("spillouts")—but sociology was not among them.[1] The rapport between sociology and economics improved somewhat in the 1970s, owing (among other things) to the work of Gary Becker. However, what caught the attention of most economists was perhaps not so much sociology as most sociologists know it, but rather the efforts of a few economists to take on topics that traditionally had interested only sociologists. Therefore, the situation in the 1970s and early 1980s was still largely the same as before.

There are several reasons for the alienation between economics and sociology during the twentieth century. For one thing, economics is a much older social science than sociology. The term "political economy" was introduced in 1615 by Montchrétien, while Comte used "sociology" for the first time in the 1830s. Economics severed its ties with reformism much sooner than did sociology, and also gained a place in the universities well ahead of sociology. In the 1930s and 1940s, economics experienced a rapid process of mathematization. On the other hand, sociology did not routinely adapt quantitative methods until after World War II. And mathematical sociology—which made its appearance in the 1960s—never became more than a minority movement.

However, it seems that this radical separation between economics and sociology is now coming to an end and that the interaction and communi-

---

[1] In a letter to the author dated March 10, 1988, Buchanan responded to my question about why sociology was not included in his article:

> My answer is simple. I do not know why I left Sociology out here. I think that those disciplines included were selected largely because I could isolate and identify features that did spill over, one way or the other, into Economics. Perhaps Sociology offered no obvious spillover, either way. . . . I agree that there is now much more intersection of interest [between economics and sociology], in part because the exchange–rational choice sociologists have now become more important. I foresee future development as blurring the distinctions between the social sciences generally, and not only between Economics and Sociology. Example: I have more in , common with Jim Coleman than with many of the more formal economists. The increasing emphasis by many economists on understanding the internal structure of organizations moves the two disciplines closer to each other.

cation between economists and sociologists is finally increasing. The trend of economists taking on traditional sociological topics—usually referred to as "economic imperialism"—continues to prevail. The fact that Becker was elected president of the American Economic Association for 1987 indicates that he no longer represents a minority perspective. After having mathematized those problems that are easily handled, the complexity of the unsolved problems also stands out with greater clarity. As a result, some economists have begun to use sociological insights in their work. George Akerlof perhaps best exemplifies the use of this practice, but there are several others as well. There are also signs that sociologists are becoming increasingly interested in economic topics. For example, after decades of slump, economic sociology is suddenly booming. An attempt to construct a new type of sociology, based on rational choice, is also being made. The key figure in this "rational choice sociology" is James Coleman, but several other people are also involved in this enterprise.

This beginning of a redefinition of the boundary between economics and sociology constitutes the major *raison d'être* for this book. I chose the interview form as a way to find out exactly what is going on at this moment at the interface of economics and sociology. What is happening today is very significant: *the border line between two of the major social sciences is being redrawn, thereby providing new perspectives on a whole range of very important problems both in the economy and in society at large*. After having been nonexistent for a large part of the twentieth century, there is now perhaps a chance for a meaningful interaction between economists and sociologists. Maybe it will even become possible again— as in the days of Adam Smith, John Stuart Mill, and Karl Marx—to get an analysis of central social problems that is informed by both economics and sociology. In a sense, then, things would simply be returning to normal, since the radical separation between economics and sociology is relatively recent.

In any case, since opportunities for fundamental change in the relations between two social sciences are quite rare, it seemed like a good idea to closely examine current developments in the form of a series of interviews with some of the major participants of this movement. The creativity and energy that are always expended at moments like this, should not be allowed to dissipate before a good debate between economists and sociologists has taken place. It is also important that many more social scientists take a good look at the issues at stake and express their opinion about the various alternatives. What is now occurring may very well affect both economics and sociology in a fundamental way.

Half of the scholars who have been interviewed for this volume are economists, and the other half are sociologists. All of the major strategies for redrawing the line between economics and sociology are represented in the book. There are interviews with those who want to extend the economic analysis to traditional sociological problems, as well as with those who want to extend the traditional sociological analysis to economic problems. Interviews with those who want to "import" some economic or sociological insights into their works have been included as well.

What unites the people who have been interviewed for this book is that they have all done work in the gray area between economics and sociology by tackling problems that cannot easily be compartmentalized into "economics" and "sociology." In the table of contents, the participants have been grouped into three rather loose categories: "the contenders," "the pioneers," and "the commentators." This classification is imposed primarily for practical purposes and it is not uncommon for a person to belong to two categories. Mancur Olson, for example, has been placed among "the pioneers," but he is of course also a "contender."

In principle, the "contenders" are those scholars who stand at the very center of the current debate. They are all well aware that the border line between economics and sociology is presently changing, and they also have a pretty firm idea of how they would like to see it redrawn. Among these people are Gary Becker, James Coleman, George Akerlof, Harrison White, Mark Granovetter, and Oliver Williamson. There is no doubt that the two key contenders are Gary Becker and James Coleman, both at the University of Chicago, and close colleagues as well as friends. Although Becker has held a joint appointment in the departments of economics and sociology since 1983, he is mainly concerned with how the neoclassical analysis can be extended to areas outside of the economy. Coleman, on the other hand, is trying to recast sociology on the basis of rational choice. Therefore, he is more concerned with maintaining certain traditional sociological features in the analysis than Becker.

George Akerlof's strategy—which he himself calls "psycho- socio- anthropo-economics"—is in many ways the opposite of Becker's. According to Akerlof, the traditional neoclassical analysis needs to incorporate certain traditional sociological insights (as well as certain psychological and anthropological insights) in order to advance. Oliver Williamson is also in favor of introducing more traditional social science into economics. His background basically stems from the tradition of behavioral economics, which was started in the 1950s at Carnegie Tech. Like Simon, Cyert, and March, he is involved in building up a novel type of economic theory on the basis of a mixture of new and old behavioral assumptions. Williamson's special brand of behavioral economics—transaction cost economics—falls somewhere between Becker's approach and a purely sociological approach.

The strategies of Harrison White and Mark Granovetter are quite similar, which is perhaps natural since Granovetter is a student of White's. Both are of the conviction that the advances of the economists into traditional sociological areas should be met by a sociological counteroffensive, which shows that sociologists are not only capable of handling their traditional problems better than the economists, but that they can also help to solve several of the problems that the economists have failed to explain. Granovetter feels that a "new economic sociology" is about to emerge, whose distinguishing mark is precisely that it tries to tackle economic problems; the "old economic sociology," he says, had much more respect for the economists' turf.

Since Becker and the others are the key players in the current debate, it was considered very important to try to find out more about their plans of action. How do they intend to go about realizing their plans? What progress can they report so far? What topics do they intend to work on in the future? These are some of the questions they answer in the interviews.

The "pioneers" include such people as Kenneth Arrow, Albert O. Hirschman, Mancur Olson, Thomas Schelling, and Neil Smelser. Like some of the founders of economics—Smith, Mill, and Marx, for example—they have all produced works that do not allow any easy compartmentalization into "economics" and "sociology." Several of these works were produced long before the current debate about the changing boundary between economics and sociology became fashionable. When they were written, many of these books seemed to be isolated products, and their authors, "lone wolves." Today they are more likely to be seen as early works in what may well turn out to be a major intellectual trend. Books that fall in this category include Kenneth Arrow's *Social Choice and Individual Values*; Smelser-Parsons' *Economy and Society*; Thomas Schelling's *The Strategy of Conflict* and *Micromotives and Macrobehavior*; Mancur Olson's *The Logic of Collective Action*; and Albert O. Hirschman's *Exit, Voice, and Loyalty*. The authors in this group have a lifetime of experience in trying to bridge the gap between a purely economic analysis and a more social analysis. Therefore, an effort has been made to tap as much of their vast knowledge as possible in the interviews.

The third group of people who were interviewed for this book have been placed in the residual category of "commentators." They have all made fundamental contributions to their respective sciences and, in the process, have come to reflect on the present interaction between economics and sociology. So even if the main thrust of their work has not necessarily been focused on the border area between economics and sociology, they are interested in problems of this type and are therefore well qualified as commentators. Among the sociologists, Daniel Bell, Aage Sørensen, and Arthur Stinchcombe fall in this category; and among the economists, one will find Amartya Sen and Robert Solow. Jon Elster, who is neither an economist nor a sociologist, has also been placed in this group. Elster is one of the few truly interdisciplinary social scientists of today, and this makes him a particularly interesting commentator.

The commentators clearly have less at stake than the contenders and are therefore well suited to pass judgment on these events. Several of them also have extensive experience within their respective fields. The combination of having no direct stake in the debate plus a firm knowledge of the foundations of their chosen disciplines should make the observations of these people quite enlightening.

Finally, it should be noted that each interview took between an hour and an hour and a half to conduct. Most of the questions were prepared in advance, although one or two extra questions were often added spontaneously. The main goal of the interviews was to have the people talk about their own research and their perception of the changing relationship between economics and sociology. Each person had been informed of the type of questions that were going to be asked well in advance of the interview. In order to put the person at ease and to make the interview more lively, it began with a few general questions. The interview focused on those works of the individual that were considered especially relevant in this context. The session usually ended with a broad question about what the person felt the relationship between economics and sociology might be like in the future. Most people were also asked what they thought of "economic imperialism" and the idea of a sociology based on rational choice. The editing of the transcripts has been kept to a minimum, and each transcript has been checked by the individual. In some cases, one or two additional questions were asked at a later date.

Background to the Present Separation between Economics and Sociology

In order to gain a better understanding of the current debate, it is useful to take a look at the history of the interaction between economics and sociology. Since this history is perhaps of more interest to the specialist than to the general reader, the latter might prefer to proceed directly to the interviews, and then to the concluding discussion at the end of the book.

As previously stated, there has been very little research on the relationship between economics and sociology. But even if many single pieces of knowledge are still missing, the main structure of the relationship can be discerned without too much difficulty. There are only a few different ways in which economics and sociology can be related to each other. One of the two disciplines can try to take over the subject matter of the other, which would constitute a case of "economic imperialism" or "sociological imperialism." Alternatively, they can each have their own distinct subject areas and ignore the other, as has been the case during the twentieth century. And finally, there can be open borders and free communication between economics and sociology, which it is hoped represents the direction in which things are currently moving. A number of economists are realizing that many economic problems are extremely complex and cannot be solved with traditional economics alone.

The early economists, such as Adam Smith, Karl Marx, and John Stuart Mill, are generally considered to have struck a happy balance between economics and sociology. They wrote about economic theory as well as social institutions with both ease and insight. It is true that "economics" and "sociology" did not exist as two distinct academic disciplines at that time, but it was of course perfectly clear to these economists when they were dealing with economic topics as opposed to social topics. What distinguished Smith, Marx, and Mill from many later sociologists and economists was their ambition to define economics in a broad manner and to be interested in the insights of the other social sciences. According to Mill, it was just common sense that "A person is not likely to be a good economist who is nothing else. Social phenomena acting and reacting on one another, they cannot rightly be understood apart" (Mill as cited in Marshall 1891, 72).

Mill's pragmatic attitude toward economic science was not popular in all circles, least of all with his colleague and one-time friend Auguste Comte. During the period 1830 to 1842, Comte published his encyclopaedic *Cours de Philosophie Positive*, in which the word "sociology" (*sociologie*) was used for the first time. It was also through this massive work that most nineteenth-century scholars came to know sociology. The thrust of Comte's argument was that knowledge and society are going through an evolutionary development from lower to higher stages, and that "sociology" represents the highest stage of human knowledge. In Comte's scheme, "economics" had no independent place, and *Cours de Philosophie Positive* actually contained a vitriolic attack on economics—that "alleged science," as Comte repeatedly refered to it (1869, 193–204). With their hairsplitting debates about concepts like "value" and "production," the economists were, in his opinion, no better than the scholastics. Apart from the work of Adam Smith, which Comte for some idiosyncratic reason exempted from his attack, he considered economics a thoroughly useless and metaphysical enterprise. The best one could do was to give it up and replace it with sociology, the "queen of all sciences."

The economists reacted very strongly to Comte's work, particularly in England, where his attack on economics was drawn into the British version of the *Methodenstreit* in the late 1800s. Alfred Marshall, John Cairnes, John Neville Keynes, and other prominent economists took Comte to task for his superficial critique. His argument was contested on point after point, and in the end nothing remained but the vain pretensions of his "sociology" (see Cairnes 1873; Marshall 1885, 33–38; 1891, 71–73; Keynes 1955, 112–41). John Neville Keynes summed up what the leading British economists thought of sociology around the turn of the century in his popular textbook *The Scope and Method of Political Economy*: "Comte charged political economy with being radically sterile as regards results. But what results has sociology, conceived as a master-science, dealing with man's social life as a whole, yet to show?" (Keynes 1955, 139).

Economists and sociologists got off to a bad start in the United States as well. By the 1890s, the *Methodenstreit* in its U.S. version—the "old" versus the "new" school of economics—was over, and what was now at issue was academic respectability. The economists were in the process of becoming professionals and wanted to rid themselves of reformism, amateurism, and the like. In brief, they wanted to have nothing to do with the sociologists (Furner 1975, 35–80, 291–312). First and foremost, the economists wanted the sociologists to stay out of economics and give up their Comtist ambition of being a "master-science." This demand led to a sharp clash between economists and sociologists around the turn of the century, which resulted in a minor flood of articles on the relationship between the two sciences (e.g., Giddings 1895; Patten 1895b; Sherwood 1897; Ward 1899). When one reads through these articles now, it is clear that the sociologists could not agree on what they meant by "sociology" and even less on what kind of relationship it should have to economics. A survey of the opinions of the sociologists on just these questions, which was conducted in the early 1890s, came to the conclusion that the situation was "chaotic" (Howerth 1895, 269).

At this time, the sociologists were particularly vulnerable to criticism from the economists, because they had not yet been able to get sociology accepted as a distinct area of study in the universities. An important confrontation with the economists took place at the meeting of the American Economic Association in 1894, which was held in New York. The economists explicitly told Albion Small and the other sociologists who were present that "sociologists have no right to stake off for themselves a portion of social science without the consent of the economists" (Patten 1895a, 108). The sociologists, who understood that their chances of getting into the universities would be slim without the support of the economists, decided to back off. They eventually got their own academic departments—but at the price of staying away from economics topics.

Sociology, which had been a science with the ambition to synthesize all knowledge, now became a "left-over science" that dealt with a series of miscellaneous topics, such as marriage, divorce, and deviance. One leading sociologist would in retrospect characterize it as follows:

> The attempt to legitimize sociology in academic circles on the ground that it had a subject matter of its own left to sociology, as Small put it, the unenviable role of studying the trivial and neglected aspects of the social world which were regarded as too insignificant to merit the attention of political scientists and economists. It meant, essentially, that the sociologists would have to feed on the crumbs that dropped off the table of these better-established academic disciplines. (Wirth 1948, 277)

The more grandiose ambitions of sociology were kept alive for a few decades longer in some European countries than in the United States. Emile Durkheim, for example, explicitly endorsed Comte's critique of the economists (Durkheim and Fauconnet 1903, 468–69; see also Durkheim 1981, 1067–68). In general, Durkheim had a strained relationship with the economists, which to some extent was caused by his backing of François Simiand's attempt to replace traditional economics with his own, rather odd version (Durkheim 1908; for Simiand, see Schumpeter 1949). Eventually, however, the Durkheimians had to capitulate and accept that economics was a distinct science, separate from sociology. But this did not take place until the 1930s, when the disintegration of Durkheimian sociology was already well under way.

The person in Europe who most accurately predicted the future relationship between economics and sociology was Vilfredo Pareto. After having made great contributions to economics, Pareto turned to sociology with vigor. His major work in the new genre, *Trattato di Sociologia Generale*, was to have a definitive impact on sociology, particularly in the United States. Of more importance in this context than Pareto's general contribution to sociology, however, was the very sharp line he drew between economics and sociology. His basic premise was that economics studies rational action, and sociology studies nonrational action—or, in Pareto's terminology, "logical" action and "nonlogical" action. According to Pareto, it was also obvious that it is much more difficult to make a good scientific analysis of "nonlogical" action than of "logical" action.[2]

---

[2] Pareto's argument on this point has been echoed by many people, especially sociologists. According to George C. Homans, for example, "Elementary economics was lucky in being able to take institutions pretty much for granted. It could leave the harder jobs of explanation to the other social sciences, and to this it may owe the fact that it has progressed more rapidly than they have" (1967, 49–50).

Around the turn of the century, it became clear that economics and sociology were also drifting apart in Germany. A few economists and sociologists, however, tried to keep the lines of communication open between the two disciplines. One of these was Joseph Schumpeter. As an economic theorist, Schumpeter identified with the neoclassical economics of the Austrian School, but he also had a lively interest in sociology. He was a member of the German Sociological Association; he collaborated with Max Weber; and he was the author of several penetrating sociological studies. To Schumpeter it was quite natural that an economist would be interested in sociology. For example, in an article on Pareto, he pointed out that "there is nothing surprising in the habit of economists to invade the sociological field. A large part of their work—practically the whole of what they have to say on institutions and on the forces that shape economic behavior—inevitably overlaps the sociologist's preserves" (Schumpeter 1951, 134).

Schumpeter considered economics a broad topic, and believed it should have good contacts with its scientific neighbors. In *History of Economic Analysis,* for example, he stated that economics consists of four "fields": "theory," "economic history," "statistics," and "economic sociology." His position on collaboration between economics and the other social sciences was simple and straightforward: "economic and noneconomic facts *are* related and . . . the various social sciences *should* be related to one another" (Schumpeter 1954, 12–24).[3]

Among the German sociologists it was Max Weber in particular who tried to keep the lines of communication open between economics and sociology. As a young man, according to Marianne Weber (1975, 200), he had decided to leave law for economics because the latter was a much younger and more flexible science. The *Methodenstreit* between the neoclassical economists and the historical economists disturbed Weber very much, and he did what he could to reconcile the two parties and to prevent a total deadlock. This was clearly stated in his famous essay " 'Objectivity' in the Social Sciences," which was published in 1904 when Weber became the editor for *Archiv für Sozialwissenschaft und Sozialpolitik.* It was here that he launched the notion of an "ideal type," which is generally seen as an attempt to mediate between the analytical and the historical modes of analysis. In the same essay, Weber (1949, 65; 1951, 163) also argued that *Archiv* should be devoted to "the science of social-economics" ("*die sozialökonomische Wissenschaft*"), by which he roughly meant a broad type of economics, including not only neoclassical theory, but also economic history and economic sociology. The same attempt to rec-

---

[3] It should be stressed that Schumpeter was in no way interested in moving economics and sociology unduly close together. "Cross-fertilization might easily result in cross-sterilization," as he put it in his *History of Economic Analysis* (Schumpeter 1954, 27).

oncile the opposing factions in German economics characterizes the giant handbook of economics—*Grundriss der Sozialökonomik*—which Weber undertook to edit in the early 1900s. In the introductory essay to this work, he said that he had decided to invite contributions from all the different methodological perspectives, since "in the last hand all roads [in economics] come together" (Bücher et al. 1914, viii). Among the contributors to the handbook one can, for example, find neoclassical theorists like Schumpeter and von Wieser, historical economists like Bücher and Sombart, and sociologists like Robert Michels and Weber himself.

By the 1920s and 1930s, it was already evident that sociology and economics were drifting apart, despite efforts to the contrary by theorists like Schumpeter and Weber. The idea that economics addresses only rational behavior, and sociology addresses only irrational behavior—which for Pareto had been a convenient way of separating the two disciplines—was now turned into a reason for economists to ignore sociology. In the influential *Foundations of Economic Analysis* by Paul Samuelson (1947, 90), we thus read that "many economists would . . . separate economics from sociology upon the basis of rational or irrational behavior."[4] By the end of the 1940s, economists and sociologists knew little about each other's works and were often hostile to each other. In the late 1940s, when Schumpeter was writing *History of Economic Analysis,* he noted that

> ever since the eighteenth century both groups [that is, economists and sociologists] have grown steadily apart until by now the modal economist and the modal sociologist know little and care less about what the other does, each preferring to use, respectively, a primitive sociology and a primitive economics of his own to accepting one another's professional results—a state of things that was and is not improved by mutual vituperation. (Schumpeter 1954, 26–27)

During the period 1930 to 1950, there seems to have been virtually a complete separation between economics and sociology. In concrete terms this often meant that the economists tried to analyze economic problems while abstracting from social forces, and that the sociologists tried to analyze social problems while abstracting from economic forces. During these years, the United States replaced continental Europe as the center of the social sciences, and the lines of communication between economists and sociologists were for various reasons much worse in America than in Europe.[5] At the most there was a handful of American scholars who were

---

[4] In a letter to the author dated January 23, 1986, Paul Samuelson writes, "Yes, my p. 90 *Foundations* remark [about the difference between economics and sociology] did trace to Pareto."

[5] It was also in Europe and not in the United States that a more sociologically oriented type of economic analysis would be created during this period, especially through the works of

interested as well as competent in both sciences. Among the sociologists, W. F. Ogburn and Talcott Parsons can be mentioned, and among the economists, Frank Knight in particular had a broad knowledge in the other social sciences. One of the few instances of interaction between economists and sociologists during these years took place between Knight and Parsons. Symbolically enough, the two had been brought together by their interest in Max Weber, and they corresponded quite a bit with each other, especially in the 1930s.[6] Knight translated Weber's *General Economic History* and basically felt that economists should be knowledgeable in both theoretical logic and the history of economic institutions. One of the metaphors Knight (1927, xv) liked to use in this context was that of the "methodological triangle" with its three "corners": "general deductive theory," "psychological and historical interpretation," and "statistical study." At this time, Parsons was also "very much occupied . . . with problems on the border line of economics and sociology," as he put it in a letter to Adolph Löwe (Parsons 1940). Many of his articles from the 1930s reflected this interest and contained an insightful discussion of the relationship between economics and sociology. From a current perspective, it is interesting to read Parsons's discussion from 1934 in *The Quarterly Journal of Economics* of "economic imperialism," a term which, it seems, Ralph William Souter had introduced into economic discourse in the early 1930s.[7] Parsons basically felt that there were more disadvantages

---

Keynes and the various members of the Stockholm School (see in this context, e.g., Lekachman 1957; Shackle 1967; and Wiley 1983). A special mention should also be made of Adolph Löwe's little book from these years, *Economics and Sociology: A Plea for Cooperation in the Social Sciences* (1935).

[6] I am grateful to William Buxton for having drawn my attention to this correspondence, which can be found in the archives of Chicago University and Harvard University. See HUG(FP) 42.8.2, box 3, at the Harvard University Archives, and box 61, folder 14, of the Frank Knight Papers at the Chicago University Archives. In this context it can also be noted that Weber apparently had little impact on Knight. According to a letter from Edward Shils to the author, dated April 22, 1988, "Although Frank Knight studied Max Weber's *Wirtschaft und Gesellschaft* intensively—at least certain parts of it, particularly the chapter which is devoted to the fundamental sociological categories of economics—it had practically no influence on Frank Knight's own economic analysis."

Later in life, Knight came to regret that he had not let himself be more influenced by Weber. Just after his retirement, when asked by a student, "If you could do it again, what would you do differently?" he replied, "There has been the work of one man whom I have greatly admired. If I were to start out again, I would build upon his ideas. I am referring of course to Max Weber." (Schweitzer 1975, 280).

[7] See Souter 1933, 94–95. The key section is the following:

The salvation of Economic Science in the twentieth century lies in an enlightened and democratic "economic imperialism," which invades the territories of its neighbors, not to enslave them or to swallow them up but to aid and enrich them and promote their autonomous growth in the very process of aiding and enriching itself.

than advantages to economic imperialism. He summed up his position in the following way: "economic imperialism . . . results not only in enriching these neighbouring 'countries,' which of course it does, but in putting some of them into a strait jacket of 'economic' categories which is ill-suited to their own conditions" (Parsons 1934, 512).

The Knight-Parsons dialogue ended in 1940 with an angry public exchange. Perhaps by this time Knight had also had enough of Parsons's penchant for abstract theorizing. In any event, Knight was the originator of one of the better jokes about sociology, and he may very well have had Parsons in mind when he formulated it: "Sociology is the science of talk, and there is only one law in sociology. Bad talk drives out good talk" (Knight as cited in Samuelson 1983, 161).[8]

During the period 1950 to 1980, there was very little interaction between economists and sociologists, perhaps even less than before. However, there was one exception, and that was at Harvard, where in the early 1950s some young economists and sociologists got together.[9] The sociologists included Francis X. Sutton, Talcott Parsons, and Neil Smelser; and the economists included James Duesenberry, Carl Kaysen, and James Tobin. Each of these groups became curious about what was going on in the other science. The result was a course, "The Sociological Analysis of Economic Behavior," which was taught from 1951 to 1956 at Harvard, first by Duesenberry and Sutton and later by Duesenberry and Smelser. Several books were also produced, including *The American Business Creed* by Sutton, Harris, Kaysen, and Tobin; *Economy and Society* by Smelser and Parsons; and *The Sociology of Economic Life* (1963) by Smelser. The years between 1951 and 1954 represented the high point of this collaborative enterprise; after that a certain fatigue and disillusionment seems to have

---

Under such circumstances, occasional armed conflict among the sciences is inevitable. Such conflicts must be conducted according to the rules of civilized warfare; and it is the duty of each science to subordinate its strategy, as best it knows how, to the ultimate goal of the harmonious unification of knowledge. Mistakes and injustices are bound to occur from time to time; but the "science" which cannot maintain its integrity and vitality in such an environment deserves to perish. And, for *any* science, a cowardly isolationist pacifism which cries peace! peace! when there is no peace is the stigma of intellectual disintegration and decay.

[8] Another good joke about sociology from this period is Schumpeter's comment that parts of Parsons's *Structure of Social Action* "become fully understandable only if translated into German." See Schumpeter's letter dated December 23, 1936, to the Committee on Research in the Social Sciences in the Harvard University Archives, UAV 737.32, box 6, folder "Parsons' Mss: Criticism of Readers." (The quote is reprinted by permission of the Harvard University Archives.)

[9] Information for the following section comes from interviews with James Duesenberry, Carl Kaysen, Neil Smelser, Francis X. Sutton, and James Tobin. The interviews were conducted during the spring of 1988.

set in. Sutton, for example, claims that the effort failed because no high quality research was produced that professional economists would take seriously. It also seems that Parsons's and Smelser's analysis in *Economy and Society* was not very highly regarded by the other people involved in this attempt to unite economics and sociology.

Aside from this effort at Harvard, economists and sociologists continued to work in isolation from each other during this time. This often led the two disciplines to develop something of a caricature of the other science. The economists, as Schumpeter put it, developed a "primitive sociology" and the sociologists, a "primitive economics." This can be seen, for example, by looking at the works in industrial sociology and labor economics from these days (e.g., Granovetter 1988, 11). But this was not always the case, and the emergence of "behavioral economics" at about this time was clearly an exception. At Carnegie Tech, a group of brilliant scholars led by Herbert Simon began to develop a new type of economic theory, which was much more informed by sociology (and psychology) than neoclassical economics. By the mid-1960s the three great contributions of behavioral economics had been formulated: the notion of bounded rationality; the behavioral theory of the firm; and a new view on organization theory.

Behavioral economics, however, did not succeed in changing mainstream economics, where the old separation between economics and sociology continued as before.[10] The absence of a dialogue between economists and sociologists, combined with a feeling among the economists that their science was clearly superior, is perhaps what accounts for the emergence of "economic imperialism" at about this time. In the late 1950s, the first two works in this genre appeared: Gary Becker's *The Economics of Discrimination*, and Anthony Downs's *An Economic Theory of Democracy*. They were soon to be followed by many others, and during the 1960s and the 1970s the economic perspective was used to analyze a host of new topics. By the 1980s, "economic imperialism" had made forays into the following areas: law (e.g., Coase, Posner, Demsetz); history (e.g., Fogel, North); organization theory (e.g., Alchian-Demsetz, Williamson); sociology (e.g., Becker, Olson); education (e.g., Becker, Schultz); and political science (e.g., Downs, Buchanan, Niskanen, Tullock).[11]

[10] Another interesting attempt to bring economics and sociology a little bit closer to each other took place in the 1950s at Columbia University under the guidance of Paul Lazarsfeld. The classic book on game theory, *Games and Decisions* by R. Duncan Luce and Howard Raiffa, was for example written as part of a program at Columbia called the Behavioral Models Project, which had been started in 1952 on the initiative of Lazarsfeld and Herbert Solomon. Lazarsfeld also brought William Baumol and William Vickrey to Columbia to teach him Markov chains and utility theory. His irritation at his fellow sociologists for their "ideological bias against business" is clear from his writings, especially "Reflections on Business" (1959).

[11] The literature on economic imperialism is extensive and growing. For good overviews,

Some of the works from the period 1950–1980 that are important to the dialogue between economists and sociologists were produced by economists who are *not* identified with economic imperialism. Albert O. Hirschman, Kenneth Arrow, and Thomas Schelling belong in this category. They have all raised questions in economics that are relevant for sociology—but in a way that is much less hostile to traditional sociology than economic imperialism.

As a result of the pressure created by economic imperialism, sociologists eventually decided to approach economic topics on their own. The first one to do so was Harrison White in the 1970s. When presenting his research on "Markets as Social Structures" at a meeting of the American Sociological Association in 1979, he said that, since Becker and other economists had begun to analyze sociological problems, sociologists should take on economic problems (White 1979). Granovetter's work in economic sociology can to some degree also be seen as a reaction to the economists' excursions into sociology (Granovetter 1985; see also Oberschall and Leifer 1985). It should also be noted in this context that White's and Granovetter's works only represent the tip of the iceberg, insofar as "new economic sociology" is concerned. Many sociologists are currently working on economic topics, and economic sociology is booming.[12]

Similar progress may soon take place for "rational choice sociology." James Coleman is the leading scholar here, but several other sociologists—both American and European—are involved as well.[13] From a theoretical perspective, there might be sharp differences between the "new economic sociology" and "rational choice sociology." In reality, however, the lines are not all that clear and the two are interrelated in interesting

---

see especially Tullock 1972; Stigler 1984; Hirshleifer 1985; Tullock and McKenzie 1985; Udéhn 1986; Radnitzky and Bernholz 1987.

[12] Some works in this genre are: Makler, Martinelli, and Smelser 1982; Stinchcombe 1983; Zelizer 1983, 1985; Adler and Adler 1984; Kanter 1984; Heimer 1985; Etzioni 1988. See also the references cited in the interview from 1986 with Mark Granovetter, and in Swedberg 1987, 63–119.

[13] For a sample of Coleman's writings, see, e.g., Coleman 1984, 1986b, 1987a, 1987b, 1988a, 1988b. Also in this context, see Hechter 1983, 1987; Lindenberg 1985, 1988; Opp 1978, 1983, 1985. The center for rational choice sociology in Europe is in Holland, more precisely The Interuniversity Center for Sociological Theory and Methodology (ICS). ICS was founded in 1986 by the Universities of Groningen and Utrecht and currently has twenty-four graduate students and a scientific directorship consisting of four professors (Siegwart Lindenberg, Frans Stokman, Albert Verbeek, and Reinhard Wippler). According to a letter dated December 12, 1988, to the author from Siegwart Lindenberg, ICS "has been built with the aim of integrating rational choice sociology with quantitative empirical research. This combination does not exist very often because RC people are mostly not so handy with setting up, conducting and analyzing empirical research and vice versa."

and unpredictable ways. This is also true for economic imperialism and its interaction with traditional social science. From one viewpoint, economic imperialism is clearly an expression of economics turning inward and isolating itself. But from another viewpoint, it represents the beginning of a dialogue between economics and the other social sciences.

On Interpreting the Interviews

Interviews of the type contained in this book can be interpreted in several ways. There is, for example, the "rhetoric of economics" approach, which has been made popular through the works of Donald McCloskey (1983, 1986), and Arjo Klamer (1984). The emphasis here is on the disjunction between economics, as it is presented in various official contexts, and the way economists actually "do" economics. The basic idea is that the philosophy of science, which is embodied in the official rhetoric, differs from the "workaday" rhetoric of most economists. From this perspective, interviews become a way of getting at the more truthful and interesting type of economic discourse. This is reflected, for example, in Klamer's interview style in his enjoyable book *The New Classical Macroeconomics.* He fires his questions very quickly, switches to new topics, and in other ways tries to break through "the official rhetoric." The interview style in this book differs in several ways from that of Klamer. Fewer questions were asked, and the persons who were being interviewed were pretty much allowed to proceed at their own pace. The main point was always to get them to discuss topics about which they had thought a great deal, but about which they would not necessarily write. Whether this approach was successful is something the reader should decide. My own evaluation can be found at the end of the book in the chapter entitled "Concluding Discussion."

It is not necessary to read the interviews in the order in which they have been placed in the book. Part of the enjoyment in reading this kind of book is that one can pretty much dip into the text wherever one pleases. The reader is nonetheless strongly urged to start out by reading the interviews with Gary Becker and James Coleman, since it is their effort to create a new Economic-Sociological Man that constitutes the natural focus of the book.

Finally, I hope that the reader will enjoy the interviews. Some of today's most interesting economists and sociologists here give freely of their ideas on two of the great themes in social science: *economy* and *society.* What is at stake today is how these two concepts can be brought closer to each other and how a fruitful dialogue may be opened up between economists and sociologists. If that would happen—and there now seems to be a chance that it will—we can look forward to a very interesting time in economics as well as in sociology.

References

Adler, Patricia A., and Peter Adler, eds., 1984. *The Social Dynamics of Financial Markets*. Greenwich, Conn.: JAI Press.

Arrow, Kenneth J. 1963a. *Social Choice and Individual Values*. 2d ed. New Haven, Conn.: Yale University Press. Originally appeared in 1951.

Becker, Gary. 1957. *The Economics of Discrimination*. Chicago: University of Chicago Press. 2d ed. 1971.

Buchanan, James M. 1966. "Economics and Its Scientific Neighbors." In *The Structure of Economic Science*, edited by S. R. Krupp, 166–83. Englewood Cliffs, N.J.: Prentice-Hall.

Buchanan, James M., and Gordon Tullock. 1962. *The Calculus of Consent: Logical Foundations of Constitutional Democracy*. Ann Arbor: University of Michigan Press.

Bücher, Karl, et al. 1914. "Vorwort." In *Grundriss der Sozialökonomik. I. Abteilung, Wirtschaft und Wirtschaftswissenschaft.* by Bücher, et al., vii–ix. Tübingen: J.C.B. Mohr.

Cairnes, John. 1873. "M. Comte and Political Economy." In *Essays in Political Economy*, 265–311. London: Macmillan.

Coleman, James S. 1984. "Introducing Social Structure into Economic Analysis." *American Economic Review* 74(2):84–88.

————. 1986b. "Social Theory, Social Research and A Theory of Action." *American Journal of Sociology* 91:1309–35.

————. 1987a. "Microfoundations and Macrosocial Behavior." In *The Micro-Macro Link*, edited by Jeffrey C. Alexander, et al., 153–76. Berkeley: University of California Press.

————. 1987b. "Norms as Social Capital." In *Economic Imperialism: The Economic Approach Applied Outside the Field of Economics*, edited by Gerard Radnitzky and Peter Bernholz, 135–55. New York: Paragon House.

————. 1988a. "Free Riders and Zealots: The Role of Social Networks." *Sociological Theory* 6:52–57.

————. 1988b. "Social Capital in the Creation of Human Capital." *American Journal of Sociology* 94:S95–S120.

Comte, Auguste. 1869. *Cours de Philosophie Positive*. vol. 4. Paris: J. B. Ballière.

Downs, Anthony. 1957. *An Economic Theory of Democracy*. New York: Harper and Row.

Durkheim, Emile, and Paul Fauconnet. 1903. "Sociologie et Sciences Sociales." *Revue Philosophique* 55 (Janvier à Juin):465–97.

————. 1908. "Discussion at Société d'Economie Politique." *Journal des Economistes* 18:108–21.

————. 1981. "The Realm of Sociology as A Science." *Social Forces* 59 (June):1054–70.

Etzioni, Amitai. 1988. *The Moral Dimension: Toward A New Economics.* New York: Free Press.

Furner, Mary O. 1975. *Advocacy & Objectivity: A Crisis in the Professionalization of American Social Science, 1865–1905.* Lexington: University Press of Kentucky.

Giddings, Franklin H. 1895. "Utility, Economics and Sociology." *Annals of the American Academy of Political and Social Science* 5 (July 1894–June 1895):398–404.

Granovetter, Mark. 1985. "Economic Action and Social Structure: The Problem of Embeddedness." *American Journal of Sociology* 91:481–510.

————. 1987. "Interview: On Economic Sociology." *Research Reports from the Department of Sociology, Uppsala University* 1987:1.

————. 1988. "The Old and the New Economic Sociology: A History and an Agenda." Paper presented at the first annual seminar of the Center for Economy and Society, University of California at Santa Barbara.

Hahn, Frank, and Martin Hollis, eds. 1975. *Philosophy and Economic Theory.* Oxford: Oxford University Press.

Hechter, Michael, ed. 1983. *The Microfoundations of Macrosociology.* Philadelphia: Temple University Press.

————. 1987. *Principles of Group Solidarity.* Berkeley: University of California Press.

Heimer, Carol A. 1985. *Relative Risk and Rational Action: Managing Moral Hazard in Insurance Contracts.* Berkeley: University of California Press.

Hirschman, Albert O. 1970. *Exit, Voice, and Loyalty: Responses to Decline in Firms, Organizations, and States.* Cambridge: Harvard University Press.

Hirshleifer, Jack. 1985. "The Expanding Domain of Economics." *American Economic Review* 75 (December):53–68.

Hogarth, Robin M., and Melvin M. Reder, eds. 1986. *Rational Choice: The Contrast between Economics and Psychology.* Chicago: University of Chicago Press.

Homans, George C. 1967. *The Nature of Social Science.* New York: Harcourt, Brace and World.

Howerth, Ira W. 1895. "Present Condition of Sociology in the United States." *Annals of the American Academy of Political and Social Science* 5 (July 1894–June 1895):260–69.

Kanter, Rosabeth Moss. 1984. *The Change Masters: Corporate Entrepreneurs at Work.* London: George Allen and Unwin.

Keynes, John Neville. 1955. *The Scope and Method of Political Economy.* New York: McGraw-Hill. Originally appeared in 1891.

Klamer, Arjo. 1984. *The New Classical Macroeconomics: Conversations with the New Classical Economists and Their Opponents.* Brighton: Wheatsheaf Books.

Knight, Frank H. 1927. "Translator's Preface." In *General Economic History,* by Max Weber, xv–xvi. New York: Greenberg Publishers.

Lazarsfeld, Paul F. 1959. "Reflections on Business." *American Journal of Sociology* 65:1–31.

Lekachman, Robert. 1957. "The Non-Economic Assumptions of John Maynard Keynes." In *Common Frontiers of the Social Sciences*, edited by Mirra Komarovsky, 338–57. Glencoe, Ill.: Free Press.

Leontief, Wassily. 1966. "Note on the Pluralistic Interpretation of History and the Problem of Interdisciplinary Co-operation." In *Essays in Economics: Theories and Theorizing.* 3–11. New York: Oxford University Press.

Lindenberg, Siegwart. 1985. "An Assessment of New Political Economy." *Sociological Theory* 3 (Spring):99–113.

Lindenberg, Siegwart, et al., eds. 1986. *Approaches to Social Theory.* New York: Russel Sage.

———. 1988. "Contractual Relations and Weak Solidarity: The Behavioral Basis of Restraints on Gain-Maximization." *Journal of Institutional and Theoretical Economics* 144:39–58.

Löwe, Adolph. 1935. *Economics and Sociology: A Plea for Co-operation in the Social Sciences.* London: George Allen and Unwin.

Luce, R. Duncan, and Howard Raiffa. 1957. *Games and Decisions: Introduction and Critical Survey.* New York: John Wiley.

Makler, Harry, Alberto Martinelli, and Neil J. Smelser, eds. 1982. *The New International Economy.* Beverly Hills, Calif.: SAGE Publications.

Marshall, Alfred. 1885. *The Present Condition of Economics.* London: Macmillan.

———. 1891. *Principles of Economics.* vol. 1. London: Macmillan.

McCloskey, Donald N. 1983. "The Rhetoric of Economics." *Journal of Economic Literature* 21 (June):481–517.

———. 1986. *The Rhetoric of Economics.* Madison: University of Wisconsin Press.

Mill, John Stuart. 1987. *Principles of Political Economy.* Fairfield, N.J.: Augustus M. Kelly. Originally published in 1848.

Oberschall, Anthony, and Eric Leifer. 1986. "Efficiency and Social Institutions: Uses and Misuses of Economic Reasoning in Sociology." *Annual Review of Sociology* 12:233–53.

Olson, Mancur. 1965. *The Logic of Collective Action: Public Goods and the Theory of Groups.* Cambridge: Harvard University Press. 2d ed. in 1971.

———. 1969c. "The Relationship between Economics and the Other Social Sciences." In *Politics and the Social Sciences*, edited by S. M. Lipset, 137–62. New York: Oxford University Press.

Opp, Karl-Dieter. 1978. "Das 'ökonomische Programm' in der Soziologie." *Soziale Welt* 29, 2:129–54.

———. 1983. *Die Entstehung sozialer Normen. Ein Integrationsversuch soziologischer, sozialpsychologischer und ökonomischer Erklärungen.*Tübingen: Mohr Siebeck.

———. 1985. "Sociology and Economic Man." *Zeitschrift für die gesamte Staatswissenschaft* 141:213–43.

Pareto, Vilfredo. 1965. "L'Economie et la Sociologie au Point de Vue Scientifique." In *Oeuvres Complètes,*vol. 2, 147–61. Geneva: Librairie Droz.

Parker, William N., ed. 1986. *Economic History and the Modern Economist.* Oxford: Basil Blackwell.

Parsons, Talcott. 1934. "Some Reflections on 'The Human Nature and Significance of Economics.' " *Quarterly Journal of Economics* 48:511–45.

———. 1940. Letter to Adolph Löwe November 22. Harvard University Archives HUG (FP) 15.2, box 13, folder "Löwe, Adolf."

Parsons, Talcott, and Neil J. Smelser. 1956. *Economy and Society: A Study in the Integration of Economic and Social Theory.* New York: Free Press.

Patten, Simon N. 1895a. "Discussion of Albion Small, 'The Relation of Sociology to Economics.' " *Publications of the American Economic Association* 10, Supplement (March):107–10.

———. 1895b. "The Relation of Economics to Sociology." *Annals of the American Academy of Political and Social Science* 5 (July 1894–June 1895):577–83.

Radnitzky, Gerard, and Peter Bernholz, eds. 1987. *Economic Imperialism: The Economic Approach Applied Outside the Field of Economics.* New York: Paragon House.

Samuelson, Paul A. 1947. *Foundations of Economic Analysis.* Cambridge: Harvard University Press.

———. 1983. "Frank Knight, 1885–1972." In *Economics from the Heart: A Samuelson Sampler.* 160–61. New York: Harcourt Brace Jovanovich.

Schelling, Thomas C. 1960. *The Strategy of Conflict.* Cambridge: Harvard University Press. Reprinted with a new preface in 1980.

———. 1978. *Micromotives and Macrobehavior.* New York: W. W. Norton.

Schumpeter, Joseph A. 1949. "Die 'positive' Methode in der Nationalökonomie." In *Aufsätze zur ökonomische Theorie,* 549–52. Tübingen: J.C.B. Mohr.

———. 1951. "Vilfredo Pareto, 1848–1923." In *Ten Great Economists: From Marx to Keynes,* 110–42. New York: Oxford University Press.

———. 1954. *History of Economic Analysis.* London: George Allen and Unwin.

Schweitzer, Arthur. 1975. "Frank Knight's Social Economics." *History of Political Economy* 7:280–92.

Shackle, G.L.S. 1967. *The Years of High Theory: Invention and Tradition in Economic Thought 1926–1939.* Cambridge: Cambridge University Press.

Sherwood, Sidney. 1897. "The Philosophical Basis of Economics: A Word to the Sociologists." *Annals of the American Academy of Political and Social Science* 10 (July–December):206–40.

Souter, Ralph William. 1933. *Prolegomena to Relativity Economics: An Elementary Study in the Mechanics of an Expanding Economic Universe.* New York: Columbia University Press.

Stigler, George J. 1984. "Economics—The Imperial Science." *Scandinavian Journal of Economics* 86:301–13.

Stinchcombe, Arthur L. 1983. *Economic Sociology.* New York: Academic Press.

Sutton, Francis X., et al. 1956. *The American Business Creed.* Cambridge: Harvard University Press.

Swedberg, Richard. 1987. "Economic Sociology: Past and Present." *Current Sociology* 35:1–221.

Tullock, Gordon. 1972. "Economic Imperialism." In *Theory of Public Choice,* edited by James M. Buchanan and Robert D. Tollison, 317–29. Ann Arbor: University of Michigan Press.

Tullock, Gordon, and Richard B. McKenzie. 1985. *The New World of Economics: Explorations into the Human Experience.* Homewood, Ill.: Richard D. Irwin.

Udéhn, Lars. 1986. "Is Economic Theory Universally Applicable in the Social Sciences?" Unpublished paper, Department of Sociology, Uppsala University.

Ward, Lester F. 1899. "Sociology and Economics." *Annals of the American Academy of Political and Social Science* 13 (January–June):230–34.

Weber, Marianne. 1975. *Max Weber: A Biography.* New York: John Wiley.

Weber, Max. 1949. " 'Objectivity' in Social Science and Social Policy." In *The Methodology of the Social Sciences*, 49–112. New York: Free Press.

————. 1951. *Gesammelte Aufsätze zur Wissenschaftslehre.* Tübingen: J.C.B. Mohr.

White, Harrison C. 1978. "Markets as Social Structures." Paper presented at the annual meeting of the American Sociological Association, Boston.

Wiley, Norbert F. 1983. "The Congruence of Weber and Keynes." In *Sociological Theory 1983*, edited by Randall Collins, 30–56. San Francisco: Jossey-Bass Publisher.

Wirth, Louis. 1948. "American Sociology, 1915–47." In *Index to Volumes I–LII, 1895–1947 of the American Journal of Sociology*, 273–81. Chicago: University of Chicago Press.

Zelizer, Viviana. 1983. *Morals and Markets: The Development of Life Insurance in the United States.* New Brunswick, N.J.: Transaction Books.

————. 1985. *Pricing the Priceless Child: The Changing Social Value of Children.* New York: Basic Books.

I   *The Contenders*

1 *Gary S. Becker*

THE KEY PERSON in any discussion of the contemporary relationship between economics and sociology has to be Gary Becker.[1] He was not only the first to apply the neoclassical analysis to noneconomic topics—he did this already in the early 1950s—but he has also continued to expand the economic analysis in a brilliant and pioneering way. In a programmatic article entitled "The Economic Approach to Human Behavior," Becker describes his method like this: "The combined assumptions of maximizing behavior, market equilibrium, and stable preferences, used relentlessly and unflinchingly, form the heart of the economic approach as I see it" (1976, 5).

The range of topics to which Becker has applied this approach is exceptionally wide. His first major work, written when he was in his early twenties, is entitled *The Economics of Discrimination* and represents an attempt to account for discrimination through a conceptual apparatus inspired by the neoclassical theories of foreign trade and consumer behavior. His second major inroad into noneconomic territory came in 1960 with an analysis of fertility. Becker's suggestion that one could conceptualize children as "durable consumer goods" evoked especially strong reactions, as he describes in the interview. A minor revolution also erupted upon publication of a 1968 article in which Becker suggested that the rational choice perspective could be applied to crime. Since the 1960s, Becker has continued to produce brilliant and controversial analyses. Many of these, especially *Human Capital*, but also *A Treatise on the Family*, now belong to the standard repertoire in economics. In the former work, Becker develops the idea that education can be seen as a special form of investment, and in the latter he tries his hand at such topics as marriage and divorce, polygamy, and monogamy. In a famous article from 1977, coauthored with George Stigler, the rational choice analysis is further extended to tradition, addiction, fashion, and advertisement.

The following interview with Gary Becker was conducted in his office at the Department of Economics at the University of Chicago on April 13, 1988.

[1] The following information comes from Gary Becker's vita, Blaug 1985; Shackleton 1981; and *Who's Who in Economics* 1986. For the reaction by sociologists, see especially Duncan 1958; MacRae 1978; Berk and Berk 1983.

Sociologists and other social scientists who are not economists have responded to Becker's work with a mixture of enthusiasm, admiration, and hostility. A fairly balanced assessment of Becker's work from a socio- logical point of view can be found in Duncan MacRae's review essay in the *American Journal of Sociology* from 1978. MacRae sums up his opinion with the remark that what Becker does "might constitute both a challenge and a source of fruitful innovations (in sociology)" (1978, 1244). A more caustic tone can be found in a survey article by two sociologists of the so-called New Home Economics of which Becker is one of the principal architects. The authors (Berk and Berk 1983, 375) conclude that "in many ways family sociology deserves the New Home Economics." A more en- thusiastic reading of Becker's "economic-sociology" (as he calls it in this interview) has clearly been made in the prestigious sociology department at the University of Chicago where, in 1983, Becker was offered—and still holds—a joint appointment in sociology and economics.

Becker was born in 1930 in Pottsville, Pennsylvania, the son of a busi- nessman. He graduated from Princeton University in 1951 with a major in economics and a minor in mathematics. Two years later, he earned an A.M. in economics at the University of Chicago, and in 1955, a Ph.D. at the same university. After a few years at Chicago as an assistant professor (1954–1957), he moved to Columbia University, where he remained for more than a decade (1957–1969). He then returned to the University of Chicago, where he has remained to date. Becker was president of the American Economic Association in 1987.

•

Q: Many economists and sociologists are familiar with your work but know little about its background and what inspired it. Could you say what made you decide to become an economist and which of your teachers were the most influential? I know, for example, that you received your graduate degrees in economics here at Chicago . . .

A: It goes back a bit further than that—to when I was an undergraduate at Princeton. At that time I was just beginning to develop, and I had an interest in both mathematics and social problems. During the first year, I took an economics course as a requirement, and I then saw that one could apply mathematics to economics. That was really what converted me to economics.

I have always felt fortunate that I took this course in economics. I read an introductory textbook by Samuelson, *Economics*; and it was the micro sections that I liked the most. They were concise and mathematically for- mulated, and yet they dealt with interesting problems. So that was what started me to try to combine the interest in social problems with a more mathematical or rigorous way of looking at things. Mathematics was always my main interest in high school, and this partly continued at Princeton. In effect, I half majored in economics and half majored in mathematics as an undergraduate at Princeton.

I might add one thing which is relevant for sociology. When I was a senior at Princeton, I developed a crisis with regard to my interest in economics. It seemed too formal to me, and I felt that it wasn't really dealing with important social problems. As a result I flirted with the idea of going into sociology. I never took a sociology course, but I did know Marion Levy, who was and still is a sociologist at Princeton. I also began reading some sociology; in particular, I read Talcott Parsons, of whom Levy was a disciple. I found Parsons too difficult. I had this feeling that either he must be over my head or there was something wrong there. I wasn't sure which; I wasn't developed enough. Much later, Parsons came out to speak at Chicago, and I was asked to comment on him. This was one year before he died, and he was the keynote speaker at a forum that the sociology department holds every spring. So I said what my impression of his work had been when I read some of it as a student. I put it slightly differently though, and said that after reading Parsons, I decided sociology was just too difficult for me.

In any case, the experience with reading Parsons soured me on sociology, and I went back to economics. I was still not sure when I was at Princeton whether economics was really a useful tool for understanding social problems—I didn't get that emphasis from the people who were teaching me micro, although they were very well known and good economists. It was when I came to Chicago that I started to believe that economics could really be an important tool for understanding social problems. I was greatly influenced by some of the people in the economics department. If I had to mention one person, it would certainly have to be Milton Friedman. He was my teacher in microeconomic theory and he influenced me in that direction. In addition to his research, I want to stress that he was a *great* teacher, and that he had an enormous influence on most people who came to Chicago. He certainly did on me. He revitalized my interest in economics and made me see that you can attack social problems with economics. I did not have to move out of economics to deal with relevant problems, which I had thought when I was a senior at Princeton. I also had Gregg Lewis and T. W. Schultz as teachers, and they were also very influential. Subsequently, there was also George Stigler, who was not at Chicago at that time. He became an enormous influence on me too.

So I began to seek out social-economic problems, and after a while I got the idea of looking at discrimination from an economic perspective. It was actually very early in my graduate studies when I saw that one could use the tools of economics to say something—or try to say something—about discrimination, which economists had not done very much with.

Q: Chicago has a famous sociology department. U.S. sociology was more or less born here in the early twentieth century, and since then, the department has been of very high quality although it might have been in a kind of transitional state when you were here in the 1950s—in between Robert Park's type of sociology and Jim Coleman's, so to speak. Did you have any contact at all with the sociology department when you were a graduate student in economics?

A: Unfortunately, I had very little contact with the sociologists. I did have a little bit of contact after I made my thesis proposal to work on discrimination. I had moral and other support from some of the economists at Chicago, especially from Friedman, Lewis, and Schultz. However, some people in the economics department at that time were uneasy about me working on what was considered a sociological problem, so they put Everett C. Hughes—a well-known sociologist, who was then in Chicago—on my committee. Since he was on my committee, I had a little interaction with him. But I must confess that while I did not get the feeling that he was hostile to what I was doing, it was very hard for me to communicate with him because I was trying to use these economic tools and he was looking at problems from a very different point of view. So I did not get as much out of him as I should have been able to. But at least he was not negative about what I was doing.

While I was a graduate student in economics I also attended the lectures of various people in the sociology department. But I did not take any courses, and I must say to my regret that I got much less out of it than I could have. There was little interaction going on between the economics department and the sociology department at that time in Chicago.

Q: Your Ph.D. thesis from 1955, which a few years later was published as *The Economics of Discrimination*, is an extremely important work insofar as the interaction between economics and sociology is concerned. Here, more or less for the first time, the traditional division of labor between modern economics and sociology was challenged, namely, that economists should only deal with "economic" problems and sociologists with "social" or "noneconomic" ones. What inspired you to make this move into a noneconomic area? Behind every book there is a story; what is the story behind *The Economics of Discrimination?*

A: I am sure that my teachers—the ones I have just mentioned—had a big influence on me in writing that book. There was something about the atmosphere I found in Chicago that was very important to me; it was almost tailormade for my interests. More precisely, it was this belief by some of the people at the economics department that economics not only helps understand why people buy cars and so on, but that it also has this broader applicability. This belief gave me the moral support necessary to try something different.

Considering discrimination more directly, I remember getting the following idea at one point: If one can assume that everyone has a taste for discrimination against members of a minority that is measured by a "discrimination coefficient," one can then go pretty easily from tastes to observable wage differences between members of the majority and minority. These wage differences would reflect the size of the discrimination coefficient that people have. I remember getting that idea and being very excited. I thought it was something I could take off with and use as a vehicle for analysis. You see, until this point I had wanted to work on social problems. But there can be an enormous gap between wanting to do something and knowing how to go about doing it. But now I had come up with an idea of how to take my economics, as it were, and yet say something about social problems, in this case discrimination.

And then I just started working on discrimination. I had enough confidence in myself, although I was only about twenty-two, that although I recognized this was not traditional economics and I felt much hostility subsequently from economists outside of Chicago, I believed that I was saying something. And that by saying something useful, there would be a payoff to me in the long run. I had an enthusiasm, and important too was the enthusiasm in the economics department that economics was an important science that could say a lot of things. I never wavered in my belief that I wanted to work on discrimination for my dissertation. I got this idea about discrimination early in my career as a graduate student—in my second year, I think—and I worked it through for my dissertation. After that, I revised the dissertation and published the book.

Q: In the preface to the 1971 edition of *The Economics of Discrimination*, you say that there was quite a bit of resistance to your ideas among economists, but less so among sociologists. Your book, it seems, was reviewed in more sociological magazines than in economic ones. Since the 1950s, you have continued to do economic work in traditionally noneconomic areas—you have written on crime, fertility, the family, and so on—and I would like to ask you about the reactions by economists and sociologists to this later work. Do you feel your line of work is more accepted today?

A: There is no doubt that the application of economics to sociology is much more acceptable today than in those days. I will tell you a little about what I went through. Initially there was a lot of hostility. I recall going up to MIT for a job interview. I was very young; it was at the end of my third year of studies. I met one of the preeminent younger economists in the profession and told him what I was working on. He listened to me and then he said that he thought I was a neoclassical economist. I said, "I *am* a neoclassical economist," and that my work was an attempt to apply neoclassical economics to discrimination. He was very skeptical, although he was a very able and polite person. I encountered this reaction often in those days.

It was ten years after the publication of my book before discrimination, or minority, economics started to become a big field in economics. In the preceding period there was very little of this subject.

But there were also things that gave me encouragement in those early days. To my surprise, several reviews by sociologists were highly favorable. I remember one in particular by Otis Dudley Duncan (1958), who was at Chicago as an assistant professor when I was a graduate student. I knew him slightly, and we had spoken on a number of occasions. He wrote a very positive review. One or two other reviews were also very favorable, though I don't remember them as well. The good reviews encouraged me, even though other reviews by sociologists were negative. There were also two or three highly favorable reviews by economists. The review by M. W. Reder in the *American Economic Review* was insightful and closely analyzed various economic aspects of discrimination. Also very positive were the reviews by Armen Alchian in the *Journal of the American Statistical Association,* and by Donald Dewey in the *Southern Economic Journal.* Although a couple of reviews by economists were quite negative, the reviews in the prime journals were very encouraging. When taken with the reception I got in sociology, I felt some vindication.

When I left Chicago in 1957, I had already spent three years as an assistant professor. Chicago wanted me to stay, but I felt that I should get away from Chicago and see how I could handle things on my own. So I turned down a good offer from Chicago, and instead took a job at Columbia University. I wanted to go to the New York area, and Columbia is a fine university. They hired me mainly on the merits of my recommendations and what they had seen of my book and other publications. I don't think the book had actually come out yet at that time, so I guess it was the manuscript they got to see. Columbia was a comfortable department for me, and I was fortunate to get such a good job. I continued my research, mainly at the National Bureau of Economic Research, then in New York, which was an excellent place to do research.

The next two problems I took up were fertility and human capital. They were also partly or mainly sociological. The profession was certainly opposed to the population stuff. At the conference where I gave my first paper on population, I said I was treating children as "durable consumer goods." There was laughter in the audience (Becker 1960). The laughter came as much from the economists as from the sociologists and the demographers. Although most people present did not like the paper, Milton Friedman and a few other people spoke up in its favor. I found the whole thing discouraging, but I felt that I was right and the critics were wrong. And fortunately I had enough confidence or delusions about myself at that time. Otherwise it could have been a severe blow.

The work on human capital got a mixed reception. There were some negative reactions but also positive ones. It wasn't received with nearly as much hostility or negativity as my work on population. Among the noneconomists, the educational people were initially opposed. Some economists were also negative. But this time I wasn't alone. There were other economists working on human capital, especially Ted Schultz and Jacob Mincer, and both did pioneering work on the economics of education and other types of human capital. The efforts of the whole group helped to get human capital accepted.

My work on the allocation of time was very well received in the profession, and I didn't have any trouble this time. Two areas, however, where I ran into a lot of opposition to applying the economic approach were politics and the family. For my work on politics I need to go back to the 1950s. Already in 1958 I had published a paper on the application of economics to politics (Becker 1958). I thought it had much promise, but nobody paid it much attention. I wrote a longer and better version in 1952 or 1953 when I was a graduate student, after being stimulated by Schumpeter's *Capitalism, Socialism and Democracy*. Unfortunately, this longer version was rejected at that time by the *Journal of Political Economy*, the eminent journal edited by the economics department at Chicago, after telling me that they would publish it. One of their referees, my teacher Frank Knight, did not like it. Since then, much good work applies economics to political science. I sometimes feel that I should kick myself for not publishing the longer paper in another journal. I was applying economics to politics as early as anyone. But the rejection hurt. I put the paper aside for several years and then published a short version of it in 1958.

Q: So you were ahead of Anthony Downs, whose *Economic Theory of Democracy* didn't appear till 1957 . . .

A: Perhaps slightly ahead. My early fifties and 1958 papers took a similar approach, although Downs's book was more thorough and better. The *JPE* made what must be said to be a mistake in rejecting my paper in 1953, but did publish a paper of Downs's in 1957. However, I didn't want to make a career as a political scientist, so I went on to other topics, until much later when I returned to politics.

Let me now come to the family. I have worked on divorce, marriage, fertility, and so on. This time too, the initial response from many economists was negative. But I began to work on the family mainly in the 1970s. By that time, I was more confident than I had been as a graduate student, and I had much more support from other economists and some sociologists and psychologists. Too many academics are reluctant to gamble in their research, so they stay with generally accepted approaches and topics. In particular, most economists are reluctant to deviate too far from what other economists are doing. Therefore, they consider work on the economics of the family to be "far out." But I think it is fair to say that rational choice has provided many insights into the family, and the critics have been proven wrong. Fortunately, by the 1970s I had confidence in my choice of topics, and was convinced that the critics were just too "conservative." I could not have survived all the opposition if I had not felt pretty confident about what I was doing. Indeed, I would have changed the type of research I did.

Today, the economics profession is much more accepting of the use of economic theory in many areas outside the traditional boundaries, even though many economists are still negative. Of course, most sociologists too are negative. But not even in my wildest dreams ten years ago did I think that I would be offered a position in the sociology department at Chicago. When I made my comment on Parsons's talk in the late 1970s, which I told you about earlier, toward the end I also made the following suggestion. I said that economics has great power, that it can be applied to sociology, and that there should be a course in the sociology department on microeconomics for sociologists. There was this big audience out there, and they started booing me. Until then they had liked my talk; I had been complimentary to Parsons and sociology; I wasn't trying to get into a fight with Parsons. But at that point the audience booed me. And after I had finished, Morris Janowitz of the sociology department, who was chairing the session, said to me, "I liked the *first* half of your talk."

So you can see why I never expected the Department of Sociology at Chicago, clearly one of the premier sociology departments, to offer me a joint appointment. I never sought it out, mind you. But when they did offer me a joint appointment a few years ago, I was happy to accept it for several reasons. The offer was proof of the flexibility of the department at Chicago. And second, it was an important sign to sociologists and economists that my type of work was much more acceptable now, at least to some eminent sociologists. This is evident from current research in sociology. I regularly see papers in sociology journals that use a rational choice approach to crime, education, the family, and many other subjects. For example, the current issue of the *American Journal of Sociology* has a very good empirical study criticizing my work on the allocation of effort (Bielby and Bielby 1988). I disagree with some of this paper, but it is a fine piece of work that shows how much dialogue there is now between economics and sociology. Whether supportive or critical, sociologists now pay much more attention to the work of economists who apply a rational choice framework to sociological questions.

Q: What exactly does your joint appointment entail? I notice, for example, that your office is still located in the economics department. Do you teach any courses in the sociology department? Do you hold seminars?

A: There is no question that I am still mainly in the economics department. My budget is in the economics department. Everybody realizes that and no one expected anything different. But I do a number of things for the sociology department. Of course, I attend meetings of the sociology department, and I have some input into appointments they make. I also interact with the younger faculty and a few of the senior people. Jim Coleman and I have a lot of contact.

Shortly after my appointment, Jim Coleman and I started a seminar on rational choice methods in the social sciences. At the meeting yesterday, for example, a political scientist from Chicago—David Laiten—made a presentation. It is an interdisciplinary seminar that mainly attracts faculty. Many economists, sociologists, political scientists, lawyers, and philosophers attend.

We have also introduced a program within the sociology department on rational choice methods that students can take as one of their fields of concentration. The program has not yet attracted many students, and it is easy to see why. They have to take economics courses, and therefore tool up on mathematics as well as on economic concepts. So it demands a large investment from students. But we are getting some students involved. My courses are now listed in sociology. In particular, the course I give in the spring quarter on human capital, population growth, and economic growth always attracts a few graduate sociology students. This quarter I have three or four, which is larger than usual.

Q: Do you think that sociology departments will increasingly hire economists or do you think that your case is unique? For example, there is clearly a trend for business schools to hire more sociologists.

A: That is true. The Chicago Business School, for example, has had more than one sociologist. As to economists being hired by sociology departments, I'd like to believe it is a trend, and I think it will be in the long run. At the moment, however, I do not know of other economists in the United States who have joint appointments in economics and sociology. The number who do will increase very slowly.

The joint appointment, however, has been useful for me, and I think it has been useful for the sociology department. Several of the younger sociologists at Chicago are doing work that interacts with the kind of things that I am interested in. We have, for example, a young sociologist who is working on women in Japan, and she is interested in human capital. There are also those who work on demographic and stratification issues. The joint appointment increased the interaction between these faculty members and economists, and this has benefitted both groups.

Q: What about the opposite trend—economic departments hiring sociologists? Schumpeter, for example, said that economics should be broad enough to encompass "economic sociology." Do you believe that this is a possibility?

A: There certainly aren't any senior sociologists yet who have been hired by economics departments. I believe there are going to be "economic-sociologists" hired in the future, but let me explain what I mean by "economic-sociologist." There are already economists who have learned some sociology and use concepts from sociology in their work.

Q: Who are you thinking of?

A: People like Michael Piore, Albert Hirschman, maybe David Ellwood at the Kennedy School, and clearly George Akerlof. There are also others I could name.

You asked me if we are going to see people who are professionally trained as sociologists hired in economics departments in the future. I don't think we will see that trend except perhaps for a few sociologists who get a strong grounding in rational choice theory or statistical methods. Otherwise it is too hard for economics departments to integrate sociologists in a useful way.

One has to realize that there is still much hostility among economists toward sociologists. Many economists have said to me: "Frankly, why did you accept an appointment in a sociology department?" They say it partly to tease me, but there is also the hostility to sociology. Fortunately, this hostility is decreasing; many excellent economists are positive toward sociology. For example, Sherwin Rosen has helped edit a theme issue on "Sociology and Economics" of the *American Journal of Sociology* (see Winship and Rosen 1988). Others too are aware of the value of interaction between economics and sociology, and have a favorable attitude to sociology.

Q: Is this hostility among economists decreasing slowly or quickly in your opinion? Economists, after all, have been hostile to sociology for a long time . . .

A: It is decreasing, and was stronger when I was a graduate student. One of my teachers, Frank Knight, formulated "Gresham's Law of Sociology: Bad talk drives out good." But the hostility is not decreasing rapidly enough.

Q: And you feel that sociologists are more friendly to economists than vice versa?

A: Sociology is bifurcated, as far as I can tell. My interpretation of why many sociologists are more receptive than in the past revolves in a way around Talcott Parsons. I may be all wet on this, but I'll state it anyway because of the importance of the issues we are talking about. When I was a graduate student, Talcott Parsons was the King of Sociological Theory, at least in the United States. Top students like Merton were greatly influenced by Parsons. He was the king, and all I heard in my undergraduate encounters with sociology was "Talcott Parsons, Talcott Parsons." Sociology supposedly had this powerful apparatus supplied by Parsons that was going to explain social behavior and even include economics as a special case.

Parsonian sociology has turned out to be a disappointment. In some sense, the whole enterprise was basically a failure. Given this, what direction is sociological theory now going to take? It seems to be going in several directions. There are, for example, strong elements of Marxism among some sociologists. A few are emphasizing history, others are trying to develop network models, and some are atheoretical and stick close to statistical methods and do not really worry much about how to interpret the facts. (The work of the statistical sociologists is important, but they need a theoretical framework.) And then there is a small minority saying, "Rational choice has something to add. After all, we have exchange theory in sociology that is akin to rational choice." And there are also other sociologists who are not working along these lines, but who are willing to say, "Let's see what rational choice has to add; maybe there is something to it."

This is my interpretation of why sociologists are now more receptive to economists, and in particular, why the sociology department at Chicago voted me a joint appointment. Of course, only a few in the sociology department believe rational choice is the way to go; most, I'm sure, are quite negative. But not many sociologists are confident about what is the right direction to go at the moment. A major exception is Jim Coleman, who knows economics as well as being an outstanding sociologist. He has a strong command of rational choice and he is obviously strongly sympathetic to economics. There is an increasing number of sociologists with Jim Coleman's sympathies. They are still small in number but they can be found all over the Western world: in some parts of the Netherlands, in Germany, at various universities in the United States, and so on.

Q: Now that you have seen both the sociological culture and the economic culture, how would you compare the two? Are economists more creative? And sociologists more open-minded? How do you see it?

A: There are many able and creative sociologists, including several of my colleagues. For example, at Chicago, I have enormous respect for Jim Coleman, Ed Laumann, and Bill Wilson. We have very good discussions and interact at our seminars and in other ways. There are also excellent sociologist-demographers, such as Sam Preston of the University of Pennsylvania. And some very promising younger sociologists, such as Mary Brinton and Peter Hedström.

What are the differences between the two cultures? The average analytical ability of economists is better. Economics does attract more talented students on average, at least in the sense of students with better analytical capacities and better training in formal skills. People familiar with both sociologists and economists would definitely agree with that.

On the other hand, what I find attractive among sociologists is the following: Economics has a powerful engine of analysis and most economists stick pretty close to that engine. But what about the problems that the engine cannot push forward? Maybe it will be able to say something one day—I am an optimist—but now it can't. Sociologists are far more willing than economists to discuss these big and broad questions. And they do it in an intelligent and thoughtful way, even though their progress in understanding these issues is very slow.

Let me give you an example. One of the most exciting seminars on rational choice dealt with religion. A young economist, Larry Iannoccone, gave a paper, and a fine sociologist, Andrew Greeley, commented upon it. It was a great seminar: both paper and commentary were excellent. But Larry is the only economist who is doing serious work on religion, while many other sociologists also do serious work on religion. So sociologists work more on these broader and important questions. These are questions that it is tough to make progress on, and sociologists are only making slow progress. But I find it stimulating to hear about their work in these areas. Most economists still work on pretty narrow questions. That narrowness may partly explain the progress made by economics, but it caused my initial rebellion against economics, and it is still there.

Economics tends to focus on issues like the pricing of cars or of securities. The stock market and other traditional economic subjects are important, but there is more to social science than these problems. Many social problems are as important or even more important. An economist should also be willing to investigate these social issues. Sociologists do that, and they sometimes do it better than economists because they are willing to do so without trying to build a solid theory. I do not believe that sociologists will go very far without a theory. But it is still valuable to have people grope their way on important issues. Maybe that will suggest an avenue of analysis, and a great sociologist or economist will come along with powerful insights. That is one of the things I like about being with sociologists. They consider broader problems that are not discussed in economics—neither in seminars, papers, nor in my personal interactions with economists. For this and other reasons, it has been very useful to me to be in the sociology department at Chicago.

Q: Your work is often associated with "economic imperialism," although you rarely use this term yourself (see Becker 1971, 2). Is it a term you approve of? And, more importantly, what exactly does it mean? Does it mean that economics can and should be extended to what by tradition have been viewed as noneconomic topics? Or is it that economics, by virtue of its powerful analytical tradition, will be able to solve a lot of problems that the other social sciences have failed to solve?

A: People like to pigeonhole work, so I am called an "economic imperialist." What it means to most people is this: the application of rational choice theory or economic theory to problems that would traditionally be treated by sociologists, political scientists, historians, or anthropologists. Not just by sociologists, mind you; I also include anthropology, history, and especially political science. The rational choice approach has had a very important influence on political science. Quite a few political scientists these days get trained as much in economics as in political science.

This definition of "economic imperialism" is probably a good description of what I do. Of course, it is necessary to recognize that every problem is unique. It is not as if one is a mechanic, and in the family you would use concept C of rational choice theory, and in slavery, concept D. Each time one approaches a novel problem, it is necessary to think hard about the possible ways to analyze it.

Q: How about the comparison to sociology? Will economics be able to solve all those problems that sociology has failed to solve because it is such a "soft" science? Is rational choice really that powerful in your opinion?

A: Yes, in the limited sense that rational choice can solve *more* of them than have been solved thus far. I don't know what the limits are. In my introductory essay to *The Economic Approach to Human Behavior,* I lay down a grand claim, and I still think that rational choice is a very powerful weapon. But I didn't mean to say that everything in social science can be handled by rational choice theory *as we know it today.* It is clear—and I say that in that essay—that rational choice has so far contributed little to the solution of many problems in social science, like war and religion. Maybe some day they will be solved with rational choice theory, but not now. My claim is that we can go a lot further by applying rational choice theory to many of these problems than we have been able to do so far.

What will the situation be like in twenty years? Maybe somebody will come along with a more general and powerful theory, which includes rational choice as a special case, and that will have different behavioral implications in some of these intractable areas. I am open-minded about this. Things like that are impossible to know, but theories do evolve over time.

Q: In addition, we are currently witnessing the emergence of different types of rational choice. There is, for example, Coleman's sociological version, which is based on "control" and "interest." What is your reaction to the fact that all these different types of rational choice exist today?

A: I think the differences between the various schools are much smaller than the similarities. Basically, what the rational choice people do is to start with some unit of behavior or actor that they assume is behaving rationally. By "behaving rationally," I mean "maximizing" consistent behavior that looks forward and tries to anticipate as far as possible what the future will bring. This is common to all versions of rational choice that I know of.

I would add that the actors have stable preferences over time, that people's preference functions don't change over time. I think that this assumption represents a huge asset, surely not a handicap. Even with stable preferences, the analysis can consider addiction, social interactions, and other complicated phenomena. I am just now doing some work (with Kevin M. Murphy) on rational addictive behavior.

The last component of rational choice theory, a tough one to formulate but common to all approaches, is how different units interact. Here you get into market equilibrium and game theory. The information available to participants is an important factor in their interaction. Rational choice theory assumes that people have imperfect information—that they have an optimal amount of information—and that they spend resources acquiring information to the point where it isn't worthwhile to acquire any more. That means a lot of ignorance—"rational ignorance"—and there is a lot of rational ignorance in any social situation. This is my view of what is common to all variants of rational choice theory. I am sure Jim Coleman's version is a bit different and so too would be those of others. But the basic components are pretty similar even among different schools of rational thought.

Q: When I have spoken to sociologists about rational choice, it has become clear to me that some of them have what could perhaps be called a "sociological concept of rationality." That would mean the following: A sociologist often investigates a social situation and tries to establish that what looks like irrational behavior to the outsider is indeed rational from the perspective of the participants. What is your reaction to this way of approaching the situation, that is, empirically investigating behavior to see if it is rational rather than just assigning rationality to the actors in the beginning of the analysis?

A: If you recall, the speaker last night at the rational choice seminar was David Laiten, who spoke on why one specific language gets chosen as the official language in a multilingual situation. He said that he wasn't a rational choice person until he concluded that he could best explain the behavior he was investigating with the rationality assumption. And that is OK to me. There are people who are more agnostic about rationality, and they will only go in that direction when they think the data are better explained that way than through some alternative approach. And then there are others like myself whose first instinct is to start with the assumption of rationality and see how far you can go with it. I always try to see how far I can push rational choice theory, until I am satisfied or give up on a problem.

So I start with the assumption that behavior is rational, and ask, "As I apply this to a particular problem, is there behavior that I *cannot* explain with the rationality model?" Since rationality can be pretty flexible and the data are often limited, I don't frequently encounter decisive evidence against rationality. Anyway, that is my way of doing things. Others are more agnostic about the scope of rationality, so they will approach a problem by asking, "Does this look like rational behavior or is it better interpreted in a different way?" Part of the difference, therefore, is the degree of *commitment* or *confidence* one has of finding rational behavior when investigating a particular set of phenomena.

Most economists have a strong commitment to rationality for behavior inside the scope of traditional economics. They are, however, dubious about how far one can go with rationality outside of traditional areas. Some economists who work on nontraditional topics are dubious about the role of rationality in other nontraditional topics. But other people, like Richard Posner, Gordon Tullock, Jack Hirshleifer, Mancur Olson, and myself, are more confident about its scope. So you have a lot of different opinions about the scope of rationality even among economists, and certainly between economists and sociologists. Economists are more confident than sociologists about rationality. This is natural since sociology started as a reaction against economics and the assumption of rationality.

Q: One consequence of what you are saying is that, if there is no difference between the sociological and the economic approach to rational choice, then one cannot really have what used to be called "economic sociology" because "economic sociology" (or, as you write it, "economic-sociology") would be the same as economic theory . . .

A: There is no basic difference. However, sociologists bring the influence of other people into their analysis of any person's behavior and also look at how social changes affect people's behavior. Economists, on the other hand, are prone to assume that people's preferences are independent of what other people are doing. I personally don't accept that. I think that the social side is very important, and agree with the sociologists on this approach.

What one person does *is* influenced greatly by what other people are doing. People don't want to look out of line; they don't want to be an object of ridicule; and they do want prestige. For example, most economists stick to traditional problems partly because they don't want to look ridiculous and look like they are not doing the right thing. This is not just an attribute of economists; it's an attribute of *people*. Sociologists emphasize that a lot more than economists do, and they are right to do so. There is still the problem of how to bring social interactions into the analysis in a fruitful and useful way (I made an effort in a 1974 paper; see Becker 1974). But there is no question in my mind that here the sociologists are more on the right track than are economists.

Q: Through your work you have helped to break up the traditional division of labor between economics and sociology. What do you think will replace it? In your opinion, what will happen in, say, the next ten years in the relationship between economics and sociology? I believe that sociologists are likely to try out rational choice for perhaps ten years. But if it doesn't pay off, they will just stop and try something else. Sociologists have done that a few times, with systems theory, mathematical sociology, and so on.

A: I agree with you that if rational choice doesn't pay off within a certain period of time, sociologists will lose interest in it. And I think rightly so. My own feeling is that this is not going to happen and that rational choice will pay off soon in certain additional fields. Some fields where it has already contributed and where it will pay off even more in the future are: the family, crime (or deviant behavior), discrimination, industrial sociology, collective choice, and stratification. These are important parts of sociology, although collective choice has been studied more in economics and political science than in sociology.

The nature of future interactions between economics and sociology is not clear, but I believe that an increasing number of economists will be using rational choice theory to work on "sociological problems." And there will also be an increasing number of younger sociologists who are trained in rational choice and who will have some confidence in their understanding of rational choice theory. They are not going to become economists; they will still be trained in sociology departments and will still be sociologists. But they will be comfortable in using rational choice theory and in reading the literature by economists and others on rational choice. These sociologists are going to be interacting increasingly with economists. A possible model for such a development in sociology are political scientists like John Ferejohn, Morris Fiorina, Kenneth Shepsle, and others who have learned much rational choice theory and have considerable interaction with economists interested in collective choice.

I don't want it to sound as if the whole thing is going to be a one-way street with the sociologists learning rational choice from economists. I have said that I have learned many things from sociologists and so too will other economists who work on sociological problems. I have already mentioned the sociologist's concern with big questions and with the influence of social interactions.

Let me also add a bit about social surveys. Sociologists have been much better at organizing surveys than economists, partly because they started much earlier than economists. Economists are finally beginning to catch up, and have even surpassed sociologists as far as the purely statistical side of survey analysis is concerned. But economists are still not nearly as good as sociologists in creative thinking when it comes to surveys; economists tend to stick to large surveys run by governments and private organizations. They seldom put together small surveys of their own. There is going to be further influence in survey construction from sociology to economics.

So to sum up thus far, the common denominator in much of the contact between economics and sociology will be rational choice theory as developed mainly, but not entirely, by economists. But other things will come from sociology, and an increasing number of economists and sociologists will be interacting with each other. Of course, most will be little influenced by what is going on in economic-sociology. But more and more economists and sociologists will want to and will be able to communicate with each other.

Does this mean that more economists will become members of sociology departments? As I said before: Yes, I think so, but it will be a slow development and there will not be many of these appointments. And will there be any sociologists in economics departments? Again: yes, there will be a very small number. There is already at least one example; Peter Mueser was a student in sociology at Chicago who was very much influenced by economists. He attended our workshops and he learned a lot of economics. And his first appointment was as an assistant professor of economics—not of sociology—at Johns Hopkins. There will be other sociologists like Mueser. The number of sociologists in economics departments will be extremely small, and not many economists will be in sociology departments. But more economists will be working on sociological problems and more sociologists will be working with rational choice theory.

Q: In your vision, then, there will be small groups of economists and sociologists interacting on the basis of their common interest in rational choice. But most economists and sociologists, you say, will continue as they always have and ignore one another. It does not sound to me as if rational choice as you see it will lead to a more unified social science.

A: No, not in the next ten or fifteen years. But it depends on what the time horizon is, and on the successes during the next decade or two. I do believe that the rational choice framework is going to be very important in sociology. I think it already *is* very important in sociology, but it is going to be even more so. Rational choice theory will also continue to be very important in political science, so that you are going to get much more of a unified social science than there is now. But obviously it will be far from a complete unification.

Take political science, where we can be more objective when discussing the use of rational choice methods. Most political scientists today are not much influenced by a hard rational choice analysis. But some political scientists are greatly influenced—including some with the most prestige in the profession. At Harvard, you have Morris Fiorina and Kenneth Shepsle, both of whom have been recruited during the last few years. They are quite knowledgeable of and heavily influenced by economics. Both, I think, have been trained at Rochester, which is a rational choice political science department. Or take Carnegie Tech's political science department, or the program in political economy that is being created at the Stanford Business School. There are also other centers in this country where you'll find political scientists working with rational choice theory.

The whole movement is growing. And, I hear that the rational choice political scientists are getting the biggest salaries and are in the greatest demand these days. Actually, these "political scientists" are half economists and half political scientists; I don't know what you should really call them. Maybe just people who are using rational choice on political problems.

In the longer run, there are going to be sociologists like that as well. Whether they will get the prominence such people already have in political science, I don't know. I don't see any reason why they wouldn't—I am optimistic that eventually rational choice sociologists will be very important members of the sociology profession.

I have already indicated that traditional sociology's concern with big questions and with social influences on individual behavior will greatly affect the evolving nature of economic-sociology. In this and other ways, traditional sociology will most definitely influence even rational choice approaches to economic and sociological phenomena. However, I am skeptical whether major *theoretical* concepts from traditional sociology will have a large influence on the development of economic-sociology and the interaction between economists and sociologists. But sociologists will have a large influence if they get solid grounding in rational choice theory and develop confidence in its power to open up to analysis stubborn social issues.

References

Alchian, Armen A. 1958. "Review of Gary Becker, *The Economics of Discrimination.*" *Journal of the American Statistical Association* 53:1047–48.

Becker, Gary. 1957. *The Economics of Discrimination.* Chicago: University of Chicago Press. 2d ed. 1971.

———. 1958. "Competition and Democracy." *Journal of Law and Economics* 1:105–09.

———. 1960. "An Economic Analysis of Fertility." In *Demographic and Economic Change in Developed Countries*, 209–31. Princeton, N.J.: Princeton University Press, for the National Bureau of Economic Research.

———. 1964. *Human Capital.* New York: Columbia University Press. 2d ed. 1975.

———. 1968. "Crime and Punishment: An Economic Approach." *Journal of Political Economy* 78:189–217.

———. 1971. *Economic Theory.* New York: Knopf.

———. 1974. "A Theory of Social Interactions." *Journal of Political Economy* 82:1063–93.

———. 1976. "The Economic Approach to Human Behavior." In *The Economic Approach to Human Behavior*, 3–14. Chicago: University of Chicago Press.

————. 1981. *A Treatise on the Family.* Cambridge: Harvard University Press.

————. 1988. "Family Economics and Macro Behavior." *American Economic Review* 78:1–13.

Berk, Richard A., and Sarah Fenstermaker Berk. 1983. "Supply-Side Sociology of the Family: The Challenge of New Home Economics." *Annual Review of Sociology* 9:375–95.

Bielby, Denise B., and William T. Bielby. 1988. "She Works Hard for the Money: Household Responsibilities and the Allocation of Work Effort." *American Journal of Sociology* 93:1031–59.

Blaug, Mark. 1985. *Great Economists since Keynes.* Brighton: Harvester Press.

Dewey, Donald. 1957. "Review of Gary Becker, *The Economics of Discrimination.*" *Southern Economic Journal* 24:494–96.

Downs, Anthony. 1957a. *An Economic Theory of Democracy.* New York: Harper and Row.

————. 1957b. "An Economic Theory of Political Action in a Democracy." *Journal of Political Economy* 65:135–50.

Duncan, Otis Dudley. 1958. "Review of Gary Becker, *The Economics of Discrimination.*" *American Journal of Sociology* 63:548.

MacRae, Duncan, Jr. 1978. "Review Essay: The Sociological Economics of Gary S. Becker." *American Journal of Sociology* 83:1244–70.

Reder, M. W. 1958. "Review of Gary Becker, *The Economics of Discrimination.*" *American Economic Review* 48:495–500.

Samuelson, Paul A. 1961. *Economics.* 5th ed. New York: McGraw-Hill.

Schumpeter, Joseph A. 1950. *Capitalism, Socialism and Democracy.* 3d ed. New York: Harper and Brothers.

Shackleton, J. R. 1981. "Gary S. Becker: The Economist as Empire-Builder." In *Twelve Contemporary Economists*, edited by J. R. Shackleton and Gareth Locksley, 12–32. London: Macmillan.

Stigler, George J., and Gary S. Becker. 1977. "De Gustibus Non Est Disputandum." *American Economic Review* 67:76–90.

Winship, Christopher, and Sherwin Rosen, eds. 1988. "Organizations and Institutions: Sociological and Economic Approaches to the Analysis of Social Structure." *Supplement to the American Journal of Sociology* 94:S1–S268.

2 *James S. Coleman*

IF THERE IS one person in the current debate on the relationship between economics and sociology who plays a similar role in sociology to that of Gary Becker in economics, it has to be James Coleman.[1] To the general public Coleman is no doubt best known for his research on education, especially through the two coauthored books *Equality of Educational Opportunity* and *High School Achievement.* However, at the same time, Coleman has been involved in a theoretical search for a new foundation for modern sociology. In 1964 this resulted in the publication of the influential *Introduction to Mathematical Sociology.* After the 1960s, Coleman began looking more seriously in the direction of rational choice for inspiration. During the last few years, this tendency has intensified, and in 1986 he published a programmatic article on the use of rational choice in sociology entitled "Social Theory, Social Research, and Theory of Action." The basic argument here is that sociological theory has stood still for half a century and needs a totally new theoretical foundation. Together with Becker, who Coleman was instrumental in bringing to the sociology department at the University of Chicago, he has also during the last few years begun to build up an institutional structure for rational choice sociology. For example, he helped develop a new magazine called *Rationality and Society,* which was first published in 1989. This new journal "aims to foster a new era in sociological analyses." For many years, Coleman has also worked on a major theoretical treatise in rational choice sociology, entitled *Foundations of Social Theory.* The publication of this work will represent an exciting event in modern sociology. The interview with Coleman was conducted while the manuscript for this new book was just being completed. In the course of the interview, Coleman presents some of the key ideas in *Foundations of Social Theory* and explains a few points, that are likely to cause discussion.

The following interview with James Coleman was conducted in his home in Hyde Park in Chicago on November 27, 1987.

[1] The following is based on Hunt 1985; Coleman's vita; and his "Autobiographical Sketch, I & II" 1985.

James Samuel Coleman was born in Bedford, Indiana, on May 12, 1926. He first attended Emory and Henry College (1944–1946), and earned a B.S. at Purdue University in 1949. He then decided to totally change his profession from a chemical engineer to a sociologist. He was later to write in an autobiographical article: "My life can be divided into two parts, before I first entered Fayerweather Hall (the building in which sociology is housed at Columbia), that is before Fayerweather (B.F.), and after Fayerweather (A.F.)" (Coleman 1985, 1). He was a research associate at the Bureau for Applied Social Research in 1953-55 and got his Ph.D. in sociology in 1955. Coleman first worked at the University of Chicago (1956–1959) and then at Johns Hopkins University (1959–1973). Since 1973, he has been Professor of Sociology at the University of Chicago.

•

Q: You began your career as a chemical engineer. Why did you study chemical engineering and what made you decide to switch over into sociology?

A: I had always been pointed toward science and engineering, both by my parents and by my interest in mathematics, chemistry, and physics in high school. My parents had aspirations for me to attend MIT, but no money for that, and anyway, World War II intervened, with very crowded universities after the war. I got into the University of Louisville on a football scholarship, but only got as far as football practice before enrolling in Indiana University, where I was admitted in 1946 in the last minute. I studied chemistry there but after one semester, transferred to Purdue University to study chemical engineering.

After graduating, I went to work in 1949 as a chemist at Eastman Kodak in Rochester, New York. But I soon became dissatisfied with the fit-and-try approaches to problems in organic chemistry that I was confronted with (there was relatively little theoretical work in these areas at that time). I decided to go back to school, either in physical chemistry, which I had especially enjoyed as an undergraduate, or in social psychology, which I had come to be interested in by taking an evening course at the University of Rochester. I finally decided upon the latter, because regarding myself as relatively indolent, I decided to choose the area that was of greater intrinsic interest to me, and could thus claim a greater fraction of my attention throughout life. That is how I came to study sociology.

Q: Did you take any courses in economics during all of this? Or you perhaps came into contact with it in some other way?

A: I took one course in economics as an undergraduate, which led me to regard it as truly a "dismal science." And I had little exposure to economics while at Columbia in graduate school (I did sit in desultorily on a course of George Stigler's or William Vickrey's on price theory, but wasn't much stimulated by it). I did have some exposure, however, to game-theoretical ideas, at the Bureau of Applied Social Research, both through exposure to von Neumann and Morgenstern's book, and because it was then and there that Duncan Luce and Howard Raiffa were working on *Games and Decisions* (sec Neumann and Morgenstern 1944; Luce and Raiffa 1957). I had some interaction with Herbert Simon, who was applying some ideas from economics to sociological problems. Also, through Paul Lazarsfeld, I had some interaction with Vickrey, with Franco Modigliani, and with William Baumol. Some of the tasks Lazarsfeld set me to work on involved exploration of the role that "utility" played in economic theory. So I read some in economics at that time. Yet, I did not see much value in carrying over the economist's paradigm of rational action into sociology. That was in large part because I was essentially a Durkheimian, seeing the central problems of sociology in the study of how properties of a social system affect individuals within that system. It was only after I left Columbia that I got intrigued with a set of problems, and a way of looking at them, that led me toward the path that I now take.

Q: Could you tell a little about this path that led to rational choice—what your sources of inspiration were and the like?

A: It is a little bit hard to reconstruct that. There certainly were several early points which were quite important. Probably the first was my listening to Homans at the University of Chicago, either in 1957 or 1958. It was a presentation of a paper that was published in the *American Journal of Sociology* in 1958, on social behavior as exchange (Homans 1958). It was Homans' first movement in this direction, and it struck me as a very important new direction. That was one element. Another element was that I got a grant from the Carnegie Corporation in early 1960 or 1961 to use games—actually, social simulation games—for high school education. I got very interested in developing such games, and in the process of developing them, I came to the realization that one could think of what was peculiarly sociological as not the actions of the players—you could take them as given—but laying out the rules of the game; the structures within which the persons acted: giving them goals, and laying out an incentive structure for them, and letting the system function. So I began to see games as a sort of precursor to social theory, or, as a certain kind of social theory. I had been a Durkheimian from graduate school on, but I had been distressed for some time that much of the sociological work in the Durkheimian tradition was work which looked at only one side of the sociological problem, that is, the way in which the social environment affects the individual and individual behavior. That was not all of Durkheim's program, but it certainly was part of it. It was about the impact of society on individual action, or on individual orientations, and was best exemplified by *Suicide*. The other side is something which in the early days of my career I never saw as very important: the way in which a person's actions combine to create a functioning of the system. This is much more a Weberian orientation; that is, Weber was closer to a kind of action theory than probably any other major social theorist.

So two important events in my thinking about these matters were the Homans presentation that I heard here in 1957 or 1958 and the development of the games program in 1960–1961. Then there was another important development, although this was somewhat later in the process, and that was some comments I made on a paper by Talcott Parsons on the concept of influence (see Parsons 1963). Although I thought that Parsons did a lot of things very badly (if you read my paper you know how I felt about it), nevertheless he got me thinking about certain things about the functioning of systems (see Coleman 1963). One of the nice things about Parsons is that even though his explanations are functionalist, he was interested in the functioning of the social system, which lots of sociologists were not at that point.

Q: I would now like to ask a few questions on rational choice. The first has to do with methodological individualism. In several of your works you talk not only of "the natural actor" but also of "the corporate actor," that is, a collective actor. How does this square with methodological individualism?

A: Let me first say something about the corporate actor. The kind of general program that I have is the following. One can, I think, take corporate actors as given for the purpose of some kinds of analyses or for certain kinds of theoretical purposes. At the same time, for other purposes, one has to take them as problematic. In other words, I say that methodological individualism can work at more than one level. True methodological individualism takes natural persons—the actions of natural persons—as the only starting point and looks at the system of action that occurs among these. But at the same time, one can use the same theoretical framework if one were to start with corporate actors and make a micro-to-macro transition to systems of these corporate actors. For example, for some purposes, one could carry out an analysis of a system of action among firms as actors, without going down to the individuals within the firm. Now, that is not to say that one should not at certain points investigate the functioning of these corporate actors and treat their functioning as problematic. But for some investigations, one would be, I think, justified in taking corporate actors as having all the properties of an actor. By having properties of an actor, I mean acting in a way to which we can attribute purpose to them; that is, acting in a consistent way, and therefore not acting in a way that is somehow aberrant or peculiar, but in a way which could be conceived of as purposive. Then one can examine the way in which the systems of those actors function. The micro-to-macro framework is a *relative* framework. At whatever level one finds actors acting purposively, one can take that as a micro level and examine the functioning of the system of those actors. But, as I say, for the fundamental explanation, one also wants to take those actors as problematic.

Q: This answers my question about methodological individualism. Now let me ask a question about purposive action, which is another important principle of rational choice sociology. Economists usually just assign a hypothetical rational purpose to the actor. Is this also your stance?

A: I am more inclined not to do that, but rather to infer purpose from behavior; that is, to look at actions, and infer purpose from these. And that can be done either through qualitative observation or through quantitative observation. So the qualitative–quantitative distinction is not really important for this theoretical framework. Investigations either in a qualitative or a quantitative domain are equally important and appropriate.

One of the things that I have always been distressed by is the fact that most quantitative work is work in which it is the behavior of individuals which is taken as the thing to be explained. We therefore are not really explaining the functioning of the system but just the behavior of individuals. One of the things I have gotten very excited about just in the last couple of months is the way in which one can begin to use quantitative data to explain not the functioning of individuals, but the functioning of the system. Even though the data may be at the level of individuals, you can study the functioning of the system. Now, that has always been more true of qualitative observations, that is, it has always been easier somehow to look in a qualitative way at the behavior of individuals and to somehow synthesize one's observations in one's mind, so that one is actually describing the functioning of the system. If you look at a classic work like *Street Corner Society*, you will find that William Foote Whyte was really studying that group of boys or gang as a system, even though he was making observations on individuals. We have never been able to do that very well quantitatively. One of my aims is to bring together qualitative and quantitative work, so that quantitative work does not go off in a nontheoretical direction.

Q: Methodological individualism and purposive action are common to most forms of rational choice. But to this you add, if I may cite your coming book *The Foundations of Social Theory*, the two concepts of "control" and "interest." In fact, they play an extremely important role in your new social theory. The way I understand it is that you basically use these two concepts to reinterpret some of the central concepts of sociology, such as authority, power, and social movements. In fact, you erect a magnificent theoretical building with the help of these two building blocks. I have two questions here. First, would you accept this interpretation of your theory? And second, could you say a little about the way you define these two key concepts, "control" and "interests"?

A: Your reading is certainly right. What I attempt to do is to have an extraordinarily simple system at the micro level, in which you have only two kinds of elements: actors on the one hand, and something I call "events" and sometimes call "resources" and sometimes call "goods" on the other hand. So there is a little bit of slipperiness there with respect to that. The two things that connect them are "interest" and "control." The principal role of "interest" in the theory is that it is the driving force, somewhat like utility is in neoclassical economic theory. In fact, in part five of the book, I show the direct connection between interest and utility in my formal model. So the connection is just a mathematical one. Interest turns out to be a parameter associated with a particular resource or good in a Cobb-Douglas utility function. So it is directly connected to utility, and it plays the same role in the theory as utility does in neoclassical economic theory. The thing that utility does is that it *activates* the actors. The principle of action depends on utility, on maximization of utility. The principle of action here is that the actor acts in the way which will best realize his interest. This is equivalent to saying that he maximizes his utility, but I like to think of it in terms of interest because interest, I think, corresponds more nearly to the natural way in which we think about persons' orientations to action.

As to "control," there are really two slightly different things I mean by that. As can be seen in the manuscript I am working on, one of these comes to have a larger and larger place in my chapters. The two components to control are "rights to control" and "de facto control." Let us think of resources as the thing being controlled. Resources are anything that people are interested in. If I have "de facto control" over certain resources, then I can exchange those. I can do whatever I want: I can consume them or whatever. If I have "rights to control," it is a different story. The right to control is, for example, this: if I make a promise to someone that I will do what they say, I transfer to them the right to control my actions. If I make a contract with an employer by giving him the right to control my action, it should be noted that my actions have a special character in that they are nonalienable. Since they are nonalienable, it is necessary that I retain de facto control over them. That means that there is a separation between rights of control and de facto control. That is also the case in norms.

I see the development of norms as the transfer of rights of control of an action from the actor to other parties who are affected by the action. The actor still retains de facto control of the action, but if there is a norm which is generally accepted the others have a right to control it. So if there is a non-smoking norm which comes to be generally accepted, then a person who wants to smoke still can pull out a pack of cigarettes and light; but he knows that if he does this, he will be subject to challenge. Ordinarily, if he does so, and if he accepts the legitimacy of that norm, he will ask someone before he lights the cigarette, "Is it all right with you if I smoke?" He asks for the right to smoke because, in fact, the right is now in *their* hands. Before the norm existed he did not ask because the right was in *his* hands. But now the right is in their hands so he asks for that right back, and they may or may not give it to him. If he smokes without asking for that right, then he can expect to be santioned in some way, and he can expect that the others would feel justified in doing this.

Q: Would it be possible for your version of rational choice to constitute the basis for all the social sciences? The sense I get from your writings is that you would indeed answer "yes" on this question—at least as far as history, law, and economics are concerned; psychology is a different story. Would you agree with this answer?

A: I think you have answered the question very much as I would. I would see the theory of rational social action as a potential foundation for all the social sciences except psychology, because psychology is concerned with a different system. It is concerned with the person as a system, whereas sociology, law, economics, political science are concerned with the social system as a system. They are concerned with different parts of the social system in a sense, but nevertheless their object of study consists of a system in which the elements are actors—either natural persons or corporate actors of some sort—and the system is a system of action among actors. Psychology is a different kettle of fish because it is concerned with how you can conceive of the action of a natural person. So I would not pretend to have much to say about psychology.

Sometimes I have an idea that there can come to be a psychology in which the same structure exists *internal* to the individual, and the values of particular resources or events for the system are his interests, since he is the system. But that is only a kind of fanciful dream, and I really don't have it that well-developed in my mind. It is consistent with the notion . . . No, I don't wan't to go into that. You're exactly right: I really don't have anything to say about psychology. One of the things I actually do not find terribly interesting is all the work in variations upon rationality that is being done now. For example, Jon Elster (1984) does a lot of this; Gary

Becker (1981) is very much interested in these variations; and Tversky and Kahneman (1981) and a lot of other cognitive psychologists are interested in variations upon ways in which people are not rational. I am not interested in that at all; I'd much rather take a very simple structure at the level of the actor, and then construct this edifice onto it.

Q: You have always been fascinated by law, it seems to me, and legal thought has influenced your work in various ways. Would it be correct to say also that the structure of your theory of social action is influenced by your interest in this area?

A: Yes, very much so. In fact, the closest correspondence to law and the closest link to law which I have developed in the chapters of the manuscript for my new book *Foundations of Social Theory* is a chapter you probably haven't seen. It is the new chapter 30 ("Externalities and Norms in a Linear System of Action"). What is interesting about this chapter is that it is a chapter on norms but it shows very closely the connection between norms and law, at least law conceived as the law and economics people do, as leading toward a socially efficient outcome and law. I also have a footnote in this chapter saying that if I were dedicating the chapters in my book, I would dedicate this one to Richard Posner and Ronald Coase. I would dedicate it to them for a very perverse reason, because Ronald Coase in his paper on the problem of social cost argues that independent of how rights are distributed, market transactions will lead to a socially efficient outcome (Coase 1960). Posner argues that the role of a judge is to bring about those socially efficient outcomes, which are not brought about because of transaction costs (e.g. Posner 1983). So I say that there is a kind of inconsistency between these two, even though they are both part of the law and economics field. I showed this chapter to Posner, and he gave me a set of extended comments on it. In these he generally agreed with the things that I had said, although at some points I really come into serious conflict with the law and economics people. But he insisted that there was no disagreement between his orientation and that of Coase, which certainly in principle there is not, even if I am right about this peculiarity. So I see a very close connection at the interface between norms and law, and all of this new chapter 30 is devoted to this problem. I see that chapter as very central to my book because a lot of things culminate in that chapter.

Q: Are there any legal questions other than the link between norms and law that you find important in this context?

A: Yes, there is especially the law of agency. I see this aspect of legal thought as probably less valuable to sociologists than the other ones that I have just been discussing, because the law of agency is, I think, a quite limited realm of law. Nevertheless, the reason I got interested in the law of agency was that here was the common law, dealing with a sociological problem: how one person can get another person to act in his interest, and what are the problems that arise in this particular structure. This fits in very nicely with the fundamental conceptual structure which I have developed. The agent mixes his resources, which are ordinarily skills, and the resources of the principal, but he is intended to use this combination of resources wholly in the interest of the principal. And where all the problems in the law of agency arise is in the fact that his own interest intrudes. He does not always act in the interest of the principal, but sometimes in his own interest. So the whole question becomes whether it is possible to have one person combine his resources with those of another and act in the interest of another, and under what conditions this is possible. I think this is a very interesting question. That is the way I first got interested in law.

Q: And what about moral philosophy à la Rawls? Isn't that also another aspect of law that has preoccupied you?

A: Your question about moral philosophy is really not so much about law, but rather raises some philosophical questions. What I think is interesting about moral philosophy is that it has always had an underlying theory of action; it has always been based on a theory of action. One of the reasons sociology lost contact with moral philosophy is because sociology really lost contact with any kind of coherent theory of action. To reconstitute a theory of action for sociology would allow it to come back into contact with some of these questions which are normative and which ought not to be ignored by sociology. Sociologists tend to be blind to normative questions. I don't think they should be.

Q: Let me ask about your relationship to neoclassical economics. It seems, first of all, that your theory has been profoundly influenced by neoclassical economics, and that you have a very high opinion of its achievements. But there also seem to be some differences of opinion between you and the economists. You emphasize, for example, the importance of power, which is a topic that neoclassical economics by tradition avoids. You also sometimes note that economic theory does not have a place for interaction (as does game theory).

A: There is much to be said on this issue. First, let me say that I have great admiration for neoclassical economics. This is for the same reason that I have extreme admiration for Newtonian mechanics. I see neoclassical economics as an elegant, almost logical system, as an elegant system of action. My real hero is not Isaac Newton, but James Clerk Maxwell. He took Newtonian theory and developed from it a theory of gases, the Maxwell-Boltzmann distribution law of molecular velocities. I was fascinated by Maxwell because he was also concerned with the micro-macro

problem. He had a very simple and neat theoretical framework of dimen-
sionless molecules of any gas acting according to the laws of motion, each
with a certain mass and velocity. And from this he constructed a theory of
gases. My admiration for neoclassical economics derives from my admiration for Newtonian mechanics and its extension to statistical mechanics.

My differences with neoclassical economics lie primarily in two areas.
One area you pointed to, and that is that they have no place for power and
no concept of power. This was one of the points where Posner and I
differed. The thing that I have to make very certain that I emphasize in
chapter 30—I practically will have to beat the neoclassical economists
over the head with it—is the whole problem of the interpersonal comparison of utility. This is something which economists claim they cannot cope
with, and which they do not cope with; they say you cannot carry out
interpersonal comparisons. My central point here is that in any action system, the constitutional allocation of rights is what gives (implicitly or explicitly) the interpersonal comparison; and that this interpersonal comparison gives different weights to different persons' interests. Basically
this constitutional allocation of rights ends up in the formal model giving
certain weights to different persons' interests. The weight that it gives to
different persons' interests is another term for power. So it is very explicit
in this theory that even if you keep to the extraordinarily simplifying assumptions of neoclassical economics—perfect information; perfect mix-
ing of persons in the market, so there is no segmentation in the market, no
structuring of the market; and so on—the differential weighting of different persons' interests constitutes the interpersonal comparison, which I
think economists have been looking for all this time. And that constitutes
power, which in my system plays the same role as wealth in the economic
system. In other words, in my system—if it were applied to economics—
power and wealth are equivalent. But when you deal not just with economic resources but also with other resources (including things involving
collective actions), then it can be better interpreted as "power" rather than
as "wealth." So that is a very fundamental difference that I have with the
neoclassical economists.

The other fundamental difference I have with economists is that I think
they took the wrong path in the micro-to-macro transition. They took a
path in which they left the utility function as a general function. They did
not specify the utility function except to specify it qualitatively. They put
two constraints on it: that the first derivative is positive and that the second
derivative is negative, so you end up getting a typical declining marginal
utility. What this has done is that it has restricted them in most of their
theoretical work—until economics got very mathematical—to dealing
with two or three goods at one time. Neoclassical economics as a price

theory can almost be identified with plane geometry! I think that was a mistake. What that cost them was the ability to cope with a larger system. The economists repaired this, and had all sorts of devices to do that. But I think the correct thing to have done, which would have gotten them a lot farther, would have been to make a simplification by assuming a particular utility function. If you assume the right utility function, a Cobb-Douglas utility function, then you can get what I call "a linear system of action." Nearly all of econometrics is studying partial equilibrium; but if you assume the right utility function, you can study "general equilibrium." You can study equilibrium of the system, even though it is a subset of the whole system, and not just the supply side or the demand side. And you can do this quantitatively. That's what I am most excited about right now: the fact that if you do make this specification of the utility function, then you are able to do quantitative analysis which is unlike most quantitative sociological research in the sense that it does not focus on individual behavior, even though the variables are measured on individuals. Instead it focuses on the behavior of the system. But economists did not do that. And as a consequence, in their econometric analysis, they seldom deal with general equilibrium but instead with partial equilibrium.

So those are my two major disagreements with mainstream economics. You mentioned a third one, which has to do with game theory and the fact that neoclassical economics does not use game theory. It does not—but certainly the kind of neo-neoclassical economics does, so that is not really any kind of central difference.

Q: There is one question which a colleague of mine, Tom Colbjørnsen, wanted me to ask you. He wondered whether it is true that in the future the sociologist might very well be reduced to becoming a kind of "scout for the economists"? The sociologist finds something of value to the economist—say norms in the workplace—and brings this information back to the economist, who works it into his or her models, only to send the sociologist out into the field again to find something new of interest, which can then be used by the economist, and so on.

A: I think the answer is "no." I think that the economists have shown certain kinds of fundamental narrowness and blindness, and that it will rather turn out that economics will become a kind of subdiscipline of sociology in the future.

Q: I was going to ask you what you think about economic sociology and whether you approve of it, but from your answer I think this is self-evident.

A: There is an old aphorism that war is too important to be left to the generals. Well, economics is too important to be left to the economists. I think there ought to be an economic sociology just like there is a political sociology. I think that somehow sociologists were scared off . . . maybe not scared off economic sociology, but somehow the economists came to create the illusion that there were no sociological processes in what is narrowly construed as "economic behavior." The minute you begin to look at these things, however, there clearly are. Economists cannot explain bank panics; sociologists have come a lot closer to that than they do. Economists cannot explain all kinds of things. And I think that they are beginning to recognize that now. So I think that economic sociology is almost virgin territory, which is really a very important direction to pursue.

Q: My final question has to do with your present work on a rational choice theory of social action. What is needed to complete it?

A: One of the things that has been inhibiting me for a long time from completing my manuscript is that I was not able to see how I could connect the theoretical work to research of the sort that I am used to, that is, to some kind of quantitative research. Now I have found that I can do that. So one whole branch of work ought to be to use the same kind of quantitative tools that we have been using for studying individuals to begin to study organizations and social systems. That would be the empirical side of my argument. The theoretical side I have just begun to sketch out, but it is as if I am just beginning the task. I am, for example, probably least satisfied with respect to authority systems. If I have done anything with respect to authority systems, the principal thing has been to do what I always accused Parsons of doing, and that is just to create a set of categories. I have defined "simple" and "complex authority systems," "conjoint" and "disjoint authority relations." I have tried to do a little bit more than that; there are some things that do not appear in the version that you have looked at. These include the conditions under which what we think of as charismatic authority will arise, and a few other things like that.

But I am really dissatisfied with that also. All I will have done is kind of show the building blocks for the structure, and the structure remains to be built. All I will have done is point to a direction. For example, part one of my manuscript shows how rights come to be exceedingly important in this way of looking at things. You may have seen a paper I wrote, called "Political Money," which is reprinted in the collection *Individual Interests and Collective Action*. It asks the question, what are the differences between political power and money as economic power? How can you logically characterize the differences between these two? I have later developed the points in that article as one of the chapters in the book, which is called "Forms of Rights and Forms of Power," and I think it represents a kind of scratching the surface of a whole theoretical development about the "forms of rights." I think a very deep exploration of rights on the border lines between political philosophy and sociology is an extremely fertile field.

So to get back to your question: what needs to be done to complete my theory of social action? The answer is that I see this work as only having begun development of the appropriate theoretical structure. What is necessary for any discipline is an internally consistent theoretical core of concepts. Sociology does not have that core. My book is an attempt to provide it. But it's only a core, only the beginning of the theory.

References

Becker, Gary. 1981. *A Treatise on the Family.* Cambridge: Harvard University Press.

Coase, R. H. 1960. "The Problem of Social Cost." *Journal of Law and Economics* 3:1–44.

Coleman, James S. 1963. "Comment on 'The Concept of Influence' (by Talcott Parsons)." *Public Opinion Quarterly* 27:63–82.

———. 1964a. "Collective Decisions." *Sociological Inquiry* 34 (Spring):166–81.

———. 1964b. *Introduction to Mathematical Sociology.* New York: Free Press.

———. 1966. "Foundations for a Theory of Collective Decisions." *American Journal of Sociology* 71:615–27.

———. 1973. *The Mathematics of Collective Action.* Chicago: Aldine Publishing.

———. 1974. *Power and the Structure of Society.* New York: W. W. Norton.

———. 1975. "*Review Essay:* Inequality, Sociology and Moral Philosophy." *American Journal of Sociology* 80:739–64.

———. 1982. *The Assymetric Society.* Syracuse, N.Y.: Syracuse University Press.

———. 1984. "Introducing Social Structure into Economic Analysis." *American Economic Review* 74(2):84–88.

———. 1985. "An Autobiographical Sketch, I & II." Unpublished manuscript.

———. 1986a. *Individual Interests and Collective Action.* Cambridge: Cambridge University Press.

———. 1986b. "Social Theory, Social Research, and a Theory of Action." *American Journal of Sociology* 91:1309–35.

Coleman, James S., et al. 1966. *Equality of Educational Opportunity.* Washington, D.C.: U.S. Government Printing Office.

Coleman, James S., Thomas Hoffer, and Sally Kilgore. 1982. *High School Achievement: Public, Catholic, and Private Schools Compared.* New York: Basic Books.

Durkheim, Emile. 1951. *Suicide: A Study in Sociology.* New York: Free Press. Originally appeared in 1897.

Elster, Jon. 1984. *Ulysses and the Sirens: Studies in Rationality and Irrationality.* Rev. ed. Cambridge: Cambridge University Press. Originally appeared in 1979.

Homans, George C. 1958. "Social Behavior as Exchange." *American Journal of Sociology* 63:597–606.

Hunt, Morton. 1985. "The Dilemma in the Classroom: A Cross-sectional Survey Measures the Effects of Segregated Schooling (on James S. Coleman)." In *Profiles of Social Research*, 51–97. New York: Russel Sage.

Luce, R. Duncan, and Howard Raiffa. 1957. *Games and Decisions: Introduction and Critical Survey.* New York: John Wiley.

von Neumann, John, and Oskar Morgenstern. 1944. *The Theory of Games and Economic Behavior.* Princeton, N.J.: Princeton University Press.

Parsons, Talcott. 1963. "On the Concept of Influence." *Public Opinion Quarterly* 27:37–62.

Posner, Richard A. 1983. *The Economics of Justice.* Cambridge: Harvard University Press.

Tversky, Amos, and Daniel Kahneman. 1981. "The Framing of Decisions and the Psychology of Choice." *Science* 211:453–58.

Whyte, William Foote. 1943. *Street-Corner Society.* Chicago: University of Chicago Press.

3

George A. Akerlof

GEORGE AKERLOF (1940–) is the youngest of the economists interviewed in this book. His contribution to the debate between economics and sociology can be described as the very opposite of Becker's. Instead of trying to use the economists' model to explain noneconomic behavior, Akerlof is concerned with introducing elements from the noneconomic social sciences directly into the economic analysis. The basic premise is that if you use new behavioral assumptions in economics, several of the problems that have long baffled economists will come closer to a solution. Among these, Akerlof considers unemployment to be by far the biggest challenge.

The approach that Akerlof advocates can best be studied in his collection of essays entitled *An Economic Theorist's Book of Tales*. The most famous of these is "The Market for 'Lemons'," which illustrates Akerlof's general approach in that a new behavioral assumption, asymmetric information among the economic actors, is introduced directly into a conventional neoclassical model—and with surprising results. The book argues enthusiastically that the very absence of economic models that take noneconomic social science seriously today allows for a whole new field to be opened up: "psycho- socio- anthropo-economics." If economists can come up with a natural research agenda here, Akerlof says, this new field might become as exciting as mathematical economics. In this interview Akerlof is, among other things, asked about the background to his book of tales: what has been accomplished in this new type of economics since the book appeared in 1984, and how he sees the future relationship between economics and sociology.

George Akerlof is the son of Gösta Akerlof, a Swedish chemist and inventor who emigrated to the United States in the 1920s, and Rosalie Hirschfelder Akerlof. He was born in New Haven, Connecticut in 1940. He earned his undergraduate degree from Yale University in 1962, and his Ph.D. in economics from MIT in 1966. Since 1966, he has mainly worked at the University of California at Berkeley. He has also spent some years

The following interview with George A. Akerlof was carried out in Palo Alto, California, on April 30, 1988.

abroad as an economist. During the period 1967 to 1968 he was as at the Indian Statistical Institute in New Delhi, and from 1978 to 1980 he was at the London School of Economics. He has held various nonacademic positions, including one at the Federal Reserve Board from 1977 to 1978.

•

Q: How did you become interested in economics? Did any teacher play a key role in this?

A: I guess I was always interested in economics. I am not sure that it was any specific teacher who influenced me to go into economics. It was more likely that some teacher could have influenced me the other way around. When I entered Yale in 1958, they had you fill out some form about what you wanted to do. It was the first day of my freshman year, and I filled out that I wanted to be a professor of economics. Later I was actually quite surprised that I knew something like that so much in advance.

But I think that I have always had an economic view of social relations and of history. This goes quite far back. When I was eight and lived in Pittsburgh, Pennsylvania, I remember that in either second or in third grade you were supposed to write a letter to Santa Claus and say what you wanted. I wrote to Santa Claus and said that I wanted a factory. Well, there were lots of factories in Pittsburgh, and my idea of course was that if you had a factory, you didn't need to ask for all these other things, like toys and so on.

So I can remember having been interested in economics at a very young age. And this continued. I recall in my junior or senior year in high school that we had to write a big history paper. I think most people wrote their papers on something political. I wrote mine on Ivar Kreuger.

Q: What about the teachers you have had in economics? Which were the most important to you at MIT in graduate school?

A: Robert Solow was by far the most important. But I didn't have that many teachers. One reason, I think, was that there were fewer people on the MIT faculty than there are now. So there were Solow and Samuelson, of course, and they were pretty influential. Modigliani was also at MIT, but the first year I was there he was teaching in the business school. It was only in the later years that he began to have a lot to do with the economics students. But I was never that influenced by him.

So Solow was very influential. This was at a time when MIT was into growth theory. If you go back and look at the issues of *The Review of Economic Studies* in those years, it is genuinely shocking because there is almost nothing but growth theory. And that is not an exaggeration. But Solow was an excellent teacher, and he is a really good economist.

I also took a course in algebraic topology at Harvard from a very good mathematician, Raoul Bott. I think that Bott and Solow were the two people who influenced me the most. Bott was important because he didn't just teach you algebraic topology, which may or may not have been interesting, but somehow he also taught you how to think about mathematics. He succeeded in making you see what was the key to a mathematical idea, and the rest he considered to be details. I have had a large number of math courses, and teachers differ quite a bit in their styles. Some people just go through the details and the proofs. Bott, who was clearly the best person I ever had, rather laid out what the key idea was.

Q: What about courses in social sciences other than economics? Did you, for example, take any courses in sociology?

A: I didn't take any at all as a graduate student. I think I took two courses outside the economics department at MIT. Remember that one only takes courses for two years, so we are talking about eight courses. I took the course in algebraic topology I have already mentioned and which lasted for two terms. And then I took a course in optimal control theory in the electrical engineering department.

Q: So it wasn't really until after your graduate education was over, that you started to read the sociology upon which you draw in your writings?

A: That's right. I had had a reasonable amount of history but I had never read anything in the other social sciences. But let me give you a little bit of background and history here. I think I had read virtually nothing in psychology, sociology, and anthropology until one year after graduate school. I came to Berkeley in 1966 and then I went to India for a year. On the way back from India I got a copy of Ruth Benedict's *The Chrysanthemum and the Sword* on Japan. I really liked that, and I then started to read a lot of cultural anthropology.

After being to India I understood that economic systems don't necessarily work as they do in standard economics, where markets always clear. The caste system somehow provided me with an alternative model for how economic systems might work, and I wrote a paper on that called "The Economics of Caste and of the Rat Race and Other Woeful Tales." I had finished the paper by 1973 and it then came out in 1976. During these years in the 1970s I was getting more interested in sociological types of issues, but I didn't read any formal sociology. I think that most of what I read was actually in anthropology.

It wasn't really until I gave a seminar at Yale in 1978 on the caste idea that I began to seriously read sociology. What happened was this. At the seminar Tjalling Koopmans asked me if I had read any sociology. No, he probably put it more politely and asked whether there was any relevance of sociology to my work. I of course said, "Oh yes!" But when I thought about it, I realized that I literally didn't know what sociology was. At the time I was working at the Federal Reserve in Washington, so when I came back from Yale I went to the George Washington University (G.W.U.) Bookstore and got the textbook for the intermediate sociology course. It was a book by Lewis Coser called *Masters of Sociological Thought,* which was actually very good. So then I decided I really liked sociology and I got hold of Merton's *Social Theory and Social Structure.* I read this book very carefully—twice as a matter of fact, making lots of notes in the margin—and I liked it very much. And then I read George Homans (e.g., 1950). Merton and Homans are the two people in sociology I have found easiest to read and to understand. I have actually been looking for more people like that, but they seem hard to find.

Q: What about Max Weber? Did he make any impression on you?

A: Not quite so much. I think I liked Durkheim better, and I have actually used him a little bit. But I don't think I have ever used Weber. What happened was this. When I got back to Berkeley in 1980—I taught at the London School of Economics for two years, from 1978 to 1980—I tried to take some sociology courses. I took the first year graduate class, and we read Weber, Marx, and Durkheim. I actually didn't find them that useful. Somehow I think that sociology has a very different approach to theory from economics. In sociology it is still a little bit like the way economics was taught under Schumpeter. You go through the classics, and you try to figure out what the classics say. Somehow it is hard to have patience with that, once you have been trained as an economist. Maybe I just never had the patience with the sociological classics although I have gone through the classics in economics. Incidentally, I think that today you would find that virtually no students have gone through the classics in economics. Somehow it is a different way of thinking today.

Q: From *An Economic Theorist's Book of Tales* it is clear that you have developed a very distinct approach to economic theory in which social influences play an important role, not to say the key role. When did it occur to you that it was possible to do economic theory this way? When was "psycho- socio- anthropo-economics," as you call it, invented?

A: I think it emerged gradually. The first thing I wrote in this genre was "The Market for 'Lemons'." That paper has been quite popular. It was easy to write, and I have never quite understood why the main idea wasn't obvious. Somehow that paper gave me a style for how to do economics. People seemed to like it, and that makes you think about what's good and bad in it. I guess I liked it myself too.

I think I duplicated it—not one hundred percent self-consciously but at least subconsciously—in doing "The Economics of Caste and of the Rat Race." That paper was a little bit more sociological than "The Market for 'Lemons'," although the latter was in some sense sociological too, at least in relation to the economics of the time. But maybe I should go into a little bit of history here. As of 1966, when I wrote "The Market for 'Lemons'," there was almost nothing about information in economics. There was no reason why there should not have been, but there just wasn't. It was simply not part of the tradition; you can say there was a taboo against writing about information in economics. So I sent my article off to various journals—and what happened is an indication of the extent of that taboo.

I first sent it to *The American Economic Review*. They sent back a rejection, saying that the paper was amusing but they didn't want to publish such trivial stuff. I then sent it to *The Journal of Political Economy*. They rejected it too, and said that it was wrong. From what I can remember—unfortunately I don't have these letters any more—they claimed that according to my argument there couldn't be a market for eggs either. How could there be a market for something like eggs, they said, if people were so worried about quality? So they felt that what I said was wrong; the paper shouldn't be published. That may have been a thoughtful review. Anyway, after that I sent it to *The Review of Economic Studies*, where actually one of the editors had suggested that I send it. But they turned it down too. They said that they didn't want to publish such trivial stuff. And then I sent it to *The Quarterly Journal of Economics*, where it was luckily accepted.

The whole process clearly took some time, and I think the reason was this taboo against discussing the role of information in economics and, more generally, against introducing new topics into economics. Somehow there are certain frameworks that people are supposed to think in and which are acceptable. If you go outside these, then people don't know exactly how to deal with it. You'd think that people in this situation would be leaning over backwards and say, "Well, this paper might have some merit to it and maybe we should publish it." But people seem in fact more likely to do the opposite.

So to get back to the topic: How did I develop the approach of "psycho-socio- anthropo-economics?" "The Market for 'Lemons' " gave me a kind of format, a way of thinking about things, or at least a style which seemed to make it possible to do things where maybe you could bring in new ideas into economics. The next step was the article on "The Economics of Caste and of the Rat Race." I actually did not believe that the part on caste could be published. So in some sense what I did was I took the rat race part and just added the caste to it. I don't think that they go very well together actually. But one of the reasons they are there is that I knew that the rat race part was acceptable. The caste part I sort of just put in, but in my opinion it was that part that was the interesting bit. The rat race part was basically just "The Market for 'Lemons' " revisited, while the caste bit had a new structure. Caste economies are very different from traditional, competitive economies of traditional economics.

I guess at that point, after having written two essays of this sort, I thought I understood the style. The whole process is difficult, and there are really two problems involved in something like this. One is that you have to have a style which is acceptable. The other is that you have to have some ideas. And the two are probably independent.

Q: What exactly do you mean by "style" in this context?

A: I don't know quite what I mean by "style." But you have to have some kind of way of writing your ideas and of putting them into frameworks, which are acceptable. I think one of the things that my models have and that some other people's models don't have is that, because I have such a good classical training in economics, what I was able to do was to combine some new elements with a very standard sort of neoclassical economics. And I think that this combination of old and new is a good thing; I don't think it's a bad thing. What you want to do, is to point out how you can modify the way people are currently thinking if they had just a little bit of a broader mind. Or, say, if they were concerned with certain issues which are very important in the way other people think. Economists, for some reason or other, want to isolate the world into only economic issues. But it is possible—in fact, it is probable—that noneconomic issues are going to alter what the fundamental structure of economics looks like.

Finally, one of the things that has interested me the most in economics is unemployment. I have always felt that this was both an interesting problem—interesting because standard economic theory finds it difficult for unemployment to exist—as well as an important and potentially solvable economic problem. You want to work with problems which you think are interesting in some way, and which you can do something interesting with. By "interesting" I mean something other than what would appear to someone with just good common sense. In all of the papers that make up *An Economic Theorist's Book of Tales*, irrespective of what they may come out looking like in the end, the basic concern has been, "What does unemployment look like?" "The Market for 'Lemons'," for example, might be about microeconomic structures, but what got me thinking along those lines was that I wanted to know why there was such a big cycle in purchases of consumer durables. The cycle in durables is a cause for fluctuations in aggregate demand and therefore in unemployment. I was thinking about why the purchase of cars was so variable. And for that I had to answer why in fact people purchased cars rather than rented them. If people rented cars, then I thought—and this is probably not true but it could possibly be true—that the purchases would be much more stable over the course of the business cycle.

Q: I have difficulty in seeing that all the essays in your book are inspired by unemployment. One of my favorites—"Loyalty Filters"—seems, for example, to be much more focused on general issues of what's right and wrong.

A: I should maybe have said that *almost all* have been motivated by unemployment. "Loyalty Filters" is about something else, which I thought was very important and that the economists were missing. "Loyalty Filters" is about how people change as a result of their experiences. If such changes occur, standard welfare theory is considerably altered.

Q: In one place you and Janet Yellen write that in 1982 you "provided the first explicitly sociological model [of unemployment] leading to the efficiency wage hypothesis" (Akerlof and Yellen 1986, 8). Could you explain what is "sociological" about this hypothesis? Also: How do you feel that your hypothesis from 1982 is holding up in today's debate about unemployment?

A: What is sociological about the model is that unemployment develops because of group behavior. In traditional (nonsociological) models in economics, all agents (consumers, businessmen, etc.) are individually maximizing. In my "gift exchange" model, unemployment develops because workers care about their coworkers. This limits the firm's ability to impose efficient contracts which would be market-clearing (with market-clearing contracts there is no unemployment).

I believe that some form of sociological theory is necessary to explain above-market clearing wages. Empirically, the character of wage differentials also supports such a view. The popular "insider-outsider" theory is, ultimately, based on collaboration of workers, which puts limits on contracts. In sum, there is more reason to believe, in 1988, that unemployment has sociological roots than in 1982, because of a lot of good subsequent work on efficiency wages, including the work on wage differentials and "insider-outsider" theories.

Q: When I first read your book of tales, I just assumed that your special approach to economics—"psycho- socio- anthropo-economics"—was applicable to all types of economic problems. But after reading the book more carefully a second time, I get the impression that there are only *some* issues that your approach really covers. In one place, for example, you say that "for most types of economic behavior, the economists' model is probably quite adequate" (Akerlof 1984a, 123). So what exactly is the scope of your new type of economics?

A: I think that the approach in my book is probably applicable to the big problems, to the really big things that we don't yet understand in economics. I think it is probably applicable to the question why underdeveloped countries are so poor. We don't yet have a simple economic model that explains that. There must in all likelihood be other factors which explain this than the conventional ones. And it is the same with unemployment. It seems to me that also here the dominant factors why these markets aren't clearing are sociological or psychological.

So I think that my approach can be used for the things that I really care about in economics, which are mainly unemployment in modern economies and why poor countries are so poor. I know that many economists care about a lot of other issues. I am actually always surprised at the range of issues other people care about. Most of today's economics therefore falls outside of the two areas I am interested in. And it's exactly there that conventional economics really works; it explains why you can always get spinach in New York and so on. On the whole, I think that economics is really very, very good. But economists tend to take themselves too seriously. They think that economics covers *everything*. In my opinion, however, you will need sociology and psychology to solve questions like unemployment and the poverty of certain countries. Still, it is unclear how far the good use of sociology and psychology actually extends.

Last year I taught a course with Danny Kahneman on psychology and economics. It was actually an interesting course. I think we each had our own misconceptions about what could be accomplished. He believed that you could just take his type of insights and make good economic theory out of them. So with the help of prospect theory you should be able to make interesting economic models (for prospect theory, see Kahneman and Tversky 1979). I believed that he did very nice experiments and interview type of work, and that if we listened to him, we could carry it over into economics. But I think that each of us had his disappointments. A problem with his thoughts about prospect theory is that prospect theory may be tremendously interesting, but will you get good economic theory just by using prospect theory? Well, maybe not. What you typically would have would be a story whereby people behave in a certain way; and then you add this to the economic theory. So somehow what you do is you have your old economic theory, and then you have, in addition, the fact that people behave in a certain way. And somehow you don't get something new and richer just because you have added prospect theory. What you get is what you would expect if you just add prospect theory to standard economics.

So the really tough thing with incorporating psychological, sociological, and anthropological elements into economic theory is to somehow come up with ways in which you have something interesting to say. It is not very interesting to say that people behave according to standard models and that they deviate exactly the way you would expect them to deviate, if they behave psychologically different. That's actually where unemployment becomes very interesting. Let me explain. If standard economic theory basically says that you can't have unemployment or that it's very hard to have unemployment, and if sociology or psychology in that situation explains equilibrium with unemployment, then *that* is interesting. You have somehow changed the fundamental structure of the problem in an interesting way.

Q: So what you are saying is that the basic thrust of your approach is to take, say, some sociological ideas and then incorporate them into conventional economic theory in a novel way? You can't just add economics and sociology together; there has to be some kind of surprise element in their encounter?

A: Yes, that is somehow what has to happen before you can get something that's interesting in some way. But it is not clear how many areas something interesting is really going to happen in, at least not something that is theoretically interesting. And theoretical is not the same as empirical here. I think that there are probably plenty of areas in which you can combine economics and sociology and get lots of empirically interesting results. Shiller, for example, is doing all kinds of interesting work on financial markets (see Shiller 1979, 1984). Just by getting himself out of the economists' null-hypothesis that all markets clear and that everybody is perfectly rational and maximizing, is pushing him into all of these interesting ways of asking economic questions.

Q: The way you incorporate sociological elements into economic theories still puzzles me. In your article on cognitive dissonance, for example, you say that it is necessary to "*translate* the psychological theory [of Festinger and others] into concepts amenable to incorporation into an economic model" (Akerlof 1984a, 124). But in this conversation, that doesn't seem to be what you are after. Maybe it's a kind of "mutation" you are looking for rather than "translation?"

A: Right, and that is probably why these analyses are more difficult than meets the eye. Because, frequently, putting together economics and sociology doesn't yield something that is necessarily so interesting. I referee a lot of articles, and what you often see is just not interesting. It is as if they proposed to add "a" and "b"; and that's exactly what you get: "a+b."

One thing about the economic model is that it always gives you a null hypothesis. It gives you some kind of base, and then you can figure out how all kinds of deviations would modify that. So, one of the reasons in my mind why economists don't really need to think too much about sociological and psychological phenomena—at least not from a theoretical viewpoint—is that in a lot of cases, you simply know what the results will be. You can take the standard economic model, and see how things will deviate from that when people have imperfect information, when they deviate psychologically or whatever—and you sort of know how the system is going to work out and how it will deviate from optimality. This is a very nice thing about economics, namely that it really gives you some basis with which you can compare what will happen when people behave sociologically. And in most cases, of course, you don't get a surprise. You get exactly what you'd expect.

But one of the problems with all of this is that economists, instead of taking the economic model as some kind of basis against which to compare the real world—which is going to be different with people acting differently—often think that the economic model *is* the world. What a very large number of economists do, and which is just beyond all bounds of belief, is that they simply start their work as if the economic model is the world and then go out and merrily estimate things which they should never have thought of estimating in the first place. That's why you can get a kind of economics which is very blind and foolish. A lot of rational expectations economics is based on the idea that markets clear instantly and that people have these rational expectations. But it is simply not possible to believe that people behave quite so literally according to the economic models. The interesting thing about these models is only that in some sense they give you some kind of backdrop against which you can compare the real world. And in the real world people will perhaps behave according to the model in *some* ways. But in many ways they are going to behave quite differently.

Q: In the introduction to your 1984 book you say that "psycho- socio- anthropo-economics" is not yet a field; and that to become one, it has to get a "set of problems with a natural research agenda" (Akerlof 1984, 6). Now, this was written about five years ago. What progress has been made since 1984? And has your type of economics become a field yet?

A: That's an interesting question. I think that my approach has actually had an impact on macroeconomics. I guess there are two areas where it seems to be important. One is macro, where I think that the Keynesian revival—which is considerable now—is partly due to efficiency wages and near rationality models (see Akerlof 1982; Akerlof and Yellen 1985a, 1985b, 1986). I guess that ten years ago you didn't find younger people working on Keynesian economics. But you do now. I went to the Brookings Panel Conference three weeks ago, and there were lots of people there working on Keynesian economics. And then there is the area of financial markets, where I think Shiller does the same type of work; he views financial markets very much in sociological terms. There's also Dick Thaler, who's doing a lot of work which relates macro to financial markets (see Russell and Thaler 1985; Kahneman, Knetsch, and Thaler 1986). So he is somebody else in this field. If you went back five years ago, you wouldn't find things like that.

I guess that this is just the beginning of a field. It's a little bit eclectic what people do, but that's of course what this field is supposed to be. I think that the work that is being done in this field is quite good, and I think it's quite interesting. Of course there is the question why it doesn't attract more graduate students. I think one reason is that the work is difficult to duplicate. It is not exactly obvious what you should do when you duplicate it. Another reason has to do with the fact that graduate training in economics is very demanding and technical. What is probably going to happen is that we are going to get people later in life gradually deviating into this area. I think we will be getting people who start out doing very standard classical economics and then find it unsatisfying because it doesn't answer their questions that well.

Let me also add something else about the course with Kahneman. It is clear that the idea we had that there was a simple recipe there for good work was wrong. But there is one student, Mark Carey, who is getting something great out of the class and who is going to do a really superb thesis. The topic involves an interpretation of the farm crisis, which I think will answer some very important questions. What happened is basically that the most optimistic farmers took over the market; they dominated the market and they bid up the land prices. The reason that they were able to take over the market was that they were provided with almost unlimited funding by federal agencies, which gave credit to the farmers. At the time that they did this, the banks already knew that the land prices were overvalued. The key idea in this analysis is perhaps that people have nonmaximizing behavior in some way or other; that they don't go around maximizing all the time. I think that is a key idea and that it is going to catch on.

If you go back to the dark old days—that is, to the 1970s—it was considered that proper theory meant that people were supposed to be maximizing. I think that what is proper theory today is that you have to assume that *some* people are maximizing, so that there are some people who will take advantage of profit opportunities if they are available. But you can allow all other people all sorts of deviant behavior. It is usually also the case that the maximizing people do not totally dominate the market; the nonmaximizing people have some influence too. The nonmaximizing people may even take over the market and for a while make the market. And *that* is the proper form for an economic model today.

So I think these ideas are having an influence on macroeconomics today and I think they are having an effect on finance. And that is a good share of economics. There is clearly lots of economics which is still overly dependent on maximization and a type of maximization that is much too finely tuned. And it will probably continue to be like that for a long time. But I think that there has also been a pretty rapid growth of nonmaximizing economics. And partly because it makes good common sense, I think it's going to continue to grow. Maybe it will be a little bit harder to do this new type of economics—because it's not out of a recipe book—but I think it is also going to lead to good innovating empirical work. I guess Shiller is an example of someone who's precisely doing good empirical work that way. Also this thesis which I was talking about will be a good piece of empirical work.

So on the whole I think that this new kind of economics is doing pretty well. I think it has already changed the standards for what good economic models are. But I guess we'll also have to wait and see.

Q: I would be very interested to hear your opinion about both "economic imperialism" and the attempt that is presently taking place in sociology to recast sociology on the basis of rationality. Do you feel it is at all possible to extend the economic model into the other social sciences? And what is your opinion about this "rational choice sociology"? Is that the kind of sociology you would use in your models?

A: You see I have gone the opposite way of Gary Becker. I have been trying to bring other things into economics; the other people have been trying to bring economics into the other social sciences. One wonderful thing about Becker, though, is that he has handled the most difficult and the most serious problems, like discrimination, addiction, human capital, marriage and divorce, crime and punishment. These are all the areas that I'd like to be able to work in myself. So Becker is really interesting and he is quite successful.

Still, I guess that what I want to do is always the opposite of what Becker does. I want to explain why the economy is *not* working; what interesting thing you need to bring in, so you do *not* get market clearing with discrimination; and so on. There is also the danger of bringing too much economics, rationality, and this optimizing technique into all these noneconomic fields. The technique is undoubtedly very good, but it's really important to be aware of its limitations. And one sees its limitations, especially when it is taken to extremes, which it sometimes is in economics. By extremes I mean for example the idea that markets are clearing at all times; that people have rational expectations based on the information available to them; and so on.

The rational expectations approach is basically a too simple approach, and it results in empirical predictions which are just false. The unfortunate thing about economic theory, in a sense, is that there are just a few structures which lead to all kinds of interesting mathematical work. Growth theory, which I mentioned earlier, is another example. For one reason or another people managed to write millions of papers about growth theory. The best of these are of course very interesting. Now, it is a bit similar with rational expectations. There are all kinds of little mathematical things that you can do with them. And these are a little bit interesting, mainly as a sort of exercise. However, important work and interesting exercises may be two different things.

So I think that this maximization business leads to slightly interesting exercises and it all looks very elegant when people do all this mathematics and so forth. But it may not make people wiser. And in the last analysis we all want something that makes people a little bit wiser. This maximization can be taken to excess as Samuelson's characterization of Milton Friedman—who nowadays appears to be quite moderate in all of this—indicates. Samuelson said that Milton Friedman was like somebody who had learned how to spell "banana" but didn't know where to stop. I think there is a great deal of that here; these people just don't know where to stop.

I feel that what is good about something like economics is that it gives you a framework within which to think and to analyze questions—questions which you perhaps wouldn't even know how to begin to analyze without this framework. But it doesn't tell you where to stop. There is no guide rule here, so people have to have some common sense. And common sense entails bringing in what the rest of the world thinks about. You have to have a picture of the world which combines not just what economists as economists are thinking about, but also what sociologists are thinking about, what psychologists are thinking about, and what anthropologists are thinking about. And if your picture of the world doesn't encompass those things but only maximization behavior, then you've got something wrong.

Let me also give an alternative answer to your question about economic imperialism. Suppose there are two views of people. One is that people are very purposeful, and there is maximizing behavior. Another is that people aren't machines in some sense. So when they are put in certain environments, they are going to behave in certain ways which are not maximizing. They might like to be maximizing—it might make them best off, at least individually—but since they are not machines they may just not do that. Now I really think it would be a shame to make everything purposeful and neglect the idea that people are not machines and that they often do things where they are not fully aware of what their motivations are and how they got into it. That's what "Loyalty Filters" to a large extent is about: you get into some environment, and you simply can't imagine how much you will change. You didn't imagine beforehand that you were going to be so changed, but five years later you come out a different person. It would actually be a shame to give that up for something that is methodologically good in some areas, but which is also a little bit superficial.

So I am not sure that bringing in a lot of maximization into sociology is going to be a good thing. I like what I read in sociology because people are talking about things outside of maximization. In a way I probably already know enough about maximization from economics. Nevertheless, it is always when people are doing things which wouldn't come just from maximization that I find them interesting. Maximization is fine; it is useful and it has its place. But at some point I also find it a little bit shallow, although it can be hard to say exactly what one means by a statement like that.

Q: Perhaps just that the human drama extends beyond maximization?

A: Yes, maybe that's it. I gave a talk at the American Economic Society meetings this winter, and Robert Lucas was my discussant and Bob Barro was there too (see Akerlof and Yellen 1987). I decided to be a little bit more aggressive than usual. These people accuse people who do work like me of assuming that people's behavior is nonmaximizing. So I decided to accuse them—and I think this is correct—of assuming *unhuman behavior* because according to them people are always maximizing. I don't think they liked that; especially Barro didn't seem to like it at all.

Actually it might be interesting to interview one or two people who do work on rational expectations to see why in fact they haven't used any sociology or why they think that that would be incorrect. Someone like Barro would give you a very precise answer. Their view in this case is something like the following. People don't just maximize all the time, so of course there is deviation from maximization. But "deviation" is a random term. Insofar as people deviate, it is purely random and unpredictable; and therefore there is no reason to bring it up in the analysis. They claim that we don't know enough about sociological and psychological behavior to be able to predict the random term. The only thing that we can predict with some degree of certainty is what people will be doing insofar as they are maximizing.

Now, I think that is wrong. I don't see why one should assume that deviation in this context is a random term. It is clearly dangerous to assume that something that you may not know about is going to have no effect on your system. And I don't see any reason why it should necessarily be purely random. Sociologists and psychologists usually write about why it is not random! It can be hard to apply sociological and psychological insights, I guess. But since somehow we know that maximization is simply not right all the time, it seems to me just wrong to assume that everybody is always maximizing.

Q: There is currently an opening up of the dialogue between economics and sociology. I am not necessarily sure that it will succeed; these things can be very hard sometimes. But what is your opinion? And how do you think one could help the dialogue along?

A: Well, I think that the best way to do it would be to have a success! I mean, somehow you have to show that you can answer some problems.

Q: Do you mean an empirical study?

A: It could be an empirical study or a theoretical one. It seems to me that success in this context would be something like explaining financial markets or some important macroeconomic phenomenon. Somehow showing that the new approach is useful for some question which doesn't otherwise have an easy answer. I think that we actually already are a little bit successful in showing that it is useful for macroeconomics and for financial markets to use this novel approach. I somehow think that what is needed is not a grand theory; it's detailed studies which show that the new approach is in fact applicable. Then you would have these things which will show that it can indeed be used, and people are going to think more about how you did that.

I guess Becker is an example of somebody who did good studies like that. He managed to do something that was perhaps convincing or at least something that you had to think about for a long time. He got people to think about extending economics into all kinds of other areas. I think if we do the opposite—if we get economists to use more sociology and psychology—maybe we too will succeed. But there are also problems that need to be solved. There is, for example, the difficulty that as an economist you need to know a lot before you can do this. Psychologists teach one thing and sociologists teach another. There are similar problems for the students who are not economists. There aren't many sociologists, for example, who take graduate courses in economics because it is difficult and they feel a little bit uncomfortable. Likewise, when I use sociology and psychology, I feel a little bit uncomfortable. I just don't know it as well as if I had learned it at an earlier age. There are also certain things that people learn in the other social sciences—field methods, methods of interviewing, and so forth—which are very different from our way of doing things in economics.

But I think there will be people who do this new kind of work. I think it will be good work and I think people will like it. And if people like it, they will think about it and copy it. So there is hope, I think.

References

Akerlof, George A. 1970. "The Market for 'Lemons': Quality Uncertainty and the Market Mechanism." *Quarterly Journal of Economics* 84:488–500. (Reprinted in Akerlof 1984a).

———. 1976. "The Economics of Caste and of the Rat Race and Other Woeful Tales." *Quarterly Journal of Economics* 90:599–617. (Reprinted in Akerlof 1984a).

———. 1980. "A Theory of Social Custom, of Which Unemployment May Be One Consequence." *Quarterly Journal of Economics* 94:749–75.

———. 1982. "Labor Contracts as Partial Gift Exchange." *Quarterly Journal of Economics* 97:543–69. Reprinted in Akerlof 1984a.

———. 1983. "Loyalty Filters." *American Economic Review* 73:54–63. Reprinted in Akerlof 1984a.

———. 1984a. *An Economic Theorist's Book of Tales.* Cambridge: Cambridge University Press.

———. 1984b. "Gift Exchange and Efficiency-Wage Theory: Four Views." *American Economic Review (Papers and Proceedings)* 74:79–83.

Akerlof, George A., and Janet L. Yellen. 1985a. "A Near-Rational Model of the Business Cycle, with Wage and Price Inertia." *Quarterly Journal of Economics* 100:823–38.

———. 1985b. "Can Small Deviations from Rationality Make Significant Differences to Economic Equilibria?." *American Economic Review* 75:708–20.

———, eds. 1986. *Efficiency Wage Models of the Labor Market.* Cambridge: Cambridge University Press.

———. 1987. "Fairness and Unemployment." *American Economic Review (Papers and Proceedings)* 78:44–49.

Benedict, Ruth. 1946. *The Chrysanthemum and the Sword: Patterns of Japanese Culture.* Boston: Houghton Mifflin.

Coser, Lewis A. 1971. *Masters of Sociological Thought: Ideas in Historical and Social Context.* New York: Harcourt Brace Jovanovich.

Homans, George C. 1950. *The Human Group.* New York: Harcourt Brace Jovanovich.

Kahneman, Daniel, Jack Knetsch, and Richard Thaler. 1986. "Fairness as a Constraint on Profit Seeking: Entitlements in the Market." *American Economic Review* 76:728–41.

Kahneman, Daniel, and Amos Tversky. 1979. "Prospect Theory: An Analysis of Decision under Risk." *Econometrica* 47:263–91.

Merton, Robert M. 1968. *Social Theory and Social Structure.* New York: Free Press.

Russell, T., and R. H. Thaler. 1985. "The Relevance of Quasi Rationality in Competitive Markets." *American Economic Review* 75:1071–82.

Shiller, Robert J. 1979. "Do Stock Prices Move Too Much to Be Justified by Subsequent Changes in Dividends?." *American Economic Review* 71:420–36.

———. 1984. "Stock Prices and Social Dynamics." *Brookings Papers on Economic Activities* 2:457–98.

4   *Harrison C. White*

AFTER THE "old economic sociology" of Parsons and his students had faded away and lost whatever vitality it had in the 1960s, many years passed before sociologists again became interested in economics. And when they did, it was to a large extent due to what Harrison White had been doing at Harvard in the 1970s—both in his own work and through the inspiration he gave to his students. White's work on stratification in the late 1960s—especially his idea of "vacancy chains"—was a first move in the direction of more economic topics. Then, from the mid-1970s on, he made the decision to directly try to model markets as social structures. This was an unprecedented move in modern sociology and helped to set off a whole new trend among younger sociologists that Mark Grano-vetter—one of White's students—would later call "new economic sociol-ogy." In this interview, White describes how he came to work on eco-nomic topics; what he thinks of contemporary economic theory; and how he looks at the relationship between economic theory and sociology.

Harrison C. White was born in 1930 in Washington, D.C., the third son of Virginia Armistead and Joel Jesse, a physician in the U.S. navy. He re-ceived a B.S. in physics at MIT in 1950, and a Ph.D. in theoretical physics from the same university in 1955. In 1960, White also got a Ph.D. in sociol-ogy at Princeton University. Since then he has worked at Johns Hopkins University (1955–1956), the Carnegie Institute of Technology (1957–1959), the University of Chicago (1959–1963), and Harvard University (1963–1986). After a brief stay at the University of Arizona (1986–1988), Harrison White is now professor of sociology and director of the Center for the Social Sciences at Columbia University.

•

Q: You began your career as a physicist and you have written on many topics besides economics, such as French painting and kinship systems. So how does your interest in economics fit into all of this? Did you, for example, study economics in college?

The following interview with Harrison C. White was conducted on March 17, 1988, at the Center for the Social Sciences at Columbia University in New York City.

A: Yes I did. Ever since I was an undergraduate at MIT in the 1940s I have been fascinated by the enormously complicated interaction and chaining of contingencies. And to me economics should be thought of as particularly concerned with long-distance chains taking place relatively promptly in production as well as in the dispersion and spread of production.

So I have been interested in economics for a long time. But I never took any courses in it as an undergraduate; I actually avoided it. In graduate school, however, I took intermediate economics from Robert Bishop, who is a standard microeconomics theorist; he had tried in the 1930s to properly model the revolutionary insights of Edward Chamberlin, but I found that out only much later. And then I took a year of graduate mathematical economics from Paul Samuelson. Now that was at a time when I think I was in my third year of graduate work in theoretical physics, so it would have been in 1952 or 1953. Taking this course with Samuelson convinced me that that I did not want to go into economics, as it was then defined. Samuelson's *Foundations of Economic Analysis* was clearly taking over economics in the 1950s and moving it, as far as I was concerned, in the wrong direction. I thought I knew why, but at the time it was only an intuitive feeling. It is only now that I am able to articulate it, I think. You see, Samuelson had the bad luck to form his ideas in the environment of the early 1940s, when the natural model to follow in science was field theory in physics. And to me that is a singularly inappropriate analogue to economic phenomena. I just hope that there is somewhere a new Samuelson today, who is learning about such things as high polymer chemistry, phase transitions, and turbulent flow. The way I see it, these are a much more natural analogue to economic phenomena.

So I did have a background in economics. It was Karl Deutsch, the political scientist then at MIT, who inspired me to switch to the social sciences with the help of a one-year fellowship from the Ford Foundation which I took at Princeton in sociology. After MIT and Princeton I went and worked in operations research as a professional analyst at the Army's Operations Research Office in Bethesda, Maryland, in 1955–1956. Some might consider operations research economics, but I don't, and I don't think economists would either. Operations research is more management science and its mathematical modeling. After Johns Hopkins I spent two years in the famous Graduate School of Industrial Administration at Carnegie. Here I did a case study of innovation in a business firm which I in 1960 presented as my Ph.D. thesis in sociology at Princeton University (see White 1980). I had chosen sociology because it seemed to me the field which went after the fundamental questions. In those days I was certainly on the fringes of economics, although what I did would probably have been considered much closer to economics in the 1920s or 1930s, when institutional studies were still prominent. Business schools had very little to do with economics in those days. The reason for this was that the intellectually respectable part of economics is microeconomics, and in the view of most business school people microeconomics has demonstrably nothing to do with observed business behavior.

On the other hand, there were people like Richard Cyert and Jim March in the GSIA at Carnegie. In those days they were trying to do microeconomics from a behavioral viewpoint and I found that much more sympathetic than mainline economics. And Herbert Simon was of course there. It was just magnificent to be a young faculty person in the same place as him! He said something I had wanted to feel for a long time, but never really dared, namely, "Why be in this unless you are having fun?" It was the first time anyone had told me that it was legitimate to have fun when you do science. In the late 1950s, Simon was still a little bit interested in the kind of things he talks about in *Models of Man* and which he then pretty much left behind. There are three Herbert Simons, you know. There is first the qualitative one with an interest in formal organization and public administration. Even to this day he is the best man in these areas and his books are the best. The second Simon is the one who was interested in behavioral science and wrote *Models of Man*. And the third Simon is the one who, unfortunately for most of us, has gone into psychology. He had already started to get into psychology when I was at Carnegie. Although with Herbert Simon it doesn't really matter what field he is into. Just having lunch with him, you know, is so refreshing.

So that was one influence of economics on me. Another significant influence came when I had spent the year 1956–1957 at the Center for Advanced Study at Stanford, where Herb Simon met me during a visit with Harold Guetzkow and offered me the Carnegie job (my only offer!). Ken Arrow was there, and his type of economics was a whole new experience to me. He just has a different type of mind than Samuelson. It is clear that Samuelson is very clever at adapting other people's formulations, but I always had a feeling that Arrow was the more original of the two. Arrow fitted my view of a scientist as someone who looks deeply into the real etiology of cause. And Arrow is just such a magnificent person! Another person who was at the Center, although not officially on the books, was Frank Knight. That was also a great experience for me, as was his book *Risk, Uncertainty and Profit*. Another book in economics that was important to me in those days was Gunnar Myrdal's study of the foundations of political economy, *The Political Element in the Development of Economic Theory*. It contains a very sophisticated look at how economics came about.

So in the 1950s I had learned this technical stuff from Samuelson, which I don't think accomplished very much. But it was nice to know and at least I could talk to people. And then I had this marvelous experience with Arrow and Knight, who introduced me to the deeper work in economics. But I should also say that in the years after I had finished my Pittsburgh field study in 1959 I was mostly interested in anthropology. I was interested in general sociology, but I thought that anthropology, especially in its English version, was one of the few places where people had really tried to do fundamental theory. So I spent a lot of time on that even at Carnegie. And then in 1959–1963 I went into an era at the University of Chicago when I worked on kinship models (see White 1963). This got me on to role structure problematics, which I thought were absolutely fundamental.

In 1963 I went to Harvard. Here I pretty much on my own tried to develop a kind of modern form of sociology. My view is that much of this work is economics. I especially did some work on mobility, and *Chains of Opportunity* was the byproduct of this. The fundamental work itself never got published, because it was not correct. I was working on a general theory called tenure-networks, which can be described as a very general way of embedding mobility in a network formulation. But it turned out not to work and I still don't know why. It may actually have been because those were still very primitive days on the computer. Anyway, when I did some very crude analyses it was clear that my predictions were not working at all.

So I gave up on that and shifted to Markov chains, which is an easy way to work. This is when I wrote the book on vacancy chains. *Chains of Opportunity* was really meant to more generally get at the nature of opportunity structures and how contingencies of opportunity fit together. And this meant that my ideas were closely allied to economics. Indeed, John Dunlop, who is a labor economist, was kind enough to have me over for a seminar. This was at the time, I guess, when Richard Freeman and many of these people were graduate students. I felt sympathetic to what Dunlop and his students were doing, partly because they were not so obsessed with price theory. So in a way I was at the fringes of economics in those days, but I did not care very much. You see, what I was after were explicit contingent mechanisms by which opportunities and chains were coupled together.

I then went on to do network models, which really grew out of my kinship models. But I was now trying to generalize them and loosen them up so they could apply to any kind of modern society. That resulted in a chain of papers (White and Lorrain 1971; White, Boorman, and Breiger 1976; White and Boorman 1976). There were also other things I did in those years, including running an interdisciplinary seminar for three years on mathematical models across the social and biological sciences. This was in 1975–1978 and I did it with NSF funding. And this was when I got involved with economics again. A number of economists, such as Stephen Marglin, Tom Schelling, Mike Spence, and Richard Zeckhauser, were interested enough and fresh enough to sit in on the seminar. We did a lot of work on phase transitions and had David R. Nelson come and talk to us. He is a brilliant young physicist, who might very well get a Nobel Prize one day for discovering two-dimensional crystals. We also learned about marvelous mathematical work that is being done on how leaves grow and how moose support themselves by foraging efficiently. And we had game theorists visiting us. We did a lot of things, including economics.

It was during these years that I got turned on by a book by Mike Spence called *Market Signaling*. This was a bit ironical since I was primarily looking at natural science models and not at economic models to get ideas. Anyway, I thought that Spence's book had an absolutely brilliant idea in it, even if he developed it the wrong way. So the core of the idea—self-reproduction through signaling—was Spence's, but since I was a sociologist, I was able to broaden it out and use it as a beginning for a general theory of interfaces or social mechanisms for exerting control.

Following what was going on in economics, Spence had thought of signaling entirely in terms of information. But in my opinion the concept of information is one of the saddest mistakes in the social sciences since World War II. The theory itself is so plausible that a lot of people have got sucked into taking it seriously and spending time on it. But to the best of my knowledge, it has never produced any useful science. It presently has the status of the old ether theory in physics, which the Michelson-Morley experiment finally killed off. That theory was very plausible too with its notion that light flowed through ether. And similarly there is this kind of myth that there is some kind of ineffable substance called "information," which goes very well indeed with some of the more unfortunate tendencies in contemporary economics to avoid serious measurements. The great thing about information is that everybody is willing to talk about it; that no one is willing to measure it; and that everybody is willing to forgive you for not measuring it. Even though I say these glib things about information, I should add that it was nonetheless in a book whose ostensible core is information that Mike Spence presented his brilliant model of self-reproduction. And Art Stinchcombe is now trying to reground organization theory on it, in a new manuscript.

Q: Through his idea of self-reproduction through signaling, Spe____ influenced your work on markets in the 1970s. But what was wrong w____ the neoclassical theory of the market to begin with?

A: It's easy to answer that. *There does not exist a neoclassical theory of the market—that's the extraordinary thing.* You do indeed have a theory of the market and an excellent one at that, but it is misleading to call it the neoclassical theory of the market. This is the pure theory of exchange, which was notably developed by Edgeworth but was part of economics well before him. A number of contemporary people have also developed this theory further. As a theory, the pure theory of exchange has all the desired features of a good theory to me. But it is a specialized theory of an exchange market, that is, it is a theory of markets, where production is not an issue. I am not an expert on mercantile behavior through the ages, but I would imagine that there are historical periods where most of what you would think of as economic phenomena were of a market kind and therefore could be handled by the pure theory of exchange. And even to this day, if you take bond sales or equivalent phenomena, there is a sense in which the pure theory of exchange is applicable to them—but not to other markets.

So economists in my opinion have never developed an actual theory of production markets. That is, they have never developed a theory about the kind of market which is around us all the time and which dominates the economy. I should say the kinds of markets, since I think there are several species. Those economists who were not very theoretically minded were perhaps under the impression that the pure theory of exchange also applied to production markets. But the more careful theorist knew of course that this is not the case; the pure theory of exchange doesn't apply to production markets. So the only real models of production markets you could find were these rather embarrassing things you can find in the old kind of microeconomic textbooks. They are really a hodgepodge of things that I don't think anyone would call theory. Another thing to notice is that there are no theorists of great repute who work on production markets. They work in the pure theory of exchange but not on production markets. At least this was true until recently. I am not really current with what has happened in economic theory since 1982, so there might be things which I don't know about.

Q: You mention 1982. What happened that year?

A: In 1982 I shifted my focus of interest and stopped reading *The Journal of Economic Theory* and scanning that literature. I am now primarily trying to model control processes in big organizations. That is not so different from what I did before since there are market interfaces within organizations, and since control is as much an issue in markets as in organizations (Eccles and White 1988; Bradach and Eccles 1989; Oberschall and Leifer 1986).

There also exist another couple of ways of looking at the theory of the market. From one viewpoint you can, for example, say that general equilibrium theory is a generalization of the pure theory of exchange. But you can also say that it has something to do with production markets. And what that means is that contemporary economics perhaps has a theory of production markets—in plural, that is. Well, you can say that if you want to be generous. And the theory of price has to some extent that flavor. You don't look too much at any tangible market but rather at an interacting system, somewhat like George Stigler does. But for me and my particular agenda, I do not trust something in which the central object—an actual market—was never explictly modeled.

A third way of looking at the theory of the market, although it hasn't affected me that much, is the line of work that began with Karl Polanyi in the early post-World War II era. This was very instructive work, I think. And there are today new studies on "industrialization before industrialization" by a group of East German economists (Kriedte, Medick, and Schlumbohm 1981). So there you have some examples of a strand of analysis which tries to take economic history and really do something theoretical with it rather than just treat it as a descriptive field. Polanyi and these other people, however, were rather sketchy and they didn't have the data down. Still, you look at these works or you look at Finley's (1973) resurrection of the controversy about the ancient economy, and it is clear that they are important works. The best current continuation of this tradition is, I think, in the sociological operationalizations in such work as Jacobs and Breiger (1988).

There is finally a fourth way of looking at the theory of the market. Since the economists had killed off the institutionalist tradition, there was in effect no intellectual basis for young economists to grow some theory out of a historical background without being trapped by it. It was hard for them to approach the problem of a theory of the market historically and see its evolutionary pattern. But I think you can see a continuous development of production markets beginning with the medieval Italian and German city systems, where for the first time you have production built in as a systematic part of the economy. So the pure theory of exchange is no longer relevant for this situation, and you are beginning to need a theory of the production market. Moving on in time through various *verlager*, *kaufmann* and putting-out systems and towards the present time, you will get close to a situation which a Leontief would recognize. The theory of Leontief is the closest equivalent in economics to a theory of the production market or rather of a system of production markets. His relations within the economics profession were, however, such that he was not going to have a very great impact. I knew him slightly at Harvard, but I didn't have that much to do with him intellectually. Anyway, the economists were not willing to listen to Leontief. Still, that would have been another way that a real theory of markets could have come about, and it would have been something along the lines of input-output combined with managerial economics. The best developer of the Leontief line today is the sociologist Ron Burt (Burt 1983, 1987); contrast his findings with good but conventional neoclassical work, for example Kwoka (1979).

But none of these potential theories worked out for me. So since the late 1970s I have published a series of articles that are essentially based on Spence and in which I have been trying to construct an analytic model of *a* specific market as a tangible mechanism in a production economy (White 1981). I have bracketed and assumed markets before and after, contrary to Leontief and to Burt, but modeled the specific market in a way that is quite general. I actually use it today when I model other kinds of interfaces.

Q: It would be interesting to hear a little bit about your future work on markets. With your references to the work of Finley and these East German scholars, it sounds as if you will be taking the historical development much more into account. Is that correct?

A: Yes. What I have been trying to do since my earlier work on markets is to follow the historical roots of the production market. If you read Weber, a lot of this is prefigured, as so many things are. On the other hand, it is true that Weber had more to say about the *verlager* system than about the production market specifically. So I have some ideas for models for some of these *verlager* systems and how they might have evolved over a few centuries in ways that are identifiable and operational. There is also a young sociologist called Bernacki, who has just done a thesis for Smelser at Berkeley. He has identified some interesting contrasts between German and British markets in the early 1900s. So there exist a number of snapshots, so to speak, which would then lead into something like a Leontief input-output model, but one that is fleshed out in an institutional system. So what I have are all kinds of bits and pieces, and I hope that some time soon I will have time to work on it. Probably I'll start by trying to write an article during the next year or so. That's all I can say about my future work on markets.

Q: How have economists reacted to your theory about production markets? I saw that you and one of your students had written an article on this topic in *The New Palgrave*. Doesn't that mean it has been accepted to some extent?

A: Well, I am delighted that my and Bob Eccles's article on production markets is in *The New Palgrave* (see White and Eccles 1987). But I am not so sure it means that my ideas are widely accepted. It is my impression that *The New Palgrave* editors, many from the Cambridge University division of applied economics, such as John Eatwell for example, are regarded as forming a separate school, more qualitative and institutionalist.

Elsewhere there is, I guess, a scattering of little bits of interest on the margin. The overwhelming feeling I have, however, is of a lack of interest. Partly that is because this is a busy world and there are lots of things to attend to. Another reason, as I have noticed when I have given papers for economists, is that they just don't see there is a theorizable problem in the existence of a production market, and in its specification as an explicit social mechanism. And among the people who are better able to cope with it, whole series of defensive mechanisms are quickly activated. To an extent the situation reminds me of what I know about medieval canon law; economics has become a system that spends about half of its energies setting up mechanisms to disallow any challenge that can be mounted to it. One could always somehow make it come out right and ignore the conundrums of life. Even a tangible and sober critique of policy impacts, like that by Ramos (1986), never even conceives that it is the theory of markets itself that is at fault.

I furthermore think that within fifteen years, by the year 2000 or so, economics as we know it will have gone through a major crisis. And it won't have been brought on by outsiders like me. There will come a time when the machine just kind of collapses out of frustration with itself. Just look at these Nobel Prizes they are handing out every year. These supposed achievements really make you wonder. I even find it hard to say what Samuelson ever did in terms of explicit scientific discovery, even if he is an amazingly intelligent and productive person. Perhaps he should have been given the Prize in literature instead—for the poetry and rhetoric with which he has formulated a consistent system.

Q: In your opinion, when did modern economics start to go wrong? As I recall, you said in an earlier conversation that the critical period was in the 1930s. Is that correct?

A: Yes, the decline set in in the late 1930s and in the 1940s. There is a declining proportion of works that have the same exciting, scientific quality after that time. The formalization process, which began at about the same time, is a clear achievement in my opinion. Indeed, one of the reasons why people didn't criticize Samuelson is that they felt the alternative was someone like John Bates Clark, that is, the old kind of vague and effulgent economics. So the attempt to formalize was fine, but the formalization should be specific and it should be right for the phenomena. Part of what instead happened was just bad luck, I think. If Samuelson had been writing in the modern era, he would probably have been tuned in to a very different kind of natural science model and would have tried to use that. And that would have been more effective.

The neoclassical revolution was a great step forward. In my view it is not so much a question whether the ideas were right or not. To me Jevons, Menger, and Walras were great figures—especially Jevons. What matters is that someone like Jevons was part of a progressive trajectory. You can't read Jevons without seeing vividly that he is trying to understand *the real economic phenomena.* He is a true scientist. When I read *The Journal of Economic Theory* I don't get that feeling. But it can have changed; I haven't read it since 1982, as I have already said.

Q: Many sociologists would be critical of the fact that neoclassical economics, as opposed to classical economics, doesn't pay much attention to institutions. What is your position there?

A: Well, I like both classical and neoclassical economics. And I think that both are needed. The important thing to understand is that the natural development would have been to try to combine them. In my opinion that's what Edward Chamberlin and Joan Robinson were trying to do in the 1930s. You can argue that Keynes was probably trying to do that too. And to this day I don't understand how things could get so much off the track.

Another way to put this is that it is important to build up theory from the actor. You see, the problem is that in a sense neoclassical theory was just right. You had classical economics, but eventually classical economics would be a dead end because it didn't provide any significant role for the actor. So there was no role for contingent developments, because only people had projects of control and visions of how resources could be used in the development of an economy. There was a kind of oppressive approach almost inherent in the classical approach, which made the economy look like an ant society. When neoclassical economics came, it was therefore so exciting. When you read Jevons, you can't help being excited because you have the feeling that the analysis can now be geared toward a rather small and changing social institution, but one which emerges in a formally specified way. It's in a way Adam Smith made operational through self-informed actions of the actors. What happened after the 1930s is that the ideas about motivational structure became ossified and people gave up on the essential problem, which is to simultaneously *embed* and *decouple* the economic process.

Q: What do you mean by "decoupling" in this context? I assume that "embed" means about the same thing as when Polanyi and Granovetter use it—roughly that economic actions are enmeshed in institutions, social networks, or some other type of social structure.

A: In this context, "decoupling" means that in order to achieve a certain production, you simply have to chop off some causal chains. You have to somehow simplify them, to dissolve their impetus through people's perceptions. If you look at the origin of present-day production, you'll find that it has in my terminology "decoupled" itself from a series of kinship and political phenomena. This has been pointed out in several studies, for example by Nadel in *A Black Byzantium*. Many people have made this observation, and I am just using the terminology of "decoupling" to emphasize that it is not just a passive phenomenon—it's *an action*. People must deliberately decouple in order to achieve some of their ends.

So that's one thing. But I shouldn't be saying that people do this to achieve their "ends," because these are more a byproduct than a cause, as Jim March has long emphasized. The question is one of achieving a kind of control. At the same time as there is a deliberate "decoupling," there is paradoxically also an "embedding." I think that I use the term "embedding" in the same sense as Polanyi and Granovetter. But I think it has many levels and meanings. I don't think that "embeddedness" should be seen as something that is inherent or automatic. "Embedding" does not happen by accident, and it can be part of control.

One of the many ways that control is achieved in a complex situation is precisely through interaction in the sense that control can lead to embedding on a more general level as one of its solutions, but you also need "decoupling" here. This is the kind of situation where mathematical theory or models are particularly important. A paradox is always best handled by putting it in a systematic mathematical model. Because then it will turn out that you can tame it; it will turn out that it isn't really a paradox.

The alternative procedure to handle this paradox would be through works like those of Habermas, Goffman, or some phenomenologists, such as Scheler or Schutz or Husserl. These people are all aware of the paradox of simultaneous "decoupling" and "embedding," but they do not have the training that would incline them to try to model it. So they just assume that the paradox can't be solved and instead they celebrate it. Take Clifford Geertz. There is a sense of this in the way he deliberately engages in "thick descriptions." If you read his early book (Geertz 1956) on the political economy of a Javanese village, you can see he was still in a kind of scientific mood. You can see that in his analysis of decoupling and embedding in that Javanese village and in his sense that there was a certain paradoxical quality to this. But after that, since Geertz didn't have a direction to go, it's as if he built a pearl around the irritant—the pearl being these "thick descriptions."

Q: There are presently several people who argue that one can use rational choice theory in sociology. What is your opinion of that? One could, for example, argue that in a sense it's an old tradition in sociology to use a rational type of analysis: you approach something that looks irrational, only to show with the help of sociology that the behavior is really quite rational.

A: As long as it's just a useful heuristic, I'm all for it.

Q: So you are for rational choice in this softer version?

A: Well, maybe it's the harder version. But on the whole, I am a little appalled by the recent resurrection of rational choice theory. From my point of view, it reminds me of going into the Empire Mountains, south of Tucson, Arizona, where there are lots of these abandoned mines, and have some new developers persuade a number of young people to go and invest their lives in these empty mines. We have been through all of this before, and I am unaware of any new great idea that can justify a renewed interest. It's not as if an Arrow had just come up with a discovery like social choice.

Jim Coleman has done some work along these lines, and I think of that as a sociological version of rational choice. I can't say it triggered anything in me, and I didn't see where he was going with it. But if anybody has earned the right to be taken seriously, it's surely him. He has time after time come up with something. I am not working along these lines myself, but I don't want to be put in a position of telling other people not to do it. That wouldn't be good science.

Q: And what is your opinion of the parallel phenomenon in economics—economic imperialism?

A: Well, first of all I don't like the term "imperialism," since I think that Gary Becker should be as openly listened to in our field as I would hope to be in their field.

Q: But it's a term the economists have chosen themselves. Becker, Tullock, and others use it. Stigler (1984) has even written an essay on economics as "an imperial science."

A: Even worse. But we sociologists shouldn't call it "imperialism" in a defensive way. And for the economists to call it that—well, imperialism has sometimes been set off exactly by a failure of a regime on its own ground! The formal apparatus which they have invested so much in learning is being taken by economists now into new areas, where it will presumably take us ten to twenty years to find out whether it is possible there at least to go beyond tautologies! Research is fortunately much more interesting than these catchwords. And Gary Becker, whose latest book is on my shelf, is always worth reading. So another thing I want to stress is that you can get some good ideas out of this neoclassical material, as Oberschall and Leifer also stress in their survey. One of my best ideas came from reading Mike Spence's book, which on principle I think is wrong in at least three different ways. But I am very glad I read it. So you should always *keep trying* and look at different things, including the things that you "on principle" think are wrongheaded.

Q: There is presently a trend of sociologists getting hired in business schools. There is Jim Baron at the Stanford Business School, Bob Eccles at the Harvard Business School, Mitchel Abolafia at Cornell, and so on. Do you think this is a good development for economic sociology?

A: Yes, very much so. I have been doing my best for some years now to get sociologists—students as well as faculty—into the business schools. At Harvard, for example, I helped to found a joint doctoral program between the business school and behavioral science. So I would very much like to see sociologists accepted at business schools and become part of them. From what I have myself seen of two business schools—first at Carnegie and then at Harvard—sociology is very well suited for much of what the business school people would really like to do and to accomplish: see for example the survey by Bradach and Eccles (1989). So business schools are natural places for sociologists to be, and sociology is the natural intellectual base in social science for business schools.

One of the things that depresses me a little is that economists are increasingly moving into the business schools. I find that somewhat astounding since I have spent some time with high-level businessmen and I have yet to meet anyone who really pays any attention to the contributions of economics except in an auxiliary way, perhaps some econometric "predictions." Obviously there are some economists in the business schools who have done good science. There is Mike Spence once again, and Michael Porter, and many others. So despite my globalistic statements there are economists who have a great deal to offer the business schools. But the business schools are increasingly importing economic theorists of a rather conventional sort, who I just don't think are flexible enough. Fuss and MacFadder for example took a brilliant innovation in production economics by the U.C.–Berkeley engineer Shepard and missed most of its power by forcing it into the conventions of economic theory. Similarly, Baumol has been stopped by his steeping in neoclassical theory from effectively developing the scientific potential of his market-crossing ideas.

It should also be said that if sociology is to have an impact on the business schools, sociologists must really get to work. They must get out there and learn business and study it. One of the reasons why I am working at this Center for the Social Sciences is that it represents one more opportunity to make sociology more oriented to field work. If there is one disastrous thing at the roots of what has happened in modern economics, it's that it has cut itself off from field observation of the sort illustrated admirably by Jevons's book on banking: the closest modern analogue has a sociologist as author (Eccles and Crane 1988). Many economists think they are doing scientific empirical work when they are massaging some time series, produced in unknown ways by unknown clerks in some government agencies. But there is a bit more to it than that.

There are of course also some economists who do brilliant field work. There is the occasional David Landes, who will go to Egypt and dig into the archives of the banks there (Landes 1979). And economics is a big profession with many applied areas. But on the whole there are not enough economists who even think it is legitimate to take the time and effort to go out and *look* at what is there. Look at it, study it, and then develop imaginative ways to conceptualize and measure it—that's what is needed in economics.

Q: You mentioned David Landes, so I guess this is a good opportunity to ask you about the relationship between economic sociology and economic history. Some argue that economic sociologists can probably get more out of being in contact with economic history than with neoclassical economics. What's your opinion there?

A: I think that economic history is very important. But sociology should be in contact with economic theory too in order to pick up good ideas. And since a lot of economic theory isn't very fruitful, at least in my mind, you don't have to spend an awful amount of time with it. What I do, and what I think sociologists in business schools should do, is to read *The Journal of Economic Literature*. That is one effective way to get tipped off to some interesting work that is going on. But you have to be alert because what's interesting might not be highly regarded within the field. Still, you can get a clue from this journal and then you can go and read the thing for yourself. And maybe you'll get some new ideas or ingenious formulations—that's the important thing.

Remember that I have been around for a long time by now. It was thirty-five years ago that I took Samuelson's course and I have developed some fairly fixed notions about economics, which it isn't necessarily in my interest to change. I may also be out of date in some respect. But even with all those blinders, I still urge sociologists to be in touch with economic theory. Part of the reason for doing this is that economic theory is quite ossified at the moment, so it's not that hard to spot the new directions. There simply aren't that many of them. Take for example the rational agents approach. Even that is worth reading. There are bound to be some clever things there and you might get an idea from it, as did Michael Hechter (1987) and Siegwart Lindenberg (1988). The rational agents approach is of course also an attempt to avoid the necessity of developing a theory of institutions. But in my own theory of markets I am using tools that come from economic theory to explicitly talk about how social institutions of a particular sort emerge. We need ideas in sociology, and some economic theorists can give us that, as for example Jerry Green.

Q: It seems to me that there is presently some kind of redefinition going on of the relationship between economics and sociology. This is evident among economists as well as sociologists. What do you believe would be the ideal relationship between economics and sociology?

A: Well, first of all it should be said that that is a utopian question. We live in the real world, where there isn't any ideal relationship between economics and sociology. Sociology is a small and relatively disregarded field. It was small and disregarded even when I started and, if anything, it is even more so thirty years later. My answer is therefore that the main opportunity will come in something like ten or fifteen years from now, when there will be a major loss of self-confidence in economics. I think that such a time will come, but I don't think it is up to us to create it. I don't see any point to that; it just doesn't make sense. It's rather up to us to get ourselves in a position so we are ready to expand and exploit when the opportunity comes. That's one answer to your question.

A second answer would be that the relationship between economics and sociology is just a standard tribal problem. We should take it for granted that we have to have a tribe called "sociology" and several tribes called "economics." It would drive us nuts if we didn't; we couldn't run our personnel systems, and so on. You also have to have a fair amount of flag waving, but you shouldn't let that muddy up your mind, because we have no reason to think that these historically evolved fields are necessarily ideal. It is quite sobering, for example, to go back to the nineteenth century and look at the structure of the university education. When you do that you realize there are whole chunks that have simply evaporated while others have been rearranged. Interdisciplinary departments are no solution either. I think it is a terrible mistake to spend a lot of time to try to put things together in some new way organizationally. That usually turns out bad. The right thing to do is to stay in your own tribe and do the reasonable work that's needed to keep your tribe going. Then you can search out interesting problems and ideas, which are often on the margins of things, and let your work evolve as it will through informal collaborations with other fields.

My third answer is that things may well be changing conceptually. I think that what you are seeing today is that you can't just talk about sociology and economics any more: *it is a triad.* I think you have to have sociology, economics, and political science. And I don't think the interesting work can be disentangled any more without bringing in at least those three. It may well be, when we get going on the historical side, that you can't leave out anthropology. But I honestly don't think that's in the cards at the moment: political science is where I see exciting new work (see Padgett and Ansell 1988; Przeworski 1980).

So I don't think you can look at what's going on in the more interesting kinds of modern social science and pull out economics as if it was something separate. Perhaps it was unfortunate that the neoclassical revolution separated out the political element from political economy, and maybe it is now time for them to come together again. But political economy can't be the solution. *You need the political, the economic, and the sociological:* without sociology to provide a kind of theoretical infrastructure, you can't really make politics and economics work together.

References

Bradach, Jeffrey, and Robert G. Eccles. 1989. "Markets versus Hierarchies: From Ideal Types to Plural Forms." *Annual Review of Sociology.* In press.

Burt, Ronald S. 1983. *Corporate Profits and Cooptation: Networks of Market Constraints and Directorate Ties in the American Economy.* New York: Academic Press.

————. 1987. "Social Contagion and Innovation: Cohesion versus Structural Equivalence." *American Journal of Sociology* 92:1287–1335.

Eccles, Robert G., and Dwight B. Crane. 1988. *Doing Deals: Investment Banks at Work.* Cambridge: Harvard Business School Press.

Eccles, Robert G., and Harrison C. White. 1988. "Price and Authority in Inter-Profit Center Transactions." *American Journal of Sociology* 94:S17–S51.

Finley, Moses I. 1973. *The Ancient Economy.* Berkeley: University of California Press.

Geertz, Clifford. 1956. *The Social Context of Economic Change: An Indonesian Case Study.* Cambridge: MIT Press.

Hechter, Michael. 1987. *Principles of Group Solidarity.* Berkeley: University of California Press.

Jacobs, Jerry A., and Ronald L. Breiger. 1988. "Careers, Industries and Occupations:

Industrial Segmentation Reconsidered." In *Industries, Firms and Jobs: Sociological and Economic Approaches*, edited by George Farkas and Paula England. New York: Plenum.

Knight, Frank H. 1971. *Risk, Uncertainty and Profit*. Chicago: University of Chicago Press. Originally published in 1921.

Kriedte, Peter, Hans Medick and Jürgen Shlumbohm. 1981. *Industrialization before Industrialization*. London: Cambridge University Press.

Kwoka, John E. Jr. 1979. "The Effect of Market Share Distribution on Industry Performance", *Review of Economics and Statistics* 61:101–9.

Landes, David. 1979. *Bankers and Pashas: International Finance and Economic Imperialism in Egypt*. Cambridge: Harvard University Press. Originally appeared in 1958.

Lindenberg, Siegwart. 1988. "Contractual Relations and Weak Solidarity: The Behavioral Basis of Restraints on Gain-Maximization." *Journal of Institutional and Theoretical Economics* 144:39–58.

Myrdal, Gunnar. 1953. *The Political Element in the Development of Economic Theory*. Cambridge: Harvard University Press. Originally published in Swedish in 1930.

Nadel, Siegfried. 1942. *A Black Byzantium: The Kingdom of Nupe in Nigeria*. London: Oxford University Press.

Oberschall, Anthony and Eric Leifer. 1986. "Efficiency and Social Institutions: Uses and Misuses of Economic Reasoning in Sociology." *Annual Review of Sociology* 12:233–53.

Padgett, John F. and Christopher Ansell. 1988. "From Faction to Party in Renaissance Florence: The Emergence of the Medici Patronage Party." Unpublished paper, Department of Poltical Science, University of Chicago.

Przeworski, Adam. 1980. "Material Bases of Consent: Economics and Politics in a Hegemonic System." In *Political Power and Social Theory: A Research Annual*, edited by Maurice Zeitlin, vol. 1, 21–66. Greenwich, Conn.: JAI Press.

Ramos, Joseph. 1986. *Neo-Conservative Economics in the Southern Cone of Latin America 1973–1983*. Baltimore: Johns Hopkins University Press.

Samuelson, Paul A. 1947. *Foundations of Economic Analysis*. Cambridge: Harvard University Press.

Simon, Herbert. 1957b. *Models of Man*. New York: John Wiley.

Spence, A. Michael. 1974. *Market Signaling*. Cambridge: Harvard University Press.

Stigler, George J. 1984. "Economics—The Imperial Science." *Scandinavian Journal of Economics* 86:301–13.

White, Harrison C. 1963. *An Anatomy of Kinship: Mathematical Models for Structures of Cumulated Roles*. Englewood Cliffs, N.J.: Prentice-Hall.

———. 1970. *Chains of Opportunity: System Models of Mobility in Organizations*. Cambridge: Harvard University Press.

———. 1978. "Markets as Social Structures." Paper presented at the annual meeting of the American Sociological Association, Boston.

———. 1980. *Research and Development as a Pattern in Industrial Management:*

A Case Study in Institutionalization and Uncertainty. New York: Arno Press. Doctoral dissertation, Princeton University, 1960.

———. 1981. "Where Do Markets Come From?" *American Journal of Sociology* 87:514–47.

———. 1985. "Agency as Control." In *Principals and Agents: The Structure of Business*, edited by John W. Pratt and Richard Zeckhauser, 187–212. Cambridge: Harvard University Press.

White, Harrison C., and François Lorrain. 1971. "Structural Equivalence of Individuals in Social Networks." *Journal of Mathematical Sociology* 1:49–80.

White, Harrison C., S. A. Boorman, and R. L. Breiger. 1976. "Social Structure from Multiple Networks: Part I. Blockmodels of Roles and Positions." *American Journal of Sociology* 81:730–80.

White, Harrison C., and S. A. Boorman. 1976. "Social Structure from Multiple Networks: Part II. Role Interlock." *American Journal of Sociology* 81:1384–1446.

White, Harrison C., and Robert G. Eccles. 1987. "Producers' Markets." In *The New Palgrave: A Dictionary of Economic Theory and Doctrine*, edited by John Eatwell, et al., 984–86. London: Macmillan.

5

Mark Granovetter

Since the late 1970s it has become increasingly common that sociologists study economic phenomena, which by tradition have interested only economists. The leading scholar in this movement, which is sometimes called "new economic sociology," is Mark Granovetter.[1] His first major contribution to economic sociology came in the mid-1970s, when he published a small book on how people in the labor market get information about vacant jobs. The method he used, and with which his work is closely identified, is that of social networks. In *Getting A Job*, for example, he tried to lay bare the exact ways in which information traveled from the employer until it reached the person who was hired. Granovetter's second major contribution to economic sociology has been his attempt in the 1980s to formulate a program for what a "new economic sociology" might look like. His main idea in this context is that economic action can be seen as "embedded" in networks of social relations. As he tells in this interview, in which he also reflects on his earlier work in economic sociology, he is now trying to complement the idea of embeddedness with the notion that economic institutions are "social constructions."

Mark Granovetter was born in 1943, in Jersey City, New Jersey, the son of Sidney and Violet Granovetter. He majored in history as an undergraduate and got his A.B. in 1965 at Princeton University. He got his Ph.D. in sociology in 1970 at Harvard University. He has worked at Johns Hopkins University, Harvard University, and is presently professor of sociology at the State University of New York at Stony Brook. He has also served as visiting professor of research at Stanford University's Graduate School of Business.

•

Q: Much of the work that you do these days is in economic sociology. Did you ever get a chance to study economics when you were a student at Princeton and Harvard?

The following interview with Mark Granovetter was conducted on May 12, 1988, at his home in Port Jefferson, New York.

[1] The following information comes from Granovetter's vita, and Granovetter 1983, 1987.

A: I took one course in economics as an undergraduate and that was in macroeconomics. I then had a scheduling conflict for microeconomics in the second term, so I couldn't take it. This was in 1962. I remember that I went to see William Baumol, who was at Princeton in those days as he still is. I asked him how I could read some microeconomics on my own, since I couldn't take the course. He told me to read a book by Henderson and Quandt called *Microeconomic Theory.* I bought the book and tried to read it, but it was extremely dry and contained the most formalistic sort of mathematical economics. So reading the Henderson-Quandt book made me think that microeconomics wasn't going to be my cup of tea after all.

In macroeconomics we used the Samuelson textbook *Economics.* It didn't make much sense to me either. Although I would not have been able to put it quite this way at the time, I felt that the reason it didn't make any sense was that I couldn't construct any story at the level of individuals which would enable me to understand the arguments that were made in this textbook. In today's sociological language I would say that there was no link between micro and macro. I could do the equations and so on and pass the exams, but I could not see what story to tell that would make any sense out of it.

I think that the combination of macroeconomics not making much sense to me and microeconomics being this very dry sort of mathematical economics turned me away from economics for quite a while. As an undergraduate I decided instead to major in history because there was a wonderful history department at Princeton. Many people majored in history, which was one of the larger departments. Sociology on the other hand was very small, and I think there were perhaps only four or five sociology majors in my whole class.

So I didn't do any more economics in college. And I didn't do any in graduate school either. When I was at Harvard I just did sociology. I had some interests in economics, however, because I was studying labor markets so I had to read a little bit of economics. But I really did not read that much. So most of what I know in economics I have learned after my formal education was over.

Q: In 1974 you published *Getting A Job,* which has become a minor classic in economic sociology. How do you look at this book in retrospect? What did you try to accomplish with this work and did you succeed?

A: Well, in a way it's an accident that I did something that is so close to economic sociology. As a student of Harrison White in graduate school, I had become very interested in social networks. Already when I was an undergraduate in history, social networks was the way I was thinking, but at that time I didn't know it had a name. I had always been very interested in social networks in historical contexts. I remember, for example, a book by the French historian Georges Lefebvre, *The Great Fear of 1789*, which I found quite fascinating. In this work, Lefebvre traced the exact social networks through which the rumors traveled about what the aristocracy was doing. These networks of rumor became "the great fear of 1789," which was a very important part of the French Revolution. It was the social network phenomenon that I found the most interesting in Lefebvre's book, because I felt it was really the proximate cause of what was happening. It explained workings or happenings; and it gave you the mechanisms. The larger forces—social classes, the general economic situation, and so on—were obviously not unimportant. But to get from them to what actual people were doing, there had to be some mechanisms. And to me, networks was one such mechanism.

Then when I got to Harvard in 1965 I found out that there was a group of people just forming around Harrison White who were interested in social networks. So I began to study with Harrison White and got very interested in social networks. For my dissertation I wanted to choose some topic that would illustrate the importance of social networks, and I considered a number of possibilities. I thought, for example, of making a study of how people found spouses. If I had done that, perhaps I would be a sociologist of the family and marriage today. But in some sense it didn't seem quite as rich a subject area as how people found jobs. I am not sure exactly why, and I think that in some ways it would probably have been just as interesting. But I was also interested in inequality and stratification, so perhaps that is why I ended up doing my thesis on how people found jobs.

At the time I had no idea if anything had been written on this subject. When I went and investigated it, I found that there was in fact a substantial literature—and all by economists. Most of the studies had the same sort of flavor, though, and found similar things, namely that most people did not find their jobs through formal means but rather through what this literature calls "friends and relatives." And with hardly any exception, as far as I can recall, they all deplored this fact as an obvious sort of inefficiency. They considered it to be a haphazard way of finding jobs, and that it could obviously not be allocating labor in a very efficient manner. So in their policy recommendation sections, most of these studies suggested some variant on formal matching schemes. In the early days they recommended that the National Employment Service be expanded, so that people could be matched more efficiently with jobs. And in the later literature they suggested national computerized matching schemes. That seemed to be a constant in this type of literature, at least until the 1970s. The fact is also that these kind of schemes have been tried many times and they have always failed—mainly because matching schemes can rarely offer the kind of *intensive* information usually found only through personal contacts.

In the 1970s economists became a bit more sophisticated. It actually had started already in the 1960s with George Stigler's work on information (see Stigler 1962; Rees 1966). And then it began to seem more reasonable that finding jobs through networks of contacts might in fact not be as inefficient as had been imagined. But I saw that there was still plenty of room for a sociological study because all the older studies, although they had established that people found their jobs through friends and relatives, saw this as an essentially haphazard way of getting information about jobs. And since this phenomenon really fell outside any sort of systematic frame of reference for rational action, the economists didn't see it as something that could be investigated systematically. So they always just reported the proportion of people who found their jobs this way and really never looked more carefully into what this really meant, and how the whole process actually worked. Coming from a sociological standpoint, it seemed to me that what happened with the "friends and relatives" was far from being haphazard and uninteresting; it would rather be very interesting to look at it systematically.

So the reason I thought that there was a good study to be done on this topic was that if you could find out exactly what it meant to find jobs through "friends and realtives" and how the whole process actually operated, then you would know a lot of important things about labor markets. So that's what I did; I tried to find out in great detail how people found their jobs.

I tried to establish the exact nature of the situation in which the information about a job was passed between my respondent and my respondent's contacts. I also wanted to find out in what way the contact person had gotten the information in the first place, so I tried to trace the information about the job from the employer to the actual respondent.

Another thing I looked at was if it mattered what part of an information network a person was in for a specific bit of information to flow to him. One of the interesting findings in this context was that many people found their jobs through people they really did not know very well, something which I later described in an article called "The Strength of Weak Ties." My argument was that this was no accident, but rather that the people you don't know very well are probably moving in circles that are different from your own and therefore less likely to have the same information as you do. The people you know very well, on the other hand, know the same people as you do and therefore have the same information.

In *Getting A Job,* I also tried to show how people had originally been connected to their contact person. I found that events early in their careers were especially significant and that it wasn't just the people you knew at the present time that mattered. Because "weak ties" are important, people you had known from earlier jobs and with whom you were barely in contact continued to be a significant source of information all through your career. What perhaps was the most interesting aspect of all of this to me was that there seemed to be a kind of snowballing effect involved. People who had moved several times early in their careers had accumulated contacts and been in several settings. And then the other people in those settings had themselves moved to new settings, something which increased the probability again of hearing about new job opportunities.

But there were also people who had not moved early in their careers and who typically were in firms where there were many other people who had not moved. The opportunities for mobility of these people were very much truncated. I, for example, had some cases of people who had been in the same firm for twenty years and who were very happy in that firm. Also the other people in the firm were very happy, and no one moved to other firms. And then suddenly the firm was bought out by another firm, and these people had an impossibly difficult time in finding new jobs since they didn't have any contacts in other firms that could certify that they were in fact good people. I also found that the employers preferred to hire people through personal contacts, just as the workers themselves preferred to find jobs that way.

Q: In 1985 you published an important theoretical article on economic sociology in *The American Journal of Sociology.* The main idea was that economic action can be seen as "embedded" in social action. What exactly does this mean and what is the advantage with this perspective?

A: What I mean by "embeddedness" is that the economic action of individuals as well as larger economic patterns, like the determination of prices and economic institutions, are very importantly affected by networks of social relationships. I think that for the economic action of individuals the embeddedness of individuals in networks of social relationships is in most contexts extremely important, and you rarely see this taken into account in economic arguments.

There are people like Gary Becker, for example, who talk about relationships and families and then try to incorporate these arguments into economic theory by using utility functions in which there is interdependence. So part of my utility function in, for example, the relationship in which you are my mother and I am your son, is not only the various things that I want for my own welfare but also the things that you want for your welfare. Now, that is one way relationships are incorporated into economic theory. I, however, think it is very narrow for two reasons. The first is that it doesn't take into account that people have *particular relationships* and not just relationships like those given by general role descriptions like mother–son, employer–worker, and so on.

People usually have a particular history in a relationship, and they deal with each other in ways which are conditioned by the specific history of their interaction. A structure of mutual expectations emerges, which defines what the expectations are in that particular relationship. So my argument is that what we have are relationships between particular concrete people rather than between abstract people as encapsulated by some kind of role identification. In this sense one can say that the use of role categories like employer–worker, husband–wife, and so on, which you can find in the work of Gary Becker, Harvey Leibenstein, and other economists, is an example of an "oversocialized" view of people. By this expression I mean the tendency to treat people in a certain category as if they all behave in the same way, namely as they are supposed to, given this role identification. The instructions for this role identification may then come from the interests that people have in the technical division of labor, as in the relationship between workers and employers, or they may simply come from the general stock of ideas which society has about the way husbands and wives should behave. In either case, however, the particular identity of people is not very much taken into account.

So that's one reason why I don't think that the way economists deal with social relationships is adequate. The other is that when you consider these pairs of people—like husband–wife, employer–worker, and so on—you haven't really escaped from a way of thinking that makes people's decisions and actions isolated from each other. All you have done is to take this tendency to "atomization," as I call it, and transfer it to a slightly higher level of analysis. So instead of having individual decision-makers, you now have isolated pairs of people. But what is really crucial for many purposes is the way the pairs themselves are embedded in networks of social relationships, because it is that which determines a lot of social action and also much of the institutional outcomes. And there is really very little way of incorporating this into the economists' argument.

Could it be incorporated? Well, the whole apparatus of utility functions, it seems to me, has in modern economics already been stretched far beyond its original use as a way of representing ordinal preferences. And I think it would be very difficult to use this apparatus to describe networks of social relationships and how these produce outcomes. Not because social networks can't be modeled technically, but because this particular way of modeling behavior is just not well adapted to it. I think it would be clumsy and awkward to adapt it to social networks. So the current technical apparatus in economics is just not very well suited to talking about social relationships and how these have an impact on economic behavior and institutions. A somewhat different approach is clearly needed, and I think that some of the arguments and techniques of sociology would be very useful here.

Q: Is the networks perspective in your opinion an effective tool in economic sociology for understanding all economic phenomena? Take institutions as an example. Aren't networks more suitable for analyzing small units ("micro") than institutions ("macro")?

A: Well, I think that there are periods in institutional development when it is very important to look at social networks. I also think that there are other periods when it is less important. Take industrial organization, for example. I have a student who did a dissertation on the electrical utility industry and whose name is Patrick McGuire (1986). He covered the period between 1880 and 1930, and one of the questions that he raises is why this industry is structured the way it is. Why is it structured as a series of large investment companies rather than in the two other ways that in the 1880s and 1890s looked equally plausible, namely that the plants should be publicly owned or that every large company would generate its own electricity? If either of these two possibilities had occurred, you obviously wouldn't have an electrical utility industry of the kind that you have today.

What McGuire argues is that in the formative period at the turn of the century, the networks of certain crucial individuals were extremely important in generating the ultimate shape of the electrical utility industry. This was especially the case with Samuel Insull and his network. When Insull in 1894 came to Chicago to take over the Chicago Edison Company, which was a small and new company, he brought with him a series of very unusual network contacts. He knew financiers in New York, Chicago, and London. He knew politicians, particularly in Chicago and New York; and he knew inventors from both the United States and England. So he had contacts in the financial world, in the political world, and in the technical world. To make a long story short, by using all of these contacts at different times, Insull was able to assemble ways of operating, organizational forms, technical developments, and financial backing in a way that no other person in the utility industry was able to do in that period, even though some people were quite aware of what needed to be done.

Now, I would argue that it was only as a result of Insull having this network and the capacity to assemble all of these technical, financial, and political resources that the industry has the form that it does today. Little by little Insull's activities and the activities of those that he was connected to foreclosed the possibility of the industry going over to public ownership as well as each firm generating its own power. The kind of argument that we make—I am working on a paper on this with McGuire and my colleague Michael Schwartz—is actually very similar to the one made by economists like Paul David (1986) and Brian Arthur (1985). And this is that certain forms of industrial organization, whether or not they are in fact the most efficient, become *locked in* at an early stage. And once they are locked in, they become improved upon little by little. David and Arthur make this argument in terms of increasing returns to scale, with the increasing returns to scale being the result of improvements made in a particular technology. But I think that it can also be made for organizational forms. Other organizational forms, which do not come into existence, therefore do not get an opportunity to be improved upon. So the particular organizational form which was originally chosen becomes gradually locked in, and other forms become locked out. And this is the case, even though it is by no means clear that the original organizational form was the most efficient one. So the argument is that even given everything one might have known in 1880 about technology and the economy, the outcome—the way the electrical utility industry would be constituted—was underdetermined.

In fact, it can be argued that what you have here is a situation which is similar to what you often have in dynamic models, where there are multiple stable equilibria. Economists have always been very reluctant, I think, to deal with models that have multiple stable equilibria; and this is one reason why dynamics is a weak point in modern economic theory. In these underdetermined economic models, it is usually very difficult to understand why the system reached the particular equilibrium it did, except by looking at some detailed historical account of how it proceeded from one point to another. And when you look at those historical accounts, the factors which determine how the system got from one point to another are usually exogenous to the economic frame of reference. That is certainly the case with the electrical utility industry. Our argument is therefore that which of the three stable equilibria this particular industry reached—namely that of investor-owned utilities—was to a large extent determined by the particular coalitions and networks that key actors like Samuel Insull had. And these networks themselves were not determined by the economic development.

From a sociological viewpoint, however, there is nothing peculiar in the fact that the evolution of the electrical utility industry, from its beginnings in the 1880s to the final outcome around 1930, depends on social networks. And these networks are *not* exogenous to the sociological analysis. It is not only that it isn't *difficult* to analyze social networks in sociology; they are typically what an economic sociologist would *want* to analyze.

Q: So what you are saying is that networks can help to account for *some* parts of the development of economic institutions?

A: Yes. And I think that when you reach 1930 and the organizational form of the electrical utility industry is already locked in, then the social networks don't matter so much. I think that one of the very crucial tasks facing economic sociologists today, if they use a structural approach of the type that I do, is to specify very clearly under what circumstances the social networks approach is not very helpful.

What I have just said about the evolution of industries could also be said about the evolution of professions. There are several ways that these can develop as well. And also here I think that the collective action that is generated in networks of social relationships and which depends on the resources that the social actors have, clearly has a crucial role to play in determining which of the possible equilibria will be reached. On the other hand, there are surely also situations in which there is really only one stable equilibrium outcome. And in situations like that, it is probably enough just to know the broad, aggregate situation. It may really be the case that the only organizational form that can arise here is in some sense called forth by the technical situation or, as Oliver Williamson would say, by something which reduces the transaction costs. There may well be situations like that. So a very important part of the task is to understand what situations are like that, and what situations rather resemble the underdetermined situation, where social networks play a key role. The formative stages of most industries probably resemble the underdetermined situation, where a social network analysis would be quite crucial.

Q: And what about the concept of the market in network analysis? Would you see markets in network terms as well?

A: It would be to go too far to replace the market with network analysis, and I think that one should rather try to combine them. I wouldn't want to say, for example, that the market situation had no impact on the electrical utility industry. I think that what the market situation actually does is to determine what the possible equilibria are. I think that the market is therefore very important in determining what is possible. But it does not necessarily determine what the final outcome is, i.e., which equilibrium is reached. In certain situations there is room for many different possibilities, and these possibilities are significantly different from one another. If in fact the electrical utility industry had evolved in the direction of public ownership in the United States, I think it would have made an enormous difference. And not only for that industry itself but also for the development of many other industries.

Q: In an earlier answer you touched a little bit on Gary Becker's work. In your 1985 article, you also discuss some of the new economics of organization, especially the work of Oliver Williamson. But what is your general opinion of economic imperialism?

A: Well, I think the idea that you can incorporate sociology as well as the kinds of subjects that sociology studies into the framework of individual, rational action is mistaken. It is mistaken because the methodological and intellectual base of neoclassical economics is just too narrow; it is even too narrow to account for the matters that economics is supposed to be about. What happens in production, consumption, and distribution is very much affected by people's embeddedness in social relations. And if that's the case at the very center of economic theory, it seems to me that it is easy to show that it is even more so for marriage, divorce, crime, and all the other subjects that sociologists study. The reason that I concentrate my own efforts on the more hard-core economic matters of production of goods and services is partly polemical, since it seems to me that if one can show that this imperialist project of certain economists isn't even appropriate within their own domain, then it is of course clear that it would have much more difficulty outside of that domain, in the more traditional sociological areas.

So I view the idea that people are able to make all their decisions and that their actions are fundamentally not affected by their interactions in networks of social relations as an extreme form of methodological individualism. I think that any project which is based on that, as the economic imperialist project is, is building an enormous superstructure on a very narrow base. And what happens when you do that is, of course, that eventually it all comes tumbling down.

Q: And what would be your opinion of the project of Coleman, Hechter, and others to recast sociology on the basis of rational choice? Would you be as critical of this attempt as of economic imperialism?

A: Well, although I find that Jim Coleman's arguments are more inspired by methodological individualism than I am comfortable with, they are certainly less so than what you find in neoclassical economics. The arguments of people like Coleman and Hechter, I think, really depend in very important ways on how people interact with one another. In my opinion they may not have taken sufficiently seriously the importance of the structure of social networks and how this structure affects the whole outcome, but they are still much more in tune with the kind of argument I am comfortable with than what the pure neoclassical economists would be.

Q: And what do you think of their hope to recast all of sociology with the help of rational choice? In a sense they are hoping for the big breakthrough . . .

A: Well, I don't think these rational choice arguments are going to revolutionize sociology. As a matter of fact, I don't think that any mathematical models that we are even close to right now are really fully adequate for that kind of revolutionizing ambition. I am certainly sympathetic to mathematical models, and I have done some myself, even some in economics (see Granovetter and Soong 1986). But I think that the level of complexity which is required is greater than most rational choice arguments are willing to permit. I am all for parsimony—I think it is very important to have parsimony—but I think that most rational choice arguments are still operating too much at the individual level and take too little account of social networks to be able to explain complex institutional outcomes. So I think that we are perhaps at greater distance from the breakthrough than Coleman and Hechter might suspect we are.

Q: In 1985 you coined the term "new economic sociology." How would you define this "new economic sociology"? What differentiates it, for example, from the old economic sociology? And what is the relationship between this new economic sociology and networks analysis?

A: Well, the old sociology of economic life had a number of different incarnations. Industrial sociology was one of these, and the other main one was the "economy and society" perspective of Parsons and his disciples. I think that although these two are in some ways very different from one another, they had in common that they did not really challenge the validity of neoclassical theory within its own domain. Neither did they try to cover the same subject matter as neoclassical economics.

So industrial sociology studied workers in industrial plants, but it didn't really study questions like how the employer could minimize his costs in production. They looked a bit at the production process but they were in many ways more interested in such subject matters as what made the workers happy; the structure of interaction within the workgroup; the norms about restrictions of the output; and so on. A book such as William Foote Whyte's *Men at Work* gives you an idea of the topics industrial sociology dealt with. They were more interested in all these things than in the way the production in the whole plant was structured. They had very little to say about the relations between labor and capital, and you certainly never heard anything about production functions. So they tiptoed around the edges of the subjects that the economists were working on. They were willing to say that the economic arguments about motivation were inadequate, but they did not really make any systematic attempt to replace them with something else.

The "economy and society" perspective of Parsons was very respectful to standard economics. In the Marshall Lectures from the early 1950s, Parsons was very explicit about his opinion that within its own domain, economics was fully adequate. And in *Economy and Society*, Parsons and Smelser say that economic theory is not only adequate, but a *model* for the other social sciences to follow. The whole argument of *Economy and Society* was that it was a remarkable thing that you could take economic theory and fit it into Parsonian categories. According to Parsons-Smelser, this somehow validated the Parsonian categories. But of course when you say it that way, you see right away that there is a presumption that the Parsonian categories needed validation and that economic theory was already valid.

So there was a very respectful attitude in most of the old economic sociology toward classical and neoclassical economic theory. And I think that the single thing that most clearly differentiates what I call the "new economic sociology" from the "old economic sociology" is that it is much less respectful of orthodox economics. "New economic sociology" is much more ready to argue that sociologists have something to say about standard economic processes and that this supplements and in some cases also replaces what economic theory has to say. Today's sociologists, partly because they are less respectful of the standard economic arguments, are more willing to look directly at the core of economics—at production, distribution, and consumption—and argue that the sociological perspective has something very important to add. They feel in other words that what economic sociology can contribute is more than just the last five percent tacked onto the end of the regression equation to sop up the little bit of variance that somehow neoclassical theory missed.

Another important difference between the old and the new economic sociology has to do with economic action being embedded in social networks. In the new economic sociology it is often argued that the embeddedness in networks of social relations contributes to the economic outcome in quite fundamental ways and not just in frictional or marginal ways. Now, it is true that within the new economic sociology you have quite a variety of works, and some of these don't use a networks approach (see Abolafia 1984; Baker 1984; Burt 1983; Eccles 1983; Fligstein 1985; Hirsch 1986; Leifer and White 1987; Mintz and Schwartz 1985; Mizruchi and Schwartz 1987; Powell 1987; Zelizer 1985). But when you look more closely at these, I think you will see that there is a certain affinity or similarity between some of them and those that explicitly use a social networks perspective. The reason for this is that they all come out of the classical sociological tradition, which says that all economic action—like any action—has a social context and that this social context is a fundamental influence on the economic action.

Take for example a work in Marxist economic sociology, such as Michael Burawoy's book *Manufacturing Consent.* Now, Burawoy doesn't talk about social networks at all in this study. But it is nevertheless quite clear that he thinks that the informal interaction on the shop floor is absolutely essential for the economic outcome. He makes the same argument in somewhat greater generality in *The Politics of Production*—and again without explicitly talking about social networks. But even if Burawoy uses a different language, there is still a clear affinity between what he does and my own work on embeddedness. One of the things I incidentally like about the new Marxist economic sociology, as represented by Burawoy, is that he tries to make clear that for Marx the social relations of production are really a crucial part of the production process. This is something I think that most Marxist economists do not see as clearly.

So although I think there are different idioms that the new economic sociology conducts its investigations in, they are all in some sense fundamentally related to one another. And somewhere down the road, we will perhaps be able to translate them all into the same kind of sociological language.

Q: You have told me that you are presently working on a major work in economic sociology. Could you say a little about its content?

A: Well, I have already touched on some of the topics I will be discussing in the book in this interview. I think that the subtitle will probably be "The Social Construction of Economic Institutions" or perhaps "The Social Construction of Economic Action"—whichever seems broader. I want to have a subtitle which has the term "social construction" in it, because what I want to try to argue is that the most complex economic institutions are social constructions. Sociologists will recognize the expression "social construction" in a way that perhaps economists will not. It is a phrase that comes out of the sociology of knowledge (see Berger and Luckmann 1966). And the general argument is that social institutions of all kinds appear to somehow be external and objective aspects of the environment; they have what the Germans call a massive "facticity" to them. This is, however, an illusion since they have all been socially constructed. But part of the social construction consists exactly of making them look like objective and external aspects of the environment.

This type of argument is usually not applied to economic institutions, but I don't see any reason why it shouldn't. Economic institutions, just like any other institutions, are social constructions. Prices are social constructions; the structure of an industry is a social construction; and professions are social constructions. The fact that we have a specific profession, say psychiatry, does not mean that it had to be that way. One of the important lessons of the sociology of knowledge is exactly that very little in society had to be the way it is. It is *socially constructed* that way, but there were probably other ways it could have been constructed too. Part of the process of construction is to make it look as if it couldn't be any other way, since society becomes more stable when people have that impression. It's when people realize that things are socially constructed that these constructions fall apart.

The image you get from standard economics and from certain kinds of sociology, on the other hand, is that economic institutions and economic forms are not social constructions. They are rather somehow automatic responses to certain conditions which require the institutions or the forms to be what they are, in order to minimize some costs or to maximize some kind of efficiency. This perspective is exactly what I was arguing against, when I was talking about the electrical utility industry. It is also clear that the argument I made there is applicable to all sorts of economic actors and institutions.

Take the profession of psychiatry as an example. The sociologist Andrew Abbott (1988) has written a very interesting account of this profession, which I think gives a good account of how we come to think of any economic institution, once it is in place, as the only way things could be. We, for example, assume that if people have difficulties in their everyday lives, they should of course see a psychiatrist. And this is just the way things are. But it wasn't very long ago that the normal assumption was that you should see your clergyman if you had trouble in coping with everyday life. One of the things that Abbott describes in his account of the evolution of the profession of psychiatry is the very vigorous and sometimes also vicious struggle between the various contending parties about who should be in power over the new profession. Lawyers, social workers, clergymen, and psychiatrists all fought with one another for the right to treat people's troubles. The way the competition was resolved was the result of the various networks of collective action that the different parties were able to call on.

In fact, if you look at the way psychiatry evolved, it is very similar to what happened in the electrical utility industry. In the nineteenth century there was a group of people who ran the mental institutions. They formed an organization, because they had been talking to each other anyway. It was called the Association of Medical Superintendents of American Institutions for the Insane. The group then started to bring its organizational resources to bear, and eventually the association evolved into what is now the American Psychiatric Association. So again we have personal networks which gradually take on an institutional form. This form then becomes locked in and eventually gets defined as a "profession."

There is no doubt that this profession has been socially constructed, but by the time the process is finished, a Williamsonian type of economist would look at it and say, "Well, the profession of psychiatry has this form because that's what's required to minimize the transaction costs." And a Williamsonian sociologist would say that it has the form it does because that's the most efficient way to deal with people's troubles. If you want to make an argument of this type, it is clear that you can always find some story about why just this organization happens to be the most efficient way of doing things. Some of the sociological literature on the professions has as a matter of fact very much that flavor. There is, for example, a functionalist literature on the professions, according to which modern professions look the way they do, because of the necessity to control expert knowledge. High-level technical developments thus require professionals to control professional activity. This would, for example, be one way of explaining why the medical profession has a kind of monopoly on who can become a doctor and so on.

But I think that a social constructionist perspective is much more valid, because it shows that there are usually different ways that professions could have been structured and that the particular way these did come out is not the only possible way. It is clear that the outcome cannot be totally inconsistent with the nature of the economic environment. Nevertheless, the outcome is not necessarily the most efficient one. And as they evolve, the professions themselves shape the economic environment in such a way that it becomes more suitable for their own professional needs. So it is not as if the environment exists once and for all, and that the professions then come into existence to suit the economic requirements of the environment. It is rather that both evolve together, and that both are socially constructed.

Q: From what you are saying, I get the impression that this idea about the economy being socially constructed is really the main idea in your new book. Would that be a correct impression?

A: Yes, the social constructionist perspective is the unifying theme in the book, and I will try to treat a large variety of economic phenomena through this general lens. I have in fact already drafted a chapter on tribal and peasant economies from this perspective, and I am working right now on a chapter on small businesses, entrepreneurship, and family and ethnic relations. I also hope to have a chapter on law and economics, and how the settlement of disputes is in fact generated through social networks in most economic settings, rather than through formal legal proceedings.

Let me just mention one argument from these chapters, namely that legal institutions come from the need for economic efficiency. This idea, which is quite popular in some circles, is in my mind typically incorrect. The general problem with functionalist explanations of this type is that they assume that if there is an economic problem, it will somehow automatically be solved. The question that is begged is how it is solved and under what circumstances it can be solved. And the reason why it is begged is that it requires you to actually pay attention to concrete actors who mobilize resources through networks of social relations. And that is a subject which is very far removed from the neoclassical way of thinking. Economists find it very hard to think in terms of social relations, either because they are preselected into the economic profession just because they are reluctant to see things that way or because they have been trained not to do it.

It seems to me that economists should not worry so much whether something can in fact be described within a purely economic framework, but rather pay attention to the phenomenon from whatever framework it can be described. I don't see why one should be so reluctant to explain economic phenomena in styles and modes of explanation that originate from other disciplines. There is no reason why disciplines need to be as narrowly encapsulated as they are today.

Q: So whichever discipline solves the problem the best is the one that should be used? And if sociology can analyze an economic problem better, it is sociology that should be used?

A: Well, I think that in most concrete cases you need both economics and sociology. In some cases you also need psychology. Now, the reward structure of all disciplines makes it difficult to use concepts from other disciplines. And the reward structure of economics is particularly resistant to this, because economics has a picture of itself as a discipline which is completely self-sufficient. It's really a kind of autarchy, and there is no sense at all that any other discipline has any comparative advantage on any aspect of economic life. Young economists to whom I talk and who are interested in sociological subjects tell me that they feel they have to be very careful about this interest and that they should not say too much about it in their writings. Because if they do, they won't be able to publish in the best journals, and they won't be well regarded in their profession.

A sociologist, on the other hand, who makes use of economic arguments, might be viewed with a certain suspicion in some circles, but will basically not have that much difficulty in publishing in the major journals. And there will always be some sociologists who find this type of work interesting. So I think that sociology is more tolerant than economics in this aspect. Part of the reason for this is that economics for a lot of very complicated reasons has a higher status within the social sciences than sociology. And I think it is this high status that makes the economists feel they are self-sufficient. The history of this self-sufficiency actually goes back a great many years and has in part to do with the fact that economics is a much older discipline than sociology. It also has to do with economics being institutionalized in the universities for a much longer time; and with economics being institutionalized outside the universities in a much more powerful way than the sociologists. Just look at the Brookings Institution, the Council for Economic Advisers, and some of the larger foundations.

So there are many reasons why economics is a higher status profession. And being a higher status profession it has the sense that it ought to avoid contamination from lower status disciplines. In some sense, it should be noticed, this feeling has perhaps served economics well, because it has enabled it to develop in a very insulated fashion for a long time. But I think that by now this strategy has reached a point of diminishing returns. And I also think that any real progress in economics in the future is going to require some substantial attempt to come to grips with the kinds of insights that the other social sciences, including sociology, are able to provide.

Q: In an interview from 1985, when you had just launched the idea of a "new economic sociology," you were very optimistic about its prospects. You drew parallels between the situation for economic sociology in the 1980s and the 1930s, when mathematics was just beginning to be introduced into economic analysis. You cited Paul Samuelson, who has said of the 1930s that in those days, "it was like fishing in a virgin lake: a whopper at every cast. . . ." Are you still as optimistic about the potentials of economic sociology?

A: Oh yes. I think that everywhere you look, there are all kinds of fascinating economic subjects that have not yet been given sociological scrutiny. So I still very much have that feeling of optimism. I don't think that we have got many whoppers yet, but I think that we are generating a whole series of insights in these economic subjects that are really new and that will make a substantial contribution to how these economic subjects are understood in the future. We are perhaps still catching relatively smaller fish in this effort, but I think that the whoppers are coming somewhere down the road. So I am certainly casting my own net wider and wider and trying to catch them!

References

Abbott, Andrew. 1988. *The System of Professions: An Essay on the Division of Expert Labor.* Chicago: University of Chicago Press.

Abolafia, Mitchel Y. 1984. "Structured Anarchy." In *The Social Dynamics of Financial Markets,* edited by Patricia A. Adler and Peter Adler, 129–50. Greenwich, Conn.: JAI Press.

Arthur, Brian W. 1985. "Competing Technologies and Lock-In by Historical Small Events: The Dynamics of Allocation Under Increasing Returns." Publication #43, Center for Economic Policy Research, Stanford University.

Baker, Wayne. 1984. "The Social Structure of a National Securities Market." *American Journal of Sociology* 89:775–811.

Berger, Peter L., and Thomas Luckmann. 1966. *The Social Construction of Reality: A Treatise in the Sociology of Knowledge.* New York: Doubleday.

Burawoy, Michael. 1979. *Manufacturing Consent: Changes in the Labor Process under Monopoly Capitalism.* Chicago: University of Chicago Press.

———. 1985. *The Politics of Production: Factory Regimes under Capitalism and Socialism.* London: Verso.

Burt, Ronald. 1983. *Corporate Profits and Cooptation: Networks of Market Constraints and Directorate Ties in the American Economy.* New York: Academic Press.

David, Paul. 1986. "Understanding the Necessity of QWERTY: The Necessity of History." In *Economic History and the Modern Economist,* edited by William N. Parker, 30–49. London: Basil Blackwell.

Eccles, Robert G. 1983. "Control with Fairness in Transfer Pricing." *Harvard Business Review* (November–December):149–61.

Fligstein, Neil. 1985. "The Spread of the Multidivisional Form among Large Firms." *American Sociological Review* 50:377–91.

Granovetter, Mark. 1973. "The Strength of Weak Ties." *American Journal of Sociology* 78:1360–80.

———. 1974. *Getting A Job: A Study of Contacts and Careers.* Cambridge: Harvard University Press.

———. 1983. "Interview: Contacts and Networks." *Working Paper Series* (University of Toronto, Department of Sociology) #41.

———. 1985. "Economic Action and Social Structure: A Theory of Embeddedness." *American Journal of Sociology* 91:481–510.

———. 1987. "Interview: On Economic Sociology." *Research Reports from the Department of Sociology.* Uppsala University 1987:1.

————. 1988. "The Old and the New Economic Sociology: A History and an Agenda." Paper presented at the first annual seminar of the Center for Economy and Society, University of California at Santa Barbara.

Granovetter, Mark, and Roland Soong. 1986. "Threshold Models of Interpersonal Effects in Consumer Demand." *Journal of Economic Behavior and Organization* 7:83–99.

Henderson, J. M., and Richard E. Quandt. 1958. *Microeconomic Theory: A Mathematical Approach*. New York: McGraw-Hill. 2d ed. 1980.

Hirsch, Paul. 1986. "From Ambushes to Golden Parachutes: Corporate Takeovers as an Instance of Cultural Framing and Institutional Integration." *American Journal of Sociology* 91:800–37.

Lefebvre, Georges. 1973. *The Great Fear of 1789: Rural Panic in Revolutionary France*. New York: Pantheon Books. Originally appeared in 1932.

Leifer, Eric, and Harrison White. 1987. "A Structural Approach to Markets." In *Intercorporate Relations: The Structural Relations of Business*, edited by M. Mizruchi and M. Schwartz, 85–108. New York: Cambridge University Press.

McGuire, Patrick. 1986. "The Control of Power: The Political Economy of Electric Utility Development in the United States, 1870–1930." Ph.D. dissertation, Department of Sociology, State University of New York at Stony Brook.

Mintz, Beth, and Michael Schwartz. 1985. *The Power Structure of American Business*. Chicago: University of Chicago Press.

Mizruchi, Mark, and Michael Schwartz, eds. 1987. *Intercorporate Relations: The Structural Analysis of Business*. Cambridge: Cambridge University Press.

Parsons, Talcott. 1986. "The Marshall Lectures (1953)." *Research Reports from the Department of Sociology*, Uppsala University 1986:4.

Parson, Talcott, and Neil J. Smelser. 1956. *Economy and Society: A Study in the Integration of Economic and Social Theory*. New York: Free Press.

Powell, William W. 1987. "Hybrid Organizational Arrangements: New Form or Transitional Development?" *California Management Review* 30(1):67–87.

Rees, Albert. 1966. "Information Networks in Labor Markets." *American Economic Review* 5:559–66.

Samuelson, Paul A. 1961. *Economics*. 5th ed. New York: McGraw-Hill.

Stigler, George J. 1962. "Information in the Labor Market." *Journal of Political Economy* 70:94–105.

Whyte, William Foote. 1961. *Men at Work*. Homewood, Ill.: Dorsey Press.

Zelizer, Viviana. 1985. *Pricing the Priceless Child: The Changing Social Value of Children*. New York: Basic Books.

6

Oliver E. Williamson

ONE OF the most powerful challenges to the traditional division of labor between neoclassical economics and sociology has come from the school of behavioral economics or the Carnegie School of Business Behavior. The three key people here are Herbert Simon, Richard Cyert, and James March. Their contributions include the notion of bounded rationality,[1] the behavioral theory of the firm, and many of the classical works in organization theory. In this book, behavioral economics is represented by Oliver E. Williamson, who can perhaps be characterized as the leading figure in the second generation of behavioral economists. It was in 1975 that Williamson published *Markets and Hierarchies*, which attracted a great deal of attention not only in economics but also in sociology. His analysis was centered around the notion of transaction costs, a concept that Ronald Coase in particular has worked on and which roughly can be defined as costs other than price incurred in trading goods and services. Williamson continued his work on transaction costs, and in 1985 the next major work appeared—*The Economic Institutions of Capitalism*. In 1986 a collection of his essays appeared under the title *Economic Organization*. At this time, Williamson also published a paper called "Economics and Sociology: Promoting a Dialogue" in which he urges that the study of economic organization will benefit from "a richer dialogue between economists and sociologists" (Williamson 1986a, 1).

Oliver E. Williamson was born in 1932 in a teachers' family in Superior, Wisconsin.[2] He got a B.S. from MIT in 1955, an M.B.A from Stanford in 1960, and a Ph.D. in economics from Carnegie-Mellon University in 1963. During the period 1963 to 1965, Williamson worked at the University of California at Berkeley; during the period 1965 to 1983, at the University of

---

The following interview with Oliver E. Williamson was conducted on June 7, 1988, at Friiberghs, a mansion outside Stockholm, Sweden.

[1] Bounded rationality means that there exist definite cognitive limits to the capacity of human beings for rational calculation.

[2] The following information comes from "An Autobiographical Sketch" in Williamson 1986b and from Blaug, *Who's Who in Economics*.

Pennsylvania; and from 1983 to 1988, at Yale University. Since 1988 he has served as the Transamerica Professor of Economic Institutions and Corporate Strategy and professor of law at the University of California at Berkeley.

•

Q: Your first degree was in engineering from MIT. What made you switch into economics and go to Stanford?

A: Well, after MIT I decided to get a Ph.D. in business administration. The field was a little vague in my mind, but I had an interest in marketing. The program I was in at MIT was actually a combined engineering and management program, so I had been exposed to management issues prior to Stanford, even if I hadn't had much exposure to economics. The Ph.D. program at Stanford at that time was being reformed by Jim Howell and some others. Jim was an outstanding teacher, and he was doing the basic economics course. When I took his course I was perfectly astonished by what I found. Not only was economics interesting, but it had a lot more structure than I had expected. It was also much more intriguing than any of the more applied subjects I was taking. I had a series of discussions with Jim, who sympathized with my predilections. He steered me towards taking more economics.

During the second semester I took a microeconomics course with Ken Arrow, which actually was an advanced undergraduate course. It was mainly a Henderson–Quandt mathematical microeconomics treatment, and I enjoyed it a lot. During the second year at Stanford I actually only took one course in the MBA program; instead I was taking graduate courses in economics, statistics, and mathematics. I gather that if it hadn't been for Jim and his sponsorship, this would have been very difficult. But that's what happened.

At about this time I also met Chuck Bonini, who was a recent graduate of Carnegie Tech and was an enthusiast of the program at Carnegie. In his view, which was an objective one really, the Ph.D. program in the business school at Stanford needed a lot of work and was not responsive to my interests. And the program in economics at Stanford—although it was an excellent one—did not have the applied aspects that were of special interest to me. So in the course of our discussions, Chuck suggested that I look into the Carnegie Tech program.

Q: Did they have an economics program at Carnegie Tech or was it a business school program?

A: Well, it was a school in industrial administration. The people who were then at Carnegie included Cyert, March, Simon, and Modigliani (who unfortunately was in the process of leaving). It was quite an impressive group. I had been awarded a Ford Foundation fellowship, which gave me a lot of latitude. You could take it wherever you wanted; it was a portable fellowship. So although my original intention was that I would continue to do my Ph.D. at Stanford, I switched over to Carnegie.

The Carnegie experience was extraordinary. I really so enjoyed it, and it is sad for me that it can't be replicated. There were also hard times of course, but it was just such an interesting place to be. Interdisciplinary work was going on, and the people I was taking courses with encouraged the students to be enterprising in their work. My major and degree were in economics, but it really was an interdisciplinary program and included a good deal of work in organization theory. Economics, quantitative theory, and organization theory—those were the three fields I had to prepare for, and I had a real interest in all of them. I especially found the intersection of economics and organization fascinating, and I felt that there would be a lot of research opportunities here.

Q: Simon, Cyert, and March—that's a very impressive list. What was your impression of them as a student?

A: I was in awe of Simon and still am. He spans an incredible range of knowledge and possesses extraordinary intelligence. Dick Cyert was an economist with genuine interests in joining economics and organization theory. I was encouraged by and enjoyed Cyert a lot. Jim March was and is an extraordinary teacher and researcher.

I received a great deal of stimulation from these three—and from Allan Meltzer as well. The message was: have an active mind; be disciplined; be interdisciplinary.

Q: Did you take any courses in social sciences like history, psychology, or sociology?

A: I took several courses in organization theory. I also read selectively the social psychology literature. The organization theory course was with Jim March. I also took a reading course with Jim March, which was in social psychology. And I took behavioral theory of the firm with Dick Cyert and mathematical social science from Herb Simon.

Q: Did you study any sociology? For example, did you read Weber in the courses on organization theory?

A: No. There certainly were outside readings in sociology in the courses of March and Simon, but Weber was not among them as I recall.

Q: *Markets and Hierarchies* is a very famous work with a famous thesis. Did you just have a sudden intuition that one could tie together markets and hierarchies with the help of transaction costs? Or was it more of a slow realization?

A: I would say that there were a series of critical experiences that I had that led up to this book. One was that I spent a year, in 1966-1967, as a special economic assistant to the head of the Antitrust Division in Washington. That was a very fascinating year for me. There were lots of wonderful, lively people around; and the head of the Antitrust Division, Don Turner, was pushing applications of economics to antitrust law. I was being asked for advice on a wide variety of cases as they came along. One of the critical issues that Turner asked advice on and which I worked on—but was not at all satisfied with—was vertical integration. There was an economics literature on this topic, which one could access, but it didn't seem to me that it went to the core issue.

So later, when I went back to Philadelphia to teach at the University of Pennsylvania, I organized a graduate seminar to study vertical market structures. This was in the late 1960s. We worked through the literature very carefully and exhaustively, I think, and I remained dissatisfied. It was completely clear to me at that juncture that the literature wasn't dealing with the critical issues. I am certain that Coase's article on the nature of the firm must have been on the reading list and that we must have thought of transaction costs as one of the factors that entered into the picture. But it wasn't at this point in time that I was persuaded of the possibilities inherent in the transaction cost approach.

It was during a course in organization theory that Julius Margolis asked me to do that I got the basic ideas for *Markets and Hierarchies.* I was actually quite pleased that Julius asked me to do this course, because organization theory was a field that I had a lot of interest in and was anxious to deepen my exposure to. So I agreed to do it. This was probably around 1969. So we went through the literature—much of it actually the market failure literature—but from a very behavioral point of view. We gave special attention to the behavioral assumptions that were ascribed to human actors, and we kept circling around these. There appeared to be some themes or regularities there, but it was difficult to discover exactly what they were. I recall telling the students that I wanted them to go home over the weekend with an assignment and to lay out the core structure of the argument in the market failure literature. I also took the assignment myself and went home and worked on it. And I persuaded myself that there really were some critical behavioral assumptions operating throughout the entire market failure literature. Bounded rationality was one of them. I don't know if I identified opportunism at the time, but we focused on two critical issues which are close to opportunism, namely limitations associated with promises and the fact that some promises need institutional supports.

What I subsequently referred to as the "organizational failures framework" emerged. The frequent transformation of what had been a large numbers exchange relation into what, in effect, was a small number dependency condition was a key feature of this framework.

I decided to continue work along these lines and to feel that the way to really bring content to all of this was to address a hard problem. So I decided to go back and look at vertical integration. I did this in a paper which was presented at the annual meeting of the American Economic Association in December 1970. The basic work on that paper was done in the summer of 1970, and it was entitled "The Vertical Integration of Production: Market Failure Considerations." I really did feel, at the time when I wrote the paper, that I had cracked the problem. I remember, as a matter of fact, telling a colleague in the spring of 1971 that I felt that I was the first person in the world that had ever understood vertical integration. This was obviously a certain exaggeration. But I did have a sense that this reformulation really got to some of the basic issues.

I was also persuaded that there was a lot of generality to my approach. So the question became, to what other kinds of issues was the same general approach applicable? Looking at contractual relations appeared to be the key. I recall coming across a book at this time, *Internal Labor Markets* by Doeringer and Piore. I remember that I went to the library to get the book and that I took it out of the shelves with some concern. The concern was really of two kinds—one, that they had seen the problem and already worked it out in my terms; and the other, that the book wasn't detailed enough for my purposes. Well, they did see the problem and they had partially worked it out. But I felt that they really didn't bring all the structure they could have brought to it. At the same time the book was sufficiently detailed that one could understand internal labor markets as possessing a more rational structure than I think a straightforward labor economics approach would support.

Q: So it was really in 1970–1971 that the key insights in *Markets and Hierarchies* were worked out. But the book wasn't published until 1975. What happened in the meantime?

A: Well, *Markets and Hierarchies* was an *enormously* difficult book to write. I am a person who goes through many drafts in most of my things, and I usually see successive improvements. But it is literally true that the penultimate draft of *Markets and Hierarchies* was better than the final draft. So I finally declared that however imperfect it was, I was into a negative returns region. So I went back to the penultimate draft and that is really what was published in 1975.

Markets and Hierarchies was very hard to write and I sympathize enormously with those who have had to read it. I have actually been reluctant to assign it to my own students. Still, it did contain an analysis which was not available elsewhere. And many people have felt that it introduced certain important issues and that it had a lot of bearing on problems they were interested in.

Q: *Markets and Hierarchies* appeared more then ten years ago. What progress do you feel has been made since 1975 with the transaction cost approach?

A: Let me first say that Ronald Coase is and continues to be an important contributor to the literature on transaction costs. And indeed there are others, such as Victor Goldberg, who have contributed to the study of regulation (Goldberg 1976). I think I have been centrally involved, but there have also been others. Klein, Crawford, and Alchian (1978) have been influential—especially since they represent "Chicago."

Now, my 1975 book was centered on two polar modes—markets and hierarchies—and although there were some intermediate forms, I was extremely skeptical that they were stable and could be adequately described. Through Victor Goldberg, however, I found out about some of the work that he and Macneil were doing on contracting. I recall reading a wonderful article at about this time of Macneil's that was published in 1974, "The Many Futures of Contracts." I read it with sheer delight. It's a very long article and basically a mixture of sociology and law with only occasional references to economics. But a lot of implicit economics is actually going on in the background. Anyway, during the academic year of 1977–1978 I was on leave at the Behavioral Sciences Center at Stanford, and I used that time to study the contract law area and see if it could be applied to my interests. It became clear to me that what Macneil calls "relational contracts" were in fact much more widespread than I had imagined and one could indeed develop a structure that would show how these fitted into the organizational scheme of things. This was done in my article "Transaction-Cost Economics: The Governance of Contractual Relations," which was published in the *Journal of Law and Economics* in 1979. I think this is a key article, because although much of what is discussed here is also discussed in parts of *Markets and Hierarchies*, the structure is more well specified. This effort to so to speak "dimensionalize transactions" seemed to me at that time and since as an important step on the road of operationalizing this whole line of study.

Subsequently I worked on an article that was published in the *American Economic Review* in 1983 as "Credible Commitments." This is really a further effort to understand how certain hybrid transactions—such as long-term contracts, franchising, reciprocity—are structured the way they are; what economic purposes are being served by them; and why certain hybrid contracts have more robust characteristics than I had earlier thought possible.

Then in 1985 I pulled together the material on which I had been working in a book called *The Economic Institutions of Capitalism*. Some of the material here deals with regulation and the limits of franchise bidding for natural monopolies. Some of it deals with the credible commitment issue; and other parts aim to enrich the view of contractual man. There is also some material on labor organizations and corporate governance in this book. These were all issues that I in one way or another had found myself working on in the early 1980s. And although I am a believer in looking at problems from several points of view, the point of view I most often ended up with was indeed the transaction cost point of view. I think that transaction cost economics actually informs all of these issues, although it doesn't exhaust them. Well, this is all in *The Economic Institutions of Capitalism*.

Q: How has the reception of your work been in the three sciences that inform it—law, economics, and organization? Has there been any critique you have found particularly useful?

A: I don't think I can complain about my reception in any of these areas, although some critics have been less instructive than others. Some critics say, for example, that I am still stuck in a *Markets and Hierarchies* setup. The fact, however, is that I have spent a huge part of my time on intermediary modes of organization. So although I surely think that there is additional work to be done here, I find it disconcerting that critics haven't caught up. Then there are critics who emphasize the need to formalize transaction cost economics. I agree that there is a need to do this and I am basically sympathetic to this line of argument. Some of this work has incidentally already been done. And more is in progress.

Another type of critique is that transaction cost economics hasn't been tested adequately. I am certainly persuaded of the need for more empirical work. The fact is, however, that there has already been a rather considerable amount of testing—there must be at least sixty empirical articles out there and more in progress. So it isn't as if there hasn't been any empirical work. The empirical work to date, moreover, has been mainly corroborative.

There are also those who claim that transaction cost economics is too narrow a formulation and that it only works out of dyadic relations. I am sympathetic to that too. My inclination is to work with simple models as much as I can, but there are clearly certain kinds of effects that don't get picked up this way and are important. One example of this, which I introduce in *Markets and Hierarchies,* is what I call the "economics of atmosphere." My feeling when I wrote the book was that this is an important phenomenon, and my feeling is the same today. Actually, I had a colleague who urged me vigorously to move ahead and work further on this. And I did write a paper, which I don't think ever was published, but it was presented at a conference that Albert O. Hirschman organized. And I am still sympathetic to doing more on this. Atmosphere does not play a prominent role in *The Economic Institutions of Capitalism,* but that isn't because I don't think it is important; it is just that I haven't made any headway with it.

Another interesting complaint along these lines is what sociologists refer to as network analysis. I was just at a conference this week in Italy, where some of these new forms of networks were under discussion that Charles Sabel and others are working on. It's my feeling that a rather huge fraction of what is going on in these network enterprises can be interpreted usefully in transaction cost terms. Actually, one of the things that is probably frustrating to noneconomists is that economics is so incredibly elastic. Once the economic content of a a concept is understood, economics finds a way to embrace it. So I anticipate that networks can probably be incorporated—at least to some degree—into an extended version of transaction cost economics. But that's just a conjecture; I don't really know.

Q: One critique of the transaction cost approach comes from Mark Granovetter, who is a key figure in network analysis. He feels that you, like many economists, automatically assume that the existing economic institutions are also the most efficient ones. According to Granovetter, the economic institutions that are around today may have survived because of some historical conjuncture; because they were hooked up to a very powerful network at some crucial time; or for some similar reason (Granovetter 1985, 1988). What would be your answer to this type of critique?

A: First of all I would like to say that those general arguments Granovetter makes about embeddedness in networks are useful, and that it is an issue to which we ought to be more sensitive. I agree that historical choices matter, but this statement needs to be given a more precise content. I think that the work of Paul David and others in conjunction with path dependency is terribly useful (David 1986). There is indeed a chance that one may end up with, say, a typewriter keyboard that is not ideal. But the fact that it is inefficient to unpack the present keyboard and replace it with another one doesn't really imply a rejection of the efficiency argument. When everything is taken into account, including the path-dependent characteristics here, we have perhaps ended up with a keyboard over which we can't affect improvements without some kind of subsidy or other assistance. That is, the market is unable to do it, and there may be no way to get from here to there that yields net social gains. But that doesn't seem to me to demonstrate that observed outcomes are, because they are imperfect, necessarily inefficient. Hypothetical inefficiency (in relation to an ideal) and operational inefficiency (in relation to a feasible alternative that can be realized with net gains) need to be distinguished. So I just don't see what the argument is here.

Q: Another sociological critique of transaction cost economics comes from Charles Perrow (1986). He argues in *Complex Organizations* that "power" in many cases can better explain what you try to explain with transaction cost analysis. What is your reaction to this argument?

A: It is certainly true that power is a consideration and that is out there. The thing I would urge is that just as transaction cost analysis needs to be operationalized, so does power. Now the definition of power, which in my opinion comes the closest to be operationalized, is what is called "resource dependency" (Pfeffer and Salanzick 1978). Resource dependency is fairly close to what I call "asset specificity" (Williamson 1985, 52–56). But a real difference between resource dependency theory and the transaction cost economics is that the latter approaches the study of contracting from the standpoint of what I call "contracting in its entirety"—that is, it looks at the whole transaction including the original negotiations. Resource dependency, on the other hand, neglects the original negotiations. It simply looks at the outcomes, and says, "Oh, my God! We've got a resource dependency outcome!"

But to get back to the power advocates: I think there is a great obligation on their part to say exactly what "power" is and how their power analysis works. One of Perrow's students, incidentally, told me that Perrow had advised him that transaction cost economics was quote "dangerous" unquote.

Q: Dangerous in what sense?

A: Well, presumably it was dangerous in the sense that the student wouldn't think about the issues in a correct way; he would have his perceptions altered permanently and be intellectually crippled. I don't think that's a mature way to see the subject matter. We should have all the viewpoints exposed and run a friendly contest of a sort, but a contest in which we expect to learn from each other.

Q: There is one more question about sociology I would like to ask you. You recently wrote a paper called "Economics and Sociology: Promoting a Dialogue" in which you say that the study of economic organization could benefit from "a richer dialogue between economists and sociologists" (Williamson 1986a, 1). Could you elaborate a bit on this statement?

A: One of the things that I think is vitally important and to which I think sociology can add is a deeper understanding of process considerations. I actually raise this issue in a paper I wrote last year to honor the fiftieth anniversary of Ronald Coase's classic article on the nature of the firm (Coase 1937). My paper is called "The Logic of the Firm" and in it I urge, among other things, that process considerations be taken into account (Williamson 1987).

It does seem to me that sociologists have been much more alert to process considerations than economists and that they indeed could alert us to what some of these critical processes are—what their ramifications are; how we should understand them; and so on. I have occasionally also made use of arguments that something is "dysfunctional," which is a venerated sociological idea. Economists need to make greater allowance for unanticipated consequences.

What I call "the fundamental transformation" is indeed a process outcome (Williamson 1985, 61–63). Actually, the neglect of this phenomenon—despite a long-standing awareness of what Alfred Marshall and others have referred to as "sunk costs"—seems to me to be one of the factors which explains the long neglect of many of the issues that come out of transaction cost economics. So, if sociologists had just said, "Look, there are many trading relations that display a lot of dependency and which don't behave in accordance with the standard market model you fellows are working out of," then we would have gotten into an examination of the relevant issues much earlier.

Another issue of a process related kind that I think is important is what I have referred to as "the impossibility of selective intervention" (Williamson 1985, 135–38). The puzzle here is, why can't a large firm do everything that a collection of small firms can do and more? If we could intervene selectively, then certainly large systems could beat small systems; more degrees of freedom are always better than less. So why can't we then implement a program of this sort? Well, I think there are some basic incentive reasons why that can't be done. I have begun to work on these issues, but there's still a lot of work that ought to be done before we feel that we have closure on this. I am also persuaded that there are many other process issues that sociologists have already worked on, but which they have not insisted that we economists attend to. We are greatly in need of a more adequate theory of bureaucracy. So I urge that sociologists call these issues to our attention, lay out their significance, and impress upon us to be responsive.

Q: Presently some attempts are being made in sociology to recast the sociological analysis on the basis of rational choice. The key person here is James Coleman in Chicago. What would your attitude be to a project of this sort?

A: In general I think a lot can be said for moving towards more of a rational action basis in sociology. This does not imply hyperrationality of the kind that is associated with much of economics. Herbert Simon's definition of bounded rationality is perhaps the most suitable, and it is also the one that I myself have found the most useful—rational behavior is behavior which is "*intendedly* rational, but only *limited* so" (Simon 1976, xxviii). This definition emphasizes intentionality and how people try to cope. But equally it emphasizes cognitive limitations.

We need to understand these limitations and ascertain what their organizational consequences are. This is something I think sociologists could help us more fully to understand. They could also advise us about what organizations can do to be responsive to this, including the possibility that certain biases sometimes get introduced which we ought to be alert to.

Now, one of the things that happens is that once we are aware that there are these systematic biases, organizations will be designed with this in mind. For this reason, I suppose, there might be some concern among sociologists that by apprising others of these systematic features, they would just become handmaidens to the organizational design specialists, who are simply going to factor these biases into a larger treatment of the problem. But I don't see that that should be a matter of great concern to sociologists. It seems to me that our knowledge of complex organizations is so primitive in relation to the complexities that are out there, that we are not going to work sociologists or anybody else out of a job for the next couple of decades.

Q: And what's your reaction to economic imperialism and Becker's work? Does that represent a good research strategy for economists and sociologists?

A: Gary's view is that one should push the apparatus of his particular type of economics as far as it will go. I think that's an interesting and useful strategy. At the same time one of the things one ought to be prepared to do is to acknowledge when it has reached its limits and when we have to bring in other points of view. And I certainly think that the behavioral assumptions are ones that we ought to be keenly aware of, and it doesn't seem to me that they are featured as strongly in Gary's work as might be appropriate. But, again, well-focused strategies are the ones we want to favor in general, and Gary's work certainly has the nice property of being sharply in focus. Now, I think that transaction cost economics has that quality to it as well—it continuously emphasizes that economizing is central, and it pushes that as far as it will go. But again, I don't think that transaction cost economics tells us everything that is interesting about organizations.

Q: The behavioral assumptions that you make in your analyses are built on what you often refer to as "human nature as we know it." This is actually a quote from *Risk, Uncertainty and Profit* by Frank Knight (Knight 1971, 270). But isn't a statement like this a bit thin to build a theory on? After all, we know somewhat more about human nature than Frank Knight did when he wrote his dissertation in the 1910s.

A: Well, Frank Knight does believe that we can use introspection to some extent. And he also makes specific reference to moral hazard, which is a technical variety of opportunism. Tjalling Koopmans has also urged that introspection is undervalued. Bounded rationality, in relation to hard problems, is something we have a lot of experience with. And both history and everyday life remind us that opportunism is out there.

Q: But Knight was hardly a psychologist and to refer to him as an authority on human nature just seems a bit thin.

A: Well, opportunism is a relatively unflattering behavioral assumption and it gives outrage to a lot of people, including my colleagues. There is actually corroborating evidence from H.L.A. Hart—but again you might say that he is not a psychologist, so why should he be quoted as an authority on these matters? Hart is a legal philosopher and he has thought quite a bit about how we characterize the human actor for purposes of trying to do legal analysis and legal philosophy (Hart 1961). He really doesn't identify opportunism as such, but he identifies a condition which is very akin to it and which I think is useful, because it takes some of the edge off of it. I myself don't assume that most people are opportunistic most of the time; I assume that *some* of the people are opportunistic *some* of the time and that it is very difficult to sort those who are opportunistic from those who are not. And one of the concerns that I have—and which H.L.A. Hart also has—is that the world should not be organized to the advantage of the opportunistic against those who are more inclined to keep their promises. I would simply say that introspection supports this view. And all of Shakespeare's tragedies and comedies support it. The alternative to opportunism is saintliness, and since we are not prepared to embrace that, then opportunism is something we have to come to terms with. Maybe a distinction between strong-form—continuous—and weak-form—occasional—opportunism is needed. If so, I refer to opportunism of the weak-form kind.

The evidence is impressive when we come to bounded rationality. But this certainly doesn't exhaust "human nature as we know it." What you find in Frank Knight and in transaction cost economics is a parsimonious description. But I think that there exist many other attributes as well, and some of these have important consequences for the analysis. So they need to be identified and factored in. And I would invite myself, my students, and others to do that.

Q: In one of your latest books you say that transaction cost economics has "enormous explanatory power" (Williamson 1986b, xviii). Could you say a little about what kind of areas you expect the transaction cost approach to be applied to in the future?

A: One of the things that is happening today is that there are a lot of young economic theorists who are interested in what is called "incomplete contracts." Now I think you can discuss "incomplete contracting" apart from transaction cost economics, but the critical assumptions that lie behind most incomplete contracting are (a) bounded rationality; (b) opportunism; and (c) the condition of asset specificity. So the carryover of transaction cost economics into the formal modeling of incomplete contracting is substantial, and I am delighted and encouraged to see that this is happening.

The study of process, which I have already mentioned, is another issue to which many people could contribute, and I would expect sociologists to be among them. There are other issues as well, including one that I see a lot of promise in and that I have begun to work on myself. That is to dimensionalize governance structures. Transactions have to be assigned a governance structure, and we have been less specific here than we should have been about what the characteristics of governance structures are. This represents an opportunity to do a lot of good work. If we are successful here, it will definitely also have a lot of impact on organization theory.

There are also good opportunities to work on issues that are referred to as strategic business behavior in business administration and to reconceptualize business strategy from a transaction cost point of view. Several people are already working on this, and others are picking up on it. Political scientists and economic historians have also been applying transaction cost economics arguments to political institutions—both domestic and international. There are also issues having to do with marketing, networks, and contract law. So altogether we observe new theory, new applications, and new empirical work taking place. There is reason to be optimistic about the future of transaction cost economics.

I should add that I am in the process of moving permanently to the University of California at Berkeley, where they have created a new field in the economics department called "the economics of institutions." Students will be able to take this as a field of concentration. My new appointment is actually a joint appointment between economics and business (it includes a law school affiliation as well). This means that there will be excellent opportunities for me to bring students from both of these fields together—students who are principally trained as economists and who are interested in institutions, and students who have a background in business but see economics as a productive way of working and who feel that the "New Institutional Economics" is the way to go. I am encouraged by all of this, but it of course remains to be seen how well this new program will work out.

Q: What about the institutional aspects of transaction cost economics itself? Do you envision it as a distinct field or as a science of its own in the future?

A: I guess I don't see transaction cost economics becoming its own science. I basically think that it needs to be supported by law, economics, and organization theory. But I also think that there will be important feedbacks from transaction cost economics to these three sciences. Organization theory has already been responsive and will probably continue to be responsive. So has antitrust and aspects of contract law. Economics, however, has been skeptical in certain respects. But I think that economists are terribly practical fellows and if you take a phenomenon which they admit is interesting, and you tell them things about it that they didn't know and the data are corroborative, then they are going to pay attention.

Q: So the bottom line is that you are optimistic about the future of transaction cost economics?

A: I am an enthusiast and very optimistic. The aspiration to create a new "science of organization," to which Chester Barnard made reference fifty years ago, is beginning to be realized. But I would emphasize that this is an interdisciplinary undertaking. Behavioral economics and the spirit of Carnegie are very much alive today.

References

Blaug, Mark. 1986. *Who's Who in Economics: A Biographical Dictionary of Modern Economics.* 2d ed. Cambridge: MIT Press.

Coase, R. H. 1937. "The Nature of the Firm." *Economica N.S.* 4:386–405.

David, Paul. 1986. "Understanding the Necessity of QWERTY: The Necessity of

History." In *Economic History and the Modern Economist,* edited by William N. Parker, 30–49. London: Basil Blackwell.

Doeringer, Peter B., and Michael J. Piore. 1971. *Internal Labor Markets and Manpower Analysis.* Lexington, Mass.: D. C. Heath Company.

Goldberg, Victor. 1976. "Regulation and Administered Contracts." *Bell Journal of Economics* 7:426–52.

Granovetter, Mark. 1985. "Economic Action and Social Structure: A Theory of Embeddedness." *American Journal of Sociology* 91:481–510.

———. 1988. "The Old and the New Economic Sociology: A History and an Agenda." Paper presented at the first annual seminar of the Center for Economy and Society, University of California at Santa Barbara.

Hart, H.L.A. 1961. *The Concept of Law.* Oxford: Clarendon Press.

Klein, B., R. A. Crawford and A. A. Alchian. 1978. "Vertical Integration, Appropriable Rents, and the Competetive Contracting Process." *Journal of Law and Economics* 21:297–326.

Knight, Frank H. 1971. *Risk, Uncertainty and Profit.* Chicago: University of Chicago Press. Originally published in 1921.

Macneil, I. R. 1974. "The Many Futures of Contracts." *Southern California Law Review* 47:691–816.

Perrow, Charles. 1986. "Economic Theories of Organization." In *Complex Organizations,* 219–57. New York: Random House

Pfeffer, Jeffrey, and Gerald Salanzick. 1978. *The External Control of Organizations.* New York: Harper and Row.

Simon, Herbert. 1976. *Administrative Behavior: A Study of Decision-Making Processes in Administrative Organizations.* New York: Free Press.

Williamson, Oliver E. 1971. "Vertical Integration of Production: Market Failure Considerations." *American Economic Review* 61:1032–57.

———. 1975. *Markets and Hierarchies: Analysis and Antitrust Implications.* New York: Free Press.

———. 1979. "Transaction-Cost Economics: The Governance of Contractual Relations." *Journal of Law and Economics* 22:233–61.

———. 1983. "Credible Commitments: Using Hostages to Support Exchange." *American Economic Review* 73:519–40.

———. 1985. *The Economic Institutions of Capitalism: Firms, Markets, Relational Contracting.* New York: Free Press.

———. 1986a. "Economics and Sociology: Promoting A Dialogue." *Working Papers.* Yale University Department of Economics, no. 25.

———. 1986b. *Economic Organization: Firms, Markets and Policy Control.* New York: New York University Press.

———. 1987. "The Logic of the Firm." Unpublished paper.

II   *The Pioneers*

7 *Kenneth J. Arrow*

KENNETH ARROW has made extraordinary contributions to the very foundations of economic analysis several times during his career. It is therefore with extra interest that one wants to hear what he has to say about the relationship between economics and sociology. In this interview, Arrow tells about his encounters with Talcott Parsons and other sociologists at Harvard and Stanford. He suggests topics that might be suitable for sociologists to work on, such as the reason why some ethnic groups are more successful in economic terms than others. Arrow also discusses some methodological difficulties involved in the problem of fitting microeconomic analysis and a more sociological perspective together; and he outlines how, in three major ways, the economic system is dependent on the social system in order to function properly. In many of his answers Arrow uses the example of unemployment to illustrate a more general point. A certain skepticism toward sociology, combined with imaginative ideas about the role that sociology could actually play in economic analysis, can be said to characterize Arrow's statements in this interview.

Kenneth Arrow was born in New York City in 1921.[1] He received his undergraduate degree in 1940 from City College, and his M.A. in 1941 and Ph.D. in 1951 from Columbia University. He first worked at Stanford (1949–1968), then went to Harvard (1968–1979), and is currently Joan Kenney Professor at Stanford (1979–). His most important contributions to economics consist of his formulation of the social choice problem; his co-invention with Gerard Debreu of the general equilibrium analysis; and his theory about the economic consequences of asymmetric information among economic agents.

•

Q: You did your undergraduate work in the late 1930s at City College and your graduate work in the 1940s at Columbia University. During this

---

The following interview with Kenneth J. Arrow was conducted in his office at Stanford University on April 28, 1988.

[1] The following information comes from von Weizsäcker 1972; Blaug 1985; Arrow 1986a; Lipset 1987; and *Who's Who in Economics*.

time, did you take any courses in the social sciences, especially in sociology? Or perhaps you read some sociology on your own?

A: No, I am afraid I did not read any sociology on my own, at least not that I remember. I didn't take any courses in sociology either. I had somewhat more of an interest in anthropology. I can't remember all that I read, but at least some of the more semi-popular books. I certainly read Margaret Mead and Ruth Benedict and probably also some works by Franz Boas. So I approached social science much more from the anthropological side than from the sociological side.

Q: And what about Marx and Weber? Did you have any opportunity to read them during this time?

A: I read Marx as a graduate student. But what I read was mainly *Das Kapital*, which I suppose is in some sense a sociological work even though the main emphasis and the basic structure are really much more economics. But there is of course a lot of sociological richness mixed in as well. I don't believe that I read Weber at all at this time. I did read Weber ten or fifteen years later, probably some time in the 1950s. I then mainly read what he had written on specific topics, such as *The Religion of China* and *Ancient Judaism.* I also read some of his shorter pieces. It must have been *The Methodology of the Social Sciences*, which appeared at about this time in English translation. I found this work more problematical. It raised deep issues of value-neutrality and of the ways we understand motives and intentions without giving the clear answers apparently supplied by logical positivism with which I was then enamored.

Q: Since you got your Ph.D. in 1951, what kind of contact have you had with sociology? Have you, for example, been interested in following what is happening in the field? Or have you collaborated with sociologists on any project?

A: My contact with sociology has been more through people. My main exposure to it took place in 1956–1957, when I spent a year at the Center for the Advanced Study in the Behavioral Sciences here at Stanford. You should remember that the main figure in its organization was Paul Lazarsfeld, who was actually there during that particular year. He was in fact also there a year or two before, but I saw especially much of him during the year I was at the Center myself, and we became quite friendly. So I had a fair amount of contact with Lazarsfeld, although it was more personal than intellectual. In the course of this I followed some of his work, mainly what he had done in statistical methodology. But I also read some of his more sociological books like the one he wrote with Katz, *Personal Influence.* I remember that I was quite impressed by this work and it gave me an interesting idea, which I have never really followed up intellectually. It is that somehow in a large amorphous economy—the sort of thing that economists postulate—personal reactions and interactions play a distinct role. Now, Lazarsfeld of course looked at the spread of opinion, but I must say that the following question occurred to me at the time: "Why shouldn't this also apply to economic relations?" Although, as I said, I have never followed this up, it has remained a nagging point in the back of my head that there is something else of a much more micronature in market transactions than what I and others allow for in our models. So I would say that Lazarsfeld's impact in this aspect represents the strongest influence of sociology on me.

Q: What about Parsons? You were at Harvard in the late 1960s and the 1970s, when Parsons was there. Did you two have any interaction at all?

A: During the time I was at the Center in the 1950s and had this exposure to sociology, I did get interested in Parsons and Shils. But this was the period when they were producing works like *Working Papers in the Theory of Action*, and I was quite turned off by that. I actually thought that the whole content of Parsons's work was very empty and grandiose. I remember hearing him speak at the Center. In fact, he was there the very same year I was. Anyway, I am afraid I did not come off with a very favorable impression. I thought that these universal fourfold categories and so on were just preposterous. And the whole thing seemed to be void of all empirical content. He had simply constructed one of those tautological schemes that are really not very useful.

Q: What about Parsons's sociological analyses of the economy, such as *Economy and Society*, which he wrote with Neil Smelser? Did you ever have an opportunity to read that?

A: Yes, I read it. But it just cast *no* light whatsoever on any kind of problem that I was interested in. Let me put it this way. I was really quite turned off and repelled by Parsons's emptiness and grandiosity. I will say this though. A few years later, when I was writing on health care I knew that Parsons had once worked on this. So I went back and read what he had written, and I remember feeling, "Now, *this* is interesting" (see Arrow 1963b; Parsons 1951). Parsons was dealing with a concrete subject here, and he was very insightful. I think this was before he got involved in grand theory making, so it represented a relatively early stage of his career. The analysis of the medical profession was totally different from this book with Smelser, which was just awful. I like Smelser personally and I think he is a bright man, but *Economy and Society* was not a useful book.

Q: Given the fact that you have had a certain exposure to sociology over the years, what is your general impression of it? Is it an immature science, an exciting science—how do you look upon it?

A: One problem with sociology that I noticed particularly through my contacts with the Harvard Sociology Department, where I knew a number of people, was that no two people seemed to be doing the same thing. First you have someone like Parsons, who was getting close to retirement at that time. And then you meet someone like Daniel Bell. Bell is classified as a sociologist, but it seems to me that his kind of essay writing on, say, the character of late capitalism doesn't belong to the same category as Parsons's works. Furthermore, you have the statistically minded people at Harvard like Lee Rainwater. I think his work is quite interesting, but I didn't see any connection between that and what the others were doing. Sociology just seems to be a very disparate field.

On the more mathematical side of Harvard sociology, the only one I had any contact with was Harrison White. Obviously he and I in some sense spoke a closer language than the others. I could understand what he was doing all right. It was just as though every sociologist was starting the subject from the beginning. I hope I am not too cruel here, but it didn't seem as if all these people were building on something. They would bring together some quantitative methods; they would make a model; or they would just do straight empirical work; or whatever it was. But it didn't seem to build on any previously established generalities of sociology, as far as I could see.

Q: You sometimes touch on social themes in your writings. Is this inspired by your readings in social science—including sociology—or is it more due to the tendency among today's economists to tackle social problems with economic methodology?

A: In my case it is more due to the former, and then especially to anthropology. There are also these general ideas of social thought all around you, which you just pick up.

Q: And how do you see the tendency of contemporary economists to apply straightforward economic methodology to social topics? Take Becker, for example, who is the leading figure here. What do you think of his approach?

A: I think that the way I would like to see the relationship between economics and social science is rather different from what I take to be Becker's program. I have not really tried to read everything Becker has done. But it seems to me that the attempt to explain all social interaction as economic interaction in a generalized sense of the word "economic," only represents one side of the coin. The other side is that a lot of the environment in which economic transactions take place is social and historical in nature. I don't know exactly how to fit these pieces together, but there are for example accounts of how special groups have played a distinct role in, say, trade. You have Chinese middlemen in Asia; Jews at certain times; Quakers during one period; and so on. And it is clearly their social characteristics that matter. In the case of the Quakers, as I understand it, the general idea was that a Quaker would keep his word, and he was therefore a very useful intermediary. He would deal with other Quakers and trade over long distances, where trust was important.

In a rational type of analysis it will be said that it is profitable to be trustworthy. So I will be trustworthy because it is profitable to me. But you can't very easily establish trust on a basis like that. If your basis is rational decision and your underlying motive is self-interest, then you can betray your trust at any point when it is profitable and in your interest to do so. Therefore other people can't trust you. For there to be trust, there has to be a social structure which is based on motives different from immediate opportunism. Or perhaps based on something for which your social status is a guarantee and which functions as a kind of commitment. How all this works is not explainable in Becker-type terms.

Q: You have written on many different topics in economics, including some that touch on social matters. Your work on social choice is a case in point. Clearly, the idea that individual preferences somehow have to be aggregated into a collective choice is also of interest to sociology. But which of your writings would you consider to be social analyses?

A: I don't think that I have done a great deal of what I would consider to be a social analysis of economics. In a couple of places in rather programmatic papers I have uttered the plea that more should be done in this direction. But that is quite different from doing it yourself. So I don't think that I can point to any specific work which represents a genuine social analysis. In one paper, which originally was a lecture and later was published as "Social Responsibility and Economic Efficiency," I discuss the idea that the system of self-seeking individuals needs some commitment, which is not of the self-seeking type, in order to exist. The general equilibrium story that I tell really can't exist without some substratum which is outside the system itself. There can, for example, be unconscious agreements not to exploit particular opportunistic considerations and the like. I firmly believe that this is an important fact but I have never been able to make a theory out of it. Now, I make a distinction between an insight—a statement so to speak about what a theory ought to do—and the theory itself. And I am of course prejudiced in favor of the idea that one should have a theory and not just talk about it. Which I don't—and therefore I have been relatively silent on these questions.

Q: From your answer it is clear that you do not consider yourself to have done any social analyses of economics. Maybe I phrased the question poorly; to rephrase, how do you view your analyses of discrimination, learning, and social choice? Don't they constitute social analyses of the economy in some sense?

A: There is no question that my work came up to the edge of social analysis, though I don't think I crossed. Whenever an economist deals with externalities, he or she is concerned about social interactions. It is implicit that the externality is mediated in some way, though the way may be simply the absence of any social control, as in the case of pollution. As I recall, in my paper on medical care, I noted such social organization as fee differentiation by physicians according to patients' income and charity hospital care, both publicly and privately provided (Arrow 1963b). In the case of racial and sexual discrimination, one assumption I explored was that of tastes for discrimination (following Becker), so that the utility function of workers included a distaste for working with blacks or women. This is social interaction, but—in typical economists' fashion—the behavior it explained was individual.

In a paper on what I called "learning-by-doing," i.e., the improvement of productivity through repeated production, I assumed that the learning was social (Arrow 1962). That is, the productivity of individual firms depended on the total amount of experience in the society. But I supplied no mechanism by which the experience of others was transmitted.

Social choice is, in my intention, a different matter. The theory was intended as a contribution to social ethics, that is, it was normative rather than descriptive. It dealt with the question, how *should* a society determine its social actions on the basis of individual preferences. It *presupposed* that there was a range of social actions, i.e., decisions which had to be made by a collectivity. It might suggest descriptively how social decision mechanisms have to avoid problems which might lead to clear violations of widely accepted norms for settling conflicts, but so far the theory has not moved in that direction.

Q: What then would be the proper way of relating economics and sociology to each other? Robert Solow, for example, argues for a position that used to be common among economists, namely, that there is an economic core surrounded, so to speak, by institutions. But Solow also says that most of today's pace-setting economists view economics as a hard science like physics. And in this type of analysis there is no or very little place for a social analysis, at least in the conventional sense. What is your opinion?

A: The answer will have to be programmatic. I think there are a number of elements involved, so there cannot just be one kind of connection between economics and sociology. One of the aspects is the fact that the transactions, which are modeled in ordinary economic theory, depend for their validation in several senses on a larger social system. By "social system" I mean a shared set of symbols, a shared set of social norms, and a set of institutions for the enforcement of the norms.

For example, one of the units in the economy is the contract. In economics we don't go into the details that surround the various transactions, but in order for me to be able to sell you something, there of course has to be a contract. There is frequently a time dimension in the contract, so there is delivery in the future. And there are elements of trust in it. In economic theory, however, we simply say "it will take place." But the question of course is, "Why will it take place?" Or, "What are we depending on for it to take place?" Well, the first thing is that the commitment has to be made in a way that is understandable. So there is the question of language in the very broad sense of the word "language," in order for a commitment to be meaningful.

Secondly, there is the idea that there has to be some kind of commercial morality for the contracts to be executed. There is an inextricable mixture of self-interest and morality here because presumably if you don't honor your contracts, there will be a long-run penalty to it. I should add that the idea of reputation solely being in one's self-interest is not really an adequate one, because the economic part only works in conjunction with the social. There are technical reasons for this, which I don't want to go into here. Let me only say again that a theory which depends merely on reputation is not enough because there will always be circumstances where it pays to violate the rule. The workings of the whole system depend on the fact that these contracts indeed will be executed. I am making commitments today on the assumption that they will be honored. I'll be pretty damaged if they are not.

And the third part of the social system are the institutions like courts and so on, which in fact enforce mechanisms like the contract and see to it that they are obeyed. The courts are indeed outside the economic system. That's a point which economists often overlook. The courts themselves are taken to be part of the economic system, as if the judicial decisions were just another commercial item. When you have a court you don't just try to bribe the judge—that's not going to make the original contract very reliable. So the assumption is that at least in the short run and for certain purposes, the social system is working in ways which in itself are *not* regulated by the market. That is, people follow norms, which are different from market norms. So the economic system—the self-seeking laissez faire system—would not work without the presence of these non-laissez faire, non-selfseeking norms. They might be self-seeking in some very long-run sense, but not in the time span we are talking about here. My view is also that you cannot simply talk about punishment; the legal system only works if most people obey it to begin with, and if its sanctions are only needed occasionally. There are plenty of examples of criminal law which show that if people don't want to obey the law, there is no amount of enforcement that is going to make them do it. So contracts are obeyed, and by and large you only need the weapon of judicial procedures in exceptional circumstances.

My point is that you need all three elements of the social system for the economic system to work: the element of communication, such as codes, symbols, and understanding; the element of shared social norms, which is the reasonable expectation that the norms will be followed even if it would be profitable not to follow them at least in the short run; and thirdly, the existing institutions for enforcement, which themselves operate outside the market system and are needed for enforcement purposes.

Q: If I understand your argument correctly, these three elements constitute some kind of preconditions for the economic system to function. So in a sense it is up to the social sciences other than economics to analyze them. However, another consequence of this kind of argument is that the economic system itself should be analyzed exclusively according to the principles of economics. Does this mean that something like an economic sociology is not a viable option in your opinion?

A: Well, one thing that I have found when I, for instance, look at old institutional economics is that it is not so much that it isn't viable; it is rather that it doesn't answer the same set of questions as conventional economics. If I want to know, for example, if a price is liable to go up, then I'll analyze the trends of supply and demand and look at the reasons why this good is wanted or not wanted; I'll see if some new substitute has been developed; and so on. Now in a social analysis you typically wouldn't look at these things. And if you did, you would have to incorporate what I would call straight economic elements into it.

But there are places where a social analysis is needed. For example, take something like the emergence of the corporation. Now, there you have an interesting bit of history. There was a period when the corporation was pretty rare in the United States as an economic entity. That was in the middle of the nineteenth century, and each one had to be incorporated separately. There were only a few in existence, such as Union Pacific Railroad and some others. After a certain period, corporations, however, started to spread, and you can see this as the emergence of a new institution. I think this is a pretty important topic but economics has not, as far as I know, analyzed this terribly well. The tendency of economists, I feel, is to regard this as a peripheral matter; it's just an epiphenomenon. The real question is about supply and the flow of goods, and *that* is what we economists are interested in. So the economists would just as well give it to someone else to work out.

Now, if you look at the works by institutionalists, there is a lot of talk about the evolution of the corporation. But I am not sure that they give you that much of an analysis of *why* the corporation emerged. And the corporation definitely has its own social structure and its own ways of being, which are really different from those of private firms. The conventional economist would probably say that economics of scale was the cause, and let it go at that. "Let's just not worry about the corporate form!" But incorporation clearly changes the whole notion of liability. It also changes the relations between the owners of the corporation in the old-fashioned sense, namely the stockholders, and the people who run the corporation. And at least it has opened up the door for a divorce between the two; it has happened in some cases, and in many others it hasn't. The main point being that the story of the corporation hasn't really been explored by economists.

Q: A couple of years ago I also asked you some questions about economics and sociology. You answered that "One must draw a distinction between an ideal analysis of social factors in economics and a realistic account of what sociology as it is now constituted can contribute" (Arrow 1986b). Does this mean that social factors do indeed play a very large role in the economy but that the real problem is how to incorporate these social facts into the economic analysis?

A: When it comes to the incorporation of sociology or anything else, there are two things which I think are important. The first is not to let difficulties interfere with doing what you can do. And the second is that it is as important to remember what you have left out in an analysis as what you have included. You should never be content. So my answer to your question is ambiguous.

I definitely think that it is important to model what you can model, and the fact that the model doesn't take care of everything that is relevant shouldn't stop you. If you insist on explaining everything, you will get nothing done. This is true in sociology, and I am sure it is true in any field. It certainly is true in economics, where it is my experience that you can get quite far by modeling and leaving certain things out, either by taking them as given or by ignoring them. You then try to draw very sharp conclusions from your simplified model. These may be unrealistic, but can still contain insights. And at least you know that the model is set; and if the conclusions are false, something has been left out. I also think that even if you have a reasonable explanation, you should not be content, as long as you know that something has been left out.

As usual in science, what you are after is a parsimonious account with considerable insight. A danger I have often found in various social analyses of the economy is the following tendency. You have a phenomenon, and therefore you introduce a cause. But the cause is often nothing more than the labeling of what has been found. You recall the dormitive principle in one of Molière's plays. It says that opium puts people to sleep because it contains a large amount of dormitive principle. During the course of a day the dormitive principle accumulates within you, and when you sleep it gradually goes away so you can wake up the following morning. I am sure that this was a satire by Molière on the science of the day. Anyway, its thrust was that a scientific explanation can be outright trivial in the sense that it just repeats the phenomenon it is supposed to explain.

Q: Perhaps we can switch to a concrete problem like unemployment. Would you say that social factors do indeed play a huge role here and that the real problem is how these social facts can be incorporated into the economic analysis?

A: Well, I have always been intrigued by the hypothesis that wage rigidity is partially caused by a feeling of justice. It also intrigues me that employers are really restrained from cutting wages. And that even when there is a big mob of unemployed workers right outside their doors which they can hire, they nevertheless don't cut the wages or they don't cut them as much as they might on the ground that somehow they cannot bring themselves to pay such low wages.

Q: So you are saying that the solutions to the problem of unemployment would be along the lines of a sociological analysis of fairness? Would that be right?

A: Well, the reason I have never done anything more with this is that this argument seems merely to say that the wages have not fallen as much as you would expect them to do. The question is really whether you have any statement there, more than that the wages have not fallen as much as they could have. I think that from a theoretical viewpoint you want at least two phenomena which can be correlated. That's what we want, and that is perhaps why the idea of a dormitive principle isn't as funny as Molière might have thought. Because it is quite clear that we do attribute causation to variables which cannot be directly observed. We do this all the time. Just take gravitation, to go back three hundred years! You can't see gravitation; there is nothing directly to observe. But it is a very powerful hypothesis in the sense that if you postulate the existence of this nonobservable quantity, you will be able to explain quite a few seemingly diverse phenomena. If the utility function worked, it would be an example of another good hypothesis. But of course it is not a very good one, because it doesn't explain very much.

In other words, if I say that there is a sense of justice and that people's economic behavior is limited by certain feelings of what is just and unjust, then I would like to be able to deduce *several* things from this one statement. Otherwise, if all I explain is one phenomenon, then I have not advanced my statement very much.

You see, what you really want to infer from the existence of what is hidden is that two observable quantities are related to each other. They are not related to each other as cause and effect; they are related to each other as the common effect of two causes. I want to get a statement which has some sharpness to it; which can be tested, refuted, and so forth. So therefore, when arguments are used which say that employers don't cut wages because of social disapproval, social disapproval better have some other consequence that someone can observe! Otherwise the argument runs the risk of being essentially tautological.

Q: How would you look on the insider-outsider theory of unemployment with its emphasis on harassment: the workers who do have jobs (the insiders) supposedly would harass the ones that don't (the outsiders), if they offered to work for less than the going wage?

A: Well, I'd like to see some evidence that harassment took place. You see here is a theory which might even be testable. Is it really true that the insiders harass the outsiders? That argument has incidentally been used to explain race discrimination in hiring years ago by Finis Welch (1967), and his argument was really a social statement. He said that when you have white and black workers together, the white workers make life very hard for the black workers. The employer would consequently find it inefficient to have integration. Welch's article would perhaps have been better if he had presented some direct evidence that the white workers were harassing the black workers. Still, it seems to me that it is an argument that is very similar to the insider-outsider argument.

Q: One of the various stereotypes that sociologists have of economists is that they rarely do empirical work. They build a very elegant and logical model, and that pretty much is the end of the analysis. Would you find this characterization true, say, in relation to the various theories about unemployment that exist today, such as the insider-outsider argument, efficiency wage-theory, and so on?

A: Your question raises a lot of questions; and the answer is neither "yes" nor "no." I think the fact is that the efficiency wage hypothesis has been subject to a lot of empirical tests. Quite a lot of literature has been devoted to it, and not all of it theoretical by any means. So there have been some empirical studies. The real question is rather what empirical evidence you use. Economists always tend to fall back on data on wages, employment, output, and so on. They do not make any attempts, for example, to directly estimate motives. Motives are only inferred by these external data.

Let me in this context mention an episode with a sociologist here at Stanford. It took place some years ago when the state passed the so-called Proposition 13, which put a ceiling on property taxes. The proposition passed in almost every county and city except for here in Palo Alto. Palo Alto was one of the few places which had a majority against it. Some economist claimed that this was obviously due to the fact that there is a very high percentage of people in Palo Alto who are beneficiaries of the government, either as civil servants or otherwise. Now this is a straightforward economic analysis. The sociologist, however, was outraged by this statement and wanted to know why we didn't go out and ask the people. Why didn't we take a poll and ask the people, "Did you vote for the proposition and are you a beneficiary of the government?" You can obviously be more subtle about the way you ask about this. But the point is that the economist felt that here was a hypothesis, which lead to certain easily observable behavior, so why do something else?

Economists tend to go in for easily observable behavior. They feel that if you have this correlation, and it obviously fits the model, then the model must be right. Sociologists will say, "You'll want to look more at individuals and their attitudes." The economist is scared of this. He'll say, "What do you expect people to say if you go around asking them questions? They are not going to say that they did something for selfish reasons." So economists regard that kind of verbal evidence as beside the point.

Q: What would your own position be here? Couldn't it be useful to ask why people do something, if only to see if the answer differs from what you'd get through some other method?

A: Well, my sense is that economists have narrowed the range of their data very excessively. Take one simple example. There are a number of economists who deny that there is something like involuntary unemployment. Some of us find that preposterous. Even without detailed sociological research we know that people are unemployed involuntarily. We see this all the time, and we are quite sure of what we see. There is also some scattered evidence. For example, you advertise a job and two hundred people turn up, something which doesn't suggest to me that they are voluntarily unemployed. Some economists will then say, "Yes, but that's really because they are asking too high wages," or something like that. This is a basic methodological issue in economics. These people will say, "Well, we have a hypothesis"—everybody is always proving a point— "and we expect all unemployment to be voluntary. People think that if they wait, they'll get a better job." Or it will be that people have been earning money for the last few years and now they want a little time off, and this may be a good time because wages will be higher next year than they are now. I am sure you have seen the stories of people like Lucas and that school. One of my colleagues here at Stanford has been working for years on intertemporal substitution in labor; or to what extent do people work harder or less hard because of expectations of future wages? It is extremely sophisticated econometric work. But the real question is maybe that people aren't working this year because there are no jobs. Lucas and others will then say, "What do you mean there are no jobs? There are always jobs at a sufficiently low wage." Well, somehow there *is* a wage at a certain level, but it is hard to explain. So sometimes you have the most obvious data, which nevertheless the economists ignore.

The people who don't believe that involuntary unemployment exists are in a way more in the full mainstream of economics than those who believe that it does. Probably a majority of economists believe that there is involuntary unemployment all right. In terms of the underlying logic of the economic analysis, the people who don't believe in involuntary unemployment are clearly pushing the logic of the economic analysis to its extreme—but it is still in the tradition. By "logic" I here mean empirical logic or the fact that they only look at a restricted range of data and do not go beyond that data on the ground that these are hard facts while all the rest is soft stuff. But there are of course also lots of economists who frequently use sociological data or survey data in a way that wouldn't qualify as strictly economics. So I don't want to generalize; there are empirical economists who are certainly going much further in this field with their sources than the more traditional ones.

Now, I partly attribute this by the way to the economics of economics. Economics differs from almost all the other social sciences in that there are certain kinds of data which are provided free of charge by the government, as a byproduct of its activities. In this sense economics is like demography. The result is that you have this rather big batch of data, and you easily develop an aversion to going out collecting anything else because anything else will be quite expensive and you also have to rethink the whole issue. Instead you have this whole machinery analyzing government data on wages, prices, unemployment, and so on.

Anyway, that is my interpretation. What happens is simply that economists gravitate towards cheap data sources. And since these official data are by no means ridiculous data sources—it's not as if they were way off base—they serve very well indeed. But I think they are also ignoring all sorts of things. And I realize there are problems about eliciting motives, as at least some sociologists do. Although I have to say that every time I get a sociological survey, my main complaint is that I can't answer the questions as asked. I think the questions are often wrong. They give you five categories and none of them fit!

Q: But there are various techniques to counter that. There is for example participant observation. You spend enough time with people to know what they mean by certain expressions, and then you put together your questions.

A: But sociologists are subject to this economic problem too! They will just send their questionnaires out; participation is a very expensive operation.

Q: Involuntary unemployment represents one area where it might be good to draw on both economics and sociology. Are there any other areas that you would recommend sociologists look at? Gender, for example?

A: I can think of quite a few places actually. But they do not belong to a single family; they are of different kinds. One of them is the one I suggested at the beginning, which is the question of the influence of the social structure on the workings of the resource allocation mechanism. For example, does the fact that Japan is a very homogeneous society while there is much more cultural diversity in the United States have anything to do with productivity? Even if economic theory doesn't allow for it, some kind of an economics of communication-information might at least offer an entering wedge here. You know, something along the lines that maybe communication is in some sense cheaper because people trust each other. Or that they can communicate more efficiently because they come from a background with common cultural norms.

A second area which economics has done very badly with is that we have large differences in performance among ethnic groups. Now, some of these differences may be there because of all sorts of classifications. I think that ethnic groups often get a certain prominence because they are simpler to identify. I am sure, for example, that among people that appear to be homogeneous there are very different levels of aspirations. Children who say this or that are encouraged to stay in school or encouraged to drop out. This is important not only for ethnic groups but also for gender differences. The economic career patterns of women are certainly different from those of men; and historically this has been even more so. I suppose this is sociology but maybe it is getting into psychology too. Some of this can be due to individual differences, even if some of it clearly must be social.

If you look at ethnic groups, it is clear that you are dealing with some kind of construct, which is somehow connected to persistent differences. Take the European countries. Somebody once remarked that if you took the Austro-Hungarian Empire around 1850 and looked at the relative income levels of its different peoples, it was about the same then as it is today! The Yugoslavs are also a very interesting group in this context. This country was created after World War I and the income levels of the groups within it are very different. The Croats and the Slovenes are at the top and the Macedonians are way down at the bottom. Now, I have heard the explanation that why the Yugoslavs went in for a decentralized economy, unlike the other Communist economies, was that this meant that you couldn't blame the central government for the regional inequality of income!

So one of the questions is, why are these groups different? India, for example, provides a lot of examples where small groups have become very successful in ways which are totally out of proportion to their number. The Parsees is one of the extreme cases, but also other groups—just fifty miles apart, you know—repeat the same process. Presumably there is some social development inherent in these groups. But that is all very vague; that is just talk. *Why* does it happen? *What* is it that explains that these groups have such different performances?

The ethnic groups among the immigrants to the United States have also developed in quite different ways. Part of this is of course due to discrimination. You can for example see what a total transformation it was when discrimination against the Orientals ceased. Some people think that the Japanese-Americans today have the highest level income among ethnic groups in the United States. Figures on that kind of stuff are pretty poor, but nevertheless they tell you something. Now what is it about the Japanese or about the Jews that sets them apart in this way? Or what accounts for the difference between West Indian blacks and native blacks? The difference between these two groups is incidentally quite strong, and West Indian blacks are typically about average income level in the United States or higher. Also in the so-called Hispanic community, there are certain groups which are much better off than others. The Puerto Ricans and the Cubans that come to the United States are very different, but both have lived under Spanish rule for four hundred years in communities based on a mixture of Indians, blacks, and some white immigrants. So what can account for the differences in economic performance between these various ethnic groups? I really don't know. But what I am saying is that there must be some kind of transmission mechanisms of attitudes or of something else that makes a difference. The whole problem is very sociological and totally inexplicable by any ordinary economic theory.

Q: I have a further question on the relationship between economics and sociology, more precisely on the use of rational choice in sociology. There is presently an attempt going on in sociology to extend the concept of rationality from economics into sociology. You have written quite a bit on rationality and sometimes you talk of "social rationality" (Arrow 1963a; 1974, 13–29). Do you think that a rational choice sociology would be a good idea?

A: I think my answer is that one shouldn't express an opinion here until one has seen the results. The rational choice model certainly contributes to our understanding, and I don't see any reason why rational choice should be confined to economic phenomena. The rational choice hypothesis is, however, a very weak hypothesis and the trouble is not so much its correctness or incorrectness, but that it says relatively little. What it says is that in and of itself there is consistency in choices made under different circumstances. In the modern point of view, it says a little bit more. What it says here is essentially that you learn from your experiences and use these in a kind of rational way to modify your beliefs. Rationality in belief formation is probably a stronger and more meaningful hypothesis than rationality in choice. And of course the learning process in turn affects the choices, because you are now making choices with a new set of assumptions about the world.

So I think the hypothesis of rational choice is certainly a reasonable one, and one undoubtedly sees rational behavior in people. You see a lot of other things too; and it is really just one factor. And even if rational choice theory was totally correct, it would only be part of a theory because the theory also has to tell you about the environmental background in terms of the choices made. The opportunities for an individual are probably self-created over time, so they are the result of previous choices. Now, you can have rational choice which nevertheless turns out to be bad in a world of uncertainty, and irrational choices which turn out to be good. Furthermore, learning is in many cases ambiguous. What you learn from your experiences may not be very clear; people learn different things. I think that rational learning, for example, does not fit into certain economic markets very well. The idea that the securities market is a totally rational market seems to be contradicted by observation, and therefore we expect this to be the case even more so with more complex social systems. The reason is that people are not only learning in a rational way; they are also forming beliefs in ways that cannot be described as thoroughly rational. So what I am arguing is that your first problem is that you are going to find that the rational choice model is not going to explain very much. And the second problem is that you are going to find some contradictions to rational learning.

Q: What is your sense of what will happen in the future when it comes to economics and sociology? Will economists perhaps start to take sociology more into account? Or will they they rather continue to create their own version of sociology, like Becker and his followers?

A: Frankly, predictions of that kind are usually not worth very much. If anything significant happens, it is going to be a surprise! And if you knew what was going to happen, you would already have done it! So let me not answer your question but give you a different answer to a different question.

My view is that the problem of the interaction between economics and sociology is not going to be solved by simply adding a few sociological variables to the already existing models in economic theory. It is going to be done by restructuring the question in some way that we have not yet fully grasped. Now, my guess is that the answers are not going to come out of the general equilibrium theory or something of that sort, but rather out of the more microscopic analysis which is implicit in some parts of game theory—what's called game theory with imperfect information. The reason is that game theory provides a somewhat better language for incorporating social elements or at least the social elements that are involved in direct social interactions like networks and things of that kind. It seems to me that there is a more natural fitting in between game theory and social analysis.

The link between game theoretical analysis and classical economics is a methodological problem. I think that if you developed a theory of this kind, the link to the traditional kind of economic analysis will run in terms of certain aggregates and not in terms of individual behavior. It is an aggregation problem, which I guess could be solved or at least approximated if we understand the microphenomenon. Whether we are about to take off or not, I don't know. I see very little evidence of it frankly. What I do see is rather a little more use of ad hoc social hypotheses in specific cases.

One of these ad hoc hypotheses has lately attracted some attention among a number of economists. What they have been trying to do is to explain savings—a very concrete problem. We are getting better and better data on savings. Of course every time that you get new data, whole theories are refuted. That is essentially what has happened. The dominant paradigm was that people essentially saved to spend in their lifetime. But today the evidence seems to be accumulating that this hypothesis is not true, and everybody seems to agree that you cannot explain savings solely on a life cycle basis. So the question is now why people die wealthy, when they could have lived better. Part of the explanation is probably an altruistic concern for the future. Another and somewhat more cynical explanation, that appeals to economists but which really is a sociological hypothesis, is that aging parents want control over their children. One paper I read did actually have data on visits by children to their parents, and it turned out to be correlated to the wealth of the parents! Now, that's an example where you try to fit sociological motives and economic behavior together.

So, to conclude, I think that the key thing when it comes to the relationship between economics and sociology is the willingness to look at new kinds of data, like in savings. I think that once you do that, you are automatically going to be forced to consider social elements. Just ask different questions, and I think that you are going to be forced into considering and drawing upon sociology. And you will probably be contributing to sociology as well.

References

Arrow, Kenneth J. 1962. "The Economic Implications of Learning by Doing." *Review of Economic Studies* 29:155–73.

———. 1963a. *Social Choice and Individual Values.* 2d ed. New Haven, Conn.: Yale University Press. Originally appeared in 1951.

———. 1963b. "Uncertainty and the Welfare Economics of Medical Care." *American Economic Review* 53:941–73.

———. 1973. "Social Responsibility and Economic Efficiency." *Public Policy* 21:303–18.

———. 1974. *The Limits of Organization.* New York: W. W. Norton.

———. 1986a. "Kenneth J. Arrow." In *Lives of the Laureates: Seven Nobel Economists,* edited by William Breit and Roger W. Spencer, 43–58. Cambridge: MIT Press.

———. 1986b. Letter to Richard Swedberg dated July 22. Reprinted in R. Swedberg, "Economic Sociology." *Current Sociology* 35 (1987):143.

Blaug, Mark. 1985. *Great Economists since Keynes.* Brighton: Harvester Press.

———. 1986. *Who's Who in Economics: A Biographical Dictionary of Modern Economics.* 2d ed. Cambridge: MIT Press.

Katz, Elihu, and Paul F. Lazarsfeld. 1955. *Personal Influence: The Part Played by People in the Flow of Mass Communication.* New York: Free Press.

Lipset, Seymour Martin. 1987. "Ken Arrow—Success without Pressure: An Interview." In *Arrow and the Foundations of Economic Policy*, edited by George R. Feiwel, 692–700. New York: New York University Press.

Parsons, Talcott. 1951. "Social Structure and Dynamic Process: The Case of Modern Medical Practice." In *The Social System*, 428–79. New York: Free Press.

Parsons, Talcott, Robert F. Bales, and Edward A. Shils, eds. 1953. *Working Papers in the Theory of Action.* New York: Free Press.

Parson, Talcott, and Neil J. Smelser. 1956. *Economy and Society: A Study in the Integration of Economic and Social Theory.* New York: Free Press.

Weber, Max. 1949. *The Methodology of the Social Sciences.* New York: Free Press.

———. 1967. *Ancient Judaism.* New York: Free Press.

———. 1968. *The Religion of China.* New York: Free Press.

von Weizsäcker, Carl Christian. 1972. "Kenneth Arrow's Contribution to Economics." *Scandinavian Journal of Economics* 74:488–502.

Welch, Finis. 1967. "Labor Market Discrimination: An Interpretation of Income Differences in The Rural South." *Journal of Political Economy* 75:225–40.

8   *Albert O. Hirschman*

ALBERT O. HIRSCHMAN is the author of several outstanding works in which economic problems are analyzed from an interdisciplinary perspective.[1] The most famous of these is probably *Exit, Voice, and Loyalty*, but *The Passions and the Interests, Shifting Involvements*, and *Essays in Trespassing* are also on their way to becoming minor social science classics. In a series of works from the 1950s and 1960s on the economic development of Latin America, Hirschman also helped to formulate what later was to become known as "dependency theory."

Hirschman was born in Berlin in 1915, the son of a well-known surgeon. He attended the Lycée français in the same city during the period 1923 to 1932. In the next few years he earned degrees at the Institut de Statistique at Sorbonne and at the École des Hautes Études Commerciales in Paris. He had a fellowship in 1935–1936 at the London School of Economics and then spent a few years in Trieste, where he earned a doctorate in economics in 1938. During the late 1930s, he was also very much involved in the struggle against fascism. He fought in the Spanish Republican Army and later with the French Army until its defeat in June 1940. In the United States, where Hirschman emigrated in 1941, he first spent some years as a research fellow in international economics at Berkeley. He then worked for the Federal Reserve Board (1946–1952) and as a consultant in Columbia (1952–1956). After this period, Hirschman worked in various U.S. universities, such as Yale University (1956–1958), Columbia University (1958–1964), and Harvard University (1964–1974). Since 1974, he has been professor of social science at the Institute for Advanced Study at Princeton.

•

Q: Your concept of economics is quite different from the one found in mainstream economics; it is basically broader and more interdisciplinary

---

The following interview with Albert O. Hirschman was conducted on February 10, 1988, at the Institute for Advanced Study in Princeton, New Jersey.

[1] For Hirschman's career, see especially Blaug 1986, 403–4; Coser 1984; McPherson 1986, 1987; Meldolesi 1987.

in nature. Can you say a little about how you came to develop this notion of economics? For example, would it be correct to say that the political and economic events of the 1930s were of decisive importance to you?

A: You are right about the last point you mentioned: the depression. I think that the reason why I got into economics was the experience of mass unemployment and political convulsion in the 1930s. I also had to think of making a living when I was a refugee in Paris and went to the École des Hautes Études Commerciales. This is still the best school for business administration in France, but in the 1930s it had a very primitive curriculum in economics proper. One learned a lot of accounting and there were some good courses in economic geography, money and banking, and also up to a point in international trade. But on the whole, the education in economics was rather poor.

My eyes were really opened to economics during this one year—in 1935–1936—I spent at the London School of Economics and during which I picked up a great deal from the various people who were teaching there. I was also already at that time writing on certain research projects of mine. Anyway, I did absorb a great deal, and I had some friends with which I discussed economic things. It was also during this year that Keynes's *General Theory* came out. I remember queuing for a copy at the London School of Economics and then going home, trying to absorb the message of the great man.

In Italy, to which I went after England and a few months in France and Spain, I was very much on my own because in order to get my doctorate, I primarily had to learn certain legal material which I had to make up for. Otherwise I had a lot of equivalencies, and I only had to finish my dissertation. The thesis was based on a research project I had undertaken in London, and which I now translated into Italian.

Q: What was the topic of your thesis?

A: It was about French monetary policy from the 1920s to the 1930s, so it was about recent monetary problems. I am very largely self-taught because, again, when I came to Italy I wanted to discuss Keynes and some other people, but I was the only one who had a copy of *The General Theory*. So I ended up discussing with myself.

Then after various upheavals I came to California in 1941. There it was a question of whether I should sit down to a regular course of graduate studies in economics or whether I should perhaps rather pursue some ideas about international trade, power, and that sort of thing which I had carried with me from Europe and which I had begun to think about. My professional activities as an economist started during the year of 1938 in Paris, just the year before the war broke out. I came back from Italy in the middle of 1938, so I had about one year before I volunteered in the French

Army in 1939. There were maybe about fifteen months that I worked as a freelance economic journalist or economic researcher in Paris. I was lucky in terms of getting in contact with a New Zealand economist, Jack Condliffe, who later on was at Berkeley as a professor in international economics and international trade and who actually got me the visa when I was in Marseilles in 1940. In Paris, just before the war, I worked for a project of his on exchange control. There was supposed to be a conference in Bergen, Norway, in 1939, which never took place. But I prepared a number of memoranda for this conference. They have never been published except for one on exchange control in Italy, which has just come out in translation in an Italian book, as my Italian friends have taken it upon themselves to publish some of the things I have written about Italy, both before and after the war.

Then at Berkeley in 1941 I took a few seminars in economics in order to find out what was going on, so to speak. But very soon I primarily concentrated on getting out a work of my own because I realized that with the war going on (or in fact it was just starting for the United States), my life was probably going to be interrupted again. And indeed it was; in 1943 I was drafted. In the two years I was at Berkeley I finished the manuscript for my first book, *National Power and the Structure of Foreign Trade.* So I did not get my American Ph.D. I decided that after all I already had a doctor's degree, and that that was good enough. This was a slightly risky decision, but one that turned out to be rather good in the end.

Q: From what I understand you read quite widely in the social sciences during your years of education—not only in economics but also in political science and sociology. Did you take any courses in these two disciplines or did you mainly study them on your own?

A: I essentially read them on my own. In Germany I started to read very widely in Marx, Engels, Lenin, Kautsky, and things of that sort. I remember that one of my first experiences in economics was to listen to a very interesting lecture by Otto Bauer on long waves. He came to Berlin and was very much taken by this long wave theory; I still remember his lecture very clearly. A number of experiences of this sort were probably important to me. I also had some friends and older people who influenced me in terms of what I was reading. And I was in the Socialist Youth Movement and in the Social Democratic Party, and there we discussed quite widely.

I also read quite a bit of Hegel in Germany because I had an older friend of mine who was a philosopher, and he started a kind of *Arbeitsgemeinschaft* or work study group when we were still in the last year of high school. I blasted my way through Hegel's *Phenomenology*, you know. So when I came to France, it was a real relief to read people like Pascal and Montaigne. . . .

Q: Was Durkheim one of the people you studied in France?

A: No, I did not read Durkheim at that time. I read rather the moralists. I enjoyed very much reading La Rochefoucauld, Pascal, Diderot, and the whole eighteenth century. I also had a very strong intellectual friendship with an Italian philosopher my sister had married, by the name of Eugenio Colorni, who later was killed by the fascists just before the liberation of Rome. I have written about this Italian part of my life in a small speech I gave in Torino in October 1987 on the occasion of receiving an honorary doctorate (see Hirschman 1987c).

Q: How about Max Weber? Was he among the people you studied during your years in Europe?

A: I read a few of Weber's famous speeches. I read them in Germany, still under the influence of the mentors I had in those days. I did not read broadly in Weber, but I read *The Protestant Ethic* as a boy.

Q: I would now like to ask you a question about the very specific way that you do economics. In *A Bias for Hope* (1971, 8), you call what you do "political economics," and you write that only "a few mavericks like myself" are working along these lines. In *Journeys Toward Progress* (Hirschman 1963, X), it says that there exists a "no man's land" at the intersection of economics, political science, and sociology; and it is clear that you situate yourself here. Finally, in *Essays in Trespassing* (1981, 13), you speak of the necessity of having "a certain turn of mind" to do your specific type of analyses. All of these statements clearly add up to quite a specific attitude toward how to do economics. So my question is: How would you characterize your vantage point and what leverage does it give you when you look at a problem?

A: I really must say that I have always started my books with one small beginning, with one kind of insight perhaps, which I felt was worth exploring and which opened up a little bit like a Chinese paper flower that you put into water. In the case of *National Power and the Structure of Foreign Trade*, there were some statistical ideas that came to me, while I was working in Paris for this Bergen Conference. But primarily, of course, I was concerned about the the potential of economic relations for the use of power, for exploitation. It was not clear to me that I would be able to come up with something that was going to be both good and new. It is always possible that what is good is not new, and what is new is not good, you know! But I had some feeling that the economists were sticking too much to the purely economic explanations of things. And political scientists saw only their side. There was no sense among either that there exist interesting areas of junction between the two—and without any loss, so to speak, of the independence of either science. Originally my ideas were almost primitive in the sense that this kind of concentration of trade that

Germany achieved in the Balkans and so on during the 1930s had not been measured, had not been noticed; it was not seen as an important development. I guess I have a kind of way of *generalizing* from very limited observations, which is something that is important in my work. I remember that my first interest was just in the percentages of the distribution of trade among different countries. The distribution differed from one country to another, and nobody had looked into that. All the other considerations came out of this first insight. Incidentally, the index of concentration that I invented became very well known later on (even if under a different name, which is another story). I remember that I invented this index on the boat that took me to New York from Lisbon in 1941, and then presented it to a friend to see what he thought about it.

I want to give you another example that might be of interest. It is from Colombia, where I was economic adviser for four years, from 1952 to 1956. It was when I looked at Colombian economic development—how certain functions are carried out or are not carried out or poorly carried out—that I made one of my first or most basic observations. It concerned the difference in performance of the airlines and the highways. Airlines perform better than highways for the reason I explained in *The Strategy of Economic Development*, that the penalty for not maintaining planes is far more serious and immediate than that for not maintaining highways (Hirschman 1958, 133–55). It was a very simple observation, but I think that the talent I have is not just to come up with an interesting observation; it is more a question of going to the bottom of such an observation and then generalize to much broader categories. I suppose that this is the nature of theorizing.

I have been lucky that way a number of times. Again, later on in *Exit, Voice, and Loyalty*, there was the example from the Nigerian railways where I noticed something strange. The railroads were since a long time being outperformed by the trucks but did not at all respond by improving their service. So, first you have to be surprised by something you notice; and then you develop a fairly general and broad concept from there. That has happened to me a few times. It has also happened in other forms in my later works on the history of ideas that I meet with a quote from Montesquieu or from someone else; and that it strikes me very strongly. Then I carry it with me for years and years, till I finally make something fairly imposing out of it. But first of all it is the capacity to be surprised, which is important.

Q: The way you phrase your answer, I feel unsure whether your way of analysis is an art or a method. Is this "trespassing" from economics into the other social sciences and then back again something that really can be taught? Or is it rather just your own very ingenious way of approaching social phenomena? Is it an art or a method?

A: Well, I think it is 80 percent art and perhaps 20 percent science or whatever you want to call it. Again, it is a certain refusal to generalize too much from a principle that belongs entirely to any one category or discipline. My contribution, as you know, has been—I think—to point out to economists that political science concepts or sociological concepts can be usefully employed also in thinking about economic problems and not only the other way around, the way some of my friends do it. I think I am still at the point at which I was when I wrote the introduction to *A Bias for Hope*. There is no master key, no master way of integrating the social sciences; it is a matter of case by case invention essentially. This is not satisfying for my colleagues or for younger people—I realize that—because one would like to have a more unified and systematic way of going about it. When I do an analysis myself I never think of economics as a whole and of sociology as a whole and how the two can meet; where are their interfaces; and so on. I do it in connection with specific phenomena. And almost inevitably I find ways in which it is *the intermingling* that explains. I of course do try to hone my mind by becoming familiar with the thinking of people in the other social sciences. Here at the Institute I have become aware of the interpretive approaches of my colleague Clifford Geertz and so on. I am interested in following other ways of thinking, but I do not do it systematically. It is rather something in the back of my mind which I take advantage of. But the actual breakthrough occurs when a specific problem is attacked; when I see that there is one way or another in which the problem escapes the shackles of the discipline.

Q: You talk about escaping the shackles of economics. Now, it seems to me that the border lines between economics and the other social sciences have changed quite a bit during the last decades. If one reads Schumpeter, for example, it seems that in the 1940s economists were much more willing to think in terms of social institutions even though their main emphasis was directed at developing economic theory. Today, on the other hand, to judge from what people like Robert Solow tell me, the pacesetting young economists show no interest whatsoever for social institutions; they behave as if their models were applicable to all societies alike. Would you agree that a change like this has occurred in economics, and how would you say it has affected your strategy of "trespassing"?

A: My problem is perhaps at this point that I am not in tremendously close touch with what is going on in the economics profession because I am at this rather isolated place in Princeton, where I am surrounded by political philosophers, anthropologists, and social historians. I do bring in some economists every year, so that I can keep somewhat in touch—or at least I have done so till my recent retirement. But even when I lived mainly among economists, I always had a strong urge to escape from "pure" economics and to explore the connections between economic and political phenomena.

You see, when I returned to this country after the war, I got myself a job in the Federal Reserve Board. I was dealing with the problems of reconstruction in Europe, primarily on the financial and monetary side. I became sort of an expert on these things. But there again, it was the *political* problem of reconstruction—the question of the uniting of Europe—that was very much in the forefront of my work. I was one of a small group in the U.S. government that was trying to think of ways in which one could create various instruments, such as the European Payments Union, that could bring the European countries closer together and prepare the ground in a kind of gradual way for closer political association.

Then I went to Colombia as an economic adviser and there the question was economic development. But very soon it became evident to me that the important question was not just the need to adopt certain reforms but how to implement the reforms, how to get certain reforms through the political system which was changing rapidly from sort of semi-democratic to dictatorial and back again. So there again the question of political feasibility and so on intruded very strongly into my thinking. You can see this in my article on inflation in *Essays in Trespassing*.

And then again in the succeeding years when all the democracies in Latin America were destroyed by military regimes, when they were taken over one after the other in the 1960s and 1970s—starting with Brazil in 1964—the question came up whether the way in which these countries had undertaken economic development had anything to do with the weakening of democratic institutions and the rise of dictatorial forms in them. This was a topic that was primarily treated by political scientists with a very limited knowledge of economics, and they came forward with a number of fairly primitive hypotheses. I entered the debate with a rather long article in the late 1970s about this problem and developed some ways one can conceivably think of these connections (see Hirschman 1981, ch. 5).

Q: Today there exist quite a variety of strategies for how to "trespass." The one that is probably the most popular is "economic imperialism," and I would like to ask you what you think of this school of thought, if one can call it that. When I read your work, I get the impression that you are somewhat critical of it. Is that correct?

A: I would put it in much stronger terms and say that I am definitely hostile to that approach. Not because I am hostile per se but because of my own ideas, as developed for instance in *Exit, Voice, and Loyalty*. It started with this work, where I made a contribution exactly to show that when one thinks of the efficiency of institutions, one has to take recourse to both economic considerations (or, let us say, to rational actor type of considerations) and to the possibility of exercising political power or "voice." Both of these can make a contribution to the workability of social institutions and to their performance. I was then in a sense attacked, primarily in a review article of this book by Brian Barry (1974), on the ground that I had not taken enough account of the argument of Mancur Olson in *The Logic of Collective Action*. I knew about the Olson book at the time, and I had actually read it. But it is true that in my book I had perhaps shoved his argument aside a bit, as sometimes happens when one tries to develop one's own argument; one can not take all possible objections into consideration at that point. And later I developed some ideas in response to this critique.

Mancur Olson's idea of collective action just struck me as nonsensical. He argues for the impossibility—not the logic but the illogic—of collective action. According to him, collective action should never happen since people act like rational actors: they always want a free ride and so on. Since my own experience of having participated in collective action was such that I found it very important, this construct of Olson just struck me as obviously absurd. There is of course some amount of evidence in favor of Olson's thesis, but there is also a great deal of evidence to the contrary. And over the years I have tried to develop, in various forms, a counter-explanation to this version of rational choice explanation.

Q: It strikes me that *Shifting Involvements* can be seen as a kind of dialogue with Mancur Olson. Would that be correct?

A: Yes, to a considerable extent. You see, what I have generally done is to just develop my own point of view. And then I have realized that my own point of view is different from some orthodoxy or ruling group of ideas, and then I have some kind of *Auseinandersetzung* or dialogue/discussion with that point of view. When I wrote *The Strategy of Economic Development*, there existed a certain orthodoxy. Today everybody talks about privatization; at that point everybody talked about planning, about the importance of planned growth, about planning for planned growth, and so on. My own experience of economic development was that this is not the way it happens in the real world; and I tried to show why it happens the way it happens—and not the way people say it should happen.

Q: Today one sometimes hears the argument that it would be possible to reorganize all the social sciences—including sociology—on the basis of rationality. This way, it is said, one would get rid of some of the more artificial boundaries between the various social sciences. What is your reaction to this line of thought?

A: Well, I think that you can get rid of some of these borders but only at the cost of tautology. In other words, you then have to include certain things into the motivation of the rational actor that are normally left outside. In "Against Parsimony," I mention the idea of collective identity, which I take from Alessandro Pizzorno. If you accept that it is rational for an actor to build up his own identity or to consolidate some collective identity, then participation in collective action and the refusal of any "free ride" become perfectly rational.

In my article I speak about this on purpose as an "investment." I do this just like people say "investment in human capital," which is considered very rational. Previously one would say, for example, that people behave very much in a puritanical and thereby economical way; that this constitutes a moral attitude; and that it constitutes its very own moral precepts. Well, according to Gary Becker and company, you just say that all people are doing is to "invest in human capital"; and then you have explained everything very "economically," with a kind of rational actor explanation. This means that conflicts such as the one between desire and duty and so on disappear. But is there really any point in doing away with these older categories? They are much more realistic and much more true. Now, if you accept the concept of "investment in identity" in addition to "investment in human capital," it is clear that the former represents an earlier stage: in order to accumulate capital, you must first have an identity on which this capital so to speak can be heaped. But then behavior like participating in a demonstration without any regard to private gain, or *not* wanting a free ride, become part of the identity. And you behave exactly in the opposite way to what a rational actor à la Olson would do. But you make it look like a rational action—and the whole thing with rational action becomes totally meaningless.

Q: Some people argue that there is a definite affinity between economic imperialism and the political conservatism of the 1970s and 1980s, and I would like to hear your comment on this. I recall, for example, that you once said that development economics was destroyed by a combined effort by the Marxist left and "the neoclassical right." Do you believe there is a link between economic imperialism and political conservatism?

A: Yes, absolutely. But some doubts about economic imperialism are beginning to emerge. At one point, there was for example the idea that in order to make people behave properly, all you needed to do was to raise the price or the cost. This was Becker's idea of crime; all you needed to do was to increase the monetary cost in the form of fines and so on. And certain things are more effective than others, depending on some functional relationship that Becker figured out. It was all very useful, and it certainly can be of help in the social analysis of certain situations. But it does *not* take into account, for example, the effect of other more important things, such as what makes people change their values. Here you find very unexpected and strange things that psychologists have looked into. I have long been interested in this but I have not written much about it. If you, for example, deter action with penalty, you do not internalize the values. Another paradoxical effect is that if you, for example, can induce people to act in a certain way *without* rewarding them, then the values they will follow are more firmly established than if they were rewarded in the first place. Rewards and penalties are consequently not exactly inducive to a change in values.

A propos the tendency to start criticizing the economic approach, there was a rather interesting article by James Q. Wilson (1985) some few years ago in *Public Interest*. He says that playing on people as if they had some kind of demand function for crime by raising the price or cost does not work. What you have to do is something else: actually change their values.

Q: Sometimes when I listen to discussions about economic imperialism I have the impression that there is a new *Methodenstreit* going on, even if it is less visible and maybe also less noisy than the original one in the 1880s. Do you see any similarities between what is happening today and the battle that Menger and Schmoller fought out a century ago? In brief, is there a new *Methodenstreit* going on today?

A: I do not think that the situation today is that similar to the German *Methodenstreit*, which was mostly a question of theory versus accumulation of facts. I think that today you rather have one kind of theory versus another kind of theory. Perhaps one could say that what you have is an imperialist pretension to rule all of the social realm by means of one simple paradigm versus people who say, "No, it's more complex than that." These latter try to maintain the theoretical structure of the field, and claim that you can understand what happens in society only by building up contending theoretical structures and see how far each one goes in terms of explaining society. There is a recent article by Mark Granovetter (1985) on the "embeddedness" of economic action which is an interesting attempt in this direction. He precisely looks at different structures—at structures coming from the rational actor approach as well as categories from the traditional, Durkheimian sociological perspective. I would also mention the work of my colleague here at the Institute, Clifford Geertz. It is informed by a structure of thought where there is a certain amount of dispute about the sharp distinction between explanation and description in social science. All of this, I would say, adds up to a bit more than the German *Methodenstreit.*

Q: By bringing up the name of Mark Granovetter, you remind me of my intention to ask you about your relationship to sociology. A little earlier you mentioned that as a young man in Germany, you studied the writings of Max Weber. And in your works there are sometimes references to sociology: to Simmel, for example, and to reference group theory. I see some books by Robert Merton on your bookshelves, and I recall that you have even received the Talcott Parsons Award! So my question is what have you found useful and valuable in the sociological literature? Has any particular sociological work influenced your thinking?

A: Well, I am probably inadequately read in the sociological literature but whenever I read it, I find things that speak to me—Durkheim and Simmel in particular, but also Weber and some of the later people. I tried to blast my way through Parsons at one point, but I had a kind of hostile reaction to his tendency to always think in terms of dichotomies: "traditional societies" versus "modern societies," and so on. I had a hostile reaction to this from the beginning, although I must say that some parts of *The Strategy of Economic Development* were nevertheless influenced by this dichotomy.

I have also had very good relations with a number of French sociologists. I found a considerable convergence between Michel Crozier's *The Bureaucratic Phenomenon* and my own *Journeys Towards Progress*. This had to do with how certain reforms come about; how the idea of crisis can be a positive factor in terms of breaking down certain structures; and so on. Later I also became interested in a number of other French sociologists.

Q: When I read your work I also find a certain convergence with contemporary sociologists other than Crozier. And on a more profound level, there is even more affinity of thought . . .

A: Yes, exactly. I have recently, for example, found a considerable convergence with the work of Pizzorno on the creation of political identity. I also find Granovetter's work very interesting. He was here at the Institute, you know, for a year and wrote his article on embeddedness. This article was very much written as a way of counteracting Oliver Williamson's attempt to create a comprehensive explanation of how organizations behave. I find Granovetter's critique of this imperialist ambition on the part of Williamson quite appealing.

So I do find a great deal of interest in the works of sociologists. Then there is also the tradition of grand theorizing—from Daniel Bell to David Riesman—which comes more easily to sociologists, or to some sociologists anyway. I do not do this kind of theorizing myself—it is not my style—but I always find it interesting as a kind of background. It is good to have around; and it is important that some people try to make sense of the larger issues.

Q: In the past few years, Granovetter has been talking about the need for "a new economic sociology." The main idea is that sociologists should start analyzing central economical phenomena and not just marginal ones like in the "old economic sociology." What is your gut reaction as an economist to this type of endeavor? Will it mainly be economists who also do the good work in economics in the future? Or perhaps is mainstream economics structured in such a way that social sciences other than economics can make important contributions as well?

A: Well, it is true that some of the most basic and important problems have always been left behind by the economists because they cannot be handled so easily. As a result there has been a kind of thinning out of economics. In effect, as I have written in my article on "interests" for the New Palgrave Dictionary, economists in a sense opted for formalism in their science (Hirschman 1987a). They did this because they couldn't handle all these powerful ideas—from Freud to Durkheim—that appeared toward the end of the nineteenth century and which were informed by the new discoveries of the irrational in human action. So they left all of them behind and tried to get away from psychology because they didn't know beans about it, as we say in the States. They just didn't know anything about psychology. Pareto is an interesting case in this context. He had one foot in the irrational, "nonlogical" camp of social science. But the other foot he put very firmly into the formalistic camp: he reformulated utility into ophelimity in order to get rid of psychology, and so on. It was an *intentional* impoverishment of economics. It was made in order to let economics continue as a science—but at the cost of contact with reality.

Q: Can you think of any specific topics that would be especially congenial to your method of "trespassing" and that you have not written about? I ask this question because I feel that there are many young scholars who are very interested in your work and who would like to follow in your footsteps.

A: Well, almost any interesting and complex topic would be suitable. There are, I suppose, still topics in international trade. Or take the question which I discuss in my latest paper on Latin America: At what point should a developing country take on such an industry as, for example, the computer industry? (see Hirschman 1987b). There is currently a big dispute between the United States and Brazil because Brazil has tried to develop its own computer industry and has invented a new form of protection; the Brazilian state simply preserves the market for the country's own industries for a number of years. I talk about this as a new way of trying to create a novel kind of international division of labor.

In many topics you find the need to combine approaches. Take what happened in the Crash of 1987. I suppose again that you cannot just explain it by purely economic factors; there must be certain other factors involved. Again there is the question of how far you can get with one type of approach and how far with another. And again I think that you have to keep your mind open to precisely *complicating* your analysis rather than pretending to understand everything and explain everything.

So I believe there are certainly a lot of discoveries still to be made in economics. The concept of contestable markets, which is probably an important contribution, is one. But even here I have a feeling that by developing this new concept you may create a certain indeterminacy, which can probably only become determinate as a result of noneconomic phenomena.

Q: In "Against Parsimony" you speak, just like now, about the need to introduce more complexity into the economic analysis. But there also seems to be an important ethical dimension to your "trespassing." This is connected, I think, to a notion of man with a very strong emphasis on moral dignity. You speak, for example, of man's "passions" and "interests" and of his "disappointment"—all rather old-fashioned terms but with a certain moral tone to them. Is this a correct reading of your work?

A: Yes, you have caught something of my intent because I also believe that we have a certain contribution to make in terms of treating human beings as something fairly precious and not just as something you can play upon. You see, if you ever could figure everything out, if you ever could have a social science that really is a science, then we would be the first ones to be disappointed. We would be dismayed because if man becomes like that, he could be figured out. And that means that he is not worth as much as we think. So in this sense I *resist* these attempts at reductionism, to use a nice term for it. People like Gary Becker and so on don't like to think of this as reductionism; they think they are all fantastic theorists who are building up science. I think that we must be prepared to see social science fail. . . . Were we ever to succeed, then mankind would have failed!

References

Barry, Brian. 1974. "Review Article of *Exit, Voice, and Loyalty.*" *British Journal of Political Science* 4 (February):79–107.

Blaug, Mark, ed. 1986. *Who's Who in Economics: A Biographical Dictionary of Modern Economics.* Cambridge: MIT Press.

Coser, Lewis A. 1984. *Refugee Scholars in America: Their Impact and Their Experiences.* New Haven, Conn.: Yale University Press.

Crozier, Michel. 1964. *The Bureaucratic Phenomenon.* Chicago: University of Chicago Press. Originally appeared in 1963 in French.

Granovetter, Mark. 1985. "Economic Action and Social Structure: The Problem of Embeddedness." *American Journal of Sociology* 91:481–510.

Hirschman, Albert O. 1945. *National Power and the Structure of Foreign Trade.* Berkeley: University of California Press.

———. 1958. *The Strategy of Economic Development.* New Haven, Conn.: Yale University Press.

———. 1963. *Journeys Toward Progress: Studies of Economic Policy-Making in Latin America.* New York: Twentieth Century Fund.

———. 1970. *Exit, Voice, and Loyalty: Responses to Decline in Firms, Organizations, and States.* Cambridge: Harvard University Press.

———. 1971. *A Bias for Hope: Essays on Development and Latin America.* New Haven, Conn.: Yale University Press.

———. 1977. *The Passions and the Interests: Political Arguments for Capitalism before Its Triumph.* Princeton, N.J.: Princeton University Press.

———. 1981. *Essays in Trespassing: Economics to Politics and Beyond.* Cambridge: Cambridge University Press.

———. 1982. *Shifting Involvements: Private Interest and Public Action.* Princeton, N.J.: Princeton University Press.

———. 1984. "Against Parsimony: Three Easy Ways of Complicating Some Categories of Economic Discourse." *American Economic Review* 74:89–96.

———. 1987a. "Interests." In vol. 2 of *The New Palgrave Dictionary of Economics*, edited by John Eatwell, et al., 882–87. London: Macmillan.

———. 1987b. "The Political Economy of Latin American Development: Seven Exercises in Retrospection." *Latin American Research Review* 22:7–36.

———. 1987c. "Torino Talk." Unpublished paper, read on the occasion of the author being granted an honorary doctorate at the University of Torino.

McPherson, Michael S. 1984. "On Schelling, Hirschman, and Sen: Revising the Conception of the Self." *Partisan Review* 51:236–47.

———. 1986. "The Social Scientist as Constructive Skeptic: On Hirschman's Role." In *Development, Democracy and the Art of Trespassing: Essays in Honor of Albert O. Hirschman*, edited by Alejandro Foxley et al., 305–15. Notre Dame, Ind.: University of Notre Dame Press.

————. 1987. "Hirschman, Albert Otto." In vol. 2 of *The New Palgrave Dictionary of Economics*, edited by John Eatwell et al., 658–59. London: Macmillan.

Meldolesi, Luca. 1987. "Alle origini del possibilismo: Albert Hirschman 1932–1952." In Albert O. Hirschman, *L'economia politica come scienza morale e soziale*, 173–215. Naples: Liguori Editire.

Wilson, James Q. 1985. "The Rediscovery of Character: Private Virtue and Public Policy." *Public Interest* (Fall) 81:3–16.

9

Mancur Olson

Mᴀɴᴄᴜʀ Oʟsᴏɴ, an economist by training, has several times made forays into the other social sciences.[1] The first effort was with his Ph.D. thesis, later published as *The Logic of Collective Action*. In this work, which has already become a classic, Olson proposed a whole new theory of groups and organizations, centered around the problematique of the free rider. A few years later he helped to publish *Toward A Social Report*, which was to be an equivalent of the annual Economic Report of the Council of Economic Advisers. His next major work, *The Rise and Decline of Nations*, addressed such problems as stagflation and economic growth. Again Olson suggested innovative solutions by extending the economic approach to the social domain. During the last few years he has been working on two books, which are soon to appear: *An Encompassing Economics*, and *Beyond the Measuring Rod of Money*. In the interview, Olson talks about these new books, and he also touches on other topics, such as interdisciplinary work and how he came to write *The Logic of Collective Action*.

Mancur Olson was born on January 22, 1932, in the tiny town of Buxton, North Dakota, in a family of farmers. He first studied at North Dakota State University, where he earned a B.S. in 1954. He got his M.A. at Oxford University in 1960, and a Ph.D. in economics at Harvard University in 1963. He first worked as an assistant professor at Princeton University (1963–1967). He then moved to Washington, D.C., where he was deputy assistant secretary (Social Indicators) at the Department of Health, Education and Welfare for two years. Since 1969 he has worked at the University of Maryland, where he is presently Distinguished Professor of Economics.

•

Q: Beginning with your first writings, you displayed an interest in topics that go beyond traditional economics, in interdisciplinary work if you so

---

The following interview with Mancur Olson took place on February 23, 1988, in Washington, D.C., in an office Mancur Olson uses when he wants to write and not be disturbed.

[1] The following is based on Mancur Olson's vita and Blaug 1985.

chose. Was this something you developed on your own or did you pick it up from your teachers at Oxford and Harvard?

A: I am unusually indebted to my teachers, but not for inspiring that portion of my work that has some constituency beyond economics. What I wanted and obtained from Harvard was a rigorous professional training in economics. Naturally, most of the economics faculty did typically specialized economics and encouraged their students to do the same. Indeed, two of my teachers there, Paul Samuelson and Robert Solow, were the leaders of the tendency in the discipline towards writing directed for technically specialized readers. Though Samuelson and Solow normally taught at the Massachusetts Institute of Technology, in my first year of graduate study two of the Harvard faculty who normally taught the first-year courses were on leave and Samuelson and Solow temporarily took their places. The superb instruction they and my other teachers at Harvard gave me shows up mostly in those aspects of my work that are usually only of interest to other economists.

Now I should also point out that before I obtained my degree, the Economics Department at Harvard did bring in one professor who is impressively interdisciplinary—Thomas Schelling. Because of an unlucky accident, I did not have any association with him until the first draft of my thesis (which was eventually published as *The Logic of Collective Action*) had been written. The United States then had conscription, and when I had been an undergraduate I had picked up a commitment to two years of military service through the Reserve Officers Training Corps (ROTC) program. The government did not choose to exercise its indenture of my time until 1961–1963. Though I had worked out the basic ideas of my thesis well before this, I mainly wrote it during those two years while serving as a lieutenant in the Air Force, and without having any thesis adviser. When I had a draft that I thought was ready for approval, I asked Otto Eckstein, from whom I had taken an interesting advanced course in Public Finance, if he would read it and serve as the chairman for my thesis committee. He kindly also sent the thesis on to Thomas Schelling, whom I didn't know because he had come to Harvard when I was in the military. Tom Schelling sent me by mail superb, severe, and detailed criticisms and required two thorough revisions of the thesis. My debt to him for this is simply profound, but he has had no influence on the choice of any of the topics I have chosen to work on.

My dons at Oxford also had a great influence on me. There I faithfully went to the lectures of two of the most famous economists of the time, John Hicks and Roy Harrod, and happily profited also from the kindly and articulate help of my tutors. But no one that I studied under at Oxford emphasized or normally did interdisciplinary work.

Q: Did you take any courses in political science or sociology during these years? In *The Logic of Collective Action*, for example, you mention Talcott Parsons. Did you take any courses with him?

A: No, I did not take any courses in sociology or political science at Harvard, but I did occasionally have useful talks with faculty there in sociology or political science. I talked with Talcott Parsons once or twice by visiting his office. He was at that time, at least as it appeared to graduate students at Harvard, perhaps as famous as any other social scientist in all the world. Parsons was kind to me and amazingly generous with his time. I talked more often with some political scientists. Probably this is partly because they were in the same building—the Littauer building—at the economics department and the reading room for its graduate students. But partly it is because I have always loved to talk politics. Two professors of government at Harvard, Samuel Beer and Robert McCloskey, befriended me and made encouraging comments on some notes I had written up at the end of the 1950s on some ideas that eventually appeared in *The Logic of Collective Action*.

I had a little formal training earlier, in my time as a Rhodes Scholar at Oxford, in political history and in philosophy. One took economics there through the Philosophy-Politics-Economics (PPE) degree, which required examinations in eight subjects, at least two of which had to be from each of the three disciplines. Though I greatly enjoyed and valued the philosophy and politics at Oxford, I nonetheless took the maximum of four examinations in the economics subjects.

Q: With these broad interests in noneconomic topics, why did you still decide to concentrate in economics?

Q: One reason for my choices about what to study and to read over the years has been the observation that the economists who do the work that is of the most value to those outside our discipline are those who have the deepest understanding of economics itself. If a person can ultimately reach the point where the hypothetico-deductive reasoning of the discipline becomes part of the software of his mind, he will naturally use this capability on a vast array of problems. Then there is a good chance that he will generate results that prove valuable to people outside his discipline.

As I see it, the record suggests that this has been supremely important in generating good interdisciplinary work by economists. John Stuart Mill and Karl Marx were past-masters of the post-Ricardian economics of their day and they also did work that had an appeal beyond the discipline.

More recently, economists like Kenneth Arrow, Gary Becker, James Buchanan, and Thomas Schelling have also made contributions that transcend the boundaries of economics, and I believe this is partly because they have assimilated economics so well. Conversely, it is those economists who do not have quite the command of the subject needed to tackle big problems that most often belittle interdisciplinary work.

Maybe what I have just said will seem preposterous to the many people who have sampled economics and found it depressing. I plead with them that even if economics seems, when first entered, like a dark cave, it is a cave that, if followed *all* the way to the end, leads to the other side of the mountain, and to a magnificent view that includes even terrain that we conventionally associate only with other social sciences.

The second thing that I have thought deserved the top priority in my education and reading is getting some basic factual knowledge of many different societies and historical periods. Here I have not learned a fraction as much as I should have, but I did take in some lectures and courses in economic history at both Harvard and Oxford, and all my life I have tried to read about other societies. I have long wished that I had the wide erudition that Joseph Schumpeter had. His great contributions to economics and to the other social sciences would not, I suspect, have been possible without his broad learning. Unfortunately, many economists today seem to think that it is enough to test any model on the U.S. government data since World War II. This parochial perspective is, in my opinion, causing enormous mischief, especially in macroeconomics.

My sense is that this problem of the lack of even the most rudimentary knowledge of other periods of history and of other societies is not nearly so widespread in the other social science disciplines as it is in economics. Probably some sociologists or political scientists are teaching courses that could pass on to economists some appreciation of the value of the incredibly broad learning that Max Weber had, and convey some sense of the value such learning would have to a technically skilled and imaginative modern economist. Every economist ought to take such a course.

Q: Did your upbringing have something to do with your broad interests? During lunch you mentioned that you came from a left-wing family, and it is my experience that lively discussions of many different topics are often valued in such families.

A: Yes, my family and perhaps above all my father was formative here. My father was an immensely curious man, interested in everything including politics. He was not at all highly educated in a formal sense; indeed, he had not finished high school. He was a very successful farmer and a man of *extraordinary* intellectual powers. And from the earliest moments

I can remember, he was discussing ideas and discussing them with his own children. He had the habit of stopping any conversation that he was having with other adults to let me or his other two children—two other boys—talk. And he always treated our speech as though it came from an adult. So there was the sense that there is nothing more important than ideas and talking about ideas. The idea that one must make sense, even if one is a child talking with adults, and contribute at their level—that was an idea I picked up at my father's knee.

Q: *The Logic of Collective Action* is a book that is centered on one very powerful idea: the notion of the free rider. Could you say a little about how you came to realize that the free rider was so important?

A: Let me answer like this. Partly because I have always been interested in politics and public affairs, I had not originally planned to be an economist. I had thought of other careers until by chance I happened to read some economics in college. The attraction of an argument with logical structure and logical subtlety and at the same time application to the real world was so great that from then on I was hooked on economics. And that attraction has still to pass. So what took me to economics was the method and the logic.

In some sense, however, I was even more interested in the substance of politics, perhaps because of my background. At one time of my youth I had even thought that I might become a politician. So when a chance arose for me to combine the intellectual attraction of economics with my interest in things political and governmental, I took it. Thus, when I read Paul Samuelson's articles on public goods in the 1950s, they struck me as tremendously interesting; and they stuck to my mind especially well. At the same time I thought—no doubt because of my farm background—about how the farm organizations, which I knew so well from the Upper Midwest, managed to support themselves. How, for example, did they get members? Well, one thing I knew as if I had taken it with mother's milk was that the farm organizations were linked with farm cooperatives and insurance companies; and that the dues in farm organizations were subtracted from the patronage dividends of the farm cooperatives or added on to the premiums of the mutual insurance companies. So I related these facts I knew as a child to the theory of public goods from Samuelson and then tried to ask how one could make a general theory of this.

Knut Wicksell—and I admittedly read Wicksell after Samuelson—had looked at the problem of how a government can rationally allocate resources. And long before Samuelson, he had worked out a rudimentary theory of public goods, so that he could answer the question, "When shall we stop spending more out of tax revenues on something?" Samuelson then looked at this problem and saw that there was a difficulty of getting people to reveal the true value to them of public services. So, starting with this situation where governments exist and asking questions like, "What is the optimal level of expenditure?", the theory of the difficulties of governmental provision of public goods got started.

But governments didn't exist before human beings did, so I took as my task to say, "How do we deal with collective action *generally*, which manifests itself not only in governments but in many different forms of organizations?" Further, "How do things like size or the number of people who cooperate affect collective action?" Samuelson, Wicksell, and everybody else who had been working on this topic took it for granted that the problem involved governments over millions of people—a large group or a "latent" group in the sense of *The Logic of Collective Action* (Olson 1971, 50–51). But one other thing you have to do if you think in a more general way is to ask, "What if there are only ten people or three large firms that want to collude? How is the problem different for them?" It is of course a lot different—and hence *The Logic of Collective Action*.

Q: You mentioned earlier that you believe economics indeed has practical consequences, an opinion that is also evident from your career. You have been deputy assistant secretary at the Department of Health, Education and Welfare, and you worked on *Toward A Social Report*. Is it correct to state that in your opinion economics should be linked to practical problems?

A: Yes. If economics is not of use to man in practical affairs, then I don't know what purpose it has. To the extent that we are concerned about esthetics (which we should be), I would suggest that other disciplines like philosophy, pure mathematics, or poetry have the greatest appeal.

Q: Let me return for a moment to the social report. In the 1960s you argued very strongly for having a social equivalent to the economic report that the Council for Economic Advisers every year presents to the president. Do you still feel that way? And also: what happened to the idea of a social report? Did it just die?

A: The work on the social report began in the administration of Lyndon Johnson, just after the United States had passed the Voting Rights Act, which first made it possible for all blacks to vote, and the Civil Rights Act, which destroyed the Jim Crow system of segregation in the South. It was also a time when a vast array of social legislation was being passed and when a high rate of economic growth was taken for granted. There had been rapid growth in the United States from World War II through the 1960s, not so rapid as in Germany and Japan but more rapid than before. So the attitude at the time I went into government to take on this assignment was one which took economic growth for granted and high levels of income for granted and which looked on the social and environmental problems of the country as more difficult, more urgent, and more important than the economic ones. The administration of Lyndon Johnson ended in January of 1969. We had thought that possibly Hubert Humphrey would be elected, but in fact he was defeated by Richard Nixon. So I resigned at the beginning of the Nixon administration. We would have liked to have a president issue our report, say in 1970 or 1971; and we assumed that the president had originally planned to do this with lots of fanfare. But our project was not the kind of thing that another administration would carry on. So we had to finish *Toward A Social Report* early, which we did. It was published in January 1969 after the defeat of Humphrey and just before the inauguration of Richard Nixon. The world was looking at Nixon's inauguration and not at the issuance of this report, so it didn't become exceptionally famous. Indeed, it was disappointing that it didn't get a wider attention.

Q: So the attempt to introduce social reports of this type died in the 1960s?

A: Yes and no. Naturally things have to be given a different name, if they are to be continued in a new administration. There was one element of continuity, and that was Daniel Patrick Moynihan, who was a consultant in our effort and who then became counsellor to Richard Nixon in the White House. He got Nixon to put forth a project under the late Raymond Bauer of the Harvard Business School that carried on this activity. But Raymond Bauer's work apparently did not meet with favor from Haldeman and Ehrlichman. So it did not get much attention, and that was the end of that activity. Then there were some statistical activities in the Office of Management and Budget that grew out of our work on a social report. These were published for a few years and have now gone to the U.S. Department of Census. The presentation of British statistics was substantially affected by what we did, and I went to London in 1967 or 1968 to talk to them about what became their counterpart effort to ours.

Q: Would you still support the idea of a social report—that there is a need for a social counterpart to the standard economic figures on economic growth, inflation, and the like?

A: Yes. On the whole I would have more or less the same view today. I suppose that I would *then* have put the priority of growth measured in per capita relatively less high than I would *now* after the country has gone through bad times since about 1973. That is to say, a country can afford more environmental quality, more social expenditure, and so on, if its economy is doing well. And since our economy is not doing as well now as it was then, that naturally affects one's priorities a little. But basically my views would be the same now as then.

Q: Your next major work was *The Rise and Decline of Nations*, which you describe as "an outgrowth of *The Logic of Collective Action*" (Olson 1982, 12). And just like *The Logic of Collective Action*, this work has been much debated. Some people argue that the whole free rider idea is wrong (Marwell and Ames 1981), and others claim that it is perhaps not wrong, but that you overly emphasize the free rider (Barry 1983; Kindleberger 1983). What is your reaction to this debate over *The Rise and Decline of Nations?* Do you see any merit to the criticism? I think that the rather soft criticism of Barry and Kindleberger is reasonable.

A: On the whole I haven't spent a lot of time with criticisms after something is published, because I get a lot of criticism beforehand. I also want to get on to the next project. So I can't claim exhaustive knowledge of all the literature growing out of these two books. My general reaction is that the readers have been marvelously indulgent. On the whole I don't complain at all about the criticisms. I gather that there are some people who say that the whole analysis in *The Logic of Collective Action* is all wrong and who will cite the occasional experiment that they think supports this. I don't know the whole experimental literature on this, for there is quite a lot of it. The sample of it that I have seen tends to fit in—broadly speaking—with my argument. I have been a great appreciator of Professor Marwell's work, and we often correspond. Some of his recent work on collective action I have particularly recommended to journals and to others that have asked for my assessment. But I wouldn't want to get into details on the literature growing out of my work, because I am not that up on it.

As for the soft criticism you speak about—that other things besides the free rider problem are also terribly important—I would say by all means. I would say be wary of pushing any one consideration too far, including the considerations that Olson has called attention to. As to Barry and Kindleberger, I would say read them and give their work a lot of attention, as surely there is something in what they say.

Q: One of the things you are working on is something you call "encompassing economics." The main idea here is that a unified approach is needed in economics and the other social sciences. You have told me that you actually had a manuscript on "encompassing economics" prepared in 1972. What stopped you from publishing it at that time?

A: What I like to think was *right* about what I said then was that we need to look at all of reality—at all of social human reality—in a unified way; and that we need to have a framework of analysis that enables us to think in a conceptually comprehensive way about the whole domain of economics and the social sciences. But this is easier said than done, and in 1972 I didn't have the necessary theorems; I didn't have the additional tools of thought that we need to see what we loosely call "economic, social, and political reality" all at once and in general. It is true that I could do this in particular cases, as I had done in *The Logic of Collective Action.* When I tried to look at things in a more general way, I however came to feel that I wasn't going deep enough. What I said was right but not deep enough—or mainly right and mainly not deep enough. I didn't then know how to do it right, and it wasn't the sort of problem that I could solve just by thinking harder for a few days.

So, notwithstanding nice offers of publication and so on, I let the ideas that I had at that time ripen in the mind. And they didn't ripen quickly. Then I got terribly interested in *The Rise and Decline of Nations,* and it took me away from these matters for a long time. Now I am back to them, and I have been working on them today. I feel that I have now developed the tools that are needed to get a little deeper with this broad vision, and that is why I am working on it.

Q: The only thing I have read of your work on "encompassing economics" is an article that was distributed in connection with your speech at Harvard on December 1, 1987, entitled "Toward a Unified View of Economics and the Other Social Sciences." From this article plus the speech itself, I have the impression that the key idea is the notion of "indivisibilities." By this you basically mean that something can't be measured easily (or at all) and that this creates theoretical difficulties. So "indivisibilities" can obscure the production function as well as the utility function. Is this reading of your work roughly correct?

A: Yes, but unfortunately the ideas don't lend themselves to short summarization. The book that literally has the title *An Encompassing Economics* is a book of essays on a vast variety of topics and, though there is a single method that led to all the essays, the conclusions on diverse subjects cannot all be summarized in a few sentences.

The notion of "indivisibilities" that you mention plays a much larger role in my other nearly finished book, *Beyond the Measuring Rod of Money: Toward A Unified Approach to Economics and the Other Social Sciences.* Relentlessly single-minded as this latter book is, it unfortunately also defies summarization in a few lines. But so far as you can put the argument in a sentence, you are right: it deals with what I call "indivisibilities." Some of these indivisibilities put human values or preference orderings in a shadow, and when we get around them we can understand why there is such a paradoxical amount of discontent and disaffection in modern high-income countries and also in traditional societies that experience rapid economic growth. Some other indivisibilities obscure some cause-and-effect relations, such as those between the inputs used by a large bureaucracy and its output or performance, and when we appreciate this we can see why bureaucracies have a lot of red tape and are also "bureaucratic" in other ways.

Q: The titles of both your books are very ambitious; in one case you speak of "encompassing economics," and in the other, of a "unified approach to economics and the other social sciences." But isn't it overly optimistic to think that one could find *one* way that would help solving not only the perennial economic problems but also questions relating to class, ethnicity, gender, bureaucracy, and so on? But maybe I am jumping to conclusions. First I should ask if you are trying to lay the foundations for a whole new approach in the social sciences, or if you are just trying to explain a few aspects of reality, as in *The Logic of Collective Action?*

A: Neither. I am so taken by the cumulative nature of science that it would be almost beyond my imagination to think that I would recast all of social science. I remember being much influenced by reading Einstein on Newton. Einstein's general modesty was momentarily overcome when he pointed out that he would get *exactly* Newton's results, when he considered the commonplace conditions that Newton took for granted. The results were a special case of his own theory and Einstein was rightly very proud of this. So the idea of recasting economics and the social sciences is repugnant to me in the same way, I suppose, that the idea of recasting physics in a way that made Newton all wrong would be repugnant to physicists. The modern physicist couldn't imagine a physics that did not build on what had gone on before, and I could scarcely imagine an economics that didn't build on what came before. As I am so fond of saying, following Newton and others: the economist stands on the shoulder of giants.

What I hope to do is not to destroy or recast what came before but to *add* something. Given that I am standing on the shoulders of giants—and if I might continue my favorite simile: I am standing on a pyramid of giants, in which giants are standing on the shoulders of other giants—then my claim is that what I add is not so very much in relationship to the height of this great pyramid of giants. It is indeed not much at all compared to that. But with what I add, plus the much, much vaster amount that we have inherited from the men of genius of the past, we can help solve all these problems. With *that* we can analyze absolutely all the problems you mentioned.

Q: Including class, ethnicity, gender, bureaucracy . . . ?

A: Exactly. That doesn't mean that there is no need for further theoretical advances and for more empirical research; those things will be needed forever. But in a way, my claim is that what I am trying to do is to help everyone get on top of the shoulders of giants. And when they are standing on the top of this pyramid of giants, I only claim to have added as it were a guy wire or a rope, which enables one to look to the side without falling off.

Q: Let me now switch over to another topic and ask you a question about the way you go about analyzing problems. You basically seem to make two moves in your analysis. First, there is the element of methodological individualism; that is, you start with an individual facing an incentive of some sort. And second, there is a bold, ingenious idea, like the free rider in *The Logic of Collective Action*, or "indivisibilities" in your forthcoming book. Is this also how you see yourself as working, and is this the way you would suggest that others work as well? Is this your equivalent, so to speak, to what Albert O. Hirschman calls "trespassing"?

A: I would not start with any desire to "trespass" in any discipline nor even to do interdisciplinary work. I have no particular belief that such work is superior to disciplinary work. I have never tried to be interdisciplinary; much of what I do is not interdisciplinary at all. Neither would I believe in avoiding interdisciplinary work. I'd rather like to start with problems that are important to human beings and to countries; problems like what makes some nations decline and others advance.

But just as important problems can fall into a given discipline, sometimes they don't. The angle one should approach a problem from depends on the problem; and the best angle is the angle from which one will make the most progress. It is my belief that one should not have any preconceptions about necessarily being either disciplinary or multi-disciplinary. The quality of work depends on the importance of the problem and the depth of the analysis—not on how it is classified.

Another part of your question had to do with scientific methodology and the role of methodological individualism. Now, I believe that to make progress in any science, it is best whenever possible to get down to primitive entities, to get down to units so primitive or simple that it is not necessary to go inside of them. I like to get down, whenever possible, to the primitive entity of economic and social life: *the individual.* Getting down to primitive entities does not mean that one is advocating or buying ideologies like rugged individualism; one is simply trying to get down to fundamentals. So if someone says that Italians don't believe in divorce because they are Roman Catholics, one makes an assertion that is very vague even though it could have some truth to it; there are many different Italians, and they don't all think the same thing. If someone says that the working class voted communist to further its interests, that overlooks the fact that there are many different people in the working class and they don't all have the same views. That is one reason why I like to get down to individuals and very much accept methodological individualism.

I would not, however, accept the characterization that one always begins with the rational actor. That is to say, the degree of rationality—or for that matter, of self-interest—is not something that is given at the outset of the inquiry. These two assumptions—the assumption of rationality, on the one hand, and the not-identical assumption of self-interest, on the other—are not inherent to the method I like to use. That is to say, the degree of rational calculation may be very slight for certain purposes, for certain people, and for certain circumstances. And in certain other cases, the degree of self-interest may be very limited. If you and I walk along the sidewalk, and we assume that the concrete beneath us will hold our feet and that the sidewalk is really made up of concrete rather than paper painted to look like concrete, then we are making an assumption because our habits probably induce us to make that assumption. Now these habits are of course the result of earlier experience and of our rational adaptation to that experience. Still, the fact remains that each time we take a step we don't calculate whether the sidewalk is of concrete or of paper painted like concrete.

So, I would try to take the degree of rational calculation and the amount of information that is used in making decisions as something that is open to empirical investigation. And the amount of information and of rational calculation it is best to assume in a given inquiry depends on the particulars of that inquiry. If one is talking about decisions that people make repeatedly, and decisions that are fairly important to them (and decisions where the individual bears the costs and benefits of the choices he or she makes), then I have found it useful to assume a high degree of rationality. If we are talking about decisions that are made rarely and that are also relatively unimportant, then I would say that individuals are much less likely to do a lot of calculation and research. In certain cases, as I have argued in some of my publications, we should assume "rational ignorance"—that ignorance is the normal state of affairs with respect to certain matters, because there are no incentives to gather information.

Self-interest, which is not entailed by the assumption of rationality, is a tremendously important force in human interaction. But I normally assume that if I am lost and need directions, people will give them to me for free. If I see someone bleeding to death in the street, chances are that someone else has already offered to help before I get there—again for free. So, it is part of my methodology that one should try to get down to primitive entities; and it is part of my methodology that one should take problems as they come and use whatever assumptions and disciplines are needed to deal with them. But it is *not* part of my methodology that one should begin with an irrational passion for dispassionate rationality, or with the assumption that human beings are always and everywhere totally self-interested.

Q: Many attempts have been made during the last ten to fifteen years to extend the neoclassical type of analysis to areas where it by tradition has not been used. Do you see your "encompassing economics" as part of this trend?

A: I would say that if you go back to the beginnings of economics—to the first one hundred years or so of the subject—the assumption was that the economist would use the tools of thought he had in a conceptually comprehensive manner. Thus, Adam Smith analyzed phenomena like incentives for lecturers at universities to teach or not to teach. He also looked at the incentives for clergymen to work or to loaf. This is all in *The Wealth of Nations*. Needless to say, John Stuart Mill wrote beautifully on representative government as well as on international trade. So the kind of thing that I like to do is what my intellectual grandparents liked to do. It is true that in the generation of my intellectual fathers—the economists who were one generation earlier than I am—economics came to be taken as a much narrower subject. From Alfred Marshall until the 1960s or so, economics became much narrower. But now it is widening, and it has widened a lot in the 1960s, 1970s, and 1980s as economists have tackled the problems of politics and created the fields of "collective choice" or "public choice." I would hope that when I have finished the book I am doing on *Beyond the Measuring Rod of Money*, there will also be a little more interest in an integrated view of economics and sociology. Other people of course, like Gary Becker, are also working toward an integrated view of these two fields. A "new social economy" is emerging that parallels the "new political economy" that got moving in the 1960s. There is more nearly a common approach now to theory in all the social sciences than there was, say, when I was a graduate student.

When I had those conversations with Talcott Parsons that you asked about, what most sociologists were doing could not be integrated with what economists were doing because a lot of the work was simply at cross purposes. Some of the things that economists were doing and some of the things Talcott Parsons was doing could not both be right. Similarly, in political science there was an utterly different approach than in economics. But if you look today at the work of sociologists—at the writings, for example, of James Coleman—and if you look at the work of a variety of political scientists, such as many of those who lately have been added to the Department of Government at Harvard, you see a methodology which is really the same methodology as the economists use. So I see this as the age when from all sides we are slowly coming together on one unified approach to all of the social sciences.

Q: Sometimes the intellectual movement we are talking about is referred to as "economic imperialism." George Stigler, for example, talks of economics as an "imperial science." What is your reaction to this "imperialism"? Is perhaps your "encompassing economics" a less aggressive version?

A: I would say that none of us should engage in imperialistic aggression. Nor should we worry about any noncoercive imperialism. The right attitude to take intellectually is the same attitude I claim is the correct one in international relations. I oppose strong countries engaging in aggression against weak countries. The relationship among peoples ought to be those relationships that arise out of mutually profitable interactions as in trade, tourism, and exchange of ideas. I am *totally* opposed to imperialism, when it means, as it often does, aggression. No dean or chair of a faculty should ever use his power to impose the economists' method on those who prefer some other method.

There are, however, some people who label too many things "imperialistic." One can go to developing countries, where there is talk of "cultural imperialism," "economic imperialism," and so on. There are, for example, efforts to exclude Western news agencies like Reuters or the United Press from some developing countries because these news agencies may carry stories that are negative about the local dictator. So, I am also weary of a too loose and pejorative use of this word "imperialism." If a word ends with "ism," it is very likely to be used too loosely.

Let me add that I don't worry about Japanese economic imperialism in the United States. I think that if the Japanese make a product that gives better value, we should buy it. And if I were in any discipline—say if I am in economics and see a tool coming from mathematics or physics—I would say that we shouldn't restrict our use of it because it comes from another discipline. And if I were a sociologist or a political scientist, I would say that we shouldn't dream of discriminating against an idea because it comes from economics any more than one should refuse to buy a car because it comes from Japan. Now, even with the broader concept of imperialism, it is also important to note that imperialism is *impossible* unless you have an advanced culture next to an underdeveloped one.

Even if imperialism comes by force (which it shouldn't), it will almost never involve powerless cultures defeating powerful ones. When there is intellectual freedom, there is no danger, at least in the long run, that poor research strategies will drive out good ones. So, I think we shouldn't engage in or worry about economic imperialism in this sense. And this is a special case of my view that one shouldn't strive to be interdisciplinary, multidisciplinary, or in this or that discipline: one should strive to tackle the problems that are important and get the answers right. If you do that, it is all you need to do—you don't need to worry about colonizing or resisting imperialism.

Q: You mentioned that roughly between 1900 and the 1960s economists showed little interest in social institutions, but that this is changing today. How widespread is that change, in your opinion? Professor Solow, for example, has told me that in his view most of today's pacesetting young economists show no interest whatsoever in social institutions.

A: I would have to answer you by using a tool of economic theory that Adam Smith emphasized. Adam Smith said that the main source of economic growth is the division of labor. He examined this, for example, in a pin factory. One of the main reasons he was opposed to tariffs and other forms of protectionism is that it diminished the degree of specialization or the division of labor. The division of labor, as he said, is limited by the market. The market is bigger with free trade than with protectionism. So with a big market or a big discipline we get more and more specialization. There is more specialization than there was thirty years ago; there is probably even more in the English language world than there is on the Continent. And probably this specialization is at its most extreme in the United States. And that does mean, "Yes, it is true that the average American economist is interested in a narrower slice of reality now than an earlier generation of economists were."

Interestingly enough, Adam Smith not only discovered the enormous potential for human betterment from specialization, he also pointed out its main disadvantage. He said that the division of labor tends to make people dull and to render them incapable of thinking very well, for example, about the larger interests of their country. So Adam Smith was for it; but he realized that the division of labor had a cost, honest man that he was. And I am for it too: we need this specialization, and it is mainly a good thing. No one who teaches students how to do research can fail to note the importance of getting people to focus on narrow and manageable questions.

But it is also true that this wonderful thing "specialization" has its costs: it leaves us a little dull. So what do we do? Struggle, I guess, and work harder. And we should indulge the occasional person who specializes a little in being unspecialized. I think that the world is fair-minded about this and also indulgent. I thought, for example, when *The Rise and Decline of Nations* went to press that critiques would say, "Olson is so audacious, so arrogant, so unmindful for the need for specialization, that he deserves to be attacked with all the forces we can muster." I expected that and I was prepared for it. But my general impression is that people have been wonderfully indulgent; that they sense that we also need to struggle to overcome the disadvantages of specialization even as we harvest the benefits.

Q: In some of your writings you stress the need for more communication between economists and sociologists. But what exactly does this mean? Does it mean that sociologists should listen to and learn from economists? Or does it mean that there should be a two-way communication between economists and sociologists? If the latter is true, what do economists want to learn from sociologists?

A: I wouldn't exclude or be astonished at sociologists coming up with any kind of achievement. If an Otis Dudley Duncan comes up with something on the problem of identifying demand and supply curves in econometrics, it is likely to be good. I wouldn't exclude anything nor would I urge sociologists to stay away from anything.

Q: You mention demand and supply curves a propos Otis Dudley Duncan. Are you saying that sociologists should have a go at economic problems?

A: Oh yes, some of them should. We could use another Herb Simon. He came out of political science rather than sociology, but we can always use more people with that level of insight, wherever they come from. Of course, most sociologists naturally will *not* work on economics. But my advice to all sociologists is: look for a problem that is interesting and important; never mind how it is classified; and tackle it. That is my advice to Mancur Olson, and that is my advice to everyone else.

Q: So you *do* think that it is a good idea that sociologists work on economic topics?

A: Yes, absolutely. Statistically speaking, there will of course be some areas where it is more likely that the great discoveries will come from the sociologists. I am struck with the tremendous amount of goods that are produced by relatively stable, nonfleeting social interaction; the goods that families, friends, and social groupings produce for one another. To take a very prosaic example: suppose we look at all the meals produced in homes. We then value these meals fairly and compare them with the value of food produced in restaurants. The value of meals produced in homes will then turn out to be of very great value; not to mention other things, like emotional support, which are less prosaic and harder to put one's finger on. So the amount of production (if I may use an economic term) that is done through close social relationships is enormous. Though I don't know enough about sociology to say for sure, I have the impression that sociologists are attuned to this; they are alert to this; and they are less likely to forget or ignore this than other people. So I would think that this traditional sociological area is one that is not by any means played out. Indeed, this is a great and mainly still unexplored continent, even by sociologists. And there are lots of things to be discovered.

Q: How do you feel that your way of doing economics ("encompassing economics") can be furthered on an institutional level?

A: I would say that we do indeed need to make special institutional provisions for overcoming the costs of specialization. We should be sympathetic to interdisciplinary programs in the social sciences, just as in the physical and natural sciences. These institutional arrangements are necessary to overcome the costs of the inevitable and unbalanced—though desirable—specialization. My experience and observations suggest that, alas, activities outside the traditional disciplines usually have poor quality control. If you, for example, look at area studies programs in the United States, they on the whole don't have the same quality control as the traditional disciplines. If you look at the new public affairs and public policy programs in this country, their quality control is also on the whole less reliable than in, say, economics, history, and physics.

So, when we set up fresh institutions to look at new specialties or to combine specializations or disciplines, we have to realize it is hard. We should look especially hard at quality control. We should realize that there has been a high proportion of failure, but we should keep on trying to do it better.

Q: If you were to give any advice to young social scientists today, what would that be? Should they head in the direction of "encompassing economics" rather than opt for mainstream economics?

A: Yes. And this is just as the best stocks to buy in the stock market are not necessarily General Motors or IBM but the companies that are maybe smaller but who have ideas which have not already been pushed to the point of diminishing returns. So, I would say to the young scholar, "Yes, invest in growth stocks." Of course, the young scholar has to be aware that there is a slower reward for things that are a little off the regular path. So, if you have a very, very high interest rate and only short-term payoffs matter, then you can of course not do this. People with weak hearts should obviously do something that is conventional and will be respectable right away, whether they are physically weak-hearted and will die soon and can't wait for long payoffs, or whether they are temperamentally weak-hearted and cannot take the danger and the delay. But the strong-hearted would be wise to make an investment in an innovative venture that can pay off in a big way in the long run.

Q: All your writings, it seems to me, are basically attempts to answer one question: What assures the well-being of collective units, especially nations? How would you summarize your thoughts on this topic today?

A: I would go so far as saying that the *main* reason, as far as my studies have been able to determine, why a country is relatively prosperous or relatively poor, is the quality of the policies and institutions of that country. It is not natural resources that made Japan or Germany great manufacturing countries. And it isn't natural resources that have made Hong Kong, Singapore, Korea, and Taiwan grow so rapidly. It is the institutions or policies that they have or have had. If one goes from Mexico to Texas, crossing the Rio Grande, one does not suddenly find that natural resources are more bountiful. So luck and natural resources, though they play a role, are secondary. It is institutions and policy that mainly determine whether nations are rich or poor; whether life is good or bad; whether a country is a country that people are trying to get into or that they try to flee from. It takes *walls* to keep people away from good institutions and from leaving bad ones.

The question then is what makes for good institutions and good policies and what makes for bad institutions and bad policies? Well, most of my writing on this subject has been about the influence of gradual accumulation of organizations for collective action to engage in redistributional struggles. The gradual accumulation of that sort of activity in a country ultimately means that the energies of the country are to a greater extent wasted in distributional struggles rather than devoted to production or to mutually beneficial exchange. So my prior work is not mainly on the influence of ideas on institutions and policies but on the influence of organized interests on institutions and policies. But the ideas, even though I haven't myself written much about them, are terribly important in determining the quality of institutions and policies; and thus in determining whether countries are poor or rich, whether they are places to leave or places to move to.

The problems caused by the accumulation of organizations for collective action, which engage in distributional struggles, are mainly problems caused by tiny organized minorities. And these organized minorities can only cause problems because the majorities do not understand the problems involved. But majorities outvote minorities; they outnumber them. So the whole problem is that majorities are being ripped off and don't understand that this is happening. They are, moreover, getting ripped off in ways which have a huge excess burden or social waste attached to them. With better research and writing in economics and in the other social sciences, this will eventually be understood. So, better ideas and better research will sooner or later have an influence on policies and institutions. And policies and institutions will determine, more than any other single thing, whether life is good or bad.

References

Bell, Daniel. 1969. "The Idea of a Social Report." *Public Interest* (Spring):72–84.

Barry, Brian. 1983. "Some Questions about Explanation." *International Studies Quarterly* 27:17–27.

Blaug, Mark. 1985. *Great Economists since Keynes.* Brighton: Harvester Press.

Kindleberger, Charles. 1983. "On the Rise and Decline of Nations." *International Studies Quarterly* 27:5–10.

Marwell, Gerald, and Ruth E. Ames. 1981. "Economists Free Ride, Does Anyone Else?." *Journal of Public Economics* 15:295–310.

Olson, Mancur. 1963a. *The Economics of the Wartime Shortage: A History of British Food Supplies in the Napoleonic War and in World War I and II.* Durham, N.C.: Duke University Press.

———. 1963b. "Rapid Growth as a Destabilizing Force." *Journal of Economic History* 23:529–52.

———. 1965. *The Logic of Collective Action: Public Goods and the Theory of Groups.* Cambridge: Harvard University Press.

———. 1968. "Economics, Sociology, and the Best of All Possible Worlds." *Public Interest* (Summer):96–118.

———. 1969a. "The Plan and Purpose of a Social Report." *Public Interest* (Spring):85–97.

———. 1969b. *Toward A Social Report.* Washington, D.C.: U.S. Government Printing Office. (Written with others).

———. 1969c. "The Relationship between Economics and the Other Social Sciences." In *Politics and the Social Sciences*, edited by S. M. Lipset, 137–62. New York: Oxford University Press.

———. 1971. *The Logic of Collective Action.* 2d ed. Cambridge: Harvard University Press.

———. 1982. *The Rise and Decline of Nations: Economic Growth, Stagflation, and Social Rigidities.* New Haven, Conn.: Yale University Press.

———. 1988a. "Introduction." Unpublished paper.

———. 1988b. "Toward A Unified Approach to Economics and the Other Social Sciences." Paper presented at Harvard University, December 1.

10   *Thomas C. Schelling*

IN ONE of his collections of essays, Thomas C. Schelling describes himself as an "errant economist."[1] The metaphor is apt and captures an important side of his work: the attempt to use economic analysis to shed new light on topics that most other economists have tended to avoid. In *The Strategy of Conflict*, which is perhaps Schelling's most famous work, he analyzes bargaining, conflict, and strategy with the help of game theory. And in *Micromotives and Macrobehavior* he discusses such issues as segregation by race, sex, and age. Another side of Schelling's work that is equally characteristic is the method he uses. It should be noted that his method is very different from, say, the way the "economic imperialists" go about their analyses of noneconomic topics. The typical Schelling analysis usually builds on the key insight of game theory, namely that an actor's behavior is directly influenced by the way the other actors behave. To this description of Schelling's method, it must immediately be added that he executes his analyses with rare subtlety and elegance as well as with a never-ending series of fascinating examples from the most diverse areas.

Given Schelling's emphasis on the interaction between actors, one would think that he would have been influenced by sociology, at least in its Weberian version where "social action" is defined as behavior that takes "account of the behavior of others." In this interview, however, he says why this is not the case; and he discusses what he believes sociology lacks. He also describes how he came to write *The Strategy of Conflict* and *Micromotives and Macrobehavior*; and he discusses the work of Gary Becker. Finally, he tells about the focus for his new research in the past few years, namely, addiction and other phenomena which include certain "lapses from rationality."

Thomas C. Schelling was born in 1921 in Oakland, California, the son of a naval officer. He got his B.A. at the University of California at Berkeley in 1943, and his Ph.D. in economics from Harvard University in 1951.

The following interview with Thomas C. Schelling took place on May 16, 1988, in his office at the Kennedy School of Government at Harvard University in Cambridge, Massachusetts.

[1] The following is based on *Who's Who in Economics*; McPherson 1984; and information from Thomas Schelling.

During the period 1948 to 1953, he worked for the U.S. government. He then became a professor of economics, first at Yale University (1953–1958), and then at Harvard University (1958–), where he currently is Lucius N. Littauer Professor of Political Economy.

•

Q: It is clear that even though your production is very interdisciplinary in nature, you have always seen yourself mainly as an economist. What was it that initially attracted you to economics?

A: I originally got interested in economics in college, at Berkeley, before the war. I was fascinated by the depression and full employment, and I thought that economics was the most important subject. I then took a couple of years off to go to South America and came back in the middle of the war. My most influential teacher was William Fellner, who died about four years ago. I took three semesters of graduate theory with him in classes that, because of the war, numbered from five to fifteen people. He was a gentleman, and he showed so much respect for his students and he was so honest and open in his thinking aloud rather than lecturing, that he could give his students an awareness of participating in the solution of theoretical problems. Working with him I just came to believe I was an economist.

I finished my studies, did some graduate work at Berkeley, and went to Washington. There I worked at the U.S. Budget Bureau for Arthur Smithies. I came to Harvard in 1946 for graduate work. I was fairly close to Alvin Hansen during these years. I actually was a teaching fellow both for him, for Edward Chamberlain, and for Gottfried Haberler. But nobody at Harvard was terribly influential, except for contemporaries—I learned a lot from other students like James Tobin, James Duesenberry, and Carl Kaysen. But I had already studied enough of economics, so I wasn't learning much from the lecture courses. I recall that Leontief taught a very helpful course in mathematical economics.

Q: Schumpeter was at Harvard in the 1940s, when you were there. Did you take any courses with him?

A: We knew each other, but I don't think anybody got much out of his courses. By then he had become a showman more than a teacher; maybe he always was. Anyway, in 1948, when I had finished off all my course work, I joined the Marshall Plan. I spent a year in Denmark, a year and a half in Paris, and three years back in Washington. I might have stayed indefinitely in the government, but I was getting tired of it. So when Yale University offered me an associate professorship in 1953, I decided to take it. So there I was—in an academic environment in economics. And that confirmed my being an economist.

Q: In between your joining the Marshall Plan in 1948 and accepting the job at Yale, you also wrote your thesis. What was it about? International economics?

A: No, it was a book called *National Income Behavior.* I wrote it nights and weekends in Europe. The book began at the suggestion of a student who was struggling verbally with problems that yielded to very elementary algebra; when I showed him, he urged me to do a short pedagogical paper on how to use algebra in national income analysis. I started, and it grew and grew and Seymour Harris got me a contract with McGraw-Hill and it continued to grow until it was everything you needed to know about the algebraic analysis of national income behavior. By the time the book was published, the market had largely evaporated; the mathematically illiterate generation of economics graduate students who returned right after the war gave way to a new generation that already had some mathematical technique. The book was sufficiently comprehensive as to be fairly widely used for several years, but as pedagogy it became obsolete.

Q: During your undergraduate and graduate studies, did you take any courses in social sciences other than economics? In sociology, for example?

A: No.

Q: In 1960 you published *The Strategy of Conflict,* which has become a classic in its field. Could you tell a little about how you came to write this book? And how do you look on it today?

A: When I was in graduate school here at Harvard I got a little interested in game theory and actually started to write something about bargaining. I showed it to Leontief, and he said that I should wait until I had read von Neumann-Morgenstern's *Theory of Games and Economic Behavior.* Then I left Cambridge and joined the Marshall Plan. Most of the time I was in the government I was dealing with negotiations. These were international negotiations, where you used promises of aid, threats of withholding aid, and things of that sort. So when I went back to academic life in 1953 at Yale I had pretty well decided that something like bargaining was what I was interested in. I soon perceived that military strategy was like a form of diplomacy and therefore was a good field of application for me. So I read memoirs from World War II and so on, and started to write what I thought was a book. When it had reached about 200 or 250 pages, I decided that I could boil it down. I compressed it as carefully as I could, and it became "An Essay in Bargaining," which is a chapter in *The Strategy of Conflict.* I then worked on another essay, which I had in my mind at that time, and it became the third chapter in the book, "Bargaining, Communication, and Limited War." Kenneth Boulding liked this third chapter, I recall. I had sent the first article to *The American Economic Review* and the editor had asked Kenneth Boulding to referee it. He liked it so much that he got in touch with me and asked me if I was also doing anything else. So I sent him the second article, which he put in the inaugural issue of *The Journal of Conflict Resolution.*

By that time I had decided that this was a fruitful field and that I wanted to stay in it. I had a year's research leave and I ended up with a very long article, which later became a whole issue of *The Journal of Conflict Resolution* and eventually also chapters 4, 5, and 6 in the book. Then, in 1958, I went to the Rand Corporation for a year and continued pretty much with the same thing there. Originally I had not written any of these articles to be in a book, but at Rand there was an editor who thought that I might put it all together into one volume. I did, and I sent it to the Harvard University Press, where they liked it.

By then—this was in 1959—I had resigned from Yale and was headed for Harvard. And from then on for the next ten years I worked on military strategy and arms control. I wrote *Strategy and Arms Control* with Morton Halperin, and later, *Arms and Influence.* I got out of this business in 1970, partly because I ceased to be a consultant for the government. I no longer had access to information, and I no longer had an audience.

How do I look at *The Strategy of Conflict* today? I still think it is a good book. I use three or four of the chapters in my lectures. Most of it is still useful. Some of the more applied chapters are perhaps a little out of date; surely the first chapter is completely out of date. But I think that chapter 3—"Bargaining, Communication, and Limited War"—is still cited a lot. The ideas in that chapter are pretty well embedded these days in political science, sociology, and to some extent also in economics. And I think the second chapter, "An Essay on Bargaining," is as good an introduction to bargaining as there is.

Q: It seems to me that in your works you have increasingly stopped referring to game theory. The core of game theory—that one actor's behavior is dependent on the other actor's behavior—is, on the other hand, still very much with you. Were you more optimistic about the use of game theory in those days than you are today?

A: I believe that in those days I was only optimistic about the usefulness of the very rudimentary or elementary game theory. In fact, I think that some of the very best game theory I ever did didn't use any paraphernalia—no matrices or anything of that sort. It was just a way of thinking about a problem.

Q: You mean like your idea in the essay on bargaining that one can precommit oneself, or "bind oneself," as you put it, in order to exclude certain options from being negotiated?

A: Yes. And in that essay I just had some diagrams at the end, sort of thrown in as an afterthought. But I didn't have any matrices in it. And chapter 3 was really about the concept of "the coordination game" (or what I later realized was the "zero-difference game"), which I still think is a worthwhile and important concept. In fact, it has been taken up and used by others. I teach a course here at the Kennedy School in which I have a lot of very elementary game theory and I still find it useful. Of all the things I have ever taught, I think it is these elementary concepts that have been the most influential. I still get letters from people who took the course fifteen or twenty years ago which tell me that it has influenced the way they think about things.

So I am still optimistic that game theory is intellectually useful—but, as I said, only at the most elementary level. Martin Shubik at Yale does very interesting work in game theory. He is one of the few people outside of pure mathematics who has continued to develop and apply game theory. I however don't find that I can use much of his work in my teaching. It is of help mainly to people who are professional theorists. I try to get my students comfortable with very elementary concepts.

Q: Which would those elementary concepts be? And which are some of your favorite examples when you teach these concepts?

A: I suppose the most elementary and pervasive concept, the one I began playing with before I left graduate school, is that binding oneself, eliminating or penalizing certain options available to oneself, can change another's expectation of what one will do and change that other's decision what to do, to one's own benefit. Burning one's bridges may deter an enemy's advance. Another relates to communication: being unable to receive or to comprehend an extortionate threat, if that inability is appreciated, may make the threat ineffectual so that it doesn't occur. The occasional need to combine threats and promises—the blackmailer's dilemma—shows up in problems of deterrence and surprise attack. And the need for clues and signals to coordinate expectations in both tacit and explicit bargaining is something of ubiquitous interest. Finally, the payoff matrix itself, though devoid of conceptual substance, is an extraordinarily powerful tool for displaying the rudiments of a two-party interaction, powerful the way double-entry bookkeeping is, or even the equation in mathematics.

Q: In 1978 you published *Micromotives and Macrobehavior*, which is your second classic. The topic is different here—you analyze things like sex, race, and so on—but the general approach seems similar to *The Strategy of Conflict* in the sense that behavior is still very much explained by the fact that when people act, they take other people's behavior into account. How did you come to switch over from international politics and economics to more sociological topics? In brief, how did you come to write *Micromotives and Macrobehavior?*

A: I sort of fell into it. I wanted to include something about the interaction between micro and macro in a course I taught, and I decided that racial segregation would be a good illustration. I spent a summer at the Rand Corporation in 1968, which had a pretty good library. I decided to take advantage of the library and go through journals in sociology, looking for articles I could use in my teaching. I went through two or three sociological journals for a ten-year span. And I found absolutely nothing.

I then decided that if I really wanted to teach racial segregation, I would have to produce the material myself. I began to play around with "tipping models," but it was hard. It was a struggle before I was able to formulate diagrammatically what I was trying to do. At about that time I flew away somewhere—I think it was to Michigan or Chicago—and when I got on the airplane to go home, I had nothing to read. I had to do something to amuse myself. I had a pencil and paper, and I began to toy with little crosses and dots on the lines. I soon found that there was more there than I could handle just with a pencil and paper. So when I came home, I did tabletop exercises, using some coins. The whole thing was still just in one line. Then I finally decided that I could also do it in two dimensions if I had blank spaces. That intrigued me. And finally I put it all together in an article, which was published in *The Journal of Mathematical Sociology* (see Schelling 1971a). The journal was just being started by Bernhardt Lieberman, who had earlier worked with me. He was the editor and he asked me for the article.

It is interesting to me, as I mention somewhere in one of my books, how much of what I have written has been on somebody else's suggestion. Emmanuel Mesthene, who was director at a Harvard Center for Technology and Society, contracted with me to write a paper for a book he was doing, called *The Corporate Society*. That paper was called "On the Ecology of Micromotives," and I put it in *The Public Interest*, where it got lots of attention (Schelling 1971b). Then Julius Margolis, at the University of Pennsylvania, asked me to give an annual lecture series that would be published as a book. So I decided I would stay on this subject. I gave the Fels lectures in 1975 and spent two years writing them up. The essay on age, chapter 5 in the book, I might have done anyway; but somebody asked me to contribute to a Festschrift for Willi Fellner, so I did that. Where the idea came from for the last chapter—"Hockey Helmets, Daylight Saving, and Other Binary Choices"—I don't remember at all.

So there they were, and I decided to just pile all these different things into a book. I thought that *Micromotives and Macrobehavior* would be a popular book—I actually thought it would make money. It didn't. Some people like it very much, but it never sold much. I often think that I should have picked a snappier title.

Q: Well, I think it is a pretty good title. And books like that usually get a second wind. Anyway, let me ask you a question on sociology. You just told about your failure to find any relevant sociological work on racial discrimination when you worked on *Micromotives and Macrobehavior*. But in *Choice and Consequence* one can find some traces of influences from sociology on your writings. The discussion of self-fulfilling prophecy is one, and the references to Erving Goffman another. So let me ask you for your general opinion about sociology.

A: When I looked into sociology, which was in the late 1960s, I was struck by the absence—perhaps not total absence, but at least great scarcity—of models of microbehavior influence. There were no models on the interaction of individuals with the collective. And I remember thinking, "That's funny, because that's all economics really is about." But I didn't find any of it in sociology. And since economics is mainly concerned with transactions involving prices, there was a huge gap in the research. There was very little on the interactions that don't have explicit prices. But it was clear to me that these should be susceptible to the kind of models that economists build, and I thought that sociologists ought to learn how to do that. So if you were to ask me what audience I had in mind when I put together *Micromotives and Macrobehavior*, I would say that it was mainly graduate students in sociology and political science. They were not being taught this kind of analysis and they could learn it; it's easy.

I tried hard to make *Micromotives and Macrobehavior* into an attractive book. I tried, for example, to use vivid and familiar examples as much as I could. I think that by now a lot more economists are actually getting into this area. I even think that to some extent these days, if economists get into, say, traffic patterns on a highway, they have begun to call that economics. The implication being that economics is whatever an economist can do; and since economists can do that kind of economics, that makes it economics! I myself, I should add, would rather try to find some other place to draw a line around economics.

Jack Hirshleifer at UCLA does work somewhat along the lines of *Micromotives and Macrobehavior*. And George Akerlof at Berkeley has gotten into some similar issues. But I think that my book has become more of a hit outside of economics than in economics. My original thought was that economists don't really need to read this, since they understand this kind of thing already. Not that they do much with it, but it is still along the lines of economics. In this sense my book was a little like Mancur Olson's book. I was Mancur's thesis adviser when he was writing *The Logic of Collective Action*, and I remember predicting that it would make no hit among economists because economists only need to read the first chapter; the rest is self-evident to them. Mancur's book is centered around a very simple idea, and it didn't seem to require a genius to produce that idea, even if nobody had quite done it before. And if you do something which has not been done before but which is sort of self-evident when you do it, you don't get much credit for it. Mancur Olson became a hero in political science and sociology, but economists disdained his first book. *The Logic of Collective Action* didn't contain any surprises for them. And I felt that way about *Micromotives and Macrobehavior.* An economist can read it and say, "Very cleverly done, but we already knew all of that." So at least the basic idea or the basic approach was already well known, when my book appeared.

Q: It really surprises me to hear that economists would have such a low opinion of your and Mancur Olson's books. I would not have thought that.

A: Another example is Albert O. Hirschman, a trained economist whose work reads like anthropology, sociology, and political science. Economists have not taken Hirschman's work nearly as seriously as other social scientists. His *Exit, Voice, and Loyalty* is now a classic among other social scientists, who have contributed bookfuls of commentary. The very simplicity of the ideas in that book makes them exciting to other sociologists but unexciting to most economists. An exception is the book by Richard Freeman and James Medoff, on labor unions, but much of their own book would not be recognized as strictly economics (see Freeman and Medoff 1982).

Q: Since it seems that we have gotten into the general topic of the tendency of economists to go into areas which by tradition sociologists, political scientists, and so on have had a monopoly on, I'll take this opportunity to ask you about economic imperialism. What is your opinion of, for example, Gary Becker's work?

A: Gary Becker has had an enormous influence, especially on people who were his students. It is really quite exceptional how many people, when they get around to writing a book of their own, refer to Gary Becker as such an inspirational teacher, way back even when he was at Columbia. Since you are Swedish, I'll take *The Harried Leisure Class* by Staffan Burenstam Linder as my example. He was one of Becker's students, and makes many references to Becker's influence.

I myself don't find Becker's work so helpful. The difference between us is that he is completely satisfied with the traditional economic model of rational behavior, while I am not. I sometimes think he lacks curiosity in

the phenomena that he studies. One of his early books was on racial segregation. It was called *The Economics of Discrimination,* and it reminds
me of an expression Schumpeter once used when he lectured on Adam
Smith. Schumpeter had no respect for Adam Smith, and I remember him
saying something like, "Adam Smith, in whose wooden hands no plant
would grow." Well, I felt something similar about Becker. I felt that he had
a piece of machinery that was cranking out results, and that he wasn't
sufficiently interested in racial segregation to look and see what was really
going on. He just decided to throw a parameter into a preference function,
giving everybody a "taste" for being with or not being with people of
another color. I thought that book just didn't get anywhere. I also feel that
what he has been doing lately on addiction is similarly uninspired by any
real interest in the subject. What he is primarily interested in is showing
that traditional economic models are all you need.

To some extent this is also true of Becker's *Treatise on the Family,* although I find this work to be much, much richer than most of the other
work. But sometimes what annoys me about Becker, and maybe your
term, "imperialism," somewhat catches it, is that he doesn't appear to
think there is anything to learn from outside economics. He is not interested in coupling the methodology of economics with the methodology of
sociology. His interest is showing that he can handle new things with
traditional economics. And I think, as you can tell from my attitude on this,
that this approach is very limited in what it can accomplish. I think, for
example, George Akerlof is more creative. He has a great curiosity. I think
that what George Akerlof does is almost the opposite of economic imperialism. He looks into sociology for concepts that he can import into economics.

Q: There exists today a movement in sociology that is somewhat parallel to economic imperialism. It is a group centered in Chicago that tries to
argue for the radical remaking of sociology on the basis of rational choice.

What would be your opinion of an attempt to remake sociology along
these lines? And can the social sciences be unified on the basis of rationality?

A: I think that rationality can be one unifying element but not more than
that. I don't think it is a complete and sufficient approach to any of these
subjects. The assumption of rationality has been very powerful in economics. It has been so powerful that many economists think you don't
need anything else. But I also think that when economists are attacked for
their obsession with rationality, say by someone like Amitai Etzioni, the
attacks are usually intended to be completely destructive. Etzioni considers rationality so far off base that you may as well throw it out and start all

over again. And of course no economist who has invested a career in models of rationality is going to discard all of that investment and look around for some place to start over.

What I would rather hope for in economics is that people might learn—a little like George Akerlof does—that there are maybe ways to couple the rationality assumption with some other phenomenon, so they can be compatible and complementary with each other. I also enjoy the work of Dan Kahneman and Amos Tversky. They are not economists but they know economics very well. They are interested in what you might call "departures from perfect rationality." And I think that because they accept a general model of rationality, they can also enrich it. They do this by relaxing rationality in certain systematic ways.

On the other hand, I think that some people, at least in political science, may have become a little too euphoric about what the assumption of rationality can do for them. That may be all right; it may be that there has to be an initial discovery stage in which people find a new tool. Robert Solow once said that if you get a new electric drill for Christmas, you'll go all around the house looking for holes that can be drilled. And I think some of my colleagues at Harvard, like Morris Fiorina and Ken Shepsle, tend to be what I would see as overconfident about how far rationality will take them. But rationality is still insufficiently familiar in political science and sociology, so a certain evangelical enthusiasm is a good thing, as long as it doesn't go too far.

Q: In what direction would you rather see research going? Would it perhaps be in the direction of "egonomics" or "self-management," that is, the various ways in which persons try to deal with their own behavior?

A: My personal feeling—and this comes when I think about what I call "self-management"—is that I would like to see economics pay more attention to the notion of the brain or the central nervous system as a biological organ that has evolved over millions of years. And it probably has evolved into a design that for some purposes may be unrational and for others antirational.

Q: You mean that the brain cannot handle certain problems in a rational way because of its historical evolution?

A: Yes. I'll give you a couple of examples. I think that if a person is thirsty enough and has been told that a drink of water will kill him, and if there is water at hand, he will eventually drink the water and die. He will do this, not because he has such a high discount rate that he will give up his whole future for a drink of water, but because the brain is programmed so that when an animal is thirsty enough, it will disregard all other goals, threats, and objects. Because, for animals and primitive people, if you don't drink, you're dead. It probably never suits the purpose of an animal to forego drinking when it is thirsty. And therefore, in order to protect the whole organism in the presence of dehydration, the brain programs the person to look for water and to drink it. And also to put everything else out of mental reach. Or, to put the same thing differently, if you knew that water would kill you—which you knew a little while ago—you would still not be able to retrieve this from memory because the brain is not interested in retrieving that kind of information from memory when you get thirsty enough. And I think quite possibly, with respect to a lot of addictive behavior, one needs to look at the stimuli that will cause the mind to focus selectively on certain desires and to neglect certain inhibitions.

Take another example. One would expect from evolutionary theory that fighting for the privilege of mating and procreation would be a stable instinct in the population because if some will fight in order to mate and others will not fight, the nonfighters will have no offspring. Only the fighters will have offspring, and their offspring will inherit the genes that make them fight. This suggests that creatures, which normally avoid danger, are programmed by evolution to ignore certain dangers in the interest of procreation. Now, it wouldn't surprise me if some of that also remains genetically programmed in human beings. So one of the reasons why sexual indiscretion may be common is that under certain stimuli—perhaps especially if one has alcohol in the bloodstream, which will anaesthetize selectively the more recently developed parts of the brain, leaving comparatively unanaesthetized certain drives—the brain is programmed in some way that in the presence of appropriate sexual stimuli, you'll simply forget the consequences. Or maybe it is that the consequences of sexual indiscretion are somehow so deep in the memory that they are just not accessible, when the sexual stimulus is right there. It is even conceivable that there are olfactory stimuli that we are unaware of. There are in insects, and it is believed that there are in some animals. In fact, when the bitch is in heat, dogs are attracted from miles by chemical signals; and by the time they arrive, they are ready to fight. I would consider the possibility that something similar is true of human beings, but sufficiently attenuated in human beings that it would only show up in some cases, not in all.

If I were to start all over again, I think I would ask for several years to study recent developments in brain science. Most of the work that attracts attention now in cognitive science is pretty much by its nature in the rationality tradition, but I don't think it has to stay that way. I think that one can also model other behavior just as one can model a rational creature that responds directly to stimuli. Take the moth, for example. It is believed that the reason why a moth circles the light is that light stimulates something inhibiting in the wing muscle on the side that the light hits and there-fore—like a person whose right arm is stronger than his left arm and who is rowing a boat—you move in circles. So you don't need the moth consciously circling the light; it can't help doing it. And I think that there may be some value in trying to think about certain kinds of human behavior in that way.

Q: The way you define rationality in your major works is mainly in terms of actors taking each other into account in predictable—and thereby rational—ways. This is a theme that goes through *The Strategy of Conflict* as well as *Micromotives and Macrobehavior*. But in this latest research of yours I can't see any of this. Does this mean that you are replacing rationality with a more biological viewpoint?

A: I wouldn't abandon the rationality approach at all. I would instead like to enlarge it or enrich it by systematically relaxing certain assumptions of rationality. Because if I abandon the concept of rationality, then I have almost nothing left over. There is nothing to which I can attach any ideas I might have about, let us say, the biological basis of behavior. I can only get interested in the biology of the brain, if I begin with a disciplined concept of rational behavior. Then I can impose some constraints or relaxations to get more out of it than the pure rational model will give you.

Q: In your recent research on "self-management," you sometimes raise moral questions. I am especially thinking of the Tanner Lectures on Human Values, which you gave in 1982 (see Schelling 1984b). Does this mean that "egonomics," or "self-management," has a moral as well as biological side? The reason I ask this is that both Amartya Sen and Albert O. Hirschman seem to be interested in resurrecting a rather old-fashioned but dignified type of moral discourse within the framework of economics.

A: My interest in what I usually call self-management is not primarily an interest in moral questions. The only reason that I got caught up in moral issues was that I gave the Tanner Lectures on Human Values in Michigan. I decided that, since I was working in this egonomics area, I would think about some suitable ethical and legal issues. And I found them fascinating. But my main interest was and still is in the ways in which people cope with their own behavior problems. I like to describe this by saying that, if you will just admit certain specified kinds of nonrational motivations, then you can have more fun with your rational model, because you can have people rationally coping with what they know will be lapses from rationality. Jon Elster is primarily interested in temptation, weakness of will, and I think that is partly because of his philosophical tradition. But I tend to be equally interested in problems of, let us say, behavior when drowsy, behavior in panic, coping with phobias, how people who mustn't fall asleep manage to stay awake, and so on. When I want to talk about the brain being momentarily not rational, I think of people who, when the alarm clock goes off, are somehow incapable of reflecting on how important it is to get out of bed. And I would prefer to say in this case that the brain isn't working in a disciplined way, rather than that people have a very high discount rate. There is also another interesting thing that takes place the night before, when you know you must get up in the morning. Namely, how do you try to arrange it so you can make yourself get up in the morning, when you know that you are not going to want to?

I think that the rational, systematic ways in which people try to cope with their own lapses of rationality are both important and fascinating. But I find that hardly anybody in economics likes the concept of "lapses from rationality." They almost always think that somehow you can take care of it through some discount rate.

I imagine that this is what I will still be working on for a few more years because it is an area where some of the more important discoveries are still to be made. The economic approach is clearly a powerful one, but it also needs to be coupled with other approaches, be they sociology or biology.

References

Becker, Gary. 1957. *The Economics of Discrimination.* Chicago: University of Chicago Press. 2d ed. 1971.

———. 1981. *A Treatise on the Family.* Cambridge: Harvard University Press.

Blaug, Mark. 1986. *Who's Who in Economics: A Biographical Dictionary of Modern Economics.* 2d ed. Cambridge: MIT Press.

Burenstam Linder, Staffan. 1970. *The Harried Leisure Class.* New York: Columbia University Press.

Freeman, Richard B., and James Medoff. 1982. *What Do Unions Do?* New York: Basic Books.

Hirschman, Albert O. 1970. *Exit, Voice, and Loyalty: Responses to Decline in Firms, Organizations, and States.* Cambridge: Harvard University Press.

Marris, Robin, ed. 1974. *The Corporate Society.* New York: Macmillan.

McPherson, Michael S. 1984. "On Schelling, Hirschman, and Sen: Revising the Conception of the Self." *Partisan Review* 51:236–47.

von Neumann, John, and Oskar Morgenstern. 1944. *The Theory of Games and Economic Behavior.* Princeton, N.J.: Princeton University Press.

Olson, Mancur. 1965. *The Logic of Collective Action: Public Goods and the Theory of Groups.* Cambridge: Harvard University Press.

Schelling, Thomas C. 1951. *National Income Behavior: An Introduction to Algebraic Analysis.* New York: McGraw-Hill.

————. 1960. *The Strategy of Conflict*. Cambridge: Harvard University Press. Reprinted with a new preface in 1980.

————. 1966. *Arms and Influence*. New Haven, Conn.: Yale University Press.

————. 1971a. "Dynamic Models of Segregation." *Journal of Mathematical Sociology* 1:143–86.

————. 1971b. "On the Ecology of Micromotives." *Public Interest* 25 (Fall):61–98.

————. 1978. *Micromotives and Macrobehavior*. New York: W. W. Norton.

————. 1984a. *Choice and Consequence: Perspectives of an Errant Economist*. Cambridge: Harvard University Press.

————. 1984b. "Ethics, Law, and the Exercise of Self-Command (The Tanner Lectures)." In Schelling, *Choice and Consequence* 83–112. Cambridge: Harvard University Press.

Schelling, Thomas C., and Morton Halperin. 1961. *Strategy and Arms Control*. New York: Twentieth Century Fund.

11

Neil J. Smelser

In MANY WAYS, Neil Smelser is the grand old man in economic sociology.[1] When U.S. sociologists made their first attempt to systematically analyze economic phenomena in the 1950s, Smelser, by coauthoring *Economy and Society* with Talcott Parsons, became one of the key participants. During the rest of the 1950s and in the early 1960s, Smelser continued to produce a series of valuable works in economic sociology on his own. When this first attempt to promote economic sociology waned in the 1960s, Smelser turned his attention to other topics. However, since the late 1970s Smelser has again been doing some work in economic sociology. In this interview, Smelser tells about his cooperation with Parsons in writing *Economy and Society* when he was a young student at Harvard; he discusses his other works in economic sociology; and he addresses the question of what economic sociology should be studying today.

Neil Smelser was born in 1930 in Kahoka, Missouri. The family was academically oriented; his father was a junior college teacher and his mother a secondary school teacher. He received his undergraduate degree from Harvard in 1952, and his Ph.D. in sociology from the same school in 1958. During the period 1952 to 1954, Smelser was a Rhodes Scholar at Oxford, where he earned a B.A. from Magdalen College at Oxford University. In 1958, he moved to the University of California at Berkeley, where he is currently employed. In 1971, Smelser graduated from the San Francisco Psychoanalytic Institute. He has also been very active in the administration of the University of California at Berkeley, in the Social Science Research Council, and in many other institutions.

•

Q: You are a sociologist who has made many contributions to economic sociology. Did you ever study economics in college or was this something that you picked up on your own?

The following interview with Neil Smelser was conducted on April 29, 1988, at the Center for the Study in the Behavioral Sciences at Stanford, California.

[1] The following information comes from Parsons 1986; Smelser 1969, 1981; and *Who's Who in America*.

A: When I was an undergraduate at Harvard in the early 1950s I took two economics courses. One was the equivalent of the first year economics course, which was offered by a number of professors on the Harvard faculty. It was in that course that I got my basic education in economics. I also took a course which was offered by James Duesenberry and Francis Sutton called Economic Sociology. That was not a very good course. They did not know what to assign and they were both too polite to one another. So while I learned some additional economics and quite a bit about some of the sociologists' work in the area of economic institutions, the course was still something of a loss for me.

I was also an undergraduate a second time at Oxford in 1952–1954, and there I read economics along with philosophy and politics. I decided to give special attention to economics. The two required courses in economics were Economic Theory and Economic Institutions, and naturally I had tutorials in each of these areas, and I was brought up to date on a great deal of contemporary thinking on the part of English economics with respect to both of them. I did something quite practical for my third paper in economics: I decided to read economic statistics. That and logic became my two elected fields of study. Both of them were very technical but gave me a better sense of the way of thinking in economics and philosophy. The economic statistics was something of a loss in one aspect though, because it overlapped so much with the statistics I had had before at Harvard. The main thing I learned from the course was the diversity of time series, something which helped me out later on.

Q: *Economy and Society*, which you coauthored with Talcott Parsons, is a landmark in economic sociology. At the time the book was written, you were a twenty-four-year old undergraduate and Parsons was fifty-two years old and probably the most famous sociologist in the world. How did you two come to collaborate? What's the story behind *Economy and Society?*

A: Talcott Parsons was a teacher of mine as an undergraduate. I took courses in Social Institutions, American Social Structure, and in The Sociology of Religion for him. He became aware of me as a student, even though I was not very active in his courses, and he was my sponsor in 1951 to go to the Salzburg seminar in American studies. I was studying economics in Oxford in 1953, and that year Parsons was also named as the Marshall lecturer. That meant that he had to give some lectures in economics. He was a very brave man because he chose the relationship between sociological theory and economic theory as his topic (Parsons 1986). I say brave because, while he had made enormous advances in sociology, he had not kept up with the economics literature. The only person that he had read in preparation for the Marshall Lectures was John Maynard Keynes. And, as many have said, Parsons didn't get Keynes right.

Our collaboration was initiated by Parsons himself. He sent me a copy of the Marshall Lectures and asked me to comment on them. This was a very big challenge for me, because, while I was very much up to date on the economics literature, I certainly was not up to date on Parsons's sociological thinking. And my tendency, since I was only a very young person of twenty-four years, was to be somewhat cautious in my criticisms and to give Parsons some economic arguments which I knew that he wasn't familiar with. Well, this proved to be helpful to him, because he was basically ignorant about contemporary economics, particularly English economics as manifested in the works of Harrod, Hicks, and some Cambridge people. So I basically gave him a bibliography and suggestions for how to improve his treatment of economics, and not embarrass himself by being so out of it with respect to economics.

The next thing that happened was that Parsons came to see me in Oxford and we spent several hours together in that initial meeting in the winter of 1953. Then, within a matter of weeks, my college roommate—William Moffat—came to England and lived around the corner from me. He was a graduate student in economics at Harvard and I showed him the Marshall Lectures. Moffat was astounded at how inadequate Parsons's treatment of Keynes was, even though the idea of Keynes having made certain assumptions about the parameters of economics seemed like a good idea to him. But Parsons's treatment was so limited that my roommate and I were able to basically rewrite one of the sections of the Marshall Lectures. We showed Parsons how he had got Keynes wrong, and how he—if he had read Keynes right—would have to revise his whole notion of boundary interchanges between economy and society. We wrote this in a long letter in March 1954 to Parsons, in which we explained what was wrong (Smelser 1954).

Parsons responded with great enthusiasm and he invited me to come to Cambridge to talk about this as well as about other things. At the time, I was applying for a junior fellowship in the Society of Fellows at Harvard, and I was trying to figure out what I was going to do my work on. So we had a multiple agenda when I went to Cambridge during the spring. But Parsons had read our letter very, very carefully and he was prepared to move ahead in terms of his interpretation of Keynes. So we set out to do that. We spent the whole day together, and we started reformulating not only Keynesian economics but its implications for the theory of action. Parsons had this tremendously active mind and he responded very positively to our comments, so by the time the weekend in Cambridge was over, Parsons and I had basically reformulated the whole idea of boundary interchange and the nature of economic theory as it had developed since neoclassical times.

Then, because of the very close tie that by now had developed between Parsons and I, he asked me to come to Salzburg, where he was teaching that summer. He paid me five dollars a day for ten days to come to Salzburg. He was teaching only a couple of times a week, so we were able to spend almost the whole day every day together. It was there in Salzburg that the book *Economy and Society* was invented. It was there that we picked up on Schumpeter's notion of development; and it was there that we reorganized the idea of factors of production and what parts of society are responsible for organizing these. So by the time we finished, we consequently had more or less completely reworked that fundamental diagram on boundary interchanges between the subsystems of society in chapter 2 of *Economy and Society* (Parsons and Smelser 1956, 68). We also began to look forward to writing on economic fluctuations as well as on economic growth, even though our ideas were not too developed at this point.

After Salzburg, I made the decision to return to Harvard and to enroll as a first-year graduate student in sociology. I did not take any further courses in economics, even though I presented the graduate records examination from Oxford as my credentials to get into Harvard. I did not score very well on that incidentally, because it was on English economics and not on American economics. Nonetheless, it didn't affect my standing. I was a student of Parsons in the required theory course at Harvard in the first year of my graduate work, and Parsons more or less invited me to write a term paper which had to do with the character of economic fluctuations and how these should be analyzed. In the meantime he hired me as a research assistant with respect to working on his book on the family (Parsons et al. 1955). And he also asked me to continue my work with him on *Economy and Society*.

Within one month after we had returned to Harvard, he had asked me to be a coauthor of *Economy and Society*. That was a justified request or invitation, I felt, because I had already worked out a fundamental change in our ideas and I was beginning to reformulate our ideas on fluctuation and growth. I was also prepared at that time to write the additional chapters that were not included in the Marshall Lectures. So we made an agreement that we should coauthor the book, and we decided on a division of labor whereby I would be responsible for certain drafting and he would be responsible for certain other drafting.

We closeted ourselves during that entire year, which was very intense for me because I was also preparing for all the rest of my examinations. We completed the manuscript in the summer of 1955, but I took it with me to Martha's Vineyard for a couple of weeks. I told Talcott that I was going to rewrite the whole thing and put it into better English. He was very gracious about it and said, "Fine. Try it. We'll see how it looks." So I rewrote all the chapters from my viewpoint as a journalist (I had worked as a journalist before going to college, you see) in an effort to make the material intelligible. And as I say, Parsons was a tremendous gentleman about accepting my revisions. It was only on one point that he objected. It had to do with chapter 5 on economic growth, which was a chapter he and I had jointly drafted. When I rewrote the chapter I tried to change its character in a fairly fundamental way. And when I showed the result to Parsons, he said to me, "Are you sure that you want to rewrite it in this manner?" And typically Parsons, he did not say that *he* objected to my rewriting but that *his daughter* objected: she didn't think it helped very much. However, I stuck to my guns and argued that my version was superior from the standpoint of readability. And Parsons accepted every change that I had made. From that point on it was simply a matter of getting the thing into production, reading the page proofs, and having the pleasure of seeing the book published when I was working away on my doctoral dissertation in England.

Q: From what I understand, it was quite exciting for you to work with Parsons on *Economy and Society*. Did you have a sense that you were making a breakthrough?

A: Yes, the whole thing was *enormously exhilirating*. And not just because I was a young person who had been singled out, prematurely you might say, in his career by someone who at that time was regarded as *the* sociologist of the twentieth century. No doubt, there was that personal dimension of it. But on top of that, there was also this tremendous excitement about ideas. The whole thing had an engaging quality that one does not very often experience in life. The ideas would flow and we would make a discovery. We would talk about Schumpeter; we would talk about Keynes; we would talk about the classics; and then we would go back to the beginning and then everything would boil over!

Q: More than thirty years have now passed since *Economy and Society* was published. What is still alive in it, in your opinion? Why should one read *Economy and Society* today?

A: Well, I would say there are several reasons. The first has to do with the fact that it is the only real statement characterizing economic theory as part of the theory of social systems. And while the theory of social systems has come under some criticism from various people, it was an absolute stroke of genius from Parsons's side to formulate economic theory as a special case of social systems theory.

At the time *Economy and Society* appeared, the economists were a little bit unfriendly to it. They didn't see what the whole point of it was. Over time, however, economists have become more friendly, and in particular as economists have begun to engage themselves in the study of economic institutions. That has been one of the major changes in economics within the past five years. In particular, the economists are interested in the institutional parameters of economic activity. Many of them have undertaken to do small group experiments in which the conditions of exchange are systematically modified. And those conditions of exchange are nothing more than the changes in the institutional definition of exchange. For example, is the exchange regarded as taking place within a barter system or within a long-term risk situation? In reconstituting the institutional parameters of economic action, the economists have discovered that the utility functions of individuals will also change in terms of their choices. This is very exciting stuff.

Q: And this line of argument, in your opinion, constitutes one of the major contributions in *Economy and Society?*

A: Yes, very much so. These economists are taking institutional variables into account and that makes it "society." Parsons and I did a thorough analysis of economic institutions in our book, and we tried to lay out the fact that exchange relations would be very different according to the institutional setup. We analyzed the consumer market, the labor market, the market for capital, and so on, while making clear that there are very different functions and utilities that go into these different kinds of exchanges. Economists are finally beginning to listen to that, and to modify their own assumptions, so that their vision of the economy has now become a view that the economy is definitely embedded in institutions, and that economic motivation cannot be understood without reference to the societal context in which it is analyzed.

So I would say that those are two of the reasons why *Economy and Society* ought still to be read: the characterization of economic theory as part of the theory of social systems, and the analysis of how economic action takes place within the context of economic institutions. A third reason is that *Economy and Society* is a landmark in the work of Talcott Parsons. He and I crystallized out the notion of system and subsystem in that work. The book was truly an important event in Parsons's way of thinking, and it never changed after we had crystallized out the ideas of subsystems, boundary exchange, and so on. All of his formulations subsequently were elaborations on what he said in this work. I should remind you, however, that our formulation was not entirely new. The idea of systems and subsystems, exchanges and equilibrium had been put forth already in Parsons's writings with Shils and Bales (see Parsons, Bales, and Shils 1953). But we brought it up to the social system level and we made it more concrete.

Q: After *Economy and Society* you kept working in economic sociology for about a decade. This was in many ways a pioneering work: you produced the first textbook in economic sociology as well as the first reader (Smelser 1963, 1965). And there was also your thesis, *Social Change in the Industrial Revolution*, which can be characterized as an example of historical economic sociology. Are there any differences between your version of economic sociology and the one that can be found in Parsons?

A: Well, with respect to my dissertation, I was responding to two types of criticism of *Economy and Society*. The first was that some people thought that the notions we put forth in *Economy and Society* could not be made empirical; that there was no way to operationalize them in terms of definite hypotheses. I was aware of these criticisms and they made a difference to my own thinking. The second criticism of Parsons's work was that there was nothing dynamic about it, that he could not analyze historical changes. So my work on my dissertation was such that I was able to make definitive empirical hypotheses and bring together a great amount of empirical material. My thesis is also a historical piece of work. As a matter of fact, historians liked it better than economists and sociologists. The book made a mark on the study of social change, and those who work in such areas as the sociology of the family, marriage, and the like often cite it.

Q: It seems to me that the attempt that Parsons, Duesenberry, Sutton, and others made in the early 1950s to get economic sociology going failed in the sense that whatever interest there was just died away in the mid-1960s. Why do you think that happened? And is it correct to see your own works in economic sociology as the end line of that attempt?

A: Yes, that is correct. One important factor is that we failed to interest economists in our own mission. And they tended to go their own merry way with respect to econometrics and other specialties in economics. And secondly, I think that there was a kind of end of the road, as far as our own efforts were concerned. Take my *Sociology of Economic Life*. It is widely regarded as a kind of definitive statement of the idea of structuring of economic behavior and institutions. In it, I pretty much exhausted the empirical literature on things like consumption, labor markets, and so on. And the question was, "Well, what do we do now?" Everybody loved it, right? But the question was, "What next?" And nobody seemed to know the answer.

Q: During the last ten or so years, you have become interested in economic sociology again. What particular topics have you looked at here?

A: The major rebirth of my interest in economic sociology came in my consideration of certain issues in higher education in the 1970s. More particularly, I was taking a look at the patterns of growth in higher education in California (see Smelser and Almond 1974). I was very much interested in the role of resources in the continuing growth of this system and in the competition for resources among the various sectors. I was absolutely astounded at the level of resources which were given to higher education in California and at the level of growth that each sector could sustain, given this pattern. At the same time I was also very much interested in how a social system, such as a system of higher education of this magnitude, could maintain itself and how competition for resources turned into a profitable line of development. So this was a continuation not only of my interest in economic resources but also of my interest in how social systems can grow and how they can come into conflict with each other when they are becoming more specialized.

Later in the 1970s, I took an interest in the market for Ph.D.s and I undertook to make an examination of that market (Smelser and Content 1980). It is a terrible market in many respects, because it doesn't behave like other markets. Practically everybody is a trade union unto himself in this matter, because the positions that academics have are so highly specialized. I was especially studying the transition from a seller's market to a buyer's market; I was studying the impact of affirmative action; and I was studying the fact that some academics were being organized into unions on that market. But above all, I wanted to make a special case study of how someone who is operating in that market is able to make strategic decisions with respect to the hiring of personnel in a department. So what I did was to analyze both the general market for academic services and then to undertake a case study as to how it worked and with respect to the filling of special positions in a specific department. So this was economic sociology from a new angle for me.

I am currently working on a very long-term project on the development of education in nineteenth-century Britain and in the United States, and I will be making much reference to the economic influences in that period. In particular, I will be interested in the family economy, and the way it shaped educational demand (or lack of demand) in that period.

Q: There is presently an attempt to revitalize economic sociology or to create a "new economic sociology." Is there something going on in economics that you think these "new economic sociologists" should be especially aware of?

A: Yes. We have a number of economists who are really raising the basic questions of our time in my opinion. And these include the question of economic interdependence, the question of the multinational corporation, and—above all—the question of international debt and its management (see Makler, Martinelli, and Smelser 1982). This means that the whole question of dependency is raised again as well as the internationalization of the world from an economic point of view. The economists are doing a lot of work in this area, but it is not altogether satisfactory because they are using the nation state as the basic unit of analysis and that is no longer advisable. However, they are particularly interested in the interdependence of economic institutions, and the role of the state in mediating these interpenetrations. And sociologists and political scientists better be aware of this development.

Numerous sociologists have undertaken to reexamine questions of dependency theory and questions of the impact of the international economy on social classes, social growth, regional differences, and so on. So economists and sociologists are really going in the same direction; they are just analyzing different facets of the same phenomena. It is also my belief that both sociologists and economists should regard the major social system of the world as the world system. Both need to point out and to analyze the ways in which this system puts constraints on national systems, and the way in which national systems cope or adapt to the exigencies of international trade and international finance. So economists and sociologists are really working hand in hand on these problems.

Q: And how do you look at "economic imperialism"? Are Becker and others making a valuable contribution in your opinion?

A: I think that particular line of analysis is fundamentally misguided. The economists of the Becker school start out from certain fundamental premises when they analyze matters like the choice of spouses or the choice of whether or not to commit a crime, and so on. That way, they impose very unrealistic assumptions on the decision-making patterns of the individuals involved. Becker, for example, believes that there is complete knowledge in the market for spouses. Every spouse who is looking for another spouse knows the market and will make his or her judgements accordingly and with respect to the economic benefits that are derived. Now, this is patently ridiculous, if you will excuse my language. In a conversation I had with Becker, I asked him, "Do we know how frequently the choice of a spouse is associated with residential propinquity or that a person is in a certain neighborhood?" You see, the pattern of spouse selection is almost completely determined by who's available and not in terms of calculations of a more or less economic sort. The calculation of whether to have children is equally nonrational from that standpoint, even though there is some reason to believe that people's calculation of whether or not to have children is economically driven.

Q: And what would your opinion be of the equivalent to economic imperialism in sociology—the rational choice type of sociology that Coleman, Hechter, and others are interested in?

A: Economics has normally involved patterns of individual choice. So economics has to do with the analysis of what is possible in life. Sociology, by contrast, has been mainly interested in examining the constraints on choice and has therefore been more geared to specifying what people cannot do or what cannot be done. Now, the move on the part of economists and others to bring rational choice back into the picture means that we have now to judge people as behaving in a rational manner and as taking their own resources and opportunities into account. I think there will be a certain amount of profit that can be gained from this type of analysis with its focus on individual and collective choice. At the same time there are great limitations to it.

James Coleman has indeed asked that sociology be rewritten, analyzing people's choices from the standpoint of rationality. I had a conversation with Coleman in Germany about a year ago in which we disagreed about this. I had written a paper in which I was making an argument that people coping with the external environment could be analyzed in the same terms as people coping with their own internal defenses. When I brought this to Coleman's attention, he resisted this line of analysis very much. Instead he made an effort to make me say that even though people were engaging in denial and repression and so on, they were still fundamentally behaving in ways that could be seen as rational. My response to that was that in that case surely *everybody* behaves rationally, because everybody is engaging in whatever line of action is possible for them. So I think that we cannot get away from the notion of the intrusion of fundamental nonrational elements in choice behavior, individual as well as collective.

Q: The concept of rationality is a key concept in economics, while it is less used in sociology. In an article you wrote some years ago, entitled "On The Relevance of Economic Sociology to Economists," you argued that there exist several notions of rationality and not just one. Could you explain that a bit?

A: I regard economic rationality as what I would call a creative simplification of the motivational characteristics of individuals. It's a simplification in the sense that it allows the economists to calculate on the basis of economic variables alone. And in this sense, systems of rationality have a real place in the world, even though they are based on a number of simplifying premises.

In the article you referred to, I came out with the view that "economic rationality" is only one form of rationality and that there also exist other forms. In particular, I picked up on Weber and took the view that there exists such a thing as "communal rationality" or that people in certain cases will behave on the basis of their particularistic ties to others insofar as the allocation of goods and services is concerned. The best model of this is of course the family, but there also exist other modes of communal rationality. Another type of rationality would be "ecological rationality," which would be aimed at preserving economic resources in the face of overutilization. My conclusion in that article was that because there are so many forms of rationality, the key problem for social science investigators is to see how these rationalities mesh with one another; how they conflict with one another; and how new kinds of rationality may emerge because people always have to weigh their priorities.

It's just not possible to simply rely on the results of economic rationality to understand the processes of collective choice and so on. You also have to take into account that there is a whole range of rationalities and that this range is such that, in order to understand how people behave in the modern world, you have to develop a superrationality. I have not found this view to be challenged by anybody, and I regard it as the key to our understanding of most decision making within social systems these days.

Q: You are the author of one of the few studies in economic sociology of a more historical type, *Social Change in the Industrial Revolution*. How do you see the relationship between economic history and economic sociology?

A: I regard economic history as being the history of economic institutions, and we simply cannot understand the character of institutionalized economic life without taking into account the history of banks, the history of firms, the history of families, and so on. Economic theorists have not been very good as historians. They tend to regard history as something which is a parameter to their own activities, and they have just not taken it seriously. I believe that a true economic sociology has to engage in the study of historical specifics and in the evolution of economic institutions in relation to other institutions.

Q: From a historical viewpoint, there have been two attempts to get economic sociology going: one around the turn of the century and one in the 1950s. Both of these failed. Today there's a third one going on. What needs to be done, in your opinion, in order to ensure the success of this third attempt?

A: I regard the future of economic sociology as resting mainly in the analysis of international economic institutions. We who work in the field of social analysis have forever regarded the basic unit of analysis as being "culture," "the nation," or "the state." But it is becoming increasingly clear all the time that these are not the basic units of analysis any more. The world is nowadays to a large extent organized on the basis of economic institutions that are international, and there are new levels of cultural and normative understanding with respect to international interaction and co-operation. There has also been an enormous spread internationally of the culture of modernization. It seems to me that when we, as social scientists, get a proper hold of the internationalization of the economy, we will be able to dig in and understand the true dynamics of economic life in the modern post-capitalistic world.

Note that everybody is involved in this process of economic internationalization. You do not find one nation in the world, including the Soviet Union, which doesn't partake of the world of international institutions because insofar as they buy into these institutions, they become part of them. The Soviet Union may fairly well dictate the price of grain in the world, but insofar as it has to pay for this grain with dollars, they are forever sensitive to changes in the international market and forever involved in making their institutions more internationally competitive. The same is true for the other socialist countries and also for Japan. I believe that it is not an oversimplification to say that we are living in an international world, and that we have to understand the character of international institutions in order to determine the fate of the world. And this represents an opportunity and a challenge to economists and sociologists and political scientists alike.

References

Makler, Harry, Alberto Martinelli, and Neil J. Smelser, eds. 1982. *The New International Economy*. Beverly Hills, Calif.: SAGE Publications.

Parson, Talcott. 1986. "The Marshall Lectures (1953)." *Research Reports from the Department of Sociology, Uppsala University* 1986:4.

Parsons, Talcott, and Neil J. Smelser. 1956. *Economy and Society: A Study in the Integration of Economic and Social Theory*. New York: Free Press.

Parsons, Talcott, Robert F. Bales, and Edward A. Shils, eds. 1953. *Working Papers in the Theory of Action*. New York: Free Press.

Parsons, Talcott, et al. 1955. *Family, Socialization, and Interaction Process*. New York: Free Press.

Smelser, Neil J. 1954. Letter to Talcott Parsons, March 10. Harvard University Archives, HUG(FP) 42.8.4 box 2, folder "Smelser."

———. 1959. *Social Change in the Industrial Revolution: An Application of Theory to the British Cotton Industry*. Chicago: University of Chicago Press.

———. 1963. *The Sociology of Economic Life*. Englewood Cliffs, N.J.: Prentice-Hall. 2d revised ed. 1976.

———, ed. 1965. *Readings on Economic Sociology*. Englewood Cliffs, N.J.: Prentice-Hall.

———. 1969. "Some Personal Thoughts on the Pursuit of Sociological Problems."
Sociological Inquiry 39:155–67.

———. 1976. "On the Relevance of Economic Sociology for Economics." In *Economics and Sociology: Towards an Integration*, edited by Tjerk Huppes, 1–26.
Leiden: Martinus Nijhoff.

———. 1981. "On Collaborating with Talcott Parsons: Some Intellectual and Personal Notes." *Sociological Inquiry* 51:143–54.

Smelser, Neil J., and Gabriel Almond, eds. 1974. *Public Higher Education in California.* Berkeley: University of California Press.

Smelser, Neil J., and Robin Content. 1980. *The Changing Academic Market: General Trends and a Berkeley Case Study.* Berkeley: University of California Press.

Who's Who in America 1986–1987. 1986. Chicago: Marquis Who's Who.

III The Commentators

12

Daniel Bell

IN MANY of his well-known sociological works from the 1950s and there-after, Daniel Bell has written on key economic issues in contemporary society.[1] Two of his many contributions in this respect are *The Coming of Post-Industrial Society*, and *The Cultural Contradictions of Capitalism*. In 1981, he and Irving Kristol edited a book of contributed essays on the theme of "the crisis in economic theory." In his own article in this volume, Bell suggests that an "interpretative economic theory" may be needed for the reconstruction of economic theory. And such a theory, he says, "might have to consider that its own analysis only makes economic sense when joined to sociology."

In this interview, Bell tells about the various stages in his education in economics—as a young boy reading Marx, as a graduate student at Columbia University, and as a junior faculty member at the University of Chicago. He discusses the strengths and weaknesses of neoclassical theory, as well as his own "interpretative economic theory" and its relationship to "the public household." Bell also addresses the question of what he considers to be the most crucial social and economic issues of the future.

Daniel Bell was born in 1919 in a working class family. He earned his B.S. from City College in New York in 1938, and his Ph.D. in 1960 from Columbia University. In the early 1940s, Bell was first staff writer and then managing editor of *The New Leader*. He taught at the University of Chicago from 1945 to 1948; from 1948 to 1958, he was Labor Editor of *Fortune* magazine, and was an adjunct professor at Columbia from 1952 to 1956. In 1958, he returned to full-time academic life, first at Columbia, from 1959 to 1969, and then as a professor at Harvard University where, in 1980, he was named the Henry Ford II Professor of the Social Sciences.

•

The following interview with Daniel Bell was conducted on May 10, 1988, in his office in William James Hall at Harvard University in Cambridge, Massachusetts.

[1] The following information comes from Brick 1986; Bell 1979; and *Who's Who in America*.

Q: Although you are a sociologist, I get the impression that you have always been interested in economics. Actually, a couple of days ago I met one of your biographers and he told me that you had already read John Stuart Mill's *Principles of Political Economy* at the age of twelve!

A: Well, that's somewhat off. I got interested in economics for a very obvious reason, namely, I joined the socialist movement at the age of thirteen. I was living then in New York, on the Lower East Side. My father had died when I was an infant, and my mother worked in a factory. She was a member of the Ladies' Garment Workers Union (ILGWU). The home milieu was socialist and trade union. My mother was not active politically. She was an immigrant Jewish woman who was literate in Yiddish, though not in English. But she was a member of the union, and the union, so to speak, was a natural fact of my life from the beginning.

So at the age of thirteen I joined the socialist movement, and inevitably one goes to socialist study groups. And here I read various works, such as Fred Henderson's *Case for Socialism*. Some pamphlets by Marx were also obligatory. The two I especially remember are *Wage-Labor and Capital* and *Value, Price and Profit*. At that time I also lived near a public library called the Ottendorfer Library, which had open stacks. And here I browsed, coming across John Stuart Mill, Herbert Spencer, and other authors. I would take them out and read them because that is part of the impetus of a socialist study circle. I also went to the Rand School, which was the socialist school in New York. It was on Fifteenth Street, near Fifth Avenue. Its full name was The Rand School of Social Science, and it had various types of classes: adult education classes, classes for the young, and so on. It was a full educational venture. There was one course in *Capital* which I took and where we read an abridged version of Marx's work, done by a man named Julian Borchardt with an introduction by Max Eastman (see Marx 1932). I remember this edition vividly because the abridgement tended to concentrate on the descriptive material—on the lengthening of the working day, on exploitation, on agricultural labor, and so on. This made it all very vivid, of course, but I would think, "What is going on here? What makes it a system?"

Q: Did you ever get an opportunity to study economics when you were a student at CCNY and Columbia?

A: There were two main immersions in economics, so to speak. The first was during the years I was a graduate student at Columbia, and the second some years later at Chicago. When I began in 1939 at Columbia, one was required to have a minor field as well as a major concentration, and my minor field was economics. I took several courses in economics at Columbia. I took courses from John Maurice Clark, the son of John Bates Clark, from an English woman named Eveline Burns and her husband Arthur R. Burns (not the more flamboyant Arthur Burns of later fame). These two were also connected to the National Bureau of Economic Research, which had been started at Columbia by Wesley Clair Mitchell. I also took work with a man named Leo Wolman, who had begun as an economist for the Amalgamated Clothing Workers Union, but had turned very conservative.

So I did get a background in economics as a graduate student. This was at the time before mathematical economics had come into the picture. In fact, two of my City College classmates were William Baumol and Kenneth Arrow, both of which I only knew vaguely. Arrow went to Columbia, but was very dissatisfied with the courses because of his mathematical background. Except for Harold Hotelling, there was no one at Columbia who did mathematical analysis. Hotelling's work was basically in statistical theory. People at Columbia were quantitative but in the empirical Mitchell style. Simon Kuznets, for example, did quantitative and empirical work and so did Milton Friedman at the Bureau. I remember Friedman did a famous study of the income of dentists as a National Bureau study.

Independently of my work in economic theory and probably because of my background and interest in Marxian theory, I also developed a fascination with economic history during this time. There is especially one book I remember very vividly: Karl Bücher's *Industrial Evolution*. This was the classic work in historical economics and I remember it as a kind of proto-Polanyi. No, it would be wrong to say that; it's rather the other way around: Polanyi was influenced by Bücher. I also read Sombart's *The Social Movement in the Nineteenth Century*, and other of the early Sombart's great works.

A third influence at Columbia was through a man whose name is almost entirely forgotten, but who was a very brilliant person: Alexander von Schelting. Von Schelting was a sociologist and a student of Max Weber's, who had written one of the first major works on Max Weber's methodology (von Schelting 1934). He was at Columbia in 1939 and I was fortunate enough to have him as a teacher. We spent the entire term on the two first chapters of Weber's *Wirtschaft und Gesellschaft*, mostly on the definitions of economic and rational actions. I learned from von Schelting something which few people know, namely, that these chapters were written last and that they were basically efforts at formalization. While people always think of Weber in terms of subjectivity—the notion of *Verstehen*—what Weber was doing was to set up an *objective* set of "meaning" categories. There are the four basic meaning complexes—*wertrational, zweckrational*, affectual, and traditional—towards which all action is oriented. In effect, Weber had moved away from the "subjectivity" which is how most commentators still read Weber, to some logical constructs of "meaning." And he thought that these categories could encompass all the relevant kinds of meaning and be the basis for a "general" theory of action. Through von Schelting I had this detailed immersion in Weber. And this was independently of Parsons, who incidentally reviewed von Schelting's book for *The American Sociological Review* (Parsons 1936). But otherwise, von Schelting left no trace behind in the United States. He taught for a year at Columbia and then he went back to Basel, Switzerland. Von Schelting subsequently wrote a book, *Russland und Europa im russischen Geschichtsdenken*, which is still a useful book to read since it works out—one of the very few books to do so—Weber's remarks on the character of patrimonial bureaucracy which was the dominant feature of Russian society.

My second immersion in economics came when I went to Chicago in 1945 to teach. My appointment was in the College, which had a unique arrangement. There were no "departments," but one was a member of a divison such as "social sciences," "humanities," etc. And there were no individual courses, but common staff-designed courses. In the social sciences, there were three year-long courses which students took in sequence. All attended the common lectures, which were given by the staff; all read the same books, though each instructor had several small discussion sections. Those were heady years because of the caliber of the staff that had been assembled. In the Social Sciences 2 course—Michael Schudson subsequently wrote a history of that endeavor—there was Edward Shils, David Riesman, Milton Singer, Morris Janowitz, Sylvia Thrupp, W. W. Cooper, and others (Schudson 1989). Shils gave the Weber lectures, Riesman the Freud lectures, and I gave the Marx lectures.

The syllabus was divided by semesters. The first part of the course was basically great theorists and their ways of thinking. We read Malthus on demography, Veblen on technology, Weber on values and the Protestant ethic, Marx on social structure, and I think Maine on law. That was the first semester. The second semester was on economic analysis. The basic readings included two things by Frank Knight. First there was his marvelous brochure called *The Social and Economic Organization* (see Knight 1965). Its main theme was very much like Parsons's idea of functional requisites. What Knight argued was that in every economy certain main functions have to be performed—such as the organization of production, of distribution, and so on. We also read parts of *Risk, Uncertainty and Profit*. To some extent, Knight himself had a skeptical view of classical and neoclassical economics. In fact, in the election of 1932, Knight voted communist. That was during the Depression; people don't know this.

Well, Knight was a very extraordinary man. And there were others like him in Chicago, who were unorthodox in their own way. Henry Simons, for example, wrote on syndicalism and wage theory (see Simons 1944). We also read Hicks's book on national income analysis, where the American part was done by Albert Hart (Hicks and Hart 1945). I think it was the first time that national income analysis was taught in an American college.

So for three years I taught economics at Chicago. I was always just one step ahead of the class, my head stuffed with cobweb models, the turnpike theorem, multipliers, and all that. And I learned a fundamental lesson: if you want to learn something, teach! Simply having to prepare for class forces you to think through what is the essential part. People have asked me over the years, "What do you teach?" And I say, "I teach what I want to learn, and I write what I have learned."

Q: In some of your writings you are quite critical of neoclassical thinking. So where does neoclassical economics go wrong, in your opinion? Is it by ignoring certain important topics—say, economic change, which you have written quite a bit about—or is it rather by using too unrealistic assumptions?

A: Well, I don't criticize neoclassical economics; I appreciate it very much. In fact, I always insist that my students learn some economics, because neoclassical economics is the one discipline in the social sciences which has a self-contained set of concepts and a basic logic, which is organized in a deductive form. And therefore it is an important way of thinking.

Very early I also realized one fundamental fact—and this I think is the difference between sociology and economics or at least neoclassical economics—and that is that *neoclassical economics detaches itself from institutions.* What's involved is the shift from "moral economy" to "political economy" to "economics." And by detaching itself from institutions, economics follows the model of classical mechanics in the sense that you don't deal with concrete bodies but with abstract properties—mass, velocity, etc.—and the equations among these, which can then be applied to any concrete body. Now, in detaching itself from institutions in this way, neoclassical economics becomes a very powerful body of concepts. The real problem is the way back. How do you go back from the model, with its self-contained system of premises, and apply it to the real world?

If I can generalize, there are several problems with neoclassical theory, if one is using it for analysis and policy. The first (as I argued in Deutsch, Markovits, and Platt 1986), is that a model is not a map. A model gives one powerful simplifications, but unless one can assume that the model can be used as a "zoom lens," as in fractals, for economic policy you want a map rather than a model. You are, so to speak, on the ground and not in the sky. The second, more important problem, is that a model—for that matter any science—assumes stable relationships that hold over time. Utility preference theory and rational choice theory assume stable relationships in their assumptions as to how people act, namely the principle of ordering preferences, or optimization and the like. Yet one of the difficulties in formulating economic policy in recent years is that the "traditional" stabilities have not held. For example, Milton Friedman has argued that the quantity theory of money is a "law," the closest thing in economics, in fact, to a law in physics. This is why he formulates the policy that any government should regulate its money supply by a fixed rule. Yet some recent studies by Benjamin Friedman of Harvard have shown the collapse of relationships connecting money to both income and prices. The *fastest* money growth since World War II, maintained for more than half a decade, occurred in conjunction with the greatest postwar *reduction* in inflation. As Ben Friedman points out, inflation predictions based on money growth failed altogether to anticipate the most significant monetary policy successes (see Friedman 1988).

These are some of the reasons why I have argued—in my essay on "Models and Reality in Economic Discourse" (Bell 1981)—that we ought to think of neoclassical *theory* as a a kind of *als-ob*, an as-if, an ideal type of *rational* behavior, what economic life would be like *if* people acted that way, or as a "standard" against which to measure actual behavior. Note, however, that sometimes people may act in ways that match the ideal either because they are socialized into such behavior, or because the system rewards them for acting that way. But that does not mean that such behavior is *intrinsic* to social actions.

Now this argument about intrinsic behavior goes back to some epistemological issues, with which I have been occasionally concerned in recent years (see Bell 1978b). It is an effort to use a distinction that goes back to Kant, or the reworking of Kant, that phenomena are either *constitutive* or *constructed*. (Kant used "regulative" for the latter, which is more ambiguous or sociologically more amorphous.) Constitutive phenomena have an intrinsic order which are "in the nature of things," though they may be difficult to discern, such as the periodic table in chemistry or the particle structure of matter, while constructed phenomena are socially defined. Thus, sex is constitutive in that it is anatomically based, though *gender*, the roles that people take, are socially defined. Economists tend to act as if the economic phenomena are constitutive of reality, and this is certainly true of the positivists like Milton Friedman, with his statement, for example, about the quantity theory of money. Yet economic behavior is more widely variable, as economists have found out when dealing with labor markets, wage theory and the like, where terms like *habits, traditional arrangements, institutions,* creep in by the back door. True, the social world is not entirely constructed. There are constraints which limit the range of actions. Much of economic behavior is shaped or limited by those constraints. But culture is much less so.

Q: So one could say that you are an institutionalist economist with sympathies for neoclassical economics?

A: Well, when I think of my own relationship to economics, I would say it is different on different levels. I am clearly interested in institutional settings: I am interested in the history of institutions, in the development of institutions, and in the ways in which they shape or reward preferences. Economists now begin to think more and more in these terms and move towards that perspective. But by and large they take preferences as *givens* and do not ask about the way they are formed.

Economic theory interests me most as a kind of *als-ob*, as an ideal type against which one can measure empirical aspects of social life. This goes back to something I think Samuelson has written about, namely, that economics deals with rational action while sociology deals with nonrational action. Now, that's a too simple distinction, but it is useful in that it at least points to some of the differences which are involved.

The one man that tried to bridge that gap between economics and sociology, interestingly enough, was Pareto. And he did it, of course, because he began as an engineer before he became an economist. As an economist, succeeding Walras at Lausanne, Pareto formalized the general equilibrium theory (*pace* Arrow and Debreu) and felt he knew all about the circulation of goods. He then turned to sociology to use the same methods to chart the circulation of elites. Pareto felt he could classify and map the sentiments and derivations and residues—the sources of nonrational behavior—to create a general theory of sociology. But the entire effort fell apart and what remained was a rich pudding of illustration and observation and generalization, but other than the scaffolding, no coherence.

Q: Isn't Pareto's argument about the difference between economics and sociology misleading in the sense that sociology only gets to deal with the nonrational sides of social life? Weber's argument that one of the key categories in sociology is rational social action seems superior to me.

A: True. But there is also an element in Weber, which is implicit and rarely explicated—except toward the end of some of his books—that there is always an irrational component to rational action. One finds it in the very concept of rationalization—that everything is becoming rationalized. When all behavior becomes completely rationalized, it often loses its bearings or ultimate meanings, because everything becomes subordinated to those "rational means." That is the meaning of the distinction between *Wertrationalität* and *Zweckrationalität*. Someone like Karl Mannheim accepts this distinction and concludes that it is "functional rationality" and not "substantial rationality" that is ruling the world. Or the Frankfurt School's argument that functional rationality dehumanizes people.

So what Weber says is that rationalization carried too far becomes irrational. To some extent this is also central in Dewey, namely, in Dewey's distinction between means and ends; or when he makes the obvious point that means and ends are inextricable from one another. When means become ends in themselves, they begin to have a nonrational element to them. So it is indeed true that Weber has all these notions of rational law, rational economics, rational accounting, and so on. But there is also the implicit notion that if these are too strongly followed, so to speak, they will in the end become nonrational.

Q: In your essay "Models and Reality in Economic Discourse" from 1981, you speak of the need for what you call "an interpretative economic theory." What exactly did you have in mind here? Perhaps a form of economic sociology?

A: No, I don't think I had economic sociology in mind when I wrote that. It was basically an effort to shift the starting point back to values in economics, to normative theory, and to say in effect: if you are going to have an ideal type model of rational action, why the conventional one? What other ones would be possible, if the value systems of society were somehow different? In a sense, all of this goes back to this idea of mine of a "public household," which is ultimately inspired by Aristotle (see Bell 1978c). Aristotle is writing a "moral economy," in which the family or the domestic household is the *ur* unit that should be replicated in the larger economy. That is what I call "the public household"—that we should conceive of our sense of obligations to each other as being members of a large communal body. Thus, it is not the conventional distinction between public and private, but a concept that embraces both, at least in the economic realm.

My ideas here are connected to the fact that I am a socialist in economics, a liberal in politics, and a conservative in culture. I am a socialist in economics because I believe that people can only identify with society if the society feels a responsibility to them. As a starting point, no society—to the extent that it is possible—should allow involuntary unemployment. So there should be a priority in the social policy to limit involuntary unemployment. What about the argument that one first needs to create wealth? Well, at various times wealth creation becomes a more important point if you have gone too far in the other direction. But the idea of public household basically means that the claims of the community are prior to other claims.

Q: So the theory of the public household is directly tied to a form of responsible capitalism?

A: Well, I think of it more as a socialist market model. I do believe in the market, but only within the framework of social goals. I have been influenced on this point by Abba Lerner, whose work I came in contact with in the 1940s, when I was the managing editor of *The New Leader*. I ran five articles by him in *The New Leader* in which he put forth various ideas that became elaborated in his *Economics of Control*. But the idea itself also has obvious parallels in Catholic social theory with its notion of a just price, a family wage, and so on. I may not share the exact premises of Catholic social thinkers like Heinrich Pesch and others, but at least they try to think in terms of other kinds of economic systems. So the important thing for me is to try to focus on a set of values, which I call "the public household," and on the institutional structures which could reinforce these.

Q: What is your opinion of economic imperialism and its prospects? And as an intellectual historian, what is your reaction to the argument that economic imperialism is an ideology of the conservative 1970s?

A: Well, I have never liked that type of easy correlation between context and ideology. It can be misleading because the ideas may have had a long history. The problem is rather, why has it got attention at the time it has? There is also the fact of the exhaustion of old ideas and the power of the new one. (In painting this happened when Cézanne broke the whole notion of the picture plane.) And even though Gary Becker is a conservative as such, I am sure that the crucial impetus in his case has been the possibility of developing a powerful idea. The basic appeal of Becker's model is its simplicity. So much of behavior is reduced to a utility preference, cost-benefit assessment. One need not worry about culture or politics; it is very *economistic*. Thus, his work may appeal to people with an anti-sociological bias, who will read it and say, "Well, here we are!" I remember an argument I had many years ago at Columbia with Sidney Morgenbesser who, always playing the devil, said, "I can destroy all of sociology with utility theory! All I need is a good ordering of the utility preferences and that takes care of everything!" Well, this is obviously the appeal of economic imperialism: it is a powerful idea with a lot of applications. And therefore it gets a lot of response.

Will it last? Here it seems to me it is a question of what it finds out. There is always a danger of over-enthusiasm. An obvious example of this is game theory. Years ago people thought that game theory would be the answer to everything. Its appeal was enormous and people like Lloyd Shapley went gung-ho with it. Serious writers like Tom Schelling applied it to international relations, Martin Shubik thought one could model almost all economic behavior in game theory terms, and Kenneth Boulding sought to elaborate a general theory of conflict on the basis of game theory. But pretty quickly you find that the best part of a theory gets absorbed into language and people say, "So, what's the big deal?" The theory loses its ability to shock and surprise. That's what has happened with much of Marxism: to think of the world in terms of power, property, and class is nowadays more or less taken for granted. And I think the same will happen with Becker and with rational choice. Ultimately, intellectual power is in the strength of the idea, its rigor, logically formalized. But so often the results of these revolutionary ideas do not always live up to their promises. And in this specific case I think the limiting factor has to do with what I said before about the difference between the constitutive and the constructed order. If you have a constitutive order you can show functional relationships, but otherwise you need great stability over time.

And this stability is absolutely crucial. Let me illustrate this with an anecdote. Some years ago—I can't remember exactly what year it was—the Bank of America asked Otto Eckstein to do a simulation of the American economy at a ten percent inflation rate for ten years. Everybody said, "But that's crazy! A ten percent inflation rate for ten years!" But Otto did it, and then they asked him and two other people to interpret the results: myself, Otto and Andrew Brimmer from the Federal Reserve. And Tom Clausen from the Bank of America said to Otto, "I know what you do. You give me all these equations that break my skull." And then he turned to Andrew: "And I know what you do too. You come from the Federal Reserve and you'll tell me why the Fed is not going to like what we are going to propose." And then he turned to me and asked, "What do you do?" And I said, "I am the exogenous variable." So he said, "What's the exogenous situation here." I replied, "The falsity of the question is to ask for a simulation rate of ten percent inflation rate." He said, "Why? Is the figure wrong?" So I said, "No, it's not that the figure is wrong. The problem is not so much the level or the rate, as the stability. The real problem with inflation, especially in this country since people have never had any experience with it, is its up-and-down quality, its yo-yo effects, its uncertainty."

This is, in fact, what gave rise to the rational expectations approach. The weakness of the existing econometric models is that they use lagged variables, and assume that the behavior of the past will remain stable in the future. Having done work in forecasting, one of the first things you learn is that there are systems breaks and all kinds of surprises. So what Robert Lucas therefore tried to do was not to use lagged variables but to put very sophisticated forms of expectations into his models which would negate or not negate each other through market clearing mechanisms. But there is a difficulty even here, and to put it in my own language: if the political discount rate is higher than the economic discount rate, then you are in trouble! You may raise the discount rate even to 15 percent, but if people know that in the next election you are not going to stick to it, there will be trouble. So until the political discount rate can match the economic discount rate, economics is not going to work or the various econometric models are not going to work.

Q: And what is your opinion about the attempt by people like Jim Coleman and others to introduce rational choice into sociology? Will they be able to make the breakthrough they are hoping for?

A: Well, I haven't really immersed myself in the rational choice literature. On one level, however, I think rational choice sociology can be seen as a move from metaphors to formalism. There are sociologists as well as other people—Clifford Geertz would be the obvious example—who think in terms of metaphors or symbolic rules. And there are others who try to formalize and who are more logically inclined. Coleman is an example of the latter, coming as he does out of an engineering background. Elster is another. But you see I never felt—and this might be where I am a man of my own temperament—that one is wrong and the other is right. The problem for me, and this goes back to my epistemological concerns I mentioned earlier, is that it is not a matter of either/or, of an interpretative versus a behaviorist/positivist approach, but which kinds of problems and issues lend themselves to what approach. Where phenomena tend towards the constitutive, and one can discern lawlike behavior, one can use a positivist methodology. Where the phenomena are largely socially constructed or symbolic, one may seek an interpretative approach. It may be that my distinctions are correct. Or it may also be my "Menshevik" temperament that seeks such accommodations!

To my mind it is also clear that the assumption of rationality is culturally shaped, and the way someone like Jim Coleman is moving away from this standpoint would be a problem for me. When you look at the values that are usually associated with the assumption of rationality, you clearly have to ask: Would these be valid also in other societies? Would they for example be valid in Muslim societies, which are strictly religious and orthodox? I would have to say "no," because they have different criteria of rationality in these societies and therefore use different rules. So rationality is quite specific to the cultural milieu.

In fact, there is a footnote in Weber's *General Economic History* in which he raises this exact question (Weber 1961, 265, 276). If you want to build a railroad in modern Western society, how do you do it? Well, it's a straight line. But what if there is a cemetery in the way? What do you do then? In traditional China, for example, you go around it, because you have respect for your ancestors. Is that nonrational? Well, from the viewpoint of the criteria that are usually put forth in rational choice, it is. And yet it is rational within the context of the Chinese way of life. This doesn't mean that rational choice is wrong. But it limits the applicability and power of this kind of approach.

But something else is at stake in the turn to the "rational choice" approach, if I think of Coleman, or Jon Elster, or Michael Hechter among its practitioners; this is the appeal of "methodological individualism" and the rejection of "collective concepts." Clearly, if one is oriented to behavior or actions, then it may be more fruitful to think of actors (even collective actors) in individual terms, for there is a danger of falling (as Durkheim almost did) into the fallacy of a "group mind." And the orientation to actors is the influence of microeconomics, which has become central once again for the economists. But if one thinks of "ritual" or "traditions" or "styles" or "collective memory"—the nutrients of culture—to which individuals respond, then a rational choice is somewhat deficient in understanding the deposits of human actions. To me there is something ironic in Jon Elster "making sense of Marx" in terms of methodological individualism (*pace* F. A. Hayek). It is like going from the "macro-Marx" to the "micro-Marx."

Q: If you were to compare economists and sociologists, what would your opinion be? For example, are economists better and brighter than sociologists?

A: I don't know if they are better and brighter. But they have a set of problems, which they can define in more exact ways, and they also have a set of tools, which they can apply to these problems. And therefore they can come up with answers. The tricky problem is of course how long and how well will these answers hold up? But regardless of that, economists can come up with answers better and faster than other people. Through the help of indifference curves, inelasticities, and so on, you can begin to deal with behavior much more quickly than sociologists, who are doing survey research, for example. The fact that you can put the economic problem more directly in mathematical form also allows you to manipulate the relations more directly.

It seems to me that economics has two advantages over sociology, though these have their limitations as well. One is that economics has a convertible metric: one can take the price of a pound of potatoes and a pound of automobile and put these into a single index to make comparisons over time. But what metric is there for the "convertability" of wealth, status, and power into comparative measures of relative standing? The second is that, not only is there a metric, but one can make the units homogenous, aggregate these, and in respect to the rates of change use the calculus. The limitation, however, is that it is difficult to build heterogeneity into such models. I recall a correspondence with Robert J. Gordon a number of years ago, following an article by him (in the *Journal of Economic Literature*, I think), where he was grappling, unsuccessfully he admitted, with building heterogeneity into wage theory and labor markets.

But I should also add that I think that there is a hierarchy of simplicity, so to speak, in the sciences. Maybe this will startle people. Anyway, I think that intellectually the easiest subject is physics, because you are dealing with a very complicated puzzle but it is not going to bark at you and bite you. And if you are a very ingenious puzzle solver, you can work out all the equations. Economics is below physics in what I call the major constitutive phenomenon order, because also here you can make things homogenous; you can aggregate them; you have a metric; and so on. Sociology, on the other hand, stands outside this order.

Now, people like Coleman and others are understandably trying to convert sociology into the same order of things as physics and economics. And so did Parsons, you know. But Parsons did it on the level of metaphors—with his AGIL scheme, pattern variables, etc.—and he lacked the metric and the element of homogeneity. But the logic was the same; the idea was to detach the sociological analysis from institutions and to get a set of concepts which would apply to any set of institutions.

To me the main difficulty here is that I don't think that sociology should do this and can do this. Or rather the other way around: it can't and it shouldn't. Sociology, in my opinion, is caught in between economics on the one hand, which can formalize, and history, on the other, which is ultimately idiosyncratic and particular. So sociology is therefore what I would call "sociographic," which means that it has to be soft and imperfect (see Bell 1978b).

Q: But doesn't sociology also have certain advantages over economic theory? One would be its sensitivity to the social elements—something that neoclassical economics seems to lack.

A: Well, I would differ in this respect: economic theory, curiously enough, is very sensitive and responsive to social elements. It reacts to the social in interesting ways, which also reveals some of its limitations. It is true that when I studied economics as a graduate student, it was at a time when economics seemed to be almost sterile. You read people like John Bates Clark on marginal productivity and so on. It was all very abstract, and economists like Eli Ginzberg and the empiricists were very impatient with it. But what happened after that, it seems to me, is that economics has been very sensitive to social developments in ways that sociology has not. Much of it was due to postwar developments once the economists felt confident that they could "manage" economies.

Let me give you two illustrations. The first is growth theory in economics. Economic growth has been a major area in economics. After World War II there was a huge spate of development plans, and people like W. Arthur Lewis, Hicks, and Kuznets were doing work in this field. Now, sociology responded with modernization theory, which was just a vague sort of ragbag of things. I am not saying that growth theory is successful, but the economists worked at it more assiduously than the sociologists did.

The other area, of course, is welfare theory. Here Pareto did pioneering work, which was almost entirely forgotten till Abe Bergson rediscovered it. So he and Ian Little and various other people did a huge amount of work on welfare theory. The tools they used were very powerful, but limiting because again there was this exclusive concentration on the allocative means problems while the contextual element of the values and other social elements, which inform the way people behave, was ignored. Still, interestingly enough, the economists went into growth theory and welfare theory well ahead of the sociologists. And some of the best work today on social behavior is being done by economists. I think of the work by Thomas Schelling on self-command as one example.

Q: Since forecasting is one of your specialties, I would like to ask you which economic problems you think will be the most important ones in the future. And are economists and sociologists likely to cooperate in their attempts to understand these problems?

A: Well, that's the same as asking, "Where do you think the world is going!" Let me start with recalling some lectures I gave at Keio University in Japan about ten years ago. In these I said that the big problem for sociology at the beginning of the twentieth century was why capitalism had been so successful in the West, and not in the Orient. Max Weber of course gave the answer: you needed something strong enough to break the bonds of traditionalism and to foster individualism, mobility, and so on. The question at the end of the twentieth century is a different one. It is: Why is capitalism so successful in Japan? Japan is traditionalist; there is little mobility; and the culture is not individualistic. The rise of East Asia as an economic force in the last quarter of the twentieth century raises, once again, the relation of culture to economy. Weber's answer may have been true for the West, but it does not apply to Japan and China. We need some new structures of explanations.

Given that context, let me say something about two other problems, which are very different from each other. One is the new framework of economic relations in the areas of production, trade, and capital. If one looks at production—and here I follow the work of Charles Sabel—the new production technologies are breaking up the old industrial society (see Piore and Sabel 1984). The new production technologies emphasize small scales and regionalization, customization, and adaptability. But the structure of trade and exchange, of capital and currency, on the other hand, are becoming more worldwide and integrated. So what you have is a mismatch of scales. Actually, it is even more complicated than that. Production is becoming more *local and regional;* trade is becoming more *continental;* and capital and currency markets are becoming more *international.* So you're going to get continental economies of scale, regional economies for production, and international economies for capital and currencies. And where will the national state be? It is caught in between all these conflicting elements.

The real problem here, from an intellectual viewpoint, is to develop some conceptual tools which can deal with these processes operating on different scales. And few sociologists are working on this. That's a pity because this is an area where you could actually have a really fruitful interaction between economics and sociology in a way that was not possible earlier. Both are needed to understand different aspects of this new set of phenomena.

The second area represents a totally different kind of problem. It is actually a very old problem which is returning in post-industrial society in a much sharper form, namely, how do you value what people do? How do I determine what your labor is worth, and what my labor is worth? A couple of years ago, for example, there was a case that went to the courts in the state of Washington. The nurses said that the teamsters were getting twice as much as they were; what's the comparable worth of our labor against theirs? Well, you say, you can apply market principles. But the problem is that what the teamsters got wasn't a market price; it had been negotiated on the basis of the monopoly power of the union.

The question that is raised here is the larger question of what are the rules for rewards on a just basis in the court of the good society? The market gives you efficiency in terms of relative scarcity and such, but is it just? Well, that's a question. If you use administrative mechanisms, how do you determine salaries? Are there technocratic rules for measurement which say: This job is worth X points and that job is worth Y points? If you just take monetary awards: Should the executive get fifty thousand dollars more than the common laborer? Should the general get thirty thousand dollars more than the private?

Well, these, it seems to me, are issues of the type that will increasingly come forth. They have come forth most strongly among women, because of the historical discrimination against women in terms of wage structure, and therefore the question of comparable worth has become a focal element in the equality for women. But there is also a more general principle involved here, which goes back to the Catholic theory of a just price versus a market wage and a market price, what in post-industrial segments I would call a knowledge theory of value.

So in response to your question, those would be two main areas that need work. One goes back to the normative question of rewards and distribution, based on the reciprocity between individuals. And the other is essentially about the organization of society under the impact of the new technologies and the new scales. There will be conflicts between the different production systems, the different trade systems, and the different capital systems. And it will be especially hard for the polity. It will face the pressures of markets and economic activities which no longer mesh harmoniously with what they do. So something is bound to crack.

Q: Is there some final summary to this?

A: Yes. It goes back to my gnomic statement that we need some new conceptual frameworks to understand world society in the next century. This past spring I gave a paper at Cambridge, England, with the cheeky title of "The Irrelevance of Marx, Weber and Durkheim" (Bell 1988). It is not that I do not have piety for my forebears. I do. But I think that our basic categories are increasingly inadequate. They arise from Western modes—from Greek concepts and Christian eschatology. Hegel, in the *Philosophy of History*, ruled out all non-Western social development on the ground that these societies had not entered "into History," which was for him the unfolding of a principle of rationality, the outcome of which would be a single unified consciousness or, in the secular version of Marx, a single world society, then a universal order, or socialism. Yet our concepts of consciousness, development, rationality—the very term "modernity"—have become questionable and limited.

On the methodological level, I do not think we can understand society in terms of *totality* or *integration*, as Marxists and Functionalists do, since society is *not* a "system." An economy may be a system, but there is no necessary connection between economy and culture. There is, as I have argued, a "disjunction of realms" (see Bell 1978b). On the ground level of the empirical terrain, the idea of *class* becomes shriveled, *legitimacy* and *charisma* become expanded without recognition, and we do not know very much about the nature of *social cohesion* in the face of the multifarious civil strifes that have engulfed all societies in the last half century. And finally, I do not think we can escape the normative issues which are inextricably woven into all the questions of analysis that we have to confront.

References

Bell, Daniel. 1960. *The End of Ideology: On the Exhaustion of Political Ideas in the Fifties.* Glencoe, Ill.: Free Press. Reissued with a new Afterword, Harvard University Press, 1988.

———. 1976. *The Coming of Post-Industrial Society: A Venture in Social Forecasting.* New York: Basic Books. Originally published in 1973.

———. 1978a. *The Cultural Contradictions of Capitalism.* New York: Basic Books. Originally appeared in 1976.

———. 1978b. "The Disjunction of Realms: Some Problems of Epistemological Dualism." Paper presented at the Boston Colloquium in the Philosophy of Science, April 4.

———. 1978c. "The Public Household: On 'Fiscal Sociology' and the Liberal Society." In *The Cultural Contradictions of Capitalism,* 220–82. New York: Basic Books.

———. 1979. "Interview with Daniel Bell, May 1972." In Job L. Dittberner, *The End of Ideology and American Social Thought,* 309–36. Ann Arbor: UMI Research Press.

———. 1981. "Models and Reality in Economic Discourse." In *The Crisis in Economic Theory,* edited by Daniel Bell and Irving Kristol, 46–80. New York: Basic Books.

———. 1986. "The Limits of the Social Sciences: A Critique of the Conference." In *Advances in the Social Sciences, 1900–1980,* edited by K. W. Deutsch, A. S. Markovits, and J. Platt, 313–24. Cambridge: Abt Books.

———. 1988. "The Irrelevance of Marx, Weber and Durkheim." Paper presented at Cambridge University, England.

Brick, Howard. 1986. *Daniel Bell and the Decline of American Radicalism.* Madison: University of Wisconsin Press.

Bücher, Karl. 1901. *Industrial Evolution.* New York: H. Holt and Company. The original edition appeared in 1893.

Deutsch, Karl W., Andrei S. Markovits, and John Platt, eds. 1986. *Advances in the Social Sciences, 1900–1980: What, Who, Where, How?* Cambridge: Abt Books.

Friedman, Benjamin M. 1988. "Lessons on Monetary Policy from the 1980s." National Bureau of Economic Research, Working Paper No. 2551, April.

Henderson, Fred. 1934. *The Case for Socialism.* Chicago: Socialist Party. The original edition appeared in 1911.

Hicks, J.R., and Albert G. Hart. 1945. *The Social Framework of the American Economy*. New York: Oxford University Press.

Knight, Frank H. 1965. "The Economic Organization." In *Theories of Society: Foundations of Modern Social Theory*, edited by Talcott Parsons, et al., 454–57. New York: Free Press. The excerpt comes from Knight's work *The Economic Organization*, 1951.

————. 1971. *Risk, Uncertainty and Profit*. Chicago: University of Chicago Press. Originally published in 1921.

Lerner, Abba. 1944. *The Economics of Control: Principles of Welfare Economics*. New York: Macmillan.

Marx, Karl. 1932. *Capital, The Communist Manifesto and Other Writings*. Edited with an introduction by Max Eastman. New York: Modern Library.

————. 1933. *Critique of the Gotha Program*. New York: International Publishers. Originally appeared in 1875.

————. 1935a. *Value, Price and Profit*. New York: International Publishers. Originally written in 1865.

————. 1935b. *Wage-Labor and Capital*. New York: International Publishers. Originally appeared in 1849.

Parsons, Talcott. 1936. "Review of Alexander von Schelting, *Max Webers Wissenschaftslehre*." *American Sociological Review* 1:675–81.

Piore, Michael J., and Charles F. Sabel. 1984. *The Second Industrial Divide: Possibilities for Prosperity*. New York: Basic Books.

von Schelting, Alexander. 1934. *Max Webers Wissenschaftslehre*. Tübingen: J.C.B. Mohr.

————. 1948. *Russland und Europa im russischen Geschichtsdenken*. Bern: A. Francke.

Schudson, Michael. 1989. "A Ruminating Retrospective on the Liberal Arts, the Social Sciences, and Social Science 2." In *General Education in the Social Sciences: Reflections on 50 Years of "Soc 2,"* edited by J. Macaloon. Chicago: University of Chicago Press.

Simons, Henry C. 1944. "Some Reflections on Syndicalism." *Journal of Political Economy* 52:1–25.

Sombart, Werner von. 1909. *Socialism and The Social Movement in the Nineteenth Century*. New York: Dutton. Originally appeared in 1896.

Weber, Max. 1961. *General Economic History*. New York: Collier Books.

Who's Who in America 1986–1987. 1986. Chicago: Marquis Who's Who.

13

Jon Elster

It MAY BE SAID that Elster's contribution to the debate between economics and sociology has been to help break down the resistance among sociologists and other social scientists to methodological individualism, to game theory, and, first and foremost, to the very idea of rational choice.[1] He has done this in a series of brilliant works, which have been pouring forth since the late 1970s and whose importance extends far beyond the debate between economics and sociology. Perhaps the two most important of these are *Ulysses and the Sirens* and *Sour Grapes*. The main idea in the former work is that certain forms of irrational behavior can sometimes be handled by precommitting oneself to a certain form of action; and in the latter, that one's preferences may be formed by the very constraints under which the choice is made.

Through his cosmopolitian education and wide ranging intellectual interests, Elster is well-equipped to play the role of a middleman in the debate between economics and sociology. In the interview, he tells how his education has taken him from his native Norway to France and to the United States; and from French and mathematics to philosophy, economics, and Marxism. Elster also discusses the relationship between methodological individualism and rational choice, and between rational choice and social norms. He also touches on the problems of interdisciplinarity. He ends with a plea for social science research where the focus is on mechanisms rather than on theories—be they rational choice, functionalism, or some other form.

Jon Elster was born in Oslo, Norway, in 1940. He got a graduate degree in philosophy at the University of Oslo in 1966, and a doctorate in social science in 1972 from Université de Paris V. During the early 1970s to the early 1980s, he worked in departments of history, philosophy, and political science in France, Norway, and the United States. Currently he teaches at the Department of Political Science at the University of Chicago (1983–),

---

The following interview with Jon Elster was conducted on May 2, 1988, in his office in Pick Hall at the University of Chicago.

[1]The following information comes from Elster's vita and Elster 1985b.

while also holding a part-time position at the Institute for Social Research in Oslo (1984–).

•

Q: When one reads your works, one is struck by their interdisciplinary and cosmopolitan quality. Does this reflect your education?

A: I did my undergraduate work in Oslo, Norway, where I studied French and mathematics. I then wrote what is more or less the equivalent to a Master's thesis in philosophy. The Norwegian system is actually such that the degree is somewhere in between a Master's degree and a Ph.D. To write that dissertation I went to France, and I wrote it in French under the partial supervision of Jean Hyppolite. The main supervision I had was by some Jesuit philosophers, who were specialists on Hegel. My dissertation was on Hegel's phenomenonology of mind. It was called *Prise de conscience dans la Phenomenologie de L'Esprit de Hegel* (*Self-Consciousness in Hegel's Phenomenology of Mind*).

I wrote that dissertation in 1966. Then I got a fellowship from the Norwegian Research Council and decided to go to France to work with Hyppolite. But he died just a few weeks after I got to Paris. And then I first thought of working with Althusser. You know, this was in the heydays of Althusserian Marxism. Well, luckily for me he was not technically qualified to supervise my dissertation. Through my old Jesuit friends I got in touch with Raymond Aron. So I went to Aron's seminar and stayed there for three years and wrote my dissertation. He didn't take a very active role in supervising my thesis, but he read the chapters and made encouraging noises. Then I put the whole thesis together and defended it in 1972. It was called *Production et Reproduction. Essai sur Marx*, and technically it was a thesis in sociology at the Université de Paris V. So that's my training: undergraduate work in French and mathematics, a master's thesis in philosophy, and a doctoral thesis in sociology.

Q: Did you study any economics during these years? My memory is that at one time you were a professor in economic history in Norway.

A: That's not exactly wrong, but it's not quite right either. What happened is that when I was working on Marx I had to teach myself both a bit of economics and a bit of economic history, since Marx was both an economist and an economic historian. I then wrote a little book in Norwegian called *New Perspectives on Economic History*. It really was more of a book on methodology, and for a few years I was working in Oslo with a number of economic historians, partly on methodological issues and partly on substantive matters.

Q: In the 1970s, there was a sudden growth of interest in rationality in sociology and in social science in general, and your works surely have helped this along. But your own interest in rationality goes back much further. What exactly was it that originally interested you in this topic? Was it a specific teacher? Or the rationalistic French intellectual culture?

A: It was definitely not the French culture. I think that French culture in the 1960s and the 1970s/was actually strongly anti-rational choice and anti-methodological individualism. No, it was all very simple. When I had to read Marx, I had to understand Marxian economics. And to understand Marxian economics, I had to understand economics in general. And to understand economics, I had to understand the foundations of economics—which turn out to be rational choice. I guess the book which sort of opened my eyes to all of this was *Games and Decisions* by Luce and Raiffa, which I read some time in the 1960s. It is a great book, and it has stayed with me ever since as a bible. A lot of things have happened since the book appeared, of course, but it is still splendid. What Luce and Raiffa especially have got right and which almost nobody gets right is the exact combination of rigor in the exposition and conceptual skepticism in the argument, in the sense of willingness to explore the conceptual problems embedded in the formulas. So they are not just mindless theorem provers but very thoughtful about what they are doing. And that is very rare in this field.

Q: What do you think is behind this wave of popularity in social science for rational choice which started in the late 1970s and which still seems to be going strong? There is, for example, a rather vulgar theory which says that the radical 1960s have been replaced by more conservative times, and that's why there is such an interest in rational choice. One could also argue that the idea of rationality was just overdue; it had proved its usefulness in economics, so why not also use it in the other social sciences? What's your opinion?

A: I don't really know. As to the first theory, it is indeed vulgar in the sense that it rests on a clear fallacy. Let me explain. There are actually three distinct issues here. There is *rational choice theory*; there is *methodological individualism*; and there is *political individualism*. Methodological individualism is the position with which I identify myself the most clearly. Now, rational choice theory presupposes methodological individualism—but not the other way around. You can be a methodological individualist and yet not believe or believe wholeheartedly in rational choice theory. That is increasingly the way in which my own thinking has been developing over the last few years. I still think rational choice theory is very important. But I also think that the theory of social norms is very important, and I have been working and writing on that for the last couple of years. And I think that any acceptable theory of social norms has to be stated within the framework of methodological individualism.

Now, political individualism—let's say liberalism—has nothing whatsoever to do with methodological individualism. They are totally independent of each other, and you do indeed find all possible combinations of them in reality. It is true, empirically speaking, that in a fourfold table which you could easily construct, some cells would be more populated than others. And it is indeed true that in this sense, liberalism and methodological individualism go together more frequently than, say, socialism and methodological individualism. This is true, and it is an interesting sociological fact, which cries out for an explanation. But there is no *logical* connection there whatsoever. Already Schumpeter (1908), who coined the term "methodological individualism," insisted on this point.

So what you find in France in the 1960s and 1970s, to go back to that example for a moment, was a massive combination of three things: there was a rejection of rational choice and emphasis instead on social norms; there was a rejection of methodological individualism and emphasis instead on methodological holism; and there was a rejection of political liberalism and emphasis instead on some kind of leftism. I think these three should really be decoupled. And as I said, you can be a methodological individualist and still take the theory of social norms seriously, just as you can be a methodological individualist and still not be a political liberal. So the problem with all these discussions at this very general level is that people lump things together conceptually that have been empirically associated with each other. So that is the response to your question about the possible relationship between rationality and conservatism.

It can also be pointed out that rational choice has sometimes already been used outside of economics. In anthropology, for example, I think the evolution has been more in the opposite direction, in the sense that there is less rational choice now than there was some years ago. In the 1950s and 1960s, there were some very good people in anthropology, who were writing within what one today would call a rational choice framework. There was Raymond Firth and even more importantly, there was Fredrik Barth. But today it seems to be cultural/functionalist/structuralist explanations that really dominate the field.

I am also not so sure that rational choice is as hegemonic today as your question seems to imply. There is also a question of what level you are talking of. If it is at the level of the *Zeitgeist*, I am not so sure it can be said to be rationalistic. If you read, for example, *The New York Times Book*

Review, which is a kind of middlebrow expression of the *Zeitgeist* in the United States, you won't find much of rational choice social science. They review social science books, but not those that are inspired by rational choice theory. If anything, I would say that the communitarian vision is stronger than rational choice here. But I also must say that I find these generalizations hopeless to discuss. The only thing that really interests me are the issues. And besides that, who cares?

Q: When one reads your works, it is clear that you have made several important contributions to modern social theory: there is your distinction between parametric and strategic rationality; the idea of precommitment as a way of handling irrationality; the notion of multiple self; and so on (see Elster 1984, 1986a). Is there an underlying theme or some hidden agenda in your work?

A: No, there is no preexisting agenda in my work. I think that the agenda is rather being constantly reconstructed *ex post*. I don't know exactly how to put this but I am just driven by sheer curiosity, I guess. Plus by a little bit of serendipity; you need a bit of serendipity. I think it would be true of many scholars to say that you can only have a small number of good ideas in your life. If you have ten, you are lucky. Two or three is more common, of course.

Q: Which would you consider to be your good ideas?

A: The notion of precommitment would be one. The idea of endogenous preference formation is another, and there is also the notion of states that are essentially byproducts (see Elster 1983, 1984). And perhaps I have got a couple more; I don't know. But the point is the following. You start with a couple of ideas—let us say three—and then you put something together. And then perhaps you get a new idea, so now you have four. But that does not simply mean that you have got a new idea; you also have three possible connections between that new idea and the three previous ones. So instead of getting just one good idea, you are actually getting three new things as well. And then you get a fifth idea, and then of course you don't just have that idea but four possible connections to your earlier ideas. So in a way you are building up a conceptual network, and it is somehow done from the inside.

Philosophers who wrote about growth in the seventeenth century had a phrase which is not used very often any more—*intussusception*. What it means is growing in the way a tree grows, from the inside—not just the way a crystal grows, by accretion. So the point is that the tree grows in all places simultaneously, not just at the outside. And I think that similarly a conceptual network expands, but not just at the outside. Every new idea adds something to it; when you have a new idea, you go back and revise what you did earlier. And in that sense the whole program or agenda is constantly being rewritten.

During these last few years I have, for example, had this interest in the theory of social norms. I think that I now take them more seriously than I used to do. And I can go back and revise and rethink some of my earlier work in the light of this new interest. Anyway, that's the way I think about the way my work develops.

Q: What is your sense of the present state of interaction between economics and sociology? It seems to me that some important changes are taking place today, and that basically the border between the two disciplines is being redrawn. So at the moment we are somewhere in between the old and the new. There is, for example, Gary Becker with one type of approach; and there is someone like George Akerlof with another. . . .

A: I think you are getting it right to cite Becker and Akerlof here because they represent two different trends. There is the imperialist trend of economics, which I would say just ignores sociological theory in its attacks on sociological problems. And then there is the trend that Akerlof represents, which takes sociological theory seriously and uses it to study economic problems. I must confess that I find the Akerlof approach much more interesting. The reason is that I have come to believe that there is a whole range of phenomena, traditionally studied by sociologists, which are quite resistant to the traditional economic approach. This is, of course, just another way of saying—for the third time in this interview—that one needs a theory of social norms to understand many of these problems. This is something which also Akerlof is referring to through his use of "custom"; he is essentially saying the same thing (see Akerlof 1980). Many phenomena, which are related to social norms, are just very difficult to make sense of in rational choice terms. Norms of revenge is an example.

But I don't mean to say that the Becker approach isn't useful. It is; of course it is useful. His work on the family is especially important and valuable. People obviously do make choices—for instance in respect to how many children to have; when to have them; and so on. Becker's analysis is very important. And I think it is good to have someone like Becker around, who really takes rational choice to its limits and beyond. He is constantly pushing the theory to its obvious limits of application. If he didn't exist, someone would have to invent him!

But I also see a danger in the mindless application of rational choice theory to everything. And therefore I think the presence of people like Hirschman, Akerlof, Leibenstein, and a few others who take sociological theory seriously is very important. They are willing to learn from sociology and not just steal the problems of sociology and incorporate them into their own domain.

Q: Let's agree that economics has lost a bit by being cut off in such a radical way from sociology, as it has been during much of the twentieth century. Doesn't the same also apply to sociology—that sociology has lost something by not being in better contact with economics?

A: I think that especially the Durkheimian tradition has had quite disastrous consequences for sociology and perhaps even more so for anthropology. We were just talking about mindless rational choice theory, but there has also been much mindless functionalism in sociology and anthropology. This went on from Durkheim to the 1960s or so. Functionalist sociology was quite intoxicating because it seemed to offer a possibility of explaining *everything*. But it was too easy in a way because if you were sufficiently clever, you could always find some consequences of a given phenomenon that were beneficial for someone or for something or in some respect and so on. You could always find something. And then you could say, "This explains it!" Now, that opened up the possibility for intellectual sloppiness, laziness, and irresponsibility. The best people in this business knew of course what they were doing; I'm not saying that everybody who did this type of work was uncritical and basically irresponsible. But they were not good because they had a good methodology; they were good *in spite of* their methodology.

Q: What about the role of Marx in the current debate between economics and sociology? None of the key participants are Marxist or seem to have much of an interest in Marx. But you do, and you recently published a work entitled *Making Sense of Marx*. So does Marxism have a role to play in this debate, and if so, what would it be?

A: The Marx that deserves to be remembered is the one in which the distinction between economics and sociology is transcended. The chapters in the first volume of *Capital* that show Marx at his very best are the ones in which he looks at the interaction between class struggle and profit-maximization within the firm. Long before, say, Akerlof and Stiglitz, he understood that rational entrepreneurs will adapt to the normatively motivated behavior of the workers. By contrast, the chapters in the third volume in which Marx attempts to do pure economics are rapidly on their way to a well-deserved oblivion. This being said, one of the unfortunate legacies of Marx is the view that rational-choice analysis is somehow suspect, because it accords too much importance to subjective matters and not enough to material factors. In particular, Marxists tend to say that preferences are unimportant compared to the objective social processes by which they are generated. To this claim, one can only respond by saying that the problem of endogenous preference formation is on everybody's research agenda, but that nobody, and certainly not Marxists, have made much headway on it.

Q: Would it be your opinion that economic problems are best analyzed by neoclassical economics? Or is there a place also for other perspectives, such as economic sociology?

A: My basic attitude towards these disciplinary distinctions is that they are pointless, boring, unproductive, and indeed counterproductive. So my basic inclination is to refuse to answer the question. That being said, I'll try to answer it. So let me back up a little and say something about interdisciplinary work in general.

What I just said about disciplinary distinctions could, I guess, be seen as a plea for nondisciplinary work. That is, let's just forget about the disciplines and focus on the problems. Who cares about the disciplines? But it is a bit more complicated than that because one of the things we have learned, I believe, over the last twenty years is the danger of premature interdisciplinary work. You cannot, for instance, teach students to be interdisciplinary. There have been experiments in this direction at some universities. There is, for example, a university in Denmark at Roskilde, that really tries to train undergraduates to be interdisciplinary. But I don't think it works, and I don't think it could work, because it seems to me that to be good in interdisciplinary work, you already have to have very solid foundations in one discipline. The main reason for this is that it is only by working with some depth in one discipline that you in a sense learn the ethics of science. That is, you learn how to be responsible; how to take the works of other scholars seriously; how to make trade-offs between breadth and depth; and so on. Yes, I think that's the best way of putting it; that to learn the ethics of science or how to be intellectually responsible, you must know everything about something. People who try to start out by learning something about everything will not get anywhere. So I certainly think that an academic community of specialists is much more desirable than one that is made up of all-round amateurs.

On the other hand, I also think that these specializations are harmful in their own ways. Both the best and the most interesting work is often done by people who couldn't care less about where they come from. But they have nevertheless internalized this ethics of responsibility, which has to do with these familiar things, such as actively seeking out counterexamples to what you are doing; listening to what other people are doing; playing the devil's advocate; not seeking out originality for its own sake; and so on. And once this ethics has been internalized, people tend to forget where they come from and just focus on the issue at hand. And that's why—to come back to your question about economic sociology—I would still say that it shouldn't really matter that much if you come from economics or if you come from sociology. The important thing is that you come from somewhere and that you have internalized the ethics of science. I am not at all sure it matters if Art Stinchcombe is a sociologist or an economist; if Jim March is a political scientist or an economist; and so on.

Q: Maybe it does. Economists and sociologists have different ways of looking at things and will sometimes come up with different answers when they look at the same problem. Let's take Stinchcombe as an example. He is a sociologist out to his fingertips, something that is quite obvious in his analyses. He is also very much aware of the differences between neoclassical economics and sociology, as when he, for example, says that economists treat rationality as an assumption, while sociologists see it as a variable (Stinchcombe 1986, 5–7).

A: That's not how I read *Economic Sociology* (1983). As far as I remember it, this book is basically all about choice, scarcity, and of course institutions. The focus more precisely is on the joint impact of institutions and scarcity of choices. Now, it is some time since I read that book and I don't have it uppermost in my mind, but it doesn't seem that rationality is much of a variable in it. Is the quote from *Economic Sociology*?

Q: No, it's from the introduction to an anthology of Stinchcombe's essays, *Stratification and Organization*. But let me ask another question, which is related. According to the principle of charity, you say that one should always start an analysis with rationality as the working hypothesis (Elster 1984, 154–56). In other words, however strange the behavior to be explained may seem to be, one should assume that it is rational. One example that you mention in this context is that peasants in underdeveloped nations often resist the introduction of better technology. My question is, then, isn't it possible that economists and sociologists use rationality in different ways? Perhaps you need two different concepts of rationality: one that is economic (*rationality as an assumption*), and one that is more social in nature (*rationality as a variable*).

A: I think it is one and the same notion of rationality that you use, independent of what discipline you are in. The strategy of finding different concepts of rationality in different areas is a strategy which I think one should oppose very strongly. There is one force of gravity and there is one concept of rationality. You shouldn't multiply entities beyond what is necessary, even if you of course can make different uses of the same concept. The example I was using about the peasants is a standard example from economics, and it has to do with risk aversion. Apparently conservative irrational behavior in this case becomes perfectly rational and intelligible once you introduce the element of risk aversion. So that example is not something which can be used in support of there being a difference between the sociological and the economic concept of rationality.

You see the way I use the notion of rationality, I just don't think it can be a variable. Rationality is very simple. It is the following: *rationality means using the best means to realize your ends*. Now, let us suppose someone says, "I am irrational," and points to the fact that he consciously and deliberately does not choose the best means to realize his ends. Well, that kind of reaction would make me question if that indeed is his end. Because it seems to me that the central evidence for imputing ends to other people is their actions. And if they choose means that are not conducive to a given end, that's the best evidence to think that they don't have that end. So it's not as if we had a choice, as it were. We *have to* assume that people are rational in order to impute ends and goals to them. This is incidentally not my idea—it basically comes from Donald Davidson (see 1980)—but it seems to me to be compelling. And I therefore think that there is no difference in rationality crossculturally and no differences across the disciplines. Rationality is in this sense just a basic fact of understanding another person.

Q: So in other words you can use rationality in sociology?

A: Yes, you have to.

Q: You write very little about Max Weber. That puzzles me a bit, especially since you at some point say that "the two main theorists of rationality are Max Weber and John von Neumann" (Elster 1979, 68). Weber is also quite relevant in this context we are discussing since it was he who most forcefully and creatively argued that rationality is part of a society's culture and ways of doing things.

A: Let me just say one thing first, to get it out of the way. The fact that culture shapes ends does not mean that rationality is a cultural variable. So, it is still the same notion of rationality that you need. And you find it everywhere; people use it in their daily life to understand each other. Any person who tries to understand another person just has to assume that that person is rational. Otherwise you'll never be able to make sense of someone else's behavior. Now, *what* sense you make—that is something which of course depends on the culture.

Insofar as Weber is concerned, I actually do cite him here and there. I have lately also been thinking about his typology of social action (see Weber 1978). There are, as you know, four kinds of behavior according to Weber. "Instrumental rationality" or "*Zweckrationalität*" is, I guess, pretty straightforward, and I think that game theoretical rationality or what I call "strategic rationality" is just an extension of that. The reason is that strategic rationality is indeed instrumental; it is "*zweckrational.*" Then there is "affective behavior." Well, Weber does not have too much to say about that. I think the role of emotions in social life is actually very little understood. Then there is "traditional behavior," and finally there is "value rationality" or "*Wertrationalität.*" Well, I am not that happy with the concept of "value rationality." I am not quite sure what it means, and how it differs from the other three. Let us take the example of voting. Why do people vote? The problcm does not make any sense on instrumental grounds. Is it then "traditional behavior"? Or is it "value rational"? What is it? I don't think that Weber spells out these notions in sufficient detail and in sufficiently precise ways to even allow us to decide.

What I think is the answer to all of this—and I am sort of obsessed with this question—is that there are really just two basic motivations of human behavior. I think that the most important is rationality, but social norms are in many ways equally important. In my opinion, social norms *combine* elements from "traditional behavior," "affective behavior," and "value rationality." They do this because social norms are non-outcome oriented; they just tell people to do things—not to do something to achieve something else. So what I am saying is that the theory of social norms incorporates elements of "value rationality" by this emphasis on the nonconsequential character of social norms; of "traditional behavior," since norms are very often perpetuated by tradition; and also of "affective behavior," since a very important mechanism in the operations of social norms are the emotions of shame and guilt, which in various ways are associated with the validation of the norms. So I really think that the fourfold Weberian classification collapses or should be collapsed into a twofold classification. It took me a long time to find this out. I have been struggling with Weber's fourfold classification for many years, but I could never really make sense of it. It never seemed like a natural classification to me. And I think it becomes more of a natural classification if you collapse it into just these two categories: instrumental rationality, on the one hand, and noninstrumental social norms, on the other.

Q: According to an old stereotype, women are irrational and men are rational. Does this mean that there is a sexist dimension to rationality? Or is that a nonsense question?

A: Yes, I think it is a nonsense question. That women are irrational just sounds like a stereotype to me. I think there are obvious differences between the sexes and the kind of irrationality and emotive behavior you can find displayed there. But I don't think men display less irrational behavior than women. I think they probably display different kinds of irrational behavior. I, however, only have a distant or thirdhand impression of the debate on this question, and all my instincts tell me it is a pseudodebate, so I haven't really gone into it. But according to my distant impression, it seems to me that there are two issues which are involved. One is, should female scholars or do female scholars work differently? Do they follow a different logic than male scholars? So, that is one of the issues.

And the second is whether women, as objects of social science, behave differently. Perhaps these two issues are somehow linked to each other or perhaps they are just mixed up with each other. Anyway, I think that both issues are largely pseudoissues.

Once again, there of course exist differences between the two sexes, but these are much more specific than what is implied by big statements like "women and men have different forms of rationality," "there is a specific feminist form of rationality," "women are more irrational," and the like. I think these propositions are too course-grained and basically too ideological to lend themselves to scientific investigation. So I sort of tend to resist that line of argument. That's why I never discuss these questions in my writings and never will.

Q: Wouldn't at least the ideology that women are more irrational than men be worth studying?

A: Yes, I think that ideology would be worth studying. It is a topic at about the third level of importance though.

Q: When I read your earlier works, I get the impression that you originally were very optimistic about the use of game theory in social science. I am thinking of your article on game theory and Marxism in *Theory and Society* in 1982. The impression I get today, however, is that you are less optimistic. Is that correct?

A: I would stick to all I have said about game theory because it seems to me that you can't understand social interaction without game theory. Game theory really has a very privileged status because it is the obvious, natural conceptual structure within which to explore what I see as the three main forms of social interactions: between actions and outcomes; between the outcomes themselves (because these can be related to each other through mechanisms such as envy and altruism); and between the actions themselves (and that is the strategic interdependence aspect of it). Game theory simply provides the natural unified conceptual framework for studying these interactions.

But in a way game theory is more a language than a theory, by which I mean that its basic theoretical postulate is simply the assumption of rationality. That assumption can be applied to different contexts, some of which are strategic. And to spell out what a strategic context is, you need the language of game theory. But it is not really a theory; it is more a language for making some necessary distinctions. So the point is not whether game theory is true or not. The point is really whether the rationality assumption is verified when it is applied to these strategic game theoretical contexts. That is the way I would put it, although I am not sure it's necessarily the best way of putting it.

I suppose that what I am saying is that I still believe that rational choice theory for various reasons is privileged. It is more fundamental for several reasons, one of which I mentioned earlier—you need it just to make sense of other people's behavior. But that perhaps only proves some overall priority of rationality. In any specific case, it is clear that you still have to inquire whether the rationality assumption really is verified. And then you have to look at the game theoretical context—at the strategic interaction—and ask whether those are contexts in which the rationality assumption is routinely verified. Perhaps I would also say today—and here I might have changed my mind somewhat—that strategic interaction is a context in which the rationality assumption is perhaps somewhat vulnerable. I say this simply because I am more impressed today than I used to be by the many cases in which the rationality assumption in strategic contexts yields indeterminate outcomes.

For a theory—or for an assumption like the rational choice assumption—to be really useful, it should ideally yield *unique* predictions. It should say: a rational actor in this situation will do *this*. Now, because of the complexity of strategic interaction, rationality quite often yields indeterminate predictions. And then, of course, it is not very helpful. So I guess I am more impressed with that than I used to be, although I do think I mention some cases of this sort in *Ulysses and the Sirens*. So in a sense it is not so much that it is a new thing, but rather that I have become more impressed with this problem over the last few years. This development is also linked to my interest in social norms, because game theoretic and strategic reasoning cannot generate stable expectations about other people's behavior. And where do we get these expectations from? We get them from social norms.

Q: Isn't there a danger that norms will end up as a kind of residual category in that line of argument? In my interview with Kenneth Arrow, he said that the problem with using social norms as an explanation—we were talking about involuntary unemployment—is that it is just a word; it explains nothing. What would your reaction be to an argument like that?

A: The real problem is whether you can identify the social norms independently of what they are supposed to explain. Let me give you a simple example of a social norm that leads to predictions that differ from what you would expect from rational choice theory. Suppose you have a little game between two persons, he or player I and she or player II (see fig. 1). Player I can choose between *a* and *b*. If he chooses *a*, the game is over. If he chooses *b*, player II can choose between *c* and *d*. Now, the payoffs are clear from figure 1. In each case the first number is the payoff for player I and the second number, the payoff for player II.

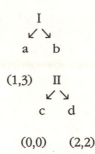

Fig. 1. *A Two-Person Game with Social Norms*

Now, let us first study the game from the point of view of rational choice theory. If player I chooses option *a*, he gets 1. If he chooses *b*, it is up to player II. In this situation, player II will obviously choose *d*. Player II will now get 2 and player I will get 2. So player I anticipates that player II will go there, and player I will also prefer that, because then he will get 2 rather than 1. So the rational choice solution is that player I chooses *b*.

From player II's perspective, this is, however, not the best it can get because she can conceivably get 3. Now why would player I want to give 3 to player II? Perhaps because player II can threaten player I. But the problem is that this threat is not credible. The notion of credible threat is central to rational choice theory. So even if player II makes a threat, when player I gets down to choose, he will not listen, because the threat is not credible. The threat is like cutting off your nose to spite your face, or, "If you don't marry me, I'll kill myself!"—well, it won't work. So player I would just ignore the threat. Now, let's suppose that player II is a member of the mafia. Members of the mafia are strongly committed to a code of honor or to norms of revenge, which tell them never to make an empty threat. If you ever make a threat, you should carry it out even if it is to your own detriment. So if player I is your standard American citizen and player II is a member of the mafia, suddenly the threat has become credible. And the reason for this is that it is backed by these social norms. Now, the interesting thing about this example is that player II—the mafioso—is not consequential when it comes to social norms; she'll carry out her threat regardless of the social consequences. And that nonconsequentialist norm has very good consequences for her, because she now gets 3 instead of 2.

So this little game should give a better illustration of the difference between social norms and rational choice than just some abstract definitions of the two. It also shows how the predictions of rational choice theory can be changed by the introduction of social norms.

Q: If you look ahead, what do you see in terms of rational choice theory and the interaction between economics and sociology? Do you think there will be some kind of breakthrough? Or will things pretty much continue as they are now?

A: Do you know the answer of Humphrey Lyttleton, the British jazz trumpeter? He was once asked, "Where is jazz going in your opinion, Mr. Lyttleton?" He answered, "Well, if I knew where jazz was going, I would already be there."

Q: Let me rephrase a bit. People like you, Jim Coleman, and a few others are in a sense holding out the hope that social science—and sociology in particular—can be profoundly restructured with the help of rational choice theory. We already know that this perspective can result in exceptionally fine works—your own and Jim Coleman's are surely examples of that—but is the rational choice approach really strong enough to accomplish a fundamental change in sociology and the other social sciences?

A: I think Jim Coleman's and my perspectives are very different. Let me as a way of answering the question say something else about the change in my perspective that I have experienced over the last few years and which goes together with the change that I just mentioned on the issue of rationality. I think that the greatest problem in the social sciences today is that of unrealistic expectations. I think there should be a shift in emphasis in the social sciences from theories to *mechanisms*. By this I mean small and medium-sized descriptions of ways in which things happen. A mechanism is a little causal story, recognizable from one context to another. "Sour grapes" and "The grass is always greener on the other side of the fence" embody mechanisms of this kind. A theory has greater pretensions: it is supposed to tell you which mechanisms operate in which situations; when, for example, people adjust their desires so as to desire only what they can get and when they adjust them so as to desire only what they cannot have. We should be very wary of grand theories, whether they be rational choice, structuralist, functionalist, Parsonian—you name it.

I like to read people like Tocqueville, Hirschman, Tversky, or Schelling because they are people who really have an acute eye for mechanisms. I think social science should become more ideographic—not going all the way to history, because I certainly think that there is a great scope for generalizations. But I think that the generalizations should take the forms of mechanisms, not theories. When you read someone like Tocqueville, he doesn't have theories; he has mechanisms. He describes causal structures, which are such that when you read them, you say, "But this is exactly like something I saw the other day in a book about China!" So I do advocate a regression here, which in my sense would represent a progress. That is, more realistic expectations will generate better social science than the grand theoretical ambitions that have been around for so long.

References

Akerlof, George A. 1980. "A Theory of Social Custom, of Which Unemployment May Be One Consequence." *Quarterly Journal of Economics* 94:749–75.

Davidson, Donald. 1980. *Essays on Actions and Events.* Oxford: Oxford University Press.

Elster, Jon. 1966. *Prise de conscience dans la Phenomenologie de L'Esprit de Hegel.* Mag. art. thesis, University of Oslo.

———. 1971. *Nytt perspektiv på oekonomisk historie.* Oslo: Pax.

———. 1972. *Production et reproduction. Essai sur Marx.* Ph.D. diss., University of Paris.

———. 1979. "Anomalies of Rationality: Some Unresolved Problems in the Theory of Rational Behavior." In *Sociological Economics*, edited by Louis Lévy-Garboua, 65–85. London: SAGE Publications.

———. 1982. "Marxism, Functionalism, and Game Theory." *Theory and Society* 11:453–82.

———. 1983. *Sour Grapes: Studies in the Subversion of Rationality.* Cambridge: Cambridge University Press.

———. 1984. *Ulysses and the Sirens: Studies in Rationality and Irrationality.* Rev. ed. Cambridge: Cambridge University Press. Originally appeared in 1979.

———. 1985a. *Making Sense of Marx.* Cambridge: Cambridge University Press.

———. 1985b. "Intervju med Jon Elster: Marxismen har framtiden för sig." *Tiden (Sweden)* 4:211–21.

———, ed. 1986a. *The Multiple Self.* Cambridge: Cambridge University Press.

———, ed. 1986b. *Rational Choice.* New York: New York University Press.

Luce, R. Duncan and Howard Raiffa. 1957. *Games and Decisions: Introduction and Critical Survey.* New York: John Wiley.

Schumpeter, Joseph A. 1908. "Der methodologische Individualismus." In *Das Wesen und der Hauptinhalt der theoretischen Nationalökonomie*, 88–98. Leipzig: Duncker and Humblot.

Stinchcombe, Arthur L. 1983. *Economic Sociology.* New York: Academic Press.

———. 1986a. "Rationality and Social Structure: An Introduction." In *Stratification and Organization*, 1–29. Cambridge: Cambridge University Press.

———, ed. 1986b. *Stratification and Organization: Selected Papers.* Cambridge: Cambridge University Press.

Weber, Max. 1978. "Types of Social Action." In *Economy and Society: An Outline of Interpretive Sociology*, 24–26. Berkeley: University of California Press.

14

Amartya Sen

AMARTYA SEN is known for having made original contributions to numerous areas in economics, ranging from technical matters to topics such as famines and welfare economics.[1] Most readers would be familiar with such works as *Collective Choice and Social Welfare* and *Poverty and Famines.* A theme common to many of Sen's works is the attempt to unite economic and philosophical questions. One of his latest books—*On Ethics and Economics*—is entirely devoted to this topic. By 1987, Sen had also published about one hundred and seventy articles on a similarly wide range of topics.

Amartya Sen was born in 1933 in Santiniketan in Bengal, India. His father Ashutosh Sen taught chemistry at Dhaka University (now in Bangladesh), and he spent his childhood in Dhaka, Santiniketan, and Mandalay (where his father went as a visiting professor). He earned a B.A. degree at Presidency College in Calcutta in 1953. He then went to Cambridge, England, for further studies. Here he was awarded a B.A. (1955), an M.A. (1959) and a Ph.D. (1959), at Trinity College. Since then he has worked as a Fellow at Trinity College (1957–1963), and as a professor of economics at the University of Delhi (1963–1971), the London School of Economics (1971–1977), and Oxford University (1977–1980), and as Drummond Professor of Political Economy and Fellow of All Souls College, Oxford (1980–1987). In the fall of 1987, he was appointed Lamont University Professor at Harvard University, where he now gives courses in both the Department of Philosophy and the Department of Economics. Sen has been president of the Econometric Society (1984), and is currently president of the International Economic Association (1986–1989).

•

Q: You have written on a variety of topics in economics: technology, famines, gender, social choice, welfare economics, and so on. What ac-

The following interview with Amartya Sen was conducted on March 1, 1988, in Professor Sen's office in the Littauer Center at Harvard University in Cambridge, Massachusetts.

[1] The following information comes from Professor Sen's vita; *Who's Who in Economics*; McPherson 1984; Ramachandran 1986; and *Harvard Gazette* 1987.

counts for this broad range of interests? Is it because you were involved in politics in your youth, perhaps? Or is there some other reason?

A: Well, first of all I am not certain that it is so unusually wide because I think that a great many economists are extremely broad in their interests. If I think of some of my teachers—like Piero Sraffa, Maurice Dobb, or Joan Robinson—all had rather wide interests in different areas. Also, some of the economists I came to know better later, like John Hicks, have written in many different fields. This is also true of many younger economists, including economists of my own generation.

Regarding my own inclination to step beyond the boundaries of economics, I think that to some extent it is indeed connected with, as you have suggested, my interest in politics. I have also been interested in philosophy—in an amateur way—from very, very early on in my life. And, in a sense, philosophy leads you to take an interest in a variety of other things. I think that both the driving force of politics and the driving force of philosophical inquiry reinforced my interest in other areas, including history, mathematics, and of course, the sciences. But, to repeat, I don't believe that there is anything particularly remarkable about the range of interests I have.

I guess I should also mention that in a sense the view that economists are rather narrow in the range of things they are concerned with is really based on concentrating on modern economics. If one looks at the classical political economists—whether it is Adam Smith or Marx or John Stuart Mill—I don't think there is any question that they had a tremendous lot of interests in different areas, dealing with some of the subjects you mentioned and also with others. Adam Smith, of course, was primarily involved in moral philosophy, but he was also concerned with history, politics, and many other matters—nutrition and so forth—in addition to fathering modern economics. John Stuart Mill was both a political philosopher and an economist, who wrote on such subjects as the position of women in society as well as the role that liberty plays in our lives and the role that it should play in them. In some ways I think that the subject of economics also *lends itself* to having broad interests. If some modern economists deny that explicitly or seem to deny it implicitly in terms of a narrow focus on their spheres of concentration, I think that this is a recent development, and I would say that that is *not* how the discipline of economics should be judged.

Q: *Poverty and Famines* is dedicated to Amiya Dasgupta and you say, to quote the book, that it was he "who introduced me to economics and taught me what it was about" (Sen 1981, v). Did you have Dasgupta as a teacher? And what exactly was it that he taught you? I looked through a

Festschrift in his honor and I got the impression that he was both a technically skillful economist and a very stringent thinker.

A: I think you are quite right: he is a wonderful economist and a very
stringent thinker. I was not taught by him at Presidency College in Calcutta
though; he never taught there. I had some distinguished teachers in economics at Presidency College (such as Bhabatosh Datta), but Dasgupta
was not there. I knew him personally because our families knew each
other. He was a colleague of my father at Dhaka University, and a very
close family friend. And he was in fact very instrumental in making me
decide to move from mathematics and physics—in which I had begun my
college education—to economics.

When I was doing this shift, I was very concerned with politics and in
a sense extremely skeptical of economic theory. What that dedication, to
which you referred, is pointing at, is really a combination of two things.
First, Amiya Dasgupta taught me the importance of theory at a time when
I was particularly skeptical of theory because it seemed rather remote. I
was much more concerned with things that looked immediately applicable and perspicuous in their relevance to the real world. He made me see
that one could make a terrible mistake even in terms of any relevance
one's work might have for practical policy making, by going *too directly*
at it and by not paying sufficient attention to the role that theorizing inevitably has to play in setting the problem right and in preparing us for facing
practical problems.

So that was one thing that he taught me. The other thing, which is
superficially thought to be contradictory and to go in the opposite direction, was his insistence that in pursuing economic theory, we have to be
very concerned with the kind of problems that ultimately are of importance to us. There is a kind of schizophrenia which operates in much of
India's economic education or which used to operate in the days when I
was a student in Calcutta. Our theory was basically derived from standard
Western textbooks. It dealt with problems that had some immediate relevance to the problems faced in advanced capitalist economies. But it did
not have a great deal of bearing on the situation with which we were
familiar in India. We took an interest in practical Indian problems, but at
the same time, our theory did not seem to relate to that. So, to some extent,
what Amiya Dasgupta was arguing was that it's not that one has to turn
against theory—quite the contrary. The real issue is to see what the point
of delivery of the theory is as to where it is going to relate to the real world:
whether it is going to be somewhere around Chicago or whether it is
going to be somewhere around Calcutta. Now, in the book with the dedication you referred to, I was using a somewhat theoretical approach in

trying to understand famines, and I felt that it had some merit in perhaps providing a bit of a correction in terms of the emphasis that was then prevalent in studies of hunger and famine. But its concentration was very much on the kind of problems that one finds in India or South Asia or in Africa; and these had tended to be neglected in standard economic theory because they are not serious problems in Europe and America any more.

So in both these respects I was very strongly reminded of my early education from Amiya Dasgupta, and I therefore felt that it was appropriate to dedicate the book to him. Indeed I am very grateful to him for having introduced me to economics and for having taken me in that direction. So it was also a wonderful occasion for me to be able to say "thank you" to him in this form.

Q: When you talk of some of the other people who have influenced you, you mention Sraffa, Robinson, and Dobb. It is thus clear that you have been exposed to Marxist thought of a very high caliber. But what about sociology? When I go through your works, I find no references to Max Weber, for example. Did you ever have an opportunity to study the classical sociologists and the later American sociologists as part of your education?

A: I have read some of Weber and some of Durkheim. But you are quite right that I can probably make my work somewhat richer—or somewhat less poor, let's put it that way—by taking more explicit note of their writings. I think that part of the problem arises from the fact that by the time I came to Weber and Durkheim and the other sociological thinkers, my basic training was to a great extent already over. I think that this is often the case with people who have been brought up in India. The strong influence on Indian thinking comes basically, on the one hand, from certain aspects of English academic background. So I had a fair acquaintance especially with utilitarianism—with Bentham and Mill—and also with other things that the English took seriously. This included a certain amount of grounding in the Western classics, including Aristotle and Plato.

On the other hand, given the preoccupations of politics in India, students got tremendously exposed to the Marxian tradition. The politics of student life—perhaps more in Calcutta than anywhere else in India but to some extent everywhere in India—takes tremendous note of the Marxian tradition. Now this happened when I was very young. I studied for my first degree in Calcutta at a time when Marx, Mill, Bentham, and Aristotle played a major part in one's thinking. By the time I came to Cambridge in 1953, I was, however, concentrating much more on what you might call economics in a relatively narrow sense because there were a lot of things that I needed to study in economics and which I also did study at that time. So in a sense that time in the mid-1950s in Cambridge was not a time when I was exploring much outside the rather narrowly conceived boundaries of economics.

The time when I was able to take an interest again in wider things was when I was a young teacher in Cambridge in the late 1950s. I then did read some of the works of Weber and Durkheim and some other sociologists, and in a sense they were influential in my thinking. Still, they never stuck to my mind as firmly as those works with which I grew up. When I am thinking, for example, of a particular point and I find it similar to a point made by somebody else but not quite the same, then my natural reference is to those things over which I have better command. And this command was acquired at a time when my receptivity was greater, namely when I read Marx or Mill, rather than later on when, as it were, the foundations of my own mental makeup had already been largely made up.

This is not to indicate that I did not get a great deal out of reading the sociological literature. I should also, by the way, mention that the gap between the sociological literature and the economic literature is partly a modern phenomenon. Weber and Durkheim might be ancient in terms of modern sociology, but they are very young in comparison with the economic writers. And one of the reasons why that is the case is that quite a lot of what would be called "sociology" today was of course then part of the writings of Bentham, Mill, Marx, and Smith—Adam Smith in particular. There isn't any particular point in asking the question as to whether this is really "economics" or "sociology" because in a sense it was both. So in some way, as far as the classical tradition is concerned, it had sociological elements in it as well as what can be seen as narrowly conceived economic elements.

Q: Some of your works deal exclusively with economic matters. There is your first book, *Choice of Techniques*, which you describe as an example of a "formal economic analysis" (Sen 1960, 7). Your second book, *Collective Choice and Social Welfare*, has a broader scope. The focus here is mainly on social choice, and at one point you say that ethics and political science must be brought into the analysis. But what about sociology? Are not the questions that are discussed within the framework of social choice also of relevance to sociology?

A: Well, I would think they must be. Their relevance is very clear and immediate to sociology, it seems to me. I guess one reason why I perhaps didn't mention this in my book is that it seems that if there is some subject to which social choice would immediately apply, one would clearly think that it is sociology. So in a sense it was almost the most obvious thing to say. And what I was really in a sense battling to establish was that social choice is of greater relevance to economics than some welfare economists would seem to think.

By the time I was beginning to write on social choice theory, it had already existed for about a decade but its formal impact on welfare economics had been very little. So partly I was arguing that social choice is of particular relevance just to welfare economics. But on top of that I was complaining of the fact that, while there was a certain amount of sympathy for social choice among modern economists, who on the whole take sociology seriously, there was a great reluctance to go into philosophy, which was regarded in a sense as being too remote from economics. Now, you have to bear in mind that when I first started doing social choice theory—I guess my first paper on this topic was published in the early 1960s and I wrote it in Cambridge—sociology was of course part of the economics tripos, so it was seen as belonging to the same general area as economics whereas philosophy was not. Earlier on, of course, it had been quite different, since economics had emerged as part of the moral science tripos. Anyhow, in the economics faculty in Cambridge, I was among the few who were very much involved at that time in ethics and who felt that we could not do serious welfare economics without addressing the ethical question more explicitly than we were doing. Therefore, I had a kind of program at that time of trying to put social choice work together with welfare economics work, on the one hand, and with moral philosophical and ethical writings on the other.

This is the way I saw it then. Sociology came into the story, but it did so as part of the broad basket which had come under the umbrella of economics. Looking back at it, I think that this is probably not the right way of characterizing it because, for one thing, sociology has become more specialized. Economics has also become very narrow, so I think the need to signal the importance of studying sociology is much clearer to me now. But at that time it did not seem to me like that. It seemed to me that the need to emphasize the necessity for looking at ethics was something which was terribly neglected and not perceived as clearly as it should be; and I was trying to make that particular point with as much force as I could.

Q: Many sociologists would probably regard *Poverty and Famines* as your most sociological work. In particular, the way you criticize the idea that it is not what you call "food availability decline" (FAD) that causes famines would seem to open up the analysis to a sociological approach. Yet if one looks more carefully at your alternative to FAD—the "entitlement" approach, or the idea that one is entitled to a certain amount of food through ownership or work—it becomes clear that this is more of a legal than a sociological concept. Why did you decide to focus so strongly on the legal aspect in *Poverty and Famines*? And in some of your latest work on hunger and famine, you have begun talking about "legitimacy." Does this mean that your analysis is now becoming more sociological?

A: The first thing I would like to say is that *Poverty and Famines* is of course concerned with a very simple but neglected problem. My later work related to legitimacy actually tries to grapple with a much more difficult problem, going into such questions as the distribution of food *within* the household and so on. In the case of *Poverty and Famines*, I was not deeply concerned with that particular and more complex issue; I was rather concerned with the fact, which I had found in a number of famines I studied, that there were millions of people who died *without there being any decline in food availability.* I was trying to explain this phenomenon in terms of the failure to *command food* rather than in terms of the decline of the supply of food. That naturally means the command as it is related to *ownership* in a private ownership economy. But also in a socialist economy you ultimately own the food that you eat, so in a sense the notion of ownership—and therefore the legal sense of entitlement—became the natural focus in that more elementary work.

Now, all of this is very elementary because once it is clear that food availability cannot possibly be the only direct factor affecting starvation but that entitlement and ownership are involved, then there isn't any great mystery about famines despite high food availability. I consequently see *Poverty and Famines* as a very elementary work. I was at that time also very much concerned with the question of measurement of poverty and the distribution of income among the poor. The latter question, which involved measuring poverty in terms of an index of deprivation, is the kind of question which also sociologists have been interested in. That particular issue was also very important for understanding famine, because often the very genesis of a famine may be connected with redistribution processes in which some of the poor groups actually gain while others go through the wall and indeed perish.

So in a sense I saw a connection between entitlements and famines which I had not seen earlier. I was quite involved with this issue, and I tried to write it up in my book. But I knew then, as I know even more clearly today, that I was really looking at the most elementary aspect of poverty, hunger, and starvation; and that in order to go beyond this part I would have to get into issues which are not so clearly economic and legal, especially the notion of legitimacy. "Legitimacy" is a particularly important and difficult concept, and it has a certain connection with legality as well as with economics. If you, for example, take the issue of the deprivation of women within the context of the relative distribution of food within the family, it is quite clear that sometimes women get deprived because the idea of what is "appropriate" or what is "right"—which has some similarity with what is legally acceptable, that is with "entitlement" in the legal sense—often tends to favor the men rather than the women and the boys rather than the girls. Men are seen as the "breadwinners," and as those who bring the earnings from outside the household into the home. This fact has an important impact on the notions of legitimacy as to who should get how much within the household in the division of food and other commodities, including the health care and medical attention that the family can provide.

In this way, the notion of "legality," which is implicit in the problems of ownership and the distribution between the families, has to get extended to the notion of "legitimacy," which includes legality *between* the families but also issues of perceived appropriateness in the form of notions of legitimacy in the distribution of food and other commodities *within* the family. So that was the linkup to which I came somewhat later. And then of course the sociological aspect became much more explicitly important in my work than it had been at an earlier stage, when I was mainly concerned with the distribution of food between families rather than within families.

So in a sense you are quite right to say that *Poverty and Famines* was dealing with problems with which sociologists would be familiar and in which sociologists would be interested. But I think that I actually failed to go into these problems in depth because I was really more concerned with some very elementary economic and legal issues. I think the book had an important point to make, and I did try to make it in as straightforward a manner as possible. In fact, in the original version of the book I had several chapters where I went into various ideas on perceived notions of rights. One part of a paper, which I later published under the title "The Right Not to Be Hungry" and which goes into some ethical issues as well as some sociological ones, was originally part of the book. But then I took these sections out of the book because I got very afraid that my main point, which is an elementary and simple one, might get lost if I also tried to address the more complicated and controversial issues involved. So I really wanted to keep it simple. As it turned out, however, I did not succeed in avoiding controversy; there was quite a bit of debate around *Poverty and Famines*. Nevertheless, the book at least has the virtue of being concerned with a very simple point.

Q: Many people probably do not know that you have made important contributions to the study of women in the economy, a topic that is currently becoming more popular in economics as well as in economic sociology. I especially recall a very fine paper of yours from 1985 entitled "Women, Technology and Sexual Divisions." Could you tell us a little about the way you view the connection between gender and the economy?

A: I would be very happy to do that, and I am honored that you think well of that paper. In it I was really concerned with the question that group associations involve elements of *cooperation* as well as *conflict* when people work together—whether it is working together in a family or in a factory or in any other kind of association. There are gains to be made by different parties through different alternative positions in these group associations. Some of these are more favorable to one of the parties, and others are more favorable to the other party; therefore, there are elements of conflict as well as elements of cooperation in these associations.

Now, all of this is for example quite explicit in the context of factories, where the relationship between the trade union and the employer's organization expresses the conflicting element. The cooperative element is present in the productivity and profitability of the firm and in the employment it can provide. But in the case of the family, the combination of cooperation and conflict is much more hidden. The cooperative elements are important and they are rightly emphasized, because families survive on the basis of mutual help. But embedded in the cooperative element are also elements of conflict. And that comes out, when the food supply is short, as to whether the boys will get more than the girls and how the food is divided between the men and the women and so forth. Now, given the very nature of the family—that people live together constantly, that they share the same room, the same cooking pot, sometimes even the same bed, and so on—it is very hard for the conflicting elements to be faced starkly. To do that would seem to be antithetical to the very nature of the family.

So the conflicting elements in families tend to be hidden, and people don't see them. What therefore happens is that there is a kind of agreed upon perception as to how these conflicts should be resolved, and this usually takes the form of some kind of legitimacy notion, which everybody accepts. In sexist societies it may take the form that the men get more than the women in the division of food or health care, and that the boys get more than the girls. But even if there is an unequal solution, this is not seen as a resolution to a conflict because the elements of conflict have to be kept below the surface. Instead, it looks as if it is just the natural order, indeed "the only sensible way" of thinking about it. That being the case, the combination of cooperative and conflicting elements must be laid bare in a somewhat different way in the family than in other groups. In particular, one has to take note of the objective reality of the subjective perception that people have, namely, their notions as to what is right, who is how well, and who deserves how much care, and so on. All these subjective perceptions have an objective role to play in the actual division of advantages within the family.

So what my 1985 paper did was to outline a model whereby the division of the benefits jointly produced in the family—through mutual cooperation with some people working outside, others inside the family and each in a sense being parasitic on the other—is dependent on a variety of parameters, including perceptions as to what is legitimate. To just mention one of the influences I discuss in that paper, namely the earnings that different members of the family have from *outside* the family. These are very perspicuous, very noticeable, and can be seen as "here some income from the outside is brought into the family." That this is the fact has a very major role in my judgement to play in the division of benefits within the family. Those who work outside the home—and that tends more often to be the men rather than the women—often happen to get a disproportionate share of the joint benefits.

Now, the amount of outside work, and earnings, of women vary of course between societies. And one of the things I tried to show in my 1985 paper is that in those societies where women are more involved in outside activities, like in Subsaharan Africa in contrast to Northern Africa or Southern Asia, they also tend to do relatively better in terms of the distribution *within* the family. I have tried to develop the empirical side of this argument in a later paper called "Gender and Cooperative Conflict." This new paper really tries to take a close look at what influences the relative distribution within the family and the factors that are involved in this, including the intermediary role of perceptions. There is of course the objectivity of earnings from outside the household, even though the work inside the home is as important or even more important for the welfare of the family. But it is *the perception* of who is doing the earnings and *the perception of legitimacy* that relate the objective factors in the division of employment to the objective factor of the division of food, health, medical care, and so on. It is exactly that close connection which I have tried to explore in the new paper on gender and conflict.

Q: If one looks at economic theory, it soon becomes clear that women play an extremely minor role in it, if any at all. Is this "invisibility" of women in economic theory due to sexism, or is there perhaps another explanation?

A: Well, I think it's difficult to say. I think you are right that women's issues have received relatively less attention in economics than one would have thought, given the importance of these problems. They do get some attention in what is sometimes called "family economics," but the dominant schools in this field have in my judgement been very narrow in their outlook. There is first the common tendency—also in the work of such great economists as Paul Samuelson—to make the assumption that the earnings of the family get distributed within the family in a way that essentially maximizes the equal welfare of everybody within it. There is also another approach, which has been pioneered by Gary Becker and a few other people. Here, family economics is seen either in terms of there being an authoritarian head of the family, whose values are shared by everybody in the family, and where things get distributed according to those values. Or, alternatively, the assumption is made that there is another market *within* the family; and that it is this added price mechanism which determines the distribution of benefits within the family. Now, both of these approaches represent very limited models, and I don't think that either of them give very much insight into what actually happens in the family. They particularly do not explicitly face the issues of perception and the impact of notions of legitimacy on the distribution of benefits within the family. So what we have is a situation where families are seen in standard economics in a rather stylized manner. They are either unimportant in the analysis or they become important—but only within a very narrow and stylized framework.

On the other hand, there are, of course, a lot of recent contributions to women's questions, but these tend to come from somewhere else than standard economics. There is a considerable influence from Marxian economics, and there is also much interest among sociologists for problems of this sort. But usually these issues are not seen as part of mainstream economics. By having separate sections of women's studies, they in a sense also get compartmentalized and fail to get absorbed into mainstream economics. Since I see myself on the whole as a mainstream economist, I think my attempt has really been to make mainstream economics take more note of these problems and not just assume them away, or deal with them in such a stylized manner that you end up with losing the very essence of these problems. There are many other persons who have also been involved in this enterprise. Still, it is an enterprise which in my judgement is well worth being involved in.

The sociological influence and the influence from Marxian political economy are important things to take note of also in mainstream economics. They are indeed part of it. Or at least they should be part of mainstream economics, not only in the context of women's questions but also in other contexts. This *integration* is in my judgement a very challenging issue with which I am very much involved.

Q: I would now like to switch over to another topic about which you have written extensively and that is of much interest to the emerging dialogue between economics and sociology, namely rationality. One of your arguments—for example in your famous essay "Rational Fools"—is that the concept of rationality in mainstream economics is too narrow; it has to be made more complex. You often stress that it is by addressing ethical questions that the concept of rationality can be given more structure. But what about also addressing *social* questions? Wouldn't that be equally relevant? In your recent book *On Ethics and Economics* you say that you are currently working on a book tentatively entitled *Rationality and Society*. . . .

A: Well, I think the content of rationality for human beings living in society—that is, for *all* human beings—has to have an inescapably social component to it. You mentioned my essay "Rational Fools," and it is incidentally not one of my favorite papers. It avoids all the main issues, and it simply grumbles at the narrowness of the formulation of motivation in economics; it is a very negative paper. But even in that negative paper there is at least a thought which can be referred to, namely that our behavior pattern can be affected by certain motivations, which can be called "commitment" and which do not necessarily relate to the pursuit of self-interest, not even to sympathy for the well-being of those who are close to us, such as family members, and so on.

There exist many kinds of commitment, such as political commitments, ideological commitments, and so on; and it is not possible to go into the substantive content of these without bringing in social considerations. My future book you referred to—and which I sometimes call *Social Rationality* and sometimes *Rationality and Society*—is concerned with taking this issue more head on. I try to argue that it is a mistake to think of our sense of identity as merely one of self—say, those associated with the proper names Amartya Sen and Richard Swedberg, respectively. Instead, we see ourselves and we see our identities as members of particular groups. And there are of course intersecting groups: we are members of a family, a class, an occupational group, a nation, a race, a community, and so on. Each of these contributes a little to our sense of identity. So in order to pursue what the role of self is in rationality—and I think the role of self is a very important one in any notion of rationality—we have to look into the issue of our identity much more closely.

This perspective provides a much richer outlook on the demands of rational action, in my judgement. It also helps to resolve some of the paradoxes of rationality, which people have earlier discussed within the context of games, such as the "prisoners' dilemma," where each individual is worse off if what looks like individual rationality is pursued. The very recognition that this is the case of course influences what we think the appropriate action should be in this context. And that is not unrelated to our identity as members of certain groups.

There is actually a very complex issue here. There is one sense in which "I am I" and "a group is a group," but there is also a sense in which I am a member of a group. One consequently has to take a much broader view of the concept of the self and of the heterogeneity that is *inescapably* implicit in the notion of the self, in order to understand the demands of rationality. This is of course a subject on which many people have written in the past, including Adam Smith, Marx, and Aristotle, just to mention a few names. These three are of course philosophers and economists, but you could also think of them as sociologists, because sociology was not a separate discipline in their days. They were as concerned with what is now the subject matter of sociology as with what is now the subject matter of economics.

In my case, studying the classical tradition has proved to be very valuable. In fact, I could only begin to understand the depth of some of these problems by seeing how long these issues have been studied in different societies, which are often rather different from ours, and how these problems have been treated with much greater richness in those days than is in some of the formulations of rationality that we today can find in standard economics. The social element in rationality is something I am indeed very much involved with just now, since I am trying to write this book on social rationality at this very moment.

Q: Some sociologists—and especially Jim Coleman—are arguing very vigorously that the concept of rationality can and should be used also as the foundation of sociology. What is your reaction to this idea? And can rationality, in your opinion, be used as the basis for *all* the social sciences?

A: Well, in a general sense I do believe that it can because I do think we have a reason for most decisions, and we indeed do use reasoning. But I think the important thing to avoid is to identify the use of reasoning in our decision making with a very restrictive model of rationality. There exist narrow models of rational choice, and very often these have fairly arbitrary restrictions which sometimes happen to be fine but which at other times are extremely misleading. There is therefore a certain risk that it will not be useful to rely on the concept of rationality. And whatever benefit one might have derived from paying attention to reasoning will be negated by the use of a narrow concept of rationality. Just take the example of what many people take to be the content of rationality, namely, certain conditions of internal consistency. I try to argue in a paper called "Consistency," which was my presidential address to the Econometric Society in 1984 and which will eventually appear in *Econometrica*, that there are no internal consistency conditions which can be thought to be invariably appropriate, irrespective of the context. In fact, the internal consistency conditions that we can insist on as part of rationality of behavior are thoroughly dependent on the external context. The idea of endogenous internal consistency is, I try to argue in that paper, in fact bizarre. Each time, there is a particular context to look at and what counts as consistent will depend on it. And quite often that context, to come back to the earlier discussion we were having, is a *social* context.

The idea of bringing in rationality in analyzing human behavior, whether in an economic or in a sociological context, is in my opinion a good idea. But at the same time that idea becomes productive rather than counterproductive only if more elbow room is given to the notion of rationality and if it is recognized that reasoning is not just following certain arbitrarily imposed consistency notions, but rather being alive to the demands that are part of reasoning, namely: What is it we are trying to achieve? What are the goals we have? What are the values we have? And what instruments do we think we have; and how do these relate to each other in a society where we all live together? Reasoning therefore takes a very complex form in integrating these various factors, and I think that if we understand rationality in this broader sense, *then* I would be sympathetic to the point you quoted Coleman as making. But at the same time, if it looks as if rationality is going to be used in a very narrow sense, in a rather mechanical way, I must say I would be very worried about it.

Q: Some of the things you have been saying remind me of Max Weber's theory of rationality, especially his distinction between "substantive rationality" and "formal rationality". Economists, however, rarely refer to Weber and to this specific distinction when they talk about rationality. Why is that so, in your opinion?

A: Maybe it is just a mistake on our part not to take Weber more seriously! I think that part of the reason may be that these two particular concepts, as I understand them, have had a fair amount of discussion in the philosophical literature which economists nowadays take more seriously than they used to. This is true both for the issue of "instrumental rationality"—which I think relates to "formal rationality"—and for rationality in a broader sense, which includes "substantive rationality." These have been discussed quite a bit, even by economists. Somebody like John Broome, for example, has been concerned with this question (Broome 1978). But he has come to it more from the philosophical end. In a sense, one reason why influences from the outside very often tend to come from philosophy rather than from sociology in the case of economics is that philosophy is the older of the two disciplines. The issue of ends and means is for example something which already Aristotle discusses extensively.

In fact, by the time Weber was writing on that subject, plenty of authors had already written on it. It may still turn out to be the case that Weber's analysis is the clearest and the best—I just don't know. But if that is so and if we have neglected Weber, we have indeed made a mistake. We do make lots of mistakes in economics, and this may be one of them! But on the other hand, I think the main reason why this particular type of distinction has not been attributed to Weber is because most of us have encountered it in some form in writings predating Weber by a couple of thousand years.

Q: Another topic on which I would like to hear your opinion, is "economic imperialism." The impression I have from reading your works is that you are fairly critical of it. In *Collective Choice and Social Welfare*, for example, you criticize Buchanan and Tullock for some of the points they make in *Calculus of Consent*, such as their insistence on unanimity as a basis for collective action. You say that you find this demand "grotesque" and point out that if this reasoning had been accepted, Marie Antoinette could have saved the French monarchy (Sen 1970, 25). And in a paper from the early 1980s on family economics, one can find some fairly harsh formulations about Gary Becker. For example, you say that "what Gary Becker does is to convert a wisecrack into a theory of all marriages and all family relations" (Sen 1983, 373). And you sum up your critique of his work like this: "What would have been a witty and insightful aphorism thus becomes [in the case of Becker] a rather odd general theory."

A: Well, let me first of all say that I would not identify the writings of someone like James Buchanan with that of Becker because I think Buchanan is very impressive in terms of the breadth of his interest. In my judgement he has done more than most to introduce ethics, legal political thinking, and indeed social thinking into economics. I have the greatest respect for Buchanan, even though I may disagree with him on a particular point. It is true that I did criticize a particular criterion, namely, the unvarying need for unanimity in collective action, put forward by Buchanan and Tullock in *The Calculus of Consent*. Today I think I was too quickly dismissive of it. If I were to rewrite my book, I would still be critical of it and reject it—but in a more reasoned and careful way.

I don't think that Becker's case is quite the same. The reason for this is that what Becker actually has done is to take a very limited set of tools that economists sometimes use and then applied these to other subjets. The thing about this "economic imperialism," as it is sometimes called, is not that these tools don't apply very well outside of economics. The main trouble is that they don't apply very well inside economics either! The situation is comparable to what would have been the case if Alexander marched off to Persia without first having established control over Macedonia. Becker's tools have been chosen on the ground of their alleged success in economics, but they are narrow and do not have much predictive and explanatory power even in economics.

Having said that, I must add that I have a certain amount of admiration for Becker's project of trying to unify the analysis in the social sciences. I think that project is right. Whatever tools prove to be appropriate in economics would in my judgement also have relevance in sociology because our subjects are so close. Sociological variables are very important in economics, and economic variables are also important in sociology. There will of course always be some differences between economics and sociology due to the particular concentration and emphasis of each. But on the other hand, the tools they use will also have much in common.

Insofar as Becker is concerned, the trouble is really that you cannot first ignore the enormous impact of sociological factors in economics and think that you have succeeded with the economic analysis, and then try to apply this narrow economic analysis outside the field of economics. The project of unification is right; the particular method of unification Becker has chosen is not. His method is based on certain very narrow and limited technologies, which have not been all that successful in economics and which will not be successful outside it either. Still I would say that there is a need for integration and that this is certainly an important project.

Q: My last question has to do with what you would consider to be the best way to go about the integration of economics and sociology. You often refer to the great eighteenth- and nineteenth-century economists—Smith, Mill, and Marx—as if you wholeheartedly agreed with their view of economics. But hasn't there been a great deal of progress in social and economic thought since then? And is your own concept of economics and the way you think this integration between economics and sociology should proceed really that similar to theirs? Doesn't your own vision, which is profoundly moral and centered on man as a reasoning creature, actually extend in both a somewhat different and more modern direction?

A: I take your point. I think indeed that there are lots of interesting and rich things to do just now in economics and where the past writings of the eighteenth and nineteenth centuries are not of great help. I think we understand much more about the nature of society today. This is partly because there have been more empirical studies and partly because the nature of society has changed, so the empirical studies that were made in the eighteenth and nineteenth centuries may not be of that much relevance any longer. So there are some problems where it certainly would be a great mistake to rely too heavily on the writings of even as wonderful writers as Smith or Mill or Marx.

But on the other hand, there are other general problems which these authors addressed extremely well, and these have tended to be neglected in modern writings. In some fields they have a kind of relevance today that is perhaps no less than what they had earlier. To give a few examples, in *The Theory of Moral Sentiments*, Adam Smith analyzes the role that the rules of conduct play in our lives and how they affect our perception of what is the right thing to do, given our own perception of our selves. I think this is a very important analysis. Similarly, there is Marx's notion that our identity is a socially determined identity and related to our membership of particular groups. There is also Mill's notion about the pervasive importance of liberty in our conception of a good life. This is again something that is very important. And I think all three of these analyses have tended to be neglected in modern economics even though Smith, Mill, and Marx still receive attention in histories of economic thought. These important ideas of theirs have had very little impact on modern economic theorizing.

Perhaps I could put my answer as saying the following three things. First, these ideas of Smith, Mill, and Marx—and of several other classical authors—remain important and should be listened to. Several problems of social living were analyzed very well by these authors, and one can benefit from reading their works. Second, since these people were actually economists—even though they were *also* moral philosophers, political theorists, or political activists (as in the case of Marx)—it is in a sense easier to integrate their ideas into economics. They also did a certain amount of integration themselves. *The Wealth of Nations* was an integrating effort on the part of Smith which he saw as an elaboration of a small part of *The Theory of Moral Sentiments*. And similarly, Marx's *Capital* draws—often implicitly—on the philosophy of Hegel, and many others, including Aristotle. The third reason why I tend to emphasize the eighteenth- and nineteenth-century economists has, I am afraid, more to do with my own intellectual history. I am simply a little better read on these authors than on many other major writers.

But I wouldn't deny at all that if we were only to rely on these authors, we would make terrible mistakes. And I think you are absolutely right that there is always a danger of falling prey to the past. These works may be relevant to some parts of modern economic theory, but much has happened in the field of modern knowledge about which the past writers, even the greatest among them, had little clue. So I am not unsympathetic to the point you are making about the need for a more modern way of integrating economics and sociology than the one advocated by Smith, Mill, and Marx. But I would still make a qualified plea for relying a great deal on the classics.

Coming back to the general question you have asked about the integration of economics and sociology, the most important point is that they both have to come to terms with the complexities of social living. Indeed, both subjects are about human life in society. Economics is ultimately not about commodities, but about the lives that human beings can lead. These lives include making commodities as well as using them, but they are not the same as commodity production, exchange, and consumption. The interest in the world of commodities is a derivative one, and the ultimate concern has to be with the lives we can or cannot lead. That is, of course, a complex concern, and the working of these lives cannot really be understood without bringing in the society in which all this takes place. One can, in fact, say that ultimately economics and sociology look at different aspects of the same phenomenon, viz. the lives of human beings in society. I believe that the task of integration of economics and sociology would be much easier if we recognize clearly how large an area of congruence we have. The immediate objects of attention are much more disparate than our respective ultimate concerns. It may, in fact, be more important to seek a fuller understanding of the commonality of our foundational interests than to seek a formal integration of the two disciplines.

References

Blaug, Mark. 1986. *Who's Who in Economics: A Biographical Dictionary of Modern Economics.* 2d ed. Cambridge: MIT Press.

Broome, James. 1978. "Choice and Value in Economics." *Oxford Economic Papers* 30:313–33.

Buchanan, James M., and Gordon Tullock. 1962. *The Calculus of Consent: Logical Foundations of Constitutional Democracy.* Ann Arbor: University of Michigan Press.

Harvard Gazette. 1987. "Amartya Sen Appointed Lamont University Professor." November 13:3.

McPherson, Michael S. 1984. "On Schelling, Hirschman, and Sen: Revising the Conception of the Self." *Partisan Review* 51:236–47.

Ramachandran, V.K. 1986. "Reorienting Economics—An Interview with Amartya Sen." *Frontline—India's National Magazine* November 29–December 12:36–48.

Sen, Amartya. 1960. *Choice of Techniques: An Aspect of the Theory of Planned Economic Development.* Oxford: Basil Blackwell.

———. 1970. *Collective Choice and Social Welfare.* San Francisco: Holden-Day.

———. 1976–1977. "Rational Fools: A Critique of the Behavioural Foundations of Economic Theory." *Philosophy and Public Affairs* 6:317–44.

———. 1981. *Poverty and Famines: An Essay on Entitlement and Deprivation.* Oxford: Clarendon Press.

———. 1982. "The Right Not to Be Hungry." In *Contemporary Philosophy: A New Survey,* vol. 2, edited by Guttorm Floistad, 343–60. The Hague: Martinus Nijhoff.

———. 1983. "Economics and the Family." In *Resources, Values and Development,* edited by A. Sen, 369–85. Cambridge: Harvard University Press.

———. 1985. "Women, Technology and Social Divisions." *Trade and Development.* New York: United Nations.

———. 1987. *Gender and Cooperative Conflict.* Helsinki: WIDER Working Paper No. 18.

———. 1987. *On Ethics and Economics.* Oxford: Basil Blackwell.

Smith, Adam. 1976. *The Theory of Moral Sentiments.* Indianapolis: Liberty Classics. Originally appeared in 1759.

15

Robert M. Solow

ROBERT SOLOW is known primarily for his innovative work on capital theory and long-term growth in which the role of technology is emphasized.[1] When he was awarded the Nobel Prize in 1987, it was this achievement in particular that was cited. He has also made important contributions to such areas of economics as fiscal policy, urban economics, and the economics of resources. "Most recently," Solow says, "I have concentrated on the ways and reasons why labor markets do not function like a classical spot market."

In this interview, Solow mainly discusses his general interest in social institutions and social norms, and how these affect economic life. Solow had previously discussed these kind of questions in connection with a session of the American Economic Association in 1984 on the relationship between economic history and economic theory. He criticized the way that many economists ignore the role of social institutions and try to treat economics as if it were "a hard science" rather than a "social science." Solow has also referred to this critique on other occasions. In his own work as an economist, it is first and foremost in his work on unemployment that he has introduced social factors into the analysis. The main problem he is struggling with here is how unemployment is at all possible. Why is it, he asks, that workers do not underbid each other rather than go unemployed? Solow's own answer is that social norms—perceptions of what is fair and unfair—must somehow be involved. That Solow's interest in this topic comes close to the concerns of sociologists is exemplified by the fact that, in 1988, he was invited to hold the prestigious Paul F. Lazarsfeld Lecture at Columbia University.

Robert Solow was born in Brooklyn, New York, in 1924, the son of Hannah Gertrude Sarney and Milton Henry Solow, a fur buyer. He received his undergraduate degree in 1947 from Harvard, where he also got

The following interview with Robert M. Solow was conducted in his office at MIT on April 26, 1988.

[1] For his two classical papers in this area, see Solow 1956, 1957. The following information is based on Blaug 1985; Parker 1986; *Who's Who in Economics*; Sweezy 1987; Feder 1987; Matthews 1988; and Prescott 1988.

his M.A. in 1949, and his Ph.D. in 1951. In 1950, he began working at MIT. He has basically worked there since that time, with an occasional break as visiting professor elsewhere. In the early 1960s, he was also a staff member of the President's Council of Economic Advisers.

•

Q: When you were an undergraduate at Harvard in the early 1940s, your first field of concentration was a combination of sociology and anthropology. Could you tell a little about how you chose to study these two topics?

A: Yes, but you have to realize that all of this is filtered through nearly fifty years of memory. I came to Harvard College in September 1940 at the age of sixteen with no very well defined interests. I can tell you what my courses were during my freshman year—that I remember. I had a year of psychology. The first half was perception, I think, and Edwin Boring was the lecturer. The second half was psychology of personality, and Gordon Allport was the lecturer. I took a year of an elementary economics course. I took a year of biology; I think I had notions of becoming a biologist. And I took German.

During all this I was interested in social science in general, and in my sophomore year I became a major in a field called "the area of the social sciences." It was sort of interdisciplinary social science, and I adopted that. During this sophomore year, I took courses with Talcott Parsons and Clyde Kluckhohn. I was probably steered into those courses by Marion Levy, who was then a graduate student in sociology and a student of Parsons. Levy was a friend of my roommate in college, and that is how I got to meet him. He came to pay a call to my roommate one day, and we got to be friends.

I also took social science courses—all this happened in about two years—with George Homans in sociology, with Henry Murray in psychology, and with Carlton Coon in anthropology. I became a friend as well as a student of Clyde Kluckhohn, and we saw each other on a social basis, especially after the war. Although I went to occasional lectures in sociology, the only sociologist I studied with any intensity was Talcott Parsons. I became friends with him too, although it is not so easy to imagine becoming a close friend of Talcott's. He was shy and formal, and I was always conscious that I was speaking to someone much older and more eminent than myself. I don't believe that he put that on. It was rather that he was such a self-conscious person, choosing his words very carefully and so on, that it was impossible to forget that he was a distinguished scholar. Clyde Kluckhohn, on the other hand, was a much more spontaneous type of person.

Q: What was your general impression of Parsons's sociology? Did you ever come across what he has written on sociology and economics?

A: Very early I read *The Structure of Social Action* by Parsons. In fact, since I got all A's during my freshman year I was entitled to a book prize, as I think Harvard freshmen all are. I could have chosen any book I wanted, but I got a copy of *The Structure of Social Action*, which was a very thick and expensive book for a poor boy.

As to Parsons and economics, one of the chapters in *The Structure of Social Action* is about Alfred Marshall. There is also one on Pareto. At that time, however, I was not aware of how distinguished an economist Pareto was. For the longest time I only thought of Pareto as the author of what is translated into English as *The Mind and Society*—his *Trattato*. It wasn't till many years later that I realized that Pareto was an extraordinary, important nineteenth-century economist, and a mathematical economist at that.

So I knew that Parsons had an interest in economics. Of the courses that I took with him, I especially remember one in the sociology of the professions. There was also a whole one-year course; I think it was called "Sociology 6" or "Social Relations 6." When it comes to Parsons—and I don't know whether I am reading this back into my mind or not—but I think I remember feeling, even as a seventeen- or eighteen-year old junior, that Parsons was surprisingly at his best when he was being concrete and less interesting when he was being a theorist. I thought his course on the sociology of professions was fascinating, but it was exciting because Parsons was a very sharp observer of the behavior of these professional people. He would typically observe something special about the way doctors or lawyers behaved, then think about it and interpret it. And I thought that was fascinating! But when he tried to do general social theory, I found it less exciting, a little dry. And as time went on, I felt that more and more.

I actually remember having a big argument with Talcott much later. This must have been in the late 1950s, so I was already a professor. It took place in Palo Alto at the Center for Advanced Study in the Behavioral Sciences, where Talcott was giving a talk on Weber and the Protestant ethic. As it happened, one of my colleagues that year at the Center was David Landes, the economic historian. He had told me about some correspondence, which he had access to, of some textile manufacturing families in two towns in Northern France called Roubaix and Tourcoing. What David had found in his research was that these people, who were Catholics, sounded very much in their letters like Weber's Calvinists (see Landes 1957, 1976). They had, according to Landes's evidence, a kind of ethic that was very similar to the Protestant ethic. So I raised this question with Talcott after the talk. I said, "Look, Weber must in a certain sense be wrong, because this set of ideas that he discusses isn't as closely tied to Protestantism as he thought." Talcott answered, "Well, you mustn't interpret Weber as meaning that the Protestant ethic has anything in particular to do with Protestantism. It has to do with some more general class of religious orientations and what not." And I remember saying, "Talcott, you are turning Weber into dishwater! Either he means Protestantism or he means nothing!" And Talcott was very angry with me. It was lèse-majesté: I had suggested that Weber might be dishwater in Talcott's interpretation. Nevertheless, we remained friends.

On the whole I think that Parsons tended to generalize too much. And when some set of facts contradicted his generalizations, he would generalize still further instead of saying, "Well, how should I alter what I've said?" He would try to weaken the assumptions to include all the embarrassing facts. And I think that is a bad way to do social science. When I later read the various works on general social theory which Talcott has written, it struck me that all these "systems" and "system boundaries" were very bad metaphors. I was really quite unhappy with this part of Talcott's work.

Q: As a young student who had sampled a bit of all the social sciences, what made you turn to economics? What tipped the balance in its favor?

A: It's hard to say. And I am not that sure how much the balance was actually tipped. I left Harvard College halfway through my junior year and joined the army. This was when I became eighteen at the end of 1942. So I was at Harvard only for the academic years of 1940–1941, 1941–1942, and then the fall term of 1942. I left simply because I wanted to fight Hitler. I decided I would rather be a soldier.

I did take a certain number of economics courses before I left. But I am not sure I did it because economics was particularly exciting. I was a fairly left-wing person, so I was interested in those things. For example, I was strongly influenced by Paul Sweezy's course on the economics of socialism. And that led me to study some labor economics. I did a lot of economics, but I don't recall that I felt committed to it. And when I left college for the war I was still, I guess, in this interdisciplinary major. When I came back from the war, I really didn't know what to do. I actually think that I chose economics, at least in part, because the girl I married had done a degree in economics. Her experience had been favorable. So I figured, you know, maybe it would suit me too.

Q: Your wife, Barbara Solow, is an economic historian, right?

A: Yes, but at the time she had just finished her undergraduate degree in economics. We got to talk, you know, about what I should do. I was discharged from the army in August 1945 and I was going to start college again in September that year, so I had to make up my mind. And it was true that I had enjoyed economics. If I were to tell you that what attracted me to doing economics was the prospect of doing a social science that was more rigorous and more like a science than the other social sciences, I would probably be exaggerating the clarity with which I saw things in those days. That would be my preferred interpretation now though. But at the time, I think I knew very little what I was doing.

Q: Since you have had some experience with both economics and sociology, how would you compare the two? And are there big differences in their professional cultures?

A: I don't know exactly how to put this, but I think that the difference in professional culture really has to do with the fact that in economics an analysis has to be reasoned out in a rigorous way and impressionism is just not a valid way to reach conclusions. Most of the sociology I read and the sociologists I talk to are more given to what used to be called "verstehende Soziologie" or "interpretative sociology." Here you rather attempt to think your way into or intuit situations. Economists have found a way to think very rigorously about the economic system as a whole; while I have found sociological thinking of society as a whole *not* to be satisfyingly rigorous. I don't think that this is necessarily the fault of the sociologists. Possibly it just can't be done. Maybe there are no comparably simple and approximately valid principles for society, apart from economics.

Q: Sometimes I get the feeling that economists look down on sociologists. Do you find that to be true?

A: Yes, economists *do* look down on sociologists. I myself seriously do not. But economists as a class do. They regard sociologists—and this goes along with what I have just been saying—as soft intellectuals; and they regard economists as hard intellectuals. And "hard" is better than "soft."

Q: So I take it that economists would feel inferior to physicists, biologists, and so on, since they are even "harder."

A: Yes, they do.

Q: According to a stereotypical belief you sometimes find among sociologists, economists don't really study reality. They build abstract models of how the economy works and then they feel that the analysis is finished. As an economist, what's your reaction to this description of economists?

A: I think that what you have just described represents an incorrect impression. But I also think that the truth about economists is almost as damaging. First, it's a mistake to think that economists don't do empirical work. In fact, I think they do too much empirical work! No, not that they really do too much; it's rather that they can talk themselves into believing any empirical conclusion, where a critically minded person would find the evidence unconvincing.

Where your sociological stereotype goes wrong is on the following point, I think. There exists a type of economic work, which is exactly as you describe it: you think of a situation; you build a mathematical model—and that's the end of the article. But there exists a much larger class of articles in economics, where you do the following. You think about a problem; you build a model; you linearize it—you treat everything as linear—and you do formal statistical analysis of real economic data; and you estimate the parameters of the models or you test hypotheses; and then you do formal statistical tests; and then you state conclusions—and *that* is the end of the article. This way of doing things is beyond any shadow of a doubt empirical work.

The problem with it, I think, is rather that it's too rare for economists to ask themselves seriously, "Will the data bear the conclusions that I want to push upon them? Am I asking questions so subtle that the statistical methods will give answers which depend on trivial characteristics of the data?" They don't ask, "Is the period of time from which I have taken the data really homogeneous? Might the relationship I am estimating have changed its form somewhere during this period?" They don't ask whether the assumption that this function is linear so that I may do standard statistical estimation on it is a reasonable estimate. They don't ask themselves—and I think this is the worst sin of them all—whether there doesn't exist a different model that would fit the data equally as well, and what does that tell me? So I think that the problem with economists is that they do too much uncritical empirical work, and that they deceive themselves with the refinements of their methods.

Q: When you talk about economics, you sometimes contrast "economics as a social science" to "economics as a hard science" (Solow 1985a, 1988c). It's clear that you prefer economics to be a social science and not of the physics-like variety. But what exactly does it mean to you that economics is a social science? The institutionalists would probably agree that economics is a social science, but their definition is not likely to be very much like yours.

A: I suspect there is a whole continuum of views about the nature of "economic science." But what I personally have in mind is that I would like to do as rigorous theoretical and empirical economics as possible. I want to preserve the analytical structure of economics, and I would also like to improve it by including or somehow incorporating into it the understanding that the objectives of individual economic behavior are modified by social institutions. Instead of supposing that the motives of workers are adequately described by pecuniary maximization of some kind, I would like to include in the very analytical description of the behavior of workers and employers the fact that they have notions of what is appropriate behavior in some contexts and might be inappropriate in other contexts. I would like to give effect to the force of social institutions in modifying or governing the behavior of participants in the economy. But I would definitely not simply want to give up the idea of doing a rigorous analysis of markets!

Q: And how do you view institutionalism? Does it represent a viable alternative in your opinion?

A: I am not certain that "institutionalism" is a coherent point of view. Perhaps it is; then I do not know exactly what it claims. My impression is that self-conscious "institutionalists" are anti-theoretical. They don't believe that generalization is possible at all. Description of institutions is all there is. I do believe that economic theory is possible and useful as a foundation for applied economics. My complaint is about much of the particular theory we have.

Q: Could you describe in greater detail what you mean when you say that economics is a social science? Incidentally, wouldn't George Akerlof use exactly the kind of mixture of rigorous economics and social influences that you seem to advocate?

A: Oh yes! George was a student of mine and a favorite one at that. And I think that George thinks he is doing the kind of economics I'd approve of—and he is right!

But to get back to the question of economics as a social science. One often hears economics being criticized on the basis that *homo economicus* is an excessively simple and unrealistic construct. And also that it is poor psychology. My answer to that has always been that economic man is not a psychological concept at all; it is a *sociological* concept. It is sociological in the sense that in our society there are certain aspects of behavior in which it is approved of as well as routine to decide things on the basis of narrow, even pecuniary self-interest. In fact, I think I once wrote, "When we say of someone that he is not in business for love, we're stating the obvious. Nobody is in business for love. Being in business is something different from being in love."

So there exist classes of human behavior, especially economic behavior, where economic man is a valid concept. And it is valid, not because anyone is born like that psychologically, but because the social norms encourage that kind of behavior. On the other hand, there also exist situations where the choice appears quite differently. If it turns out that in choosing and deciding whom to marry I am only interested in the wealth of various women, then I would be thought of not only as strange but also as unattractive.

Q: Is the viewpoint that you are talking about—economics as a social science—popular in the economic profession, or is it a minority view?

A: I think it is a minority view. It is a minority view, at least among those who publish papers in economic theory, that is, the pacesetters. If we take the economics profession to be the twenty thousand or so members of the American Economic Association, I have no idea what they would think. Probably more of them than the elite would adopt the view of economics as a social science.

Q: If we now switch to your second category of economics—economics as a "hard science"—What exactly is wrong with this approach?

A: Let me put it to you this way. Assume that I am a physicist and that I am studying the decay of electrons. You put me on an airplane, blindfold me, fly me somewhere, and parachute me to the ground together with my equipment. Now I could, if I so choose, just continue my study of the electrons without ever asking, "Where am I?" But if I am an economist who studies the labor market and the same thing happens, then it is really necessary, when I land with the parachute and propose to study the local labor force, to ask myself, "What kind of society am I in? Is this an African tribe? Are these people Australian bushmen? Are they Europeans or Japanese?" A physicist might be curious whether he is in Japan or in Australia, but he would really have no reason to believe that his results would differ or that the way he should go about doing his research would differ, depending on where he is.

I think that many economists would like to think that economics is a universal science, just like physics, and that all the sociological stuff is pointless. People maximize this or that; and that is really all you need to know. That is why I disagree with the notion of economics as physics.

Q: So, by default, those who see economics as a hard science like physics would constitute a majority of today's pacesetting economists?

A: Yes, I think so.

Q: It seems to me that the traditional border between economics and sociology is presently being redrawn. There are several ways of doing this, and the one I would like to ask you about is "economic imperialism." What opinion do you have of the work by Becker et al.? Does it fall into your category of "economics as a social science," or into its opposite, "economics as physics"?

A: My impression of the body of work you are referring to here is that it tried very hard to turn economics into the physics of society, to explain as much as possible using only narrow economics-like assumptions. I am not at all attracted by the kind of work that Gary Becker is now doing. I think that something interesting will come out of it, however, because Gary Becker is a very smart person, and even when a very smart person goes down the wrong road, something of interest will come out of it. I have read some of the literature on economic imperialism, but I haven't read it exhaustively because it doesn't interest me particularly. As I read Becker's stuff on the family, marriage, divorce, and all that, I feel that he is trying to force quite different and maybe also more complicated forms of behavior into the mold of behavior that we economists feel to be particularly suitable for economic analysis. That means: maximizing well-defined functions (of a certain kind) subject to well-defined constraints (of a certain kind). My nagging feeling is that what he gets out of this oscillates between the obvious and the false.

Q: Poor Becker!

A: Don't say, "Poor Becker!"—he is very successful with his own serious research project. And he will one day win a Nobel Prize for his work. In terms of high-quality thinking, there is no doubt that he is very, very good. I just find that when I read him, my response usually falls into one of two categories. Either I feel that I do not need all this apparatus to reach these obvious conclusions. Or I say to myself, "How could anyone believe this to be true?"

Much of the work by people like Becker—and by others too, probably including myself—falls into a certain trap, which incidentally is not a trap peculiar to economics; it's just as typical for other social sciences. The trap is this: I have a model with some parameters, and if I choose the parameters correctly, I can make the model fit some facts. That is, there is *some* evidence in favor of the truth of the model, but it is not very strong evidence unless I have some way of convincing myself that I have not done what somebody else could do with any one of thirteen different models of the same phenomena.

Q: In sociology there is presently a parallel movement to what Becker is doing in economics. It is sometimes called rational choice sociology, and the leading person is James Coleman at Chicago. The basic idea behind this movement is that you can recast sociology on the basis of rational choice. What would be your reaction to this attempt?

A: Oh, I would certainly be sympathetic to it in the sense that I think one should see how far you can go with rationality in sociology. I would apply the same rules to Jim Coleman as I would apply to myself or to any other economist, namely that before I go on modeling behavior in this sphere as rational—as obeying, that is, the axioms of rationality—I want to ask myself, "Do I really think that behavior in this sphere of social life follows that sort of rules?" And while I am sure that some social behavior indeed is rational, I am not at all sure that *all* noneconomic social behavior is rational. Just as I am not sure that all economic behavior is rational.

There is a subtlety here that I have never been able to get straight for myself. If you are imbued with the economists' way of proceeding, you first of all ask: "What are these people trying to accomplish?" This usually means, without much loss of generality, "What are they trying to maximize?" And then secondly you ask, "When they make their choices to maximize whatever it is they are trying to maximize, what constraints do they see their choices as subject to?" That's the economists' reflex way of going at any problem of human behavior. Now, there are two ways of modifying a theory like that. One is to say to yourself, "What else might they be maximizing, other than the normal economic thing?" And you can also say, "What constraints do they feel subject to other than the normal economic ones?" You can often accomplish very much the same thing by either method. Now, I prefer and I also feel more comfortable in modifying the constraints. There are two reasons for this. The first is that it is intellectually too easy to assume that they are maximizing something else. Suppose you have what looks like some peculiar behavior, and you would like to understand it and produce a model of it. It's very easy to explain this peculiar behavior if you feel that you have a free choice in terms of the goals of the people, whose behavior you are trying to explain. If people stand on their heads all the time, you may say to yourself, "Aha! What they are trying to achieve is an upside down view of the world!" But that's too easy and it usually doesn't lead to anything interesting.

The other reason why I prefer to modify the constraints is that, to my mind, it is a good way of doing sociologically interesting economics. It's neater as well. And it is also, I think, more realistic and sound to say different social institutions impose different constraints on what constitutes acceptable behavior.

Q: What would the constraints be in your example with people standing on their heads?

A: I don't know, but it might be that it's impolite to have the same vertical orientation as your social superior. It's not so much that they want to be standing on their heads as the fact that they must do it or otherwise they would be violating some norm.

Q: In your work, you have made contributions to several different areas in economics, such as mathematical economics, economic growth, capital theory, and a few others as well. In all of this—and your work on unemployment exempted for a moment—have you had any help from sociology or in some way introduced social influences directly into the analysis?

A: Only in one context that I can think of just now. And that's something I have never written about. I don't know if this is the kind of thing you have in mind, but let me describe it to you and you can judge. I used to teach a course for the graduate students at MIT on the theory of capital. Now, the mainstream theory of capital has often been criticized from a

Marxian or semi-Marxian influenced point of view by some people, who say that the normal theory of capital ignores the class structure of society. This always comes up because in the simplest orthodox model of the capitalist economy, it really doesn't matter whether it is the capitalists who hire the workers or the workers who rent the capital. Those are two equivalent setups.

Q: I guess I belong to the people who have always found that a bit weird.

A: Well, it's weird because markets are not so simple. And it is not easy to find out what the right modification is. But in order to convince myself and to convince the students of this kind of capital theory, I used to try to construct a model of a class society in my lectures. Instead of making the assumption that there are only households and firms, I would start with the assumption that there are two kinds of households; and that these two classes of households differ, perhaps systematically in their tastes for goods, in their access to credit or in some other way. And then I would try to see, in a simple mathematical model, how much difference this makes. Obviously, a society in which there are two classes of people with different tastes will not give exactly the same results as a society in which there is only one class of people with only one set of tastes. But does it fundamentally alter the basic metaphor of capital theory? Well, there are differences, of course, just as if people could live without food, the results of economic analysis would be different. But nevertheless, the fundamental type of conclusions one would come to, namely, that increased willingness to save will lower the return on capital and perhaps even lower the income of the capitalist class—they would still hold.

Q: Let's switch to unemployment. This is a problem you have worked on for a long time and which seems to interest you very much. By 1964, you had already published a book on unemployment; in 1979, you devoted your presidential address at the American Economic Association to it; and just a couple of weeks ago when you gave the Lazarsfeld Lecture, you chose to talk about unemployment. Do you have mainly an intellectual interest in unemployment, or is it rather political-social?

A: It's a mixture of both. It's first of all a social interest—I don't know if "political" is a good word in this context—and in this sense it's non-intellectual or only partially intellectual, as is clear from my Lazarsfeld Lecture. I think I have had this interest in unemployment from the very beginning—since I was a child during the Great Depression. The 1930s were the years when I was becoming conscious of what was happening in the society around me, so I think of unemployment as the characteristic pathology of the capitalist economy.

Q: I also have the impression that you find unemployment a very intriguing intellectual problem, in the sense that the normal market model doesn't work here. Is that correct?

A: Yes, that is the intellectual side of it.

Q: There currently exist several different theories in economics for how to analyze unemployment: efficiency wage theories, insider-outsider models, and so on. Where do you place your own research in all of this?

A: First of all, you have to understand that the way an economic theorist works is maybe different from the way a sociologist works. Precisely because mathematical model building is the natural mode of doing theory, it is much easier for an economist, I suspect—I don't know this for sure—to say, "Let's try this; let's try that; let's try something else! Let's try one modification after another of the conventional Walrasian market-clearing model to see what set of assumptions, what set of postulates or axioms will give us a story which looks as if it corresponds a bit better to the things we are trying to understand." So I have written papers on efficiency wage theory; I have written papers about insider-outsider models; and I am presently writing a chapter together with Frank Hahn which is trying to say that the really important way in which the labor market differs from the classical economic market is that there is an understood concept of *fairness*, which steers the behavior of the workers and even of employers. So normal market behavior is constrained by the fact that there are things that a worker will not do because he or she thinks it would be an improper way to behave; it would be *unfair* to one's mates or colleagues.

So there exist three different models, and I have written papers about all of them and always in the spirit that the labor market is clearly not like the market for fish. Well, let's be more precise. How is it unlike the market for fish and which of the ways in which it is unlike the market for fish seems most likely to give a believable account of unemployment? I think that there is a little bit of truth in all these three stories, but I have beliefs about which aspects of the problem each of these stories is most suitable for.

For instance, the efficiency wage story is a story which says that unemployment can be an equilibrium state of the labor market, essentially because without it, firms would have no way of inducing the workers to perform, to extract labor from them or forcing them to perform. I think there is something to that, but I think that it has mainly to do with the long-term level of unemployment. And I do not believe that business cycle fluctuations in unemployment can be explained in this way. On the other hand, I think that the insider-outsider models are more appropriate or more plausible as a way of explaining the cyclical level of unemployment or fluctuations in unemployment. So I don't think of these models as exclusive alternatives, but rather as different aspects of the same thing.

Q: And where does sociology come into all of this? In an earlier conversation we had about Schumpeter and economic sociology, you described yourself as a "frustrated seeker after sociological help" a propos unemployment.

A: Yes, I think that sociology could be of help in the analysis of unemployment. And especially when it comes to this fairness story, which I am really very interested in for a number of reasons. Some of these reasons, I would say, are good reasons and some are more parochial. The parochial is that Frank Hahn and I have been able to formulate this fairness part as a formal game, and I like that! It gives us economists a way of doing theory and of behaving the way we are supposed to behave. But there is also the fact that if fairness is part of the behavior in the labor market, then I need to understand how norms of social behavior evolve. And this is where sociology would come in.

Let me give you an example, which I mention in the Lazarsfeld Lecture.

What should happen as unemployment is prolonged? If what prevents unemployed workers from competing for jobs—to take away jobs from employed workers—is some social norm which forbids it, which says it's not a decent thing to do, would you then expect prolonged unemployment to cause that prohibition—that constraint—to weaken? Or would you not? If it weakens, would you expect it to weaken gradually or suddenly? Those are questions about the dynamics of social norms, and I don't think I am the person to make suggestions about how to analyze that dynamic. I would rather like to be able to read a book by a sociologist on the topic. I remembered, when I was working on this fairness model of the labor market, that in my early days at Harvard College I had read a book by Muzafer Sherif called *Psychology of Social Norms*. So I said to myself, "Maybe Sherif will tell me something I need to know." I went back and looked at the book, but it didn't tell me what I was after. It was still worthwhile—it's an interesting book—but it didn't tell me anything of value for my analysis of unemployment.

Or take another example, *Obedience to Authority* by Stanley Milgram, which I read just a few years ago. It contained a fascinating account by this Yale psychologist of experiments in which he got some people to apparently cause other people a lot of pain. Now, an economist doing these experiments would have insisted on producing a model of what would reinforce this willingness to cause pain; of what would cause that willingness to cause pain to diffuse and to deteriorate; and so on. He would have tried to give an account of how all that happens. But Milgram seemed to have no real interest in doing that or capacity to do it. Well, that's the kind of work I would want some sociologists to do.

Q: Apart from unemployment, what would be some other area where sociology could be of help to economists?

A: Another example, though not one on which I have worked, would be this long-standing problem in economic theory, namely, how to model oligopoly behavior. One could try to model the behavior of markets in which there are small numbers of sellers, each of which knows there is only a small number of sellers, and so on. The way economics has evolved, the current device for doing this would be to model it as a game. But the game has no sociological structure at all. There is nothing in it at all about how strategies evolve in situations where there are rivals who can communicate with each other, who can observe one another, maybe not perfectly but clearly up to a point. And when do people tend to collude tacitly? They are not allowed to do this—it's against the law—but we know that there are some markets in which the sellers do collude. They have some ways of signaling to each other what they are going to do; they avoid conflicts; and so on. There also are circumstances under which they clash and when one of them may destroy the other. Or there may be periods in which they don't clash, followed by periods in which they do clash. What about all this? How do rivals learn—if "learn" is the right word here—what governs their behavior? Well, I would have thought that a sociologist or a social psychologist—I don't know which discipline is the right one here—would have something to say about this or might create experimental situations in which you can learn about it. So oligopoly would be another example of a situation where human beings interact with one another, and which you would expect a sociologist or a social psychologist to have some insights into.

Q: That's a very interesting example. But, you know, sociology has so many white spots when it comes to economic sociology that it doesn't surprise me that no sociological work has been done on oligopoly.

A: Well, I can understand that sociologists might have better things they are interested in—the family, for instance. I don't require all sociologists to do this, but some!

Q: What does the future, in terms of the relationship between economics and sociology, look like to you? Will "economics as a social science" win out over "economics as physics"? And what would you personally like to see happening?

A: One can't predict the distant future of anything, let alone the way a discipline will evolve. But for the moment I am inclined to think that what we in this interview have been calling the "economics as physics" view will continue to dominate and perhaps even get stronger. Why would that be? Because economists are conditioned to like aesthetic science. They like things to be intellectually neat; it is also much easier to judge. I can say that this is an A+ piece of intellectual neatness, while this is only a B piece of intellectual neatness, whereas economics as a social science is necessarily sloppier and therefore harder to judge. I want to emphasize that "sloppy" does *not* mean unrigorous. I am as devoted to rigor as anyone. "Sloppy" means "not so neat." So my guess is that formal game theorists will continue to dominate microeconomics and equilibrium theorists—people who try to apply the standard economic model to macroeconomics—will probably continue to dominate macroeconomics.

Obviously that is not the way I would like it to go. What I think might change it—at least in my part of the field, which is macroeconomics—would be a couple of really good empirical successes of sociological economics. The weakness of that branch of the economics profession which prefers "economics as physics" and wants to study macroeconomics is that it really isn't doing that well. It has lost ground in the last few years because what has been happening in the United States and in Europe in the past seven or eight years is very hard to interpret in their preferred way. You can imagine how the fact that Germany, France, and Great Britain have had extraordinarily high unemployment rates for a long period of time is very hard to account for with a model that starts out with the idea that supply equals demand everywhere, including in the labor market! So a lot of intellectual effort has gone into evading that set of problems.

Now, it's not quite good enough for my kind of macroeconomics to say that those other guys don't have a good explanation for that. *I* need a very good explanation myself. I'm not pessimistic about getting these good explanations but I think that without them, the other type of economics—economics as physics—will for a while at least seem more exciting to a young economist who wants to make her way in the field. If she can do both kinds, she'll say, "Well, the surest thing to do is to do a brilliant piece of mathematics." So, for that reason I think that most of the advantages are in the court of economics as physics. The only counter that people like George Akerlof, myself, and some others have—apart from being right, which isn't an overwhelming advantage—would be to come up with some really good empirical successes. Then we could say, "This fits perfectly! Let's see you folks produce anything as good!" We *are* better at explaining the facts, but clearly not good enough.

Deep down, I also hope and think that the kind of economics that takes social norms and institutions seriously can also be made aesthetically attractive, can get explanatory power out of fairly simple models. Economists feel the pull of that ideal. Keats was wrong: truth is not beauty and beauty is not truth. But truth *and* beauty, that's an unbeatable combination.

References

Blaug, Mark, ed. 1985. "Solow, Robert M., 1924–." In *Great Economists since Keynes*, 232–33. Brighton: Harvester Press.

Feder, Barnaby J. 1987. "Tackling Everyday Economic Problems: Robert Merton Solow." *New York Times*, October 22.

Landes, David S. 1957. "Reviews by Works of Claude Fohlen and Others on the French Textile Industry." *Journal of Economic History* 17:262–65.

———. 1976. "Religion and Enterprise: The Case of the French Textile Industry." In *Enterprise and Entrepreneurs in Nineteenth- and Twentieth-Century France*, edited by Edward C. Carter I, et al., 41–86. Baltimore: Johns Hopkins University Press.

Matthews, R.C.O. 1988. "The Work of Robert M. Solow." *Scandinavian Journal of Economics* 90:13–16.

Milgram, Stanley. 1975. *Obedience to Authority: An Experimental View.* New York: Harper and Row. Originally appeared in 1974.

Parker, William N., ed. 1986. *Economic History and the Modern Economist.* Oxford: Basil Blackwell.

Parsons, Talcott. 1937. *The Structure of Social Action: A Study in Social Theory with Special Reference to a Group of Recent European Writers.* New York: McGraw-Hill.

Prescott, Edward C. 1988. "Robert M. Solow's Neoclassical Growth Model: An Influential Contribution to Economics." *Scandinavian Journal of Economics* 90:7–12

Sherif, Muzafer. 1936. *Psychology of Social Norms.* New York: Harper and Co.

Solow, Robert M. 1956. "A Contribution to the Theory of Economic Growth." *Quarterly Journal of Economics* 70:65–94.

———. 1957. "Technical Change and the Aggregate Production Function." *Review of Economics and Statistics* 39:312–20.

———. 1964. *The Nature and Sources of Unemployment in the United States.* Stockholm: Almqvist och Wiksell.

———. 1967. "A Rejoinder." *Public Interest* 9, Fall:118–19.

———. 1973. Review of Benjamin Ward, *What's Wrong with Economics? Journal of Economic Issues* 7:694–98.

———. 1980. "On Theories of Unemployment." *American Economic Review* 70:1–11.

———. 1984. "Robert M. Solow." In *The New Classical Macroeconomics: Conversations with New Classical Economists and Their Opponents,* by Arjo Klamer, 127–48. Brighton: Harvester Press.

―――. 1985a. "Economic History and Economics." *American Economic Review* 75:328–31.

―――. 1985b. "Insiders and Outsiders in Wage Determination." *Scandinavian Journal of Economics* 87:411–28.

―――. 1988a. "Bibliography of Robert M. Solow's Publications, 1950-1987." *Scandinavian Journal of Economics* 90:17–26.

―――. 1988b. "Unemployment as a Social Problem: From Marienthal to Maryland." Paul F. Lazarsfeld Lecture, Columbia University, New York.

―――. 1988c. "Review of *The New Palgrave: A Dictionary of Economics.*" *New York Times Book Review* March 20:3, 25.

Sweezy, Paul. 1987. "Interview with Paul M. Sweezy." *Monthly Review* 38:1–28.

16 *Arthur L. Stinchcombe*

In several respects, Arthur Stinchcombe represents a rare breed of sociologist.[1] For one thing, he is one of the few who actually succeeds in living up to the ideal among sociologists of being highly competent in both theory and methods. In a world of specialization, he has also made contributions to sociology in general, as well as to some of its subfields. Two of his most appreciated contributions to general sociology are *Constructing Social Theories*, and the essay "Merton's Theory of Social Structure". For a nonsociologist who is interested in finding out what "social structure" is all about, and also to get a glimpse of how sociologists look at theory, these two works are highly recommended.

As to Stinchcombe's more specialized works, his contributions to organizational sociology and to economic sociology are particularly noteworthy. In his first article, "Bureaucratic and Craft Administration of Production," one encounters that raw streak of originality that has become the hallmark of Stinchcombe's work. Many of the themes that stimulated his thinking in the years that followed can also be found here: the interest in different types of industrial organization; the confrontation with Weber's ideal type of bureaucracy; and the attempt to understand rationality in social terms. An early work that has a similar focus and has also become a minor classic is *Creating Efficient Industrial Administrations*. Of particular interest for the current dialogue between economists and sociologists are *Economic Sociology*, and *Organization Theory and Project Management*. Stinchcombe coauthored the latter with his wife, sociologist Carol S. Heimer. In 1986, a collection of his essays was published under the title *Stratification and Organization*. The introduction to this work contains an especially good discussion of rationality and social structure. As he discusses in the interview, Stinchcombe is currently working on a study of organization and uncertainty.

The following interview was conducted on April 14, 1988, with Arthur L. Stinchcombe in his office at the Department of Sociology at Northwestern University.

[1] The following information comes from Stinchcombe's vita; Mullins and Mullins 1973, 213–49; and various works by Stinchcombe cited in the Introduction.

Arthur Stinchcombe was born in 1933 in Clare County, Michigan, the son of a school teacher and a clerical worker. He received his undergraduate degree in 1953 at Central Michigan College, where he majored in mathematics. He earned his Ph.D. in sociology from Berkeley in 1960. He first worked at Johns Hopkins (1959–1967), and then at Berkeley (1967–1975). He subsequently worked for the National Opinion Research Center (NORC) at the University of Chicago (1975–1980), and at the University of Arizona (1980–1982). For many years he has also been connected to the Institute of Industrial Economics in Bergen, Norway (1979–). He is currently working at Northwestern University.

•

Q: As an undergraduate, you were first interested in mathematics. What made you switch into sociology? Did you ever consider becoming an economist?

A: The main thing that made me switch from mathematics into sociology was that I thought I would be of second rank as a mathematician. In sociology you can never tell whether you are first rank or second rank. Anyway, it doesn't make that much difference. The second reason, which was perhaps more fundamental, was that among the things I like to talk about and which you could talk about at Central Michigan College were people like Thorstein Veblen, Karl Marx, Herbert Blumer, George Herbert Mead, and John Dewey. You could not have a natural conversation about mathematics at this college, which was a third rate place, so my conversation was much more about sociology. Parts of it also had to do with me being radical; I was a Trotskyist of a sort as an undergraduate.

So by the time I had graduated, I had already decided not to go into mathematics. In part, I chose sociology because I was particularly enthusiastic about Thorstein Veblen as an undergraduate, and I couldn't find any economists who wanted to talk about Thorstein Veblen. Sociologists, on the other hand, would. But first, however, I went into the army. Before doing that I collected reading lists for the Ph.D. examination from several sociology departments and from the economics department at Berkeley. I tried to read the things that were in common on those sociology lists and some of the things in economics. Having a Marxist background, I thought that one should learn some economics in order to study the fundamental sociological questions.

And so I went to Berkeley. I did this in part because one of the submovements of American Trotskyism was very influenced by Dewey and the pragmatists and that was represented at Berkeley by Selznick. Herbert Blumer, who introduced the pragmatists—especially G. H. Mead—into sociology, was also at Berkeley. But I actually studied mostly with Rein-hard Bendix and S. M. Lipset; and Philip Selznick was the one who finally supervised my dissertation. My thesis, as things turned out, was not on a topic that Selznick was especially appropriate for. It was on education, and my book *Rebellion in A High School* is based on my dissertation. While I conceived of the thesis as being in economic sociology, nobody else did.

Q: The title doesn't exactly give associations to economic sociology. . . .

A: Well, the fundamental argument was that what produces discipline in a high school is the prospect of economic success for the students. Discipline consists of the pursuit of approved goals under approved rules, when this is validated through a payoff in the labor market. Whatever variation that you'll find has its basis in the articulation between the student's conception of his future and what he is doing right now. The rewards and punishments of the system got their meaning, so to speak, only from the labor market and not from the school.

Q: That sounds a bit like the argument in Bowles's and Gintis's *Schooling in Capitalist America*: the discipline in the schools is directly connected to the capitalist labor market.

A: Not really, since my analysis didn't have any larger functional argument in it like their book does. It simply said that much of the time schools fail to convince the students that they are going to connect them to a good job later on. The main reason for failing to do this is that they are not going to connect them to a good job. When the schools start to put over their ideology of discipline and hard work and so on, and they are not really offering any rewards, that's when the students don't believe them. And they properly shouldn't. That was my principal explanation of the rebellion against the rules in high school. Already at the time when I wrote the thesis, I conceived of that argument as basically being a mere translation of the argument that I planned to make about the construction industry, which was my first dissertation proposal.

Q: Are you referring to the analysis one can find in your first article, "Bureaucratic and Craft Administration of Production"?

A: Yes. My first thesis topic resulted in this article except that the labor market part of the construction industry was not yet in that article. It looked instead at the administrative side, and at the demand side of the labor market. Why, for example, do they demand craftsmen in the construction industry? I was going to do my dissertation on this question. But then I couldn't get access to the construction unions I wanted; they were very suspicious at that time of academics.

Q: Did you study any economics when you were a graduate student at Berkeley?

A: Yes, I took a microeconomics course for graduate students at Berkeley. It was taught by Andreas Papandreou. He also examined me on economics in my Ph.D. prelims. He of course is not an absolutely conventional neoclassical economist, but a lot of the things I believe about economics as a discipline, I learned from him. He has this wonderful book on the relation between models and theory (Papandreou 1962). And he did a perfectly adequate job of introducing people into the basic presuppositions of economics as a paradigm. So I studied quite a lot of economics as a formal discipline and I learned even more, I suppose, when I worked as a research assistant at the Institute of Industrial Economics at Berkeley. Bendix and Lipset were working on social mobility at that time, and Clark Kerr's aura was still there. Kerr was president of the university or something of the kind, but he was still a major mover and shaker of the Institute. So that's where I got my real world economics. If you divide my education in economics into "economics as a paradigm" and "real world economics," then I got my real world economics at the Institute of Industrial Economics, and the paradigm from Andreas Papandreou and a couple of other people. Roy Radner was also at Berkeley in those days, and I took a course in mathematical economics with him. At the Institute, about half of the graduate students—the people you learn from in that context—were economists, and the other half were sociologists.

So I had a pretty good background in economics but it was sort of by conviction; I had read lots of the literature on my own. And being in the army in 1953–1955 was probably the best part of my graduate education. I worked on the night shift at a mental hospital, and even though mental patients are very sick, they are not sick at night when they sleep. So I spent two years reading everything you could get in Denver on those reading lists for the Ph.D. in sociology and economics.

Q: Industrial organizations has been a major theme in your writings ever since you started doing research thirty years ago. What is it about this topic that fascinates you? And what is it that you have tried to accomplish in this area, from the 1959 article onward?

A: Well, the first thing that sort of struck me in reading "real world economics" was that organizations behave a lot more like individuals are supposed to do according to economic theory than individuals do. Individuals don't actually calculate that much; neither do they collect all that much information. They buy something in a store, when just across the street you can buy it for half as much. But corporations don't do that, and even households buy more rationally than individuals. So the more socially organized something is, the more closely it approximates the presuppositions of the economic paradigm.

It seems to me that this is what Weber's argument was originally about; namely, that it is *society* that has to be rationalized and that individuals can't be rationalized. Or rather, individuals become rationalized because society is rationalized and not vice versa. It is because individuals are embedded in social systems that they maximize profits and so on, and not because they naturally want to maximize profits. Individuals have only gradually improved their methods of maximizing profit. So it always seemed to me that the problem Weber posed was how do you get organizations and households to become rational and supply the things they supply in a market? How do you get them to rationally calculate and do it in a way that can be compared across the economy and in the way that is required for markets to work?

The first problem that I posed was therefore in a way to explain why it was that economics works. At that time, you should know, the basic notion among most business administration and business economics types was that there wasn't any rationality in these ancient organizations that make up the construction industry. So one of the things I tried to show was that, when you consider what kind of problems this industry faced, then you shouldn't be surprised that in order to be rational about building buildings, you had to organize it in this odd decentralized way. In brief, you had to rely on what I call a "craft administration of production," where independent craft workers make many of the key decisions on their own, as opposed to a "bureaucratic administration of production," where most things are rather decided through an ordinary hierarchy. You just couldn't go out and randomly organize Ricardian labor markets and find someone who knew how to build buildings when you didn't know how to do it.

So that was the first half of the problem I had set myself very early in my career. The second half had to do with what I call "Marxism with variables." The other side of my background had led me to be interested in what a mode of production really is, and how you could get some variations on it in order to be able to study its effects. It seemed to me that the different organization of different industries obviously resulted in different behavior. You could see that just by looking at the trade union organizations in various branches of industry. Where these were different, there emerged different conditions of class conflict. So if the mode of production was to explain differences in class conflict, it obviously had to explain differences among the industries.

Looked at from an administrative viewpoint, industries showed the same sort of thing. And it was also clear that the construction industry had to solve a very different kind of set of uncertainties and problems than, for example, the automobile industry. And since these industries organized themselves differently, they also produced different class relations.

A first extension of that part of the argument in my 1959 paper on the construction industry came in a paper on agricultural enterprises and rural class relations (see Stinchcombe 1961). I was taken by a comment which Bendix once made, that the crucial thing to remember about all industrialization is that it takes place in agricultural societies. Consequently, in order to understand the constraints under which the class system of industrialization grows, you have to understand what kind of class system the society had; and that was an agricultural one. So you could not understand the transformation to industrial societies unless you could also understand the variations in the various agricultural systems. England, for example, had a very different system from that in France, from those in the various parts of Germany, and so on.

This idea, I think, was more present in those days in Bendix's lectures than in his writings. Nevertheless, it was obvious that if you were going to study economic development—which I thought I was going to do at the time—then you needed to study the class system during the period *before* the industrialization process began. The class system was quite different in different places, and the real question was if you could explain this with the help of the same argument I had used to explain the difference between the class system of the construction industry and the automobile industry. Namely, that in different forms of agriculture you have to get different things out of the labor force; that the risks of property are different; that different kinds of contract are rational; and so on. This approach has become more popular since those days, I think. Anyway, that is where my paper on agriculture fit into the second half of the intellectual enterprise I was involved in in those days.

I should also add that Berkeley was a lot more of a Marxist place than the other sociology departments in those days. That was especially true for Bendix and the graduate students but also, relatively speaking, for the faculty. Bendix was much more interested in the Marxist approach to Marxism than in, so to speak, turning it back on its head into a sort of Hegelianism again, which he became more interested in doing later. Many Marxist students also came to Berkeley when they had decided that they after all wanted to make a living. It was definitely also the place for ex-Trotskyists to go.

Q: Have you had any help from economic theory in your research on industrial organization? From what you have said, it rather seems that it was industrial economics that made an impression on you. That seems to be the case with quite a few sociologists, incidentally.

A: Let me answer like this. It is true that the further you go towards the periphery in economics, like to industrial economics or agricultural economics, the more data there is about the real world. It's similar to when you leave Oxford and go towards the red-brick universities, or when you leave Harvard and Princeton and go towards Kansas or whatever. And I myself am more interested in the periphery of economics than in its center. Still, I wouldn't go as far as Dorothy Thomas is reported to have done, when she said that she'll use the data of the economists but not their theories!

In relation to economic theory, I must say that I have always been very suspicious of any argument that something was efficient, unless I could check it myself. I don't understand land-tenure systems unless I can see for myself how they actually work. To take an example, namely why it is that under some circumstances there might be share rents,[2] although the conventional answer is that share rents are economically irrational since they constitute an irrational contract? It is indeed correct that under certainty that would be true. But it seems to me that if you take account of risk bearing plus unavailability of insurance, it is not at all clear that share rents are economically irrational. What kind of contract is rational varies from one crop to another and from one situation to another.

At the same time, unless I could also give something which was reasonably close to a conventional economic explanation of why some contract might fit the situation, I would be suspicious of my own argument that it was rational to have this kind of a system. But I am quite sure that an economic argument doesn't have to be as good to satisfy me as it has to be to satisfy the *American Economic Review*. Some of them might also more or less be fantasy economic arguments; I don't know.

Q: What about cooperating with economists? Have any economists been involved in any of your projects on industrial organization?

A: No. But it depends on how you define "cooperation." I have sat on a lot of dissertation committees in economics and in economic history. Americans tend to have committees that go across disciplines, and you have at least a minority from outside the discipline. At Johns Hopkins there was this wonderful system, at least from the viewpoint of my own education, that you had to have a *majority* from outside the discipline. Since the economists never could scare up enough of a majority to read their dissertations, especially the mathematical ones, I got to read almost

[2] The definition of share rents is that the return from an agricultural enterprise is divided between the owner and whoever rents it according to some rental scheme, either in money or in kind. See Stinchcombe 1961, 39.

all of the economics dissertations when I was there. I also got to read many dissertations in economic history, but that was for a different reason; I got along with Alfred Chandler, who was there at the time. So that was cooperation in the sense that I criticized their works, and the economists would look at our students' dissertations.

Q: When I said "cooperation," I actually meant something more involved, like working together with economists on a project. Have you ever done that?

A: In some sense, I don't do projects. I am more of a book-writing kind of person than a project-doing one. But when I was at the National Opinion Research Center in Chicago there were data-collecting projects, which did have economists on them and which I worked on. These projects were mostly on labor markets. But except for data collections of that type, I don't do projects; I do my own work.

Q: What I was really trying to ascertain—with you as a kind of indicator—is the present state of cooperation between economists and sociologists. How would you describe that?

A: Well, I would say that cooperation between economists and sociologists is partly a status matter and partly a matter of style. Most sociologists can't read economics, and there is even some of it these days that I can't read. My son, in fact, is a mathematical economist and I can't read his work except to tell him that he hasn't defined a symbol he's using or something of that sort. I can probably read about 90 percent of the economic literature, but the average sociologist can only read 20 to 30 percent of it. And that seems to me to be a big barrier. Economists, on the other hand, can read all of the sociological literature, though of course they may not have the context to see what we think is important—sociology rarely grabs you by its elegance. There isn't anything that is sufficiently obscure about sociology, so that you have to train for a long time to read it.

It also seems to me that an economist doesn't gain anything by having successfully associated with sociologists. So why should he? Being widely accepted in sociology wasn't what got Herbert Simon the Nobel Prize. The incentive system in economics is simply not of the type that, if a body of your peers who all happen to be sociologists accept your work, you get a boost in the economics profession. But the reverse is true, and here it works the other way around. If some sociologist is doing something that you wouldn't normally do, but which a whole bunch of econometricians think is wonderful stuff, then that is a really good argument for promoting this person. The incentive system therefore doesn't encourage cooperation from the economists' viewpoint.

There is also the stylistic matter of sociologists being interested in re-searching what the economists would rather assume. Even people like Herbert Simon and Jim March have trouble with that aspect of economics. Sociologists will show that in fact businessmen don't behave according to economic theory; and the economists will say, "Well, we will assume that they behave that way anyway; it's more fruitful, you know." And that is the end of the argument, as far as the economists are concerned.

Q: Sometimes I get the impression that economists have a certain contempt for sociologists. They will, for example, sometimes tell you anecdotes in which the really funny part is that sociology is ridiculous as a science. Does this concept of economists having a certain contempt for sociologists also answer to your experience?

A: Yes, I think that's true. But I also think it is pretty appropriate. It seems to me that you have to be smarter to make a go of it in economics than in sociology. The stellar economists have a kind of command of their topic that is hard to find among sociologists. Take Kenneth Boulding, for example, who is not intolerant of sociology. You could give him a sociology problem, and he would probably do better with it than the average distinguished sociologist. So in other words, I think that some of the contempt for sociologists is justified. For another illustration of the same thing, take statistics. There were some statistical problems which sociologists had been wrestling with in vain for a long time. But as soon as they came under the economists' purview, advances were made very quickly. These were problems that had to do with things like causes going around in circles, and the like.

Q: Do you then believe that economic students are smarter than sociology students?

A: Yes, probably. Economics may simply have a more efficient selection system than sociology. To require calculus in order to go on works as a crude kind of sorting mechanism for the economists, even though a good command of calculus is only roughly correlated with broad intellectual ability. Still, it is better than nothing.

Q: When *Economic Sociology* appeared, the reviews differed quite a bit in how to perceive the book. Should it be seen, as the title actually indicates, as a broad introduction to the topic in general? Or should it rather be seen as a study where the emphasis is on the need for a more historical and comparative approach in economic sociology?

A: The book should not be read as a basic text in economic sociology. It is rather the historical-comparative approach that is the basic message of the book. But it is not necessarily the only message that needs to be said about economic sociology. Nevertheless, it represents *one* slant on that whole field, and one which I worked with for quite a while.

And it does seem to me that a lot of the more interesting things about economic behavior really do vary across countries. Take the question of why it is that the Japanese at the moment save so much more than the Americans. I don't think that the answer is that the Americans had a more anal character in the past and that they therefore saved more, or something like that. Instead I think that there are all kinds of rules and regulations relating to savings, which come out of some conception of what the whole social life is all about in these two countries and which have become institutionalized.

So it seems to me that all over the place you can find big differences in economic behavior, which have no simple explanation in terms of market competition. It clearly isn't that the Japanese are more rational in figuring things out, while we are more irrational; and that this gives us the wrong answer and the Japanese the right one. There really are culturally constructed institutional factors, and it is them that are going to explain the differences. And many of these institutions grow out of the very nature of the economic problems, as these are posed in a concrete and direct sense in these societies and not as the result of some abstract choice between savings and consumption or something of that sort. What counts are details such as how old people are provided for; what happens when a disaster hits a family; how the state intervenes in society; and so on. This is what is going to explain the difference, say, in the savings rate between the United States and Japan.

One of my objectives in *Economic Sociology* was exactly to show that different societies conceive of their economic problems differently. They create different economic institutions, and these are seen as the most obvious and natural way of doing things by the people involved. So it isn't necessarily obvious to have a capitalist mode of organization in all situations. And it isn't obvious that people who, say, spend all their time raiding others' cattle are more irrational than what we are, when we are building automobile factories or whatever.

Q: How do you view the present situation in economic sociology? It seems to me that U.S. economic sociology was more or less established in the 1950s; lay dormant in the 1960s and 1970s; and that it is now reemerging. What's your opinion?

A: It seems to me that the components of economic sociology are certainly booming today. Organizational sociology is still, more or less, doing very well. And there is still that vague feeling that there are things that we could know, given our present methodological and theoretical tools, and that we don't know. So there is a sense of there being a research program in organizational sociology, leading unto the future. The situation is similar in labor market sociology. We have made enormous advances in relating what we know about the labor markets and social mobility to what the economists know about labor markets and pricing and so on. There has also been progress in the area of class conflict and politics.

So it seems to me that, of the several fields into which economic sociology can be broken up, each is in a state of vigorous development. The notion of putting them all back together as one single subject matter and of training people in all of them plus making sure that the students know enough of economics as well as sociology; well, that just doesn't seem to be organizationally viable. But for the individual student who wants to try it on their own, it is of course viable. These students will also be easy to place in other universities since they can teach organizations, labor markets, and methods. I include methods here because labor market sociology is the field where methodological research is advancing the fastest just now.

Q: So in your opinion it's not yet time to put economic sociology back together again into one single field?

A: I don't know whether it's a question of it being time or not; it seems to me that it is just not happening. But I do think that the research in this field is among the most exciting stuff presently going on in sociology; that it is widely recognized to be very exciting stuff; and that any reputable sociology department ought to have economic sociology.

Q: Economic sociology, to switch to another topic, represents just one way of relating economics and sociology to each other. There are also several other ways to do it, and of these, "economic imperialism" is probably the most popular. What's your opinion about the research by Becker et al.? Do you reject it outright? Do you find it brilliant but wrong?

A: I suppose "brilliant but wrong" comes the closest. It seems to me that these folks in economic imperialism commit a sort of fundamental mistake, which most of their disciples in sociology also commit. And that is to have the individual as the unit to which the economic assumptions attach. It seems to me that that is not very good, and that a firm behaves much more like economists assume individuals do. I have said this already. I believed it in the 1950s, and I still believe it.

Jon Elster too has gone in the direction of the economic imperialists, which attaches the study of economic models to methodological individualism. I would argue for a different approach, namely, to identify the empirically acting units and reduce your explanation to their behavior; and not to assume that the acting unit is an individual and then reduce the behavior of the institutions to these individuals. It seems to me that that is a stupid way of approaching, say, the financial markets. The guys who operate there aren't acting for themselves; they are acting for their bank or corporation, and that's why they are acting rationally. They wouldn't be acting so rationally if they were acting for themselves.

Or, as another example, take the sexual market. It is organized in a very irrational way, in spite of Gary Becker's argument. People don't maximize very well in that market at all. They don't collect information in a rational way; they don't experiment enough with the different stores in which you can buy sexual services; and so on. It's not at all like that. But if a corporation was going to buy sexual services, and I guess some Japanese corporations do, they would be much more price-conscious and rational about it. So it seems to me that the problem with economic imperialism is not the economics part; it's the philosophical part about this reified individual.

An individual is not just one thing; it is all sorts of things. And ever since infancy its behavior gets shaped this way and that way by different pieces of the environment. The individual isn't only this rational being. Let me take an example. When you go to work, you can never remember what you decided this morning. Maybe you were supposed to call the babysitter at three o'clock. But you won't call the babysitter at three o'clock, because by that time you will be in the middle of a problem in your work. I am obviously being carried away by my enthusiasm for this argument, but it seems to me that the problem with economic imperialism isn't that lots of the time sociologists can't use the technical apparatus of economics because it is too difficult. I can use it, and I do use it lots of times. But I typically don't use it in order to try to reduce the behavior of corporations or markets or what not to the behavior of individuals. I apply it to the behavior of what are the acting units which seem to be maximizing utilities or collecting information with different methods.

That seems to me to be the right thing to do; to look for the kind of behavior that economics is good for explaining, and then use it for that. If this happens to be individuals—fine. Sometimes, of course, it does happen that individuals behave in a rational way; I wouldn't deny that. I don't even deny it as much as Herbert Simon does. But it also seems to me that very often—and much more often—it is corporations that behave in a rational way. They especially do it in the context of trying to maximize those things which are easily calculable, like how to distribute risks over time, and so on. They seem to do it much less when they are dealing with their own trade unions, for example. It seems to me, in brief, that economic imperialism should be imperialistic where it works best. But it should be modest where it works badly.

Q: Economic imperialism has also been extended to organizations, and there exist today several different economic theories of organizations. Since organizational sociology is one of your specialties, I would like to ask you some questions here. I recall, for example, that a few years ago you went into a polemic against Oliver Williamson, arguing that he makes the mistake of presenting "markets" and "hierarchies" as if the two were totally distinct phenomena, while in reality markets contain some elements of hierarchies and vice versa (Stinchcombe 1985).

A: I think that Williamson recently corrected that. His last book, *The Economic Institutions of Capitalism*, is much more along the line I advocated in my essay from 1983 (see especially Williamson 1985, 83–84).

Q: And what about agency theory, for example?

A: Agency theory happens to be my wife's—Carol Heimer's—business at the moment, so I am not doing it (see Heimer 1985). But it seems to me that it's the same story there. If you look at all the things that the economists assume, and make them into variables, then you will find things that are at the other extremes of those variables. The case my wife is interested in is people making decisions on behalf of a prematurely born child who is having major problems. Under those circumstances—where the principal presumably is the child, and the agents the parents—how do you figure out what the principal's utility functions are? And how much influence does the principal have in setting up the contract? And so on. It is clear that this problem is at the opposite extreme of the ones that agency theory normally deals with. But it illustrates—perhaps in too dramatic a form; it's so dramatic as to make it ridiculous—that not all things that we conventionally call agency come anywhere close to satisfying the assumptions that the economists make about actors.

Where agency theory does come close to do this, however, you can learn a lot from employing it. In a book I am writing just now, called *Information and Organization* or something like that, I am analyzing why universities don't actually administer their space in the sense that an operations research analyst would think it should be done: centrally; by setting up specific criteria; and so on. It seems to me that one of the problems of any university as an organization is that the people who know whether the faculty members are doing a good job are not the ones that control the university. The people who have this information are not the university's agents at all but the faculty at other universities. They constitute a particularly good source of information whether a university is doing well in some field, because you don't have the problem of the agent misrepresenting his or her performance to the principal, something which fouls up agency relations in general. This is one of the reasons, so to speak, why a university never really knows what its faculty is worth. They have to wait, or at least it used to be that way, until somebody from the outside offered the faculty member more money, before they would realize that the person was worth more.

So the problem comes from the difficulties inherent in the agency relations. When your agent knows so much more about something than you do, he or she will not report accurately what you need to know to evaluate the person; set up an incentive system; and so on. So you have to make the incentive system dependent on the people outside of the university. And that's also true—and this is the problem I am studying in particular—when the case is whether some scientist is really making good use of the reseach space he or she's got. But here you can't get your reliable outside sources to tell you if that is the case. So the usual way that we correct for our agency problems in the universities doesn't work when it comes to assigning space. I have constructed an explanation of why it is that we instead get a kind of Organization for African Unity type of structure here. The department owns its own territory, whether that makes any sense at all. It has its own people, like any nation. And when you have nations, everybody will defend their borders or there will be general anarchy.

Perhaps that was too sketchy to be convincing, but it seems to me that I have got some ideas out of the agency literature which have been useful to me and which I have exploited opportunistically. In the long run I will be dissatisfied if I can't do a more formal representation of why this problem arises in this particular agency relation of the university. On the other hand, if I can't do it formally and more in traditional terms of agency theory in the long run, at least I won't be suspicious that I am just projecting my own preference for decentralization and for not wanting to be told what to do onto a theory about the inherent nature of the university.

Q: Some people have recently been arguing that rationality can become the foundation for all the social sciences. What is your reaction to this? Is it, for example, possible to square this with your opinion that rationality is basically an assumption for economists, while it is a variable for sociologists?

A: Well, it seems to me that for some subparts of social science, rationality can work as a unifying element. It's easy, for example, for me to talk to people like Jim March, Oliver Williamson, and—to mention someone in my own field—Philip Selznick. The reason is that although we all use different approaches, we do share the basic notion that people under some conditions—conditions in which we are interested—will be trying to get more or less the best answer that they can manage; that there are social influences on what these people can manage, and what they think is best; and so on. We all think that individual cognition and collective cognition are somehow at the core of what is going on here.

But it seems to me that there also exist other kinds of behavior, which are really hard to explain this way. Why is it, for example, that marriages stay together? You could, for example, argue that what's similar between a house and a wife is that the average duration of your relation with both of them is around the same. But it doesn't seem to me that these two things are similar. It rather seems to me that erotic sentiment or the love of children don't belong to the same category as the house. If you, for example, try to explain the phenomenon of loving your children by thinking of them as an investment vehicle or something along those lines, then that whole conception is not a realistic description of what it is all about. When you have a child, it changes your preferences; and economists have no place for a change in preferences. You love that person much more than when he or she was just a sperm; there is no other way to describe it.

Q: So rationality, on the whole, functions a bit like a bridge, connecting islands of thoughts to each other?

A: Yes, but it can only connect some of the islands. And there will be rivers in between them, which you don't understand. Or that you won't understand by *that* method. It seems to me that there are lots of things that we can predict about who will love whom, how long they will love them, and what will disrupt the relationship and so on, without any appreciable intervention of rationality. Carol Heimer and I wrote a paper on love and irrationality in which we argue that many of the things you do in connection with love are not irrational, but—and that is the fundamental idea—it is only because the things that make us happy are things that can be had from loving people, that you don't have to be irrational to love people (see Heimer and Stinchcombe 1980).

But to explain why it is that these things make us happy, that is not part of the rational tradition. And it never was assumed to be part of what economics was all about; that is rather where the economists started.

These things, anyway, are clearly produced socially. Let me illustrate. One of my colleagues was telling me the other day about interviewing some admission officer about the introduction of coeducation in some school, and for whatever reason this officer said, "Undergraduates never form relations with each other if their S.A.T. scores are more than one hundred points apart." Now, this phenomenon is clearly socially produced. And it wouldn't have been true before S.A.T. scores and intellectual performances were so central to the social system. But what it does indicate, of course, is that there are some fundamental causes of the formation of these deep sentimental relations, and that it is them that shape the preference function rather than vice versa. To conceptualize phenomena of this type with an ordinary consumption function of the type you would use for a house—that just doesn't cut it. So it seems to me that we don't have to worry about economic imperialism, when it comes to these types of behavior, because the economists are not going to explain them. We sociologists are not that good at it. But at least we are not that bad!

Q: How do you view the future of the relationship between economics and sociology? Will there be more interaction? Or some kind of mutation?

A: It seems to me, broadly speaking, that the hostility of sociology and the other social sciences toward economics will disappear. I also include psychology here, even if it is true that if a psychologist can't disprove the economists' assumptions about how people behave, he or she shouldn't be encouraged to go on for a M.A., even let alone for a Ph.D.

So, the hostility toward economics will soon be gone from the social sciences. To an extent this has already happened; not quite, but almost. It seems to me, however, that one of the bad aspects of this is that rationality has come to be defined in a narrow sort of way. Now when we are agreeing to be interested in it, we are apparently going to be interested in it the way the economists are, rather than the way John Dewey or Max Weber were. This is a pity, because there are all different sorts of ways in which you can conceive of where rationality originally comes from and how it adds up and all that kind of stuff. One thing I think is particularly problematic about the current conception of rationality is the drift towards individualism. That seems bad to me.

So I am a bit worried that the rapprochement between economics and sociology is going too fast and going too far. The reason for this is that it seems to me that economists can mostly ignore the fact that the units in the market are not actual individuals. As long as they don't get too philosophical, this doesn't give them any problem. They just treat them as if they were individuals; what the hell. But it is quite different when they invade our turf and start applying this eighteenth- and nineteenth-century utilitarianism of their presuppositions to a lot of social phenomena. Then this old-time philosophy or theology comes in the way, and they quite often make a mess out of it. It seems to me that Gary Becker can't make as good a regression equation as I can about family behavior because he keeps trying to relate it all to individuals. Families aren't all individuals, they are families; and these families have their utility functions, just like individuals.

Still, it seems to me that the dialogue is open, and that economists are sort of willing to tackle practically any problem these days. How hospitals recruit interns is now a perfectly reputable part of labor market economics, and there are all sorts of odd problems like that which in the old days of Clark Kerr would not have been considered real labor market economics. So economists in some ways—maybe out of sheer self-confidence— are more flexible today than they used to be. They seem to be saying, "Surely you can't come up with anything I can't handle!" Most scientific dialogues work better if everybody has a chance at it and can chop away at each other; if everybody is listening; and if everybody reads something even if it comes from another point of view. It seems to me that there is more of that now. There is definitely more of it than when I grew up.

All this said, it still seems to me that we sociologists will in most cases have to continue to do independent work because the things that are problems to us and the things that make us say, "Aha! I have found something!" are sufficiently different from what makes economists have the same reaction. For this reason, you cannot have the same reward system for both disciplines. In the end we have got different utilities; we disagree about what's really a finding. So we can have the same technical system, but we are in different businesses.

References

Bowles, Samuel, and Herbert Gintis. 1974. *Schooling in Capitalist America: Educational Reform and the Contradictions of Economic Life.* New York: Basic Books.

Heimer, Carol A. 1985. *Reactive Risk and Rational Action: Managing Moral Hazard in Insurance Contracts.* Berkeley: University of California Press.

Heimer, Carol A., and Arthur L. Stinchcombe. 1980. "Love and Irrationality: It's Got to Be Rational to Love You Because It Makes Me So Happy." *Social Science Information* 19:697–754.

Mullins, Nicholas C., and Carolyn J. Mullins. 1973. *Theories and Theory Groups in Contemporary American Sociology.* New York: Harper and Row.

Papandreou, Andreas G. 1962. *Model Construction in Macro-Economics.* Athens: Center of Planning and Economic Research.

Stinchcombe, Arthur L. 1959. "Bureaucratic and Craft Administration of Production: A Comparative Study." *Administrative Science Quarterly* 4:168–87.

———. 1960. "The Sociology of Organization and the Theory of the Firm." *Pacific Sociological Review* 3:75–82.

———. 1961. "Agricultural Enterprise and Rural Class Relations." *American Journal of Sociology* 67:165–76.

———. 1964. *Rebellion in a High School.* Chicago: Quadrangle Books.

———. 1968. *Constructing Social Theories.* New York: Harcourt Brace Jovanovich.

————. 1974. *Creating Efficient Industrial Administrations*. New York: Academic Press.

————. 1975. "Merton's Theory of Social Structure." In *The Idea of Social Structure*, edited by Lewis Coser, 11–33. New York: Harcourt Brace Jovanovich.

————. 1983. *Economic Sociology*. New York: Academic Press.

————. 1985. "Contracts as Hierarchical Documents." In *Organization Theory and Project Management: Administering Uncertainty in Norwegian Offshore Oil*, by Arthur L. Stinchcombe and Carol A. Heimer, 121–71. Oslo: Norwegian University Press.

————. 1986a. "Rationality and Social Structure: An Introduction." In *Stratification and Organization: Selected Papers*, 1–29. Cambridge: Cambridge University Press.

————, ed. 1986b. *Stratification and Organization: Selected Papers*. Cambridge: Cambridge University Press.

Williamson, Oliver E. 1985. *The Economic Institutions of Capitalism: Firms, Markets, Relational Contracting*. New York: Free Press.

17

Aage B. Sørensen

FOR SEVERAL REASONS, Aage Sørensen is an ideal person to comment on some of the changes that are presently taking place between economics and sociology. For one thing, he is a pioneer in the new field of labor market sociology. He has also helped to develop mathematical sociology, which is a field where the ambition originally was to mathematize sociology, just as Paul Samuelson and others had revolutionized economics by mathematizing it in the 1930s. Finally, Sørensen is a student of James Coleman's and is therefore well suited to comment on Coleman's ideas about rational choice.

In this interview, Sørensen discusses recent developments in mathematical sociology. He presents a critique of neoclassical labor economics as well as of labor market sociology. A theme throughout the interview is the need for sociologists to develop a new concept of sociological theory, and here Sørensen maintains that sociologists have much to learn from economists with their emphasis on sophisticated mathematical models and mechanisms.

Aage Sørensen was born on May 13, 1941, in a teacher's family in Silkeborg, Denmark. He got his Master's degree in sociology from the University of Copenhagen in 1967. He then moved to the United States, where he earned a Ph.D. in 1971 from Johns Hopkins. The title of his dissertation was *The Occupational Mobility Process: An Analysis of Occupational Careers*. He first worked at the University of Wisconsin at Madison during the period 1971 to 1984. Since 1984, Aage Sørensen has served as chairman of the Department of Sociology at Harvard University.

•

Q: Your two specialties are mathematical sociology and labor market sociology. Can you explain briefly how you became interested in them?

A: I started to study sociology at the University of Copenhagen in 1961. At that time, there were only six to ten students in sociology and one professor, Kaare Svalastoga. He had a strong interest in quantitative soci-

The following interview with Aage Sørensen took place on March 23, 1988, in his office in William James Hall at Harvard University.

ology and was a proponent of a kind of behaviorist approach to sociology. Svalastoga also thought that mathematical modeling was very important, but I must say that I didn't learn a whole lot from him in that area. I did, however, get an interest in stratification from him, which was his main specialty.

When I had finished my Danish degree in 1967, I decided to go to America and see if I could study with Jim Coleman. I had always had a strong interest in mathematics and statistics, but I didn't really know what to do with them. And I thought that Jim Coleman could teach me how to do mathematical models. So I applied to Johns Hopkins and was accepted; I didn't apply anywhere else.

And indeed Coleman did teach me a lot of mathematical modeling, and I think I got better at it. I then tried to do a dissertation, which combined my interest in mathematics with my interest in stratification and mobility; and this is what led me to labor markets. In my dissertation I developed a little model, a simple difference equation, of what people would gain by moving from one job to another. I saw this as a question of the extent to which people were free to leave at a time when it was most opportune for them to do so, as opposed to having to leave when someone told them to leave or something like that. So in trying to explain the outcome of job-shifts, I came to the conclusion that this really had to do with what kind of employment relationship people have—whether they have a high degree of job security or not. And that, in turn, led me to worry about labor markets.

Q: Did you take any courses in economics as part of your education?

A: I actually started out studying economics at the University of Copenhagen. It didn't last too long—only about a year—and I found it kind of boring.

Then I heard of this new field, sociology, and that is how I got into sociology. I probably would have started out in sociology, if I just had known it existed, but it was a such a small and new discipline in Denmark at that time. Anyhow, I did get about a year of basic microeconomics, so I do have some background in the field. I haven't had any formal training in economics since that time, although I have read a fair amount on my own, especially human capital theory and labor economics.

Q: In the 1970s, you and your wife Annemette Sørensen, who is also a sociologist, wrote a book-long overview of mathematical sociology (Sørensen and Sørensen 1977). You describe how the field was started in the 1950s and how it then gained momentum in the 1960s. How do you see the development within mathematical sociology after 1975, where your book ends? Has any progress been made in the last ten to fifteen years?

A: Well, I am sort of unhappy about what has happened in mathematical sociology because I don't think there has been a whole lot of progress. In some sense I would say that the area has gone through something of a decline. There is still a bunch of people who call themselves "mathematical sociologists" or who would say that that is one of their specialties. And there is a considerable amount of activity in certain areas of mathematical sociology, like networks. But overall, I am skeptical and discouraged by the lack of progress.

I think that one thing which has been important in this process and made mathematical sociology less vibrant has to do with the type of mathematical sociology that was around in the 1960s. If Coleman's work is seen as the prototype for what mathematical sociology should be like in those days, then it is mainly a very rich set of stochastic process models, applied to various types of social processes. Coleman uses quite standard and well-known models, developed in the mathematical and statistical literature. He then adapts these models to various social processes and parameterizes them in order to mirror certain mechanisms in social processes. For example, one model would be that if I do one thing and if another person does something which reinforces what I do, then there is a kind of contagion effect (see Coleman 1964b, 288–429).

All Coleman's models were quite simple, but theoretically and conceptually adapted to social processes, and that is really the achievement of his *Introduction to Mathematical Sociology,* which came in 1964. It is not that his models of social processes were mathematically very original; it was rather Coleman's ability to take these models and reformulate them in terms of social processes. You also needed a good deal of creativity and ingenuity to test these models, and Coleman was very good at that too.

But what has happened since then is that in the 1970s there was a phenomenal advance in numerical computer analysis and in the availability of longitudinal data. It now is possible to estimate parameters of stochastic models directly without making the equilibrium assumptions and other simplifying assumptions used by Coleman. But this meant one did not need to be very imaginative and creative conceptually, which had been the case earlier, because you could just go ahead and estimate everything directly. For this reason, the use of stochastic models became a kind of regression problem, for example, in event history analysis. That this happened explains the lack of enthusiasm for doing any more models. The beauty went out of it, even if perhaps realism became greater.

Q: What about game theory? Wouldn't that have represented an alternative to regression models?

A: Well, game theory is a different matter altogether and has only been of borderline interest to sociologists. It is much stronger in mathematics, economics, and operational research. Sociologists would go in and out of game theory, but it never became a central activity like stochastic processes or network models. Coleman, however, made another important contribution in the 1960s with a paper on collective decisions, which led him to a set of problems with rational actor models (Coleman 1964a). He takes up classical game theoretical problems, such as the prisoner's dilemma. But I still don't think that you can say that game theory has been an important activity among mathematical sociologists. I think that American mathematical sociologists are basically either doing stochastic models; and if they are doing that, they are estimating more than modeling. Or they are doing networks, in which case they are probably more involved in modeling, but also emphasize estimation problems.

Q: One of my friends, who is a sociologist, keeps telling me that economists are much more sophisticated than sociologists when it comes to model building. Is that also your opinion?

A: Yes, I think that is true. And the reason is mainly that economic theory has been translated into mathematics to a considerable extent, and you can't really do economic theory without doing mathematics. So the language and the substance sort of go together in economics. It is almost implausible, I think, to conceive of a theoretical proposition in economics which is not formulated in a mathematical fashion today.

You should also realize that the big agenda of people like Jim Coleman and Harrison White, who were the two great pioneers in the United States in using mathematical models in sociology, was always *theoretical*. But they have never been able to push the idea that what they did was indeed "theory." Most sociologists outside of mathematical sociology rather saw them as methodologists. Sociological theory, as it is carried out by people who call themselves "theorists," is with a few exceptions completely removed from mathematical modeling. And therefore sociologists haven't had to learn mathematics. Only a few people, who have known mathematics by accident (maybe they studied it as undergraduates), have really gotten into what I would call theory development using mathematical tools.

Q: In the 1930s and 1940s, people like Paul Samuelson showed that you could take verbal propositions in economic theory and translate them into mathematical language. Are you saying that that wouldn't be possible in sociology?

A: No, I am not saying that. I think that some of the work of Jim Coleman, Harrison White, and other mathematical sociologists (including myself) is indeed sociological theory translated into mathematics. What I am saying is rather that the bulk of what is called "sociological theory" by sociologists is *not* translatable into mathematics. And also: what the mathematical sociologists have done is not recognized by these other sociologists as "theory." So there is really a discrepancy, if you want, between what is practiced as theory and what is possible to translate into mathematics. What is largely practiced as theory in sociology, is rather history of sociology, metatheory, or some kind of conceptual elaboration of what is meant by "capital," "norms," and so on. In either case, there is no need for mathematics.

Since most sociologists don't really know any mathematics, I don't think there is going to be a whole lot of progress, either for mathematical sociology or for sociological theory, as it is practiced today. Although it might be a little bold to state it so bluntly, I must say that I don't think that sociology has made a whole lot of theoretical progress for many years and certainly not compared to economics. The main reason for this, I think, is precisely that sociologists have not used mathematics to formulate their theoretical propositions.

Q: Your second major interest is labor market sociology. How do you see the relationship to economic theory here, especially neoclassical theory?

A: I admire neoclassical theory a great deal for its power to explain different phenomena, and also for its elegance. On the other hand, I have the impression that much of what it explains can also be explained by other means. What this shows is in a sense that economists have been incredibly creative in coming up with explanations for what they already knew would happen. In a sense they have formulated their theory *backwards*.

I actually think that this is the case with much of good theory. But I am in this case explicitly thinking of human capital theory, which is very important in labor market research. Gary Becker's own work is really a very elegant way of explaining certain basic, observed relationships with economic theory. But most of these relationships—and this has been a main purpose for myself to show—can equally well be explained by other means. There are other mechanisms, in brief, that can account for the observed facts. I am thinking of things like the education–earnings relationship or the age–earnings profile, to take two key observables in human capital theory for which the theory gives some explanation. There are other theories—including the theories I have worked on myself—that explain the same phenomena with very different assumptions.

Now, that is no reason to reject neoclassical labor economics. But there is something about the assumptions which are employed in neoclassical theory which makes the whole enterprise sometimes unbelievable. This has mainly to do with the assumption of openness in labor markets. Now, this assumption is made despite that there is all this evidence that labor markets are in fact structured, full of barriers to movements, and so forth. But neoclassical economists still equate them with markets for potatoes or oil or grain. We *know* that labor markets are different. We know it, for example, from classical institutionalist analyses, and we know it from Herb Simons's analysis of the employment relationship (Simon 1957a). It has also been repeated to us by the neo-institutionalists, like Oliver Williamson (1975), that the basic kind of employment relationship is very much in contradiction to what is assumed in the theory of the market that drives neoclassical labor economics. So I guess I find neoclassical labor theory very persuasive, very beautiful, and quite unrealistic.

Q: From your own work, it is clear that you are also quite critical of the various attempts by sociologists to analyze labor markets, including the "new structuralist" approach where one focuses on the structural aspects of labor markets. Could you say something about this?

A: It should first of all be said that much quantitative work in sociology on labor market phenomena really originated in the demographic tradition, which basically just set out to describe certain observed relationships in some given population. This is similar to what Otis Dudley Duncan and Peter Blau did in *The American Occupational Structure*. This work represents the invention of status attainment models, which are mainly exercises in estimating, as precisely as possible, the association between current status, first status, education, and family background. They do this, however, without providing any kind of theoretical explanation for why one should observe these relationships. That is, there is no theory about the process in classic attainment research. And there is still no theory about what produces the various associations in a lot of today's sociological work on labor markets.

The reason for this has a lot to do with the way theory is thought of by sociologists. They see it as something having to do with which variables should be included in the equations and how these variables relate to other variables—and not as something which is about which mechanisms produce the observed associations in the variables. This is where there is a huge difference between sociological research and economic research in this area; and the difference is very much to the disadvantage of the sociologist. Sociologists have not developed many powerful theoretical statements about what produces the observed associations which are at all comparable to neoclassical economics. Even though I find the neoclassical explanations unrealistic, as I said before, they certainly do give you a reason for why, e.g., education should have an effect on income. There is very little of this in the sociological literature, except for various ad hoc observations about why some relationships should be observed.

So, this is one problem with the sociological literature on these matters: there is too little effort to really explain what it is that you in fact observe. Another problem, which is related, is that you also have a tendency to see alternatives to the prevailing theories in equally simplistic ways. You basically take them into account by putting in different sets of variables. For human capital theory, you put in some education variables. For dual labor market theory, you put in some industry variables. And for internal labor market theory, you put in some organizational variables. Then you see to what extent each of these sets of variables can explain the variance, and then you say, "Well, since human capital theory does not explain all the variance we have shown it is not a good theory." But this is a kind of sledgehammer approach to theory; it basically equates theoretical power with the amount of variance it explains, and that is a terrible criterion.

So sociologists have not really been able to link theory very closely to quantitative research in labor market research. This is a major defect of sociological research in this area, including the "new structuralist" approach. This doesn't mean that all this research hasn't provided important insights and knowledge. But these have mainly been descriptive in nature. We now know a little about how different firms produce earnings and how different labor markets create mobility and career patterns—but it is all quite descriptive. It doesn't really challenge any existing theory, like neoclassical theory, and it hasn't really produced any new theory.

Q: How would you describe your own research on labor markets? It is centered, if I have understood it correctly, around "processes of allocation" and "open" versus "closed" positions (Sørensen 1977, 1983).

A: The main issue for me has been to try to contribute to the solution of the problem that I just talked about, namely, that economic theory gives you very elegant solutions but on the basis of totally unrealistic assumptions. Neoclassical labor economics produces explanations, based on quite unbelievable scenarios. So I decided to use a set of *contrasting conceptions*, where one set would reproduce the neoclassical assumptions while the other would be quite different. Both conceptions would generate a set of predictions about the same phenomena. So you would have two alternative theories with very different assumptions that would explain the same phenomenon.

Q: These are the two conceptions that are called "open" and "closed" employment relations, right?

A: Yes, this is what the argument about "open" and "closed" positions is about. What I call "open employment relationships" or "open positions" are basically positions or employment relationships that fulfill the assumptions of neoclassical theory. This means that there are no permanent, long-term, or indefinite matches between people and their jobs. People move in and out of their jobs. You can fire people at will and you can hire them at will. If somebody wants to take over your job—if your employer gets a bid from some worker who wants to do the job at a lower wage—he would hire him immediately and just fire you. So you get market competition in the manner that neoclassical theory indeed assumes that market competition takes place. And hiring labor is basically the same as buying oil on the spot market in Amsterdam: every day you have an auction where you hire the most productive labor at the lowest rate; and then you fire the ones who are less productive or who want a higher wage, and so on. This is what I call "open employment relationships."

I then try to develop a set of mechanisms for how you match people to earnings when you do *not* have this flexibility; when you instead have constraints on the ability to remove people from their positions because they have job security or tenure. When this is the case I call the situation "closed," because now you can only create new matches when there are vacancies in already existing jobs. Therefore, you get a very different kind of allocation process, which is basically governed by the degree to which people leave their jobs. And they leave their jobs because they get promoted to better jobs or because they retire from the system—that's what decides the hiring now. In this scenario, earnings will be more or less fixed; they are stable attributes to positions and people can only change their earnings or status by changing their position, not by changing themselves. So there is no longer a direct connection between your productivity and your earnings.

With this perspective you basically get the scenario, which has been described by some neo-institutionalists like Williamson (1975) and Doeringer and Piore (1971). Wages are not set by market competition; they are set by administrative decision. People are relatively secure in their jobs, and so forth. My own particular interest in this scenario has been to formulate models that will predict the outcomes you observe, and which are also predictable from neoclassical theory. I have succeeded in at least a couple of instances, namely, with respect to the age-earnings profile and, to some extent, with the association between earnings and education (see Sørensen 1977). My models indeed produce some of the same observed relationships, but they provide a very different interpretation for why they are there. In my opinion this is theoretically much more informative than just showing, as most sociologists do, that some measure of internal labor markets produces some variance in some outcome variable.

Q: And what about your future agenda in labor market sociology? Will you continue working with these "open" and "closed" positions?

A: Well, I have actually gone back and forth between different things lately. One of my publications, which relates to this model, has to do with career trajectories (Sørensen 1984). Here I am mainly concerned with if the observed increase in earnings over people's lifetime is due to the fact that they are more productive or that they have been promoted to better jobs, even though they might not have become more productive. I am concerned with empirically keeping these two interpretations apart, and I basically feel that the closed position scenario is the more plausible one.

I have also worked on other phenomena recently. I have been spending quite a bit of time on unemployment processes, and I have noticed that I can use some of the same concepts to explain things here. I am basically concerned about the extent to which different industries produce different employment processes. I think this has something to do with how open or closed the labor markets are. If they are open and jobs are freely available, then you should expect to find that unemployment is mainly terminated by people who find a better job through *search*. They look at a lot of different jobs and try to find something that will satisfy whatever preferences they have. If labor markets instead are closed, then unemployment processes will in some sense rather result in layoffs. Here people have no jobs but a claim to their old jobs. So when the firm picks up, it just moves everybody back in, and people don't do any searching in the period between. They get laid off and then they get rehired; and in between they just sit home and paint their fences. In the more open labor markets, people are more likely to run around, read newspapers, and ask their friends if they know of any better jobs. I think that these are very different processes, and I am interested in seeing to what extent one or the other type of process is likely to occur for people in different occupations, in different age groups, in different educational groups, and so on.

Q: The differences between economics and sociology are generally considered to be pretty great. In your opinion, is this also true for labor market research? Or is it perhaps so that economists and sociologists cooperate frequently in this area? I know, for example, that you have worked with economists at the Institute for Research on Poverty at the University of Wisconsin at Madison.

A: Yes, and I learned a lot from interacting with the economists in Madison. In fact, this whole idea of dealing with some of the same predictions, which you get from neoclassical theory and from other perspectives, is very much inspired by my work with economists. As to the differences between economics and sociology, I basically don't think they are that large in labor market research. Economists and sociologists do come out of different traditions, so they tend to look at different variables and so on. Sociologists might know a little bit more about mobility processes, and economists a little bit more about production functions and marginal productivity. But I really think that sociologists and economists are to a large extent dealing with exactly the same processes. They are also, I think, not necessarily providing different explanations for these phenomena.

I think the big issue here is rather that if you limit the economists to neoclassical economists, then sociologists are indeed doing much more realistic work. To some extent, to make something of a caricature of economics, it has become a science about a world that doesn't exist. So economic theory is generating very important insights about phenomena and processes that nobody can observe. And if that is indeed the situation, then sociology has a very important role to fill, namely, to empirically observe and explain what is going on. All of this would be left to the sociologists, because the other guys are living in this world that only exists in their assumptions.

But that hasn't really happened and I don't think it will happen, because there has always been another group of economists—the institutionalists and the neo-institutionalists—who do *not* assume that this dream world exists and who are much more concerned with the empirical world. In some sense we sociologists are actually neo-institutionalists. Or the neo-institutionalists are sociologists, whichever way you want it. So I don't really see any difference between sociologists and institutionalists, either when it comes to the assumptions we use or the questions we ask. The study of labor markets is therefore divided by theory rather than by discipline. On the one hand, there is neoclassical theory which generates very powerful hypotheses in a nonexisting world. And on the other, there is the institutional and sociological research, which for all I can see are indistinguishable, except for in some terminological sense. So there doesn't really exist any sociology of the labor market, which is separate from the institutional analysis; that's just not a very useful distinction to make.

Q: One of the issues that is currently being discussed in sociology is whether sociology can be recast on the basis of rational choice. What's your opinion here?

A: Well, I must say that I am not very impressed by the amount of progress that has been made this far. Some of the work in this area, however, has made me understand the world in a different way. I think, for example, that Coleman's work about collective decisions gives you a new and very useful perspective on power and dependency (see Coleman 1964a).

But on the whole I am not so sure that you have to go through this whole exercise of purposive actors and so on to come up with ideas like this. The same can be said about the current micro–macro debate in sociology. Once you are inside these models, then you see the problems very clearly—but then I am not so sure that you should start out with a rational actor model of the more extreme type.

It is true that assumptions about rationality and maximization are extremely useful in generating hypotheses, say, about behavior in the labor market. But I think that social structure can be talked about and conceptualized quite easily without starting out from a rational actor model and, so to speak, build the whole analysis from the bottom up. It may be that I haven't thought enough about this issue, but I am definitely underwhelmed by the amount of progress that has been made this far in rational actor theory. I guess I am closer to a kind of middle-range, institutional approach, where people try to do what is best for them but keep wandering into various constraints provided by the social structure. I consider this perspective to be the most fruitful. I know that this is not a particularly profound perspective, but it lets you talk about the world reasonably well. There are institutions out there and they limit people's freedom of action. They do this in a way that make people react in a certain manner and do things differently than they otherwise would. And that's why you get different career processes, and so on.

Q: It sounds like you'd much rather do middle-range mathematical modeling than rational choice sociology!

A: That's exactly true.

Q: And what is your opinion about economic imperialism? Is it an intellectually fruitful enterprise, or is it just loud and noisy imperialism?

A: Well, at least the way it is written up, it is more the latter. In Becker's work, for example, it explicitly says that there is no sociology which can't be improved by a bit of microeconomics. I also think that his stuff is sometimes methodologically contrived and a bit vacuous when it comes to predictions. Tautologies are generated en masse and so are inferences about marriage, divorce, and time uses, which are often very difficult to provide any empirical evidence for. The evidence that is provided—and this is something we talked about earlier a propos earnings—can also be interpreted in many other ways. Having said all that, however, I must also say that I admire some of Becker's work because it is creative and filled with good ideas. That it also has this imperialistic side should not detract from its good sides; the imperialistic bit is just silly.

Q: It would seem, to summarize your opinion about economics and sociology, that sociology has two things in particular to learn from economics: the way it makes use of mathematics, and the way it emphasizes the need to look for explanatory mechanisms. Is that correct?

A: Yes, but those two things are very strongly related. The beauty of much economic reasoning for me is exactly that since the economists were able to use mathematics to formulate a theory, they can derive equations from this exercise that have parameters with a theoretical interpretation. So you can make direct statements about whether a theory is true or not, because the sizes of the coefficients tell you something about what should be going on out there. To give you a simple example, which astounded me the first time I came across it. In Mincer's *Schooling, Experience and Earnings*, there is a section about the earnings–schooling relationship, in which Mincer says that there must be something wrong with one of his models because the coefficient is simply too large. Basically, he was showing that if the return to education was as large as he had estimated it be, everybody should be in school because it was such a profitable investment! Well, no sociologist would ever be able to make such a statement. There is nothing that is too large or too small in the parameters of their models.

So I think that sociologists should try to imitate the close relationship between theoretical systems and empirical observations that you can find in some economics. Our inability to make this kind of inference really is a sign of theoretical weakness. Sociologists can say that there is a set of findings showing that X relates to Y and that X does not relate to C; and they can say that this doesn't make any sense or that it makes good sense. But our criterion for saying so is that it is similar to some study by someone who probably did a good job or that it squares with common sense or that it doesn't square with common sense. Quantitative sociology is usually only theoretically informed about which variables to put in a regression type model (and the "theory" is mostly common sense). What matters is usually which is most important (an ultimately very hard question to answer). The functional form of the model and the interpretation of parameters is rarely derived from any kind of deductive reasoning. In my opinion, only a concern with the latter issues will produce genuine theoretical progress, as economics has demonstrated.

References

Coleman, James S. 1964a. "Collective Decisions." *Sociological Inquiry* 34 (Spring):166–81.

———. 1964b. *Introduction to Mathematical Sociology*. New York: Free Press.

Doeringer, Peter B., and Michael J. Piore. 1971. *Internal Labor Markets and Manpower Analysis.* Lexington, Mass.: D. C. Heath Company.

Duncan, Otis Dudley, and Peter M. Blau. 1967. *The American Occupational Structure.* New York: John Wiley.

Mincer, Jacob. 1974. *Schooling, Experience and Earnings.* New York: NBER.

Simon, Herbert. 1957a. "A Formal Theory of the Employment Relationship." In *Models of Man,* 183–95. New York: John Wiley.

Sørensen, Aage B. 1977. "The Structure of Inequality and the Process of Attainment." *American Sociological Review* 42:965–78.

———. 1983. "Processes of Allocation to Open and Closed Positions in Social Structure." *Zeitschrift für Soziologie* 12:203–24.

———. 1984. "Interpreting Time Dependency in Career Processes." In *Progress in Stochastic Modeling of Social Processes,* edited by A. Dieckman and P. Mitter, 89–122. New York: Academic Press.

Sørensen, Aage B. and Annemette Sørensen. 1977. "Mathematical Sociology." *Current Sociology* 23(2):1–158.

Williamson, Oliver E. 1975. *Markets and Hierarchies: Analysis and Antitrust Implications.* New York: Free Press.

Concluding Discussion

It has become recognized that the most promising field for research is the "no man's land" between the traditional disciplines. There is one concept which the economist or the sociologist can keep blurred, namely the concept of "economics" or "sociology"; for it can never be a premise for a rational inference. In reality, what exists are merely problems to be solved, theoretical or practical; and the rational way of attacking them is to use the methods which are most adequate for solving each particular problem.

—Gunnar Myrdal, "The Relation between Social Theory and Social Policy"

In the fall of 1987, when I set out to do these interviews, I was convinced that something of great interest was happening in the "no-man's land" between economics and sociology that Gunnar Myrdal refers to in the opening quote. I was not as sure as he seems to be that disciplines do not matter and that all there exists are problems to be solved, but I felt certain that the relationship between economics and sociology was changing and that this was significant. In an earlier book, published in the spring of 1987, I had argued that sociologists should use this opportunity of a thaw in the relationship between economics and sociology to revive economic sociology, which had been leading a very bleak existence since the 1950s. And initially my idea was to interview only a dozen or so of the "new economic sociologists," thereby drawing attention to their work and helping to give a sense of identity to this new and dynamic field. However, I was advised against this by a colleague, who felt that I should also include some interviews with economists. In retrospect, this turned out to be good advice, even if I would still maintain that the new economic sociology is worth a book of its own.

By including economists in the book, the problems I wanted to analyze were therefore scrutinized from several new angles. The economists I had picked also turned out to be such amazingly interesting people that my initial feeling of irritation at having to give up the "new economic sociology" project was gradually replaced by a feeling of working on an even more exciting problem—namely, to map out what was happening in the whole "no man's land" between economics and sociology.

The very fact that I did not know exactly what was happening in this "no man's land" seemed at first like a serious drawback to me; all I had was a vague feeling that *something* of consequence was taking place. How could I conduct interviews about something with which I was not fully familiar? Reflecting on this, however, I decided that it was just another version of the old paradox of all research, namely: how can you look for something if you by definition don't know what it is? Basically, the answer is that you just have to know in which direction to look. And what you find is usually something other than what you expected.

So I came to the conclusion that I did not have to know exactly what to ask in order to do the interviews. It also seemed to me that if I were to focus the interviews too sharply, I would not get very far anyway. It is my experience that people only tell you what they want to say; and that one does better listening carefully than trying to spear the victim with ever sharper questions. In this particular case at least, holding off on very precise questions turned out to be a good strategy. In addition, several of the people I interviewed—especially the economists—were such excellent entertainers that just sitting back and listening became a pleasure in its own right.

When I reread the interviews in transcript a half year later, I feel that they have kept this capacity to entertain, even if the voices and the gestures are gone. In my opinion, the interviews are often witty, informative, and filled with insights of various kinds. From one point of view, this very quality will perhaps be held against them—doesn't it make them that much harder to interpret? Maybe so. But I feel that what makes the interviews somewhat difficult to interpret is not so much their colorful and entertaining dimension as the fact that the interviewees are essentially trying to talk about what is happening at this very moment and what will happen in the future. And talking about an ongoing enterprise usually makes the answers hard to judge. It is the future that will finally single out what is important *now* and what will count as the "past." So in this sense there is no single correct answer to the questions raised in this book, and, consequently, no single correct interpretation of the interviews.

Having said all of this, it is nonetheless clear that the interviews are centered around certain recurring questions, and that certain themes keep surfacing. Therefore, there is something to be gained by juxtaposing the way different authors look at the same problems and by commenting on these opinions. The only caveat that is needed here is that many of the issues involved are so complex that the following attempt to present the results of the interviews may simplify things too much.

On the History of the Relationship between Economics and Sociology

The interview material contains several new pieces of information on the history of the relationship between economics and sociology. To this one should add that the present way of examining this movement is still very much open to interpretation. It is, for example, common to regard the turn of the century—when the breakthrough of neoclassical economics also took place—as the period when the decisive split between economics and sociology occurred. It is therefore refreshing to find a novel interpretation in the interview with Harrison White. He suggests that it was rather in the 1930s that economics and sociology were permanently separated, and that what then happened has something to do with the kind of economics that Paul Samuelson in particular helped to popularize. According to White, Samuelson was influenced by field theory in physics, and this theory was not a suitable model for economics. White does not claim that this is the whole explanation; there is more to the story, as he says, including the fact that mainstream economics impoverished itself by its wholesale rejection of institutionalism.

It is also clear from the answers that there have been many more encounters between economics and sociology than is hitherto known. In some cases these interactions between economists and sociologists were to leave an important imprint on the persons involved. Arthur Stinchcombe, for example, remembers with pleasure the teachings of Andreas Papandreou. The industrial economics that he came in contact with at Berkeley also made an important impression on him. Harrison White's experience at Carnegie Tech was crucial for his development, and he thrived in the atmosphere that Herbert Simon and others had created. In a sense, it is of course natural that a sociologist would be more interested in behavioral economics and institutional economics than in neoclassical theory. Harrison White's comment that much is to be gained by establishing better contacts between sociology and the business schools can be seen within this context. Business schools often have good contacts with the business community, something that today's sociologists lack. Their faculty members also know much more about business than what sociologists do. Of course, there are also certain drawbacks to trade schools, business schools included. Still, their close relationship to the economic world makes them quite attractive to sociologists.

But if it is true that sociologists have been unable to find the kind of economics they want in mainstream economics, it is also true that economists who have approached sociology with special questions in mind have failed to find an answer. The interviews contain two examples of this. Robert Solow has repeatedly tried to learn what norms are, and he has found very little help in sociological literature. And Thomas Schelling describes how he searched through many years of sociological magazines to find something on the micro–macro link, but to no avail. This was in connection with writing *Micromotives and Macrobehavior,* and what Schelling was primarily after was material on what happens with race relations when you, for example, aggregate individual attitudes to housing.

An interesting contribution to the history of the relationship between economics and sociology that is found in these interviews has to do with the role of Talcott Parsons. According to current interpretation, Parsons wrote some important articles on economics and sociology in the 1930s, and then tried to revive economic sociology in the 1950s through *Economy and Society.* However, Parsons also alienated several key economists from sociology. Many economists who came in contact with Parsons identified sociology with his works. He was indeed, as Becker puts it, the "King of Sociological Theory" in the 1950s and early 1960s. "All I heard . . . was Talcott Parsons, Talcott Parsons," Becker says. But the economists disapproved of what they found in Parsons's work. Robert Solow, who was a friend of Parsons, felt that his theoretical scheme was all wrong. Mancur Olson notes politely that what Parsons said and what the economists said could not possibly both be right. According to Gary Becker, "Reading Parsons soured me on sociology." And finally, Kenneth Arrow found Parsons's theoretical work "empty," "tautological," and "preposterous."

Economy and Society, which is usually seen as the supreme effort by Parsons to pull economics and sociology closer together, was not appreciated by Arrow either. He found it "just awful." The story of how *Economy and Society* came to be written is told in the interview with Smelser, and from this version, it is clear how little Parsons knew about contemporary economics, Keynes in particular. Reading the interview with Smelser, one also gets the impression that Parsons picked Smelser because Smelser—at the time an undergraduate student—was more up on economic theory than he himself was.

An interesting detail in the economists' appraisal of Parsons is their appreciation of his *empirical* work. Both Solow and Arrow mention how useful they found Parsons's analysis of the medical profession as opposed to his grand theoretical schemes. It is true that Parsons's work on the medical profession is of high quality. But it should also be said—to restore the balance a bit after the economists' onslaught—that Parsons's work covers a wide range of topics, and that one does not get the impression that the economists have gone through Parsons's work very carefully. His writings from the 1930s on the relationship between the social sciences (including economics and sociology) are extremely interesting. His theory of social action and his interpretation of Max Weber are two other important contributions to social science, which the economists seem to have missed.

A propos Max Weber it can be noted that the economists, surprisingly enough, seem to have had very little exposure to Weber's work. And whatever exposure they have had does not seem to have left much of an impression. It is actually only Mancur Olson who explicitly mentions Max Weber's tremendous historical learning. Robert Solow says that he does not care for Weber's "verstehende Soziologie" ("interpretive sociology"), and that David Landes has proved the Protestant ethics thesis to be wrong. Weber made no great impression on Akerlof and Williamson either, though both have had some contact with his work.

Amartya Sen's comment on Weber is interesting. He says that he studied Weber, but that he did it *after* his formal education in economics was over, and that, for this reason, Weber never became a formative influence on his thinking. One can probably generalize from this statement and say that by not including sociological material in the programs of the economics departments (and vice versa), one in fact prevents it from ever having much of an impact—it simply never becomes a natural reference. For whatever it is worth, I should also add that the only thing that really disappointed me about the economists was their reaction to Weber. The economists impressed me on practically every other score as extraordinary intellectuals; they were very sharp, knowledgeable, and often witty. But I found their reading of Weber dull and narrow-minded.

To be dull and narrow-minded is not necessarily more of a sin in social science than in social interaction. In this case, however, it is an indicator of something much more important, namely, of how little today's economists are tuned in to a genuinely social approach to economic affairs. Weber is *the* key figure in sociology, and it is he who has formulated the sociological enterprise in the most clear and forceful manner. Sociology, according to Weber, should be an interpretive social science; it should be historically inspired; and it should make use of comparative material. On all these accounts, sociology differs from contemporary mainstream economics. I would put it in the following way: By not paying more attention to Weber, the economists have failed to explore the main intellectual alternative to an overly quantified and mathematized social science.

Tribal Differences and How Distance Is Maintained

According to Harrison White, one can see sociologists and economists as two different tribes with all that that entails. Indeed, Axel Leijonhufvud has written a very funny satire on this theme, "Life among the Econ," where he describes how the "Econs" have a "fierce attachment to their ancestral grounds" and how they bring up their young "to feel contempt for the softer living in the warmer lands of their neighbors, such as the Polscis and the Sociogs." He continues:

> Despite a common genetical heritage, relations with these tribes are strained—the distrust and contempt that the average Econ feels for these neighbors being heartily reciprocated by the latter—and social intercourse with them is inhibited by numerous taboos. The extreme clannishness, not to say xenophobia, of the Econ makes life among them difficult and perhaps even somewhat dangerous for the outsider. (Leijonhufvud 1973, 327)

Here it can be pointed out, as Amartya Sen and Mancur Olson in particular do, that economics and sociology used to be fairly close to each other. In the works of Adam Smith, John Stuart Mill, and Karl Marx, economics and sociology mingle freely. This, however, is no longer the case, except perhaps in a few areas such as labor economics. Aage Sørensen thus points out that in labor economics—where neo-institutionalism is very strong—there is not much of a difference between the works of economists and sociologists.

Labor economics, however, is clearly an exception, and in most of economics the "distrust and contempt" that Leijonhufvud talks about seem to be the rule. "Distrust" is perhaps too strong a word for what Arrow feels toward sociology; "skepticism" is probably more accurate. In any event, his reaction to the sociologists at Harvard, during the years when Arrow himself taught there, was one of surprise: he was quite startled when he realized that every sociologist seemed intent to start the topic anew. According to Arrow—and on this point he is seconded by others—economists also tend to feel that sociologists will not get very far in their research by just asking people what they think. In their view, what one needs to do is to analyze the problem from a more objective angle. Robert Solow, who explicitly warns against economists who treat economics as if it were some kind of physics, agrees with Arrow on this point. To Solow, "interpretive sociology" is to be avoided; institutions and norms preferably shall be modeled in a nonsubjective manner.

If the economists feel that the sociologists are too "soft" on data, the sociologists feel that the economists do not use sufficiently good empirical data. To quote Harrison White, "If there is one disastrous thing at the roots of what has happened in modern economics, it's that it has cut itself off from genuine field observation." He continues: "Look at it, study it, and then develop imaginative ways to conceptualize and measure it—that's what is needed in economics." Stinchcombe adds another twist. He says that for the economists, data collection is very much connected to the status system of the profession. Prestigious institutions, such as Harvard and Chicago, will mainly uphold theory, while schools of less renown are more interested in collecting real data.

The economists do not seem to be too concerned about these accusations. In any case, they do not feel that economics has lost touch with empirical reality. To Solow, the real issue is rather that economists are often much too quick to settle for one specific way of modeling a problem and then consider it solved. Becker feels that, at most, sociologists are better than the economists at administering their own surveys. The economist who goes the furthest in agreeing with the sociologists is Arrow. He says that the economists have narrowed down the notion of acceptable data "excessively." The main reason for this, he says, is that economists use government data. It is also very expensive to go out and collect one's own data. To Arrow, like most neoclassical economists, there is also the danger of being too empirical. To merely go out and collect data means coming uncomfortably close to institutionalism—and to be labeled an institutionalist still seems to be a fate worse than death for most economists.

The "contempt" between the different social science tribes that Leijonhufvud talks about is discussed in several of the interviews. Solow says that economists look down on sociologists, and so does Becker. The pecking order seems to be the following: physics, mathematics, and biology all have higher status than economics; and economics has higher status than sociology, psychology, and history. The more one uses sophisticated mathematics, the higher status one has. So one way to turn a low-status social science into a high-status social science is to mathematize it. Who collaborates with whom is connected to this pecking order as well. One basically "pecks" downward and seeks collaboration upward. Sociologists achieve status from associating with economists, but not the other way around. Economists can fairly easily publish in sociological magazines, while the opposite is much more rare, and so on.

Stinchcombe says that he understands why sociologists are looked down upon; the average sociologist can only read about 20 to 30 percent of what the economists produce, while the economists can read everything the sociologists write. What Stinchcombe is referring to is the fact that sociologists are not as sophisticated as the economists in mathematics. This is indeed true. Stinchcombe's argument can, however, be challenged on another ground: the fact that someone can "read" or spell their way through a text does not mean that he or she understands what to do with it. The economists' reading of Weber is a case in point. But even if Stinchcombe slips on this issue, is he not correct in his other argument—that the stellar economists are better than their sociological counterparts? Is it not true, as he says, that people like Kenneth Boulding can arrive at better solutions to problems than the best sociologists are able to achieve? Stinchcombe is probably right on this point—but it is also true that sociology is much more ready to accept interpretations from other perspectives than is economics.

A fact that worries some sociologists is that sociology attracts much less talented students than economics. Stinchcombe touches on this issue and says that demanding a certain level of knowledge in calculus is probably what makes it easier for economics to sort out the good students from the bad students. Becker also feels that economics students are better than sociology students, especially in terms of analytical skills. Daniel Bell, on the other hand, disagrees that economists in general are so much brighter than sociologists. It is rather that problems are more easily defined in economics than in sociology. Economics also has a metric, a lot of problems can be formulated mathematically, and so on.

It is clear that there exist certain mechanisms in the sciences that prevent people from straying too far from the core. One of these is ridicule. An example of this can be found in the interview with Becker, where he tells about the reception of his paper from 1960 on children as consumer durables. Becker says that what you need in order to continue, when people ridicule your work, is self-confidence. Telling jokes is another way to convey a warning. In the introduction to this book, I cite Frank Knight's joke about sociology and Gresham's Law, as it is told in a book by Paul Samuelson. When Gary Becker's corrected transcript was returned, I found the same anecdote there. In fact, there exist several of these jokes about sociology, told by economists; and the point is invariably that sociology is ridiculous. In one of the footnotes to the introduction, Schumpeter's crack at Parsons is cited. And in Samuelson's great article on Schumpeter from 1951, "Schumpeter as a Teacher and Economic Theorist," there is another Schumpeter joke about sociology:

> And as relaxation for really old age, he [Schumpeter] spoke of writing a sociological novel in his eighties. He even once did field work on the latter: after a long and rather tiring walk, Mrs. Schumpeter with some difficulty persuaded him to ride on the subway back to Harvard Square. This, he reported, had been a very interesting experience; and what was more, when he came to write his sociological novel, he was going to do it again. (Samuelson 1951, 48)

All of these jokes are highly entertaining. There is also a message in them for the economist: stay away from sociology—or we will laugh as heartily at you as at this joke. Mark Granovetter tells about meeting young economists who feel that they have to hide their interest in sociology. By displaying it too openly, they feel that they will endanger their reputation and their chances of being published.

Undoubtedly, there also exists a bit of hostility among sociologists toward economists. However, according to Stinchcombe, who is the only one who touches on this issue, this hostility is not only diminishing but, in fact, has all but disappeared. According to Gary Becker, the hostility of economists toward sociologists is diminishing as well, even if it is a slow process. Whether the hostility between economists and sociologists will indeed disappear is hard to say. What is certain, however, is that a readjustment is by now long overdue in the relationship between economics and sociology. This means that the old conception of what the other science is all about needs to be changed. So what is so funny today will perhaps not be so funny tomorrow.

It is in any event utopian to believe that perfect harmony between economics and sociology is just around the corner. To realize this one only needs to read the interview with Robert Solow. On the one hand, Solow stresses that "economic man is a sociological concept"; that social institutions should be taken into account by economists; and that unemployment is an economic-sociological problem. But on the other hand, he distances himself very quickly from Parsons, from "interpretive sociology," and from most ways of analyzing social phenomena other than mathematical modeling. That is, he distances himself from most of sociology. So it is clear that it is just a readjustment of the relationship between economics and sociology that is overdue. But for the rest, it is probably back to the old tribal ways.

Economic Imperialism

All the interviewees in this book were asked what they think of economic imperialism. The reason for paying so much attention to this topic is that economic imperialism has, more than any other idea, helped to break down the traditional division of labor between neoclassical economics and sociology. It has convinced many mainstream economists that the time has come to extend the economic approach to a range of new topics, and that the boundaries between economics and the other social sciences should be redrawn.

When confronted with the question about economic imperialism, a couple of people pointed out that the term "economic imperialism" is not a very helpful one. To Becker, who rarely uses "economic imperialism" himself, it is just a kind of label that you use for lack of something better. Harrison White does not like the term "economic imperialism" at all—he feels that it prevents people from seriously evaluating scientific work on its own merits. Sociologists, he says, should not be defensive and label things "economic imperialism" just so they won't have to deal with them. Mancur Olson has a similar opinion. To him, "imperialism" basically denotes aggression, and it should not be used when one is talking about one science being influenced by another, intellectually more powerful science. The question that the answers of White and Olson raise is whether "economic imperialism" is not really an unnecessarily provocative term that should be replaced with something more neutral. One obvious candidate is "the economic approach," as in *The Economic Approach to Human Behavior* by Gary Becker. The opening essay in this book (which has the same title as the book) is also the closest that this intellectual movement comes to a manifesto.

In the interviews, however, the expression "economic imperialism" was used, and the reactions to it range from very positive to very negative. Gary Becker, James Coleman, and Mancur Olson identify strongly with the economic approach. Becker, who is the key figure in this whole movement, is obviously very positive and says that he has much confidence in the applicability of the economic approach to the most varied topics. James Coleman, whose ideas are by no means identical to those of Becker, is similarly hopeful. Mancur Olson has his own interpretation of "economic imperialism" and draws parallels between this approach and the work of people like John Stuart Mill and Karl Marx. "Economics," he says in a handsome, Plato-inspired metaphor, "seems, when first entered, like a dark cave [which] if followed *all* the way to the end, leads to the other side of the mountain, and to a magnificent view." When asked if it would be possible to solve all the great problems of sociology, political science, and so on with the help of the economic approach, Olson answers "yes."

Some of the people who were interviewed feel neither particularly positive nor particularly negative toward economic imperialism. Jon Elster and Oliver Williamson fall in this category, and perhaps Kenneth Arrow does as well. The rest of the participants, however, are negative to economic imperialism. Their critiques are all different except on one point: most of them explicitly make an exception for Becker's work, which they find very impressive. The typical answer can be paraphrased in the following way: "Economic imperialism is excessive in its attempts to impose the economic type of analysis on every topic—but Becker's work is definitely brilliant." After having criticized economic imperialism, one economist says that Becker will probably one day get a Nobel Prize for his work. "Brilliant but wrong" is another comment on Becker's work.

The reasons for this hostility toward economic imperialism differ from case to case. To Neil Smelser, economic imperialism is "fundamentally misguided" because of its "unrealistic assumptions," especially the assumption that the individual tries to maximize in all situations. To Stinchcombe, the gravest error of economic imperialism is its tendency to use the individual as the basic unit of analysis. According to Stinchcombe, this means that economic imperialism will not be able to handle truly collective phenomena, such as the family, mass movements, and the like. To Schelling and Hirschman, economic imperialism is just too crude. It lacks the kind of subtlety that one needs to analyze social phenomena; everything is always fed through the same machinery. Schelling also denounces the "evangelical enthusiasm" of economic imperialism, and he thinks that the present tendency to call something "economics" just because economists do it is fundamentally wrong.

Akerlof's critique is similar to that of Schelling and Hirschman in that he too reacts against the simplistic side of economic imperialism. In his own low-key manner, Akerlof says that economic imperialism is "a little bit superficial." He also turns the powerful weapon of a good joke against those who see the economic approach as the solution to every problem: "Samuelson said that Milton Friedman was like someone who had learned how to spell 'banana' but didn't know where to stop. I think there is a great deal of this here; these people just don't know where to stop."

The most severe criticisms of economic imperialism come from Amartya Sen, Harrison White, and Mark Granovetter. Their basic argument is that mainstream economics, as it exists today, cannot even solve its own problems; so how could it possibly solve those in the other social sciences? According to Sen, Becker's theory of the family is more of a wisecrack than a scientific theory. So for Becker to go into new areas of social science, Sen says, is about as wise as if Alexander the Great had tried to conquer Persia without first having secured Macedonia. White's comment is in the same vein: "Imperialism has sometimes been set off exactly by a failure of a regime on its own ground!" And Granovetter agrees: Since neoclassical economics cannot solve many of the problems within its own sphere of competence, how could it possibly aspire to solve those outside of it?

Another issue that is discussed in the interviews pertains to the link between economic imperialism and conservatism. According to Hirschman, economic imperialism is basically a conservative enterprise. One of the arguments for this is that in economic imperialism, the individual is someone who is mainly motivated by money and maximization. It is also obvious to Hirschman that economic imperialism has a clear affinity with the conservative temper of the 1980s. Elster rejects the identification of rational choice with conservatism, stressing that Schumpeter, who invented the term "methodological individualism," has already made a sharp distinction between "political individualism" and "methodological individualism." In reality, you may indeed find these two forms of individualism together—but that does not mean that there is any logical connection between them, according to Elster. Bell notes that while someone like Becker is indeed conservative, the main appeal of his approach is rather its great simplicity. Becker, in short, holds out the promise that extremely difficult problems can be solved in a fairly easy way. Bell also says that he is basically against the argument that there is a close fit between interests and ideas; ideas often have long and complicated histories.

To summarize, one can say that there exists a strong resistance to economic imperialism among the sociologists as well as the economists; that a distinction is often made between economic imperialism (which is criticized) and Gary Becker's work (which is admired); and that the issue of the relationship between economic imperialism and conservatism is complicated and not yet settled. What all of this adds up to is that the proponents of the economic approach have a great resistance to break down, since some of the key people in economics and sociology view it with very mixed feelings. That Becker is considered brilliant *despite* the hostility to economic imperialism means that his solutions to certain problems are admired, but that many scholars do not want to see his way of doing science proliferate.

Rational Choice Sociology

Another question asked of each interviewee concerns the possibility of introducing rational choice into sociology—is this a fruitful enterprise or not? In this context, it should be noted that it is really now, toward the end of the 1980s, that this is becoming an important question in sociology for the first time. Rationality was introduced into anthropology in the 1940s, and into political science and history in the late 1950s. Why it took such a long time for rationality to reach sociology is not clear; maybe it has to do with the long tradition of alienation between economics and sociology. In any case, the introduction of rationality into sociology raises many questions. Will there now be a confrontation in sociology, just as there was a confrontation between "formalists" and "substantivists" in anthropology in the 1950s? Or will the pattern rather be that of political science—an initial period of success, followed by difficulties?

One point that is clear from the interviews is that a concentrated effort to develop a rational choice sociology is presently under way at the University of Chicago. The two key figures are James Coleman and Gary Becker. An institutional structure is also being set up at the University of Chicago to give maximum support to rational choice sociology. This includes a new journal, a new book series, a seminar in rational choice methods, and various efforts to get the graduate students interested in rational choice. The journal is called *Rationality and Society* and is edited by James Coleman. It is described as "a new international journal which will focus on the growing contributions of rational-action-based theory, and the questions and controversies surrounding this growth." The book series, which is still under evaluation, is to be edited by James Coleman, Michael Hechter, and Siegwart Lindenberg. It will be the third general social science book series on rationality (the other two being *Studies in Rationality and Social Change* of Cambridge University Press, edited by Jon Elster and Gudmund Hernes; and *California Series on Social Choice and Political Economy* of the University of California Press, edited by Brian Barry, Robert Bates, and Samuel Popkin). The seminar on rational choice methods is interdisciplinary and meets once a week. It is also possible for graduate students to have rational choice as one of their areas of concentration. In order to do this, they must, among other things, take two courses in microeconomics in the economics department.

The general intellectual program in sociology of this new Chicago School is very ambitious. Basically, the goal is to set sociology straight through the introduction of rational choice. In this book, this project has been referred to as "rational choice sociology," but this is not the term that either Coleman or Becker use. In the interview, Becker calls what he is doing "economic-sociology." This concept is used in a very broad sense, and Becker, for example, explicitly includes Hirschman and Akerlof in the category of "economic-sociologists." He defines this new category of scholars as "economists who have learned some sociology and use concepts from sociology in their work." It also seems that sociologists can be "economic-sociologists." In any event Becker envisions a fairly slow growth of the number of the rational choice sociologists. There will not be many of these in the near future, but there will be some. He doubts that any major theoretical concepts will come from sociology during the process of reconstructing sociology. What the sociologists can add to the whole "economic-sociology" project are mainly two things: a sensitivity to the social dimension of individual behavior, and a much broader interest in social affairs than the economists have. According to Becker, sociologists often speculate about war, religion, and similar subjects, while economists tend to stick to a much more narrow range of problems.

The fact that Becker includes people like Hirschman and Akerlof under the umbrella of "economic-sociology" shows that he has a very broad project in mind. On the question of whether there exist other types of rational choice theories, Becker's answer also indicates that he is tolerant of different approaches. James Coleman's interpretation of rational choice is quite different from Becker's approach. Coleman advocates a much more sociological version of rational choice, which many mainstream economists would probably have difficulty in accepting. The notion of power (albeit reconstructed on a rational choice foundation) plays a key role in Coleman's theory. He also challenges the taboo against interpersonal utility comparisons, and says that economics will one day become a subdiscipline of sociology—and not the other way around, as Becker clearly thinks.

From the interview with Becker, one may get the impression that he basically intends to carry on with his own work in about the same manner as if he had *not* been offered the joint appointment in 1983. Coleman, on the other hand, is making a great effort to redirect his own work in order to give content to rational choice sociology. The result of this theoretical effort is to be found in his forthcoming book *Foundations of Social Theory*. This work constitutes a vigorous attempt to give sociology a new direction, and is in this sense similar to his *Introduction to Mathematical Sociology*.

Coleman's new book pulls together and further elaborates upon several themes he has worked on from the mid-1960s onward. Glimpses of what Coleman is trying to do can therefore be gleaned from his books on collective action, power, and "the asymmetric society" (Coleman 1973, 1974, 1982). The key idea seems to be that if the individualistic notion of "utility" is replaced by a pair of concepts, "control" and "interest," it becomes easier to make sociology of the whole thing. In Coleman's view—to give a quick summary—people are drawn to each other because one has an "interest" and the other the "control" over something. A single person can in principle have the control over something as well as an interest in it, but in many typical situations (involving authority, power, collective action, and so on), this is not the case. By replacing "utility" with "control" and "interest," the economic analysis is thus turned into rational choice sociology.

Throughout *Foundations of Social Theory*, Coleman is very sensitive to the micro-macro transition, and many of his arguments are intended to show that it is only by analyzing problems on the level of the individual that a solution can be found. It can also be noted that Coleman, unlike the economists, does not advocate just *assigning* a rational purpose to the actor; he feels that the rationality of the purpose is something that needs to be *investigated*. Coleman's version of methodological individualism is very flexible. Not only does he acknowledge the existence of corporate actors, but the focus of his analysis is as much on the social system as on the individual actor.

Practically all the economists in this book are positive toward the idea of introducing the rational choice approach into sociology. Included among these people, it should be noted, are also several of the most vocal critics of economic imperialism. The only dissenting voice comes from Albert O. Hirschman, who argues that rational choice can only be used in sociology at the price of tautology. If you label everything "rational," according to Hirschman, you can indeed use "rationality" as the explanation—but what is the point? Several of the economists are also very quick to point out that rationality should not be extended too far in sociology. Schelling, for example, says that rationality can indeed be a unifying element for sociology—but no more than that. Traditional sociological and psychological material is needed to complement the analysis.

The sociologists are clearly more divided in their attitude toward the project of a rational choice sociology than the economists. The idea does not at all appeal to Harrison White, who stresses, however, that one must under all circumstances wait and see what the rational choice people come up with before making a judgement. Sørensen is skeptical as well, and it sounds as if the whole thing has a bit of a *déjà vu* for him. He says that what he has seen thus far does not impress him. He says, "I am definitely underwhelmed by the amount of progress that has been made this far in rational actor theory." Bell, Granovetter, Smelser, and Stinch-combe are all skeptical, though they also tend to feel that some aspects of rational choice could perhaps be useful for sociology.

To the extent that rational choice sociology can be identified with an increased use of mathematics in sociology, strong doubts are expressed in particular by Sørensen and Granovetter. Both have worked with mathe-matical modeling, but neither believes that any great mathematical break-through is imminent for sociology. Sørensen discusses this issue at some length, and his brief history of the rise and fall of mathematical sociology is quite relevant in this context. To Sørensen, the real problem in sociol-ogy has much more to do with the lack of a proper concept of sociological theory than with the lack of a rational choice tradition. Sociologists basi-cally tend to equate sociological theory with the history of sociology, con-ceptual clarification, and the like, he claims. Not until a novel concept of theory is accepted in sociology will it make sense to introduce the issue of mathematization.

How then is one to evaluate the attempt by Becker and Coleman to recast sociology on the basis of rational choice? As a few interviewees emphatically state, it is basically much too early to undertake such an evaluation. At this stage, however, it is already clear that rational choice sociology represents an interesting attempt by Coleman and Becker to make something out of the present flux in the relationship between eco-nomics and sociology. The publication of Coleman's new book, *Founda-tions of Social Theory*, will also in all likelihood be a great event in sociol-ogy. The simplicity and elegance of many of Coleman's analyses, such as those of power and authority, has already impressed many fellow sociolo-gists and economists. The fact that an eminent economist like Gary Becker now works in a sociology department also represents a new and progres-sive development in sociology. But the last word still has to be that it is much too early to make any kind of judgement about the merits of rational choice sociology.

Economic Sociology

A further sign that interesting changes are under way in the no-man's land between economics and sociology is the fact that economic sociol-ogy has suddenly become popular again after years of neglect. For termi-nological purposes, it should perhaps be clarified here that "economic sociology" (no hyphen!) is something quite different from Becker's "eco-nomic-sociology" (with a hyphen!). The former approach has its roots within sociology and the main idea is to analyze economic phenomena from a sociological perspective; in "economic-sociology," one basically uses neoclassical tools to analyze sociological phenomena.

The attitudes toward economic sociology that are found in the interviews differ quite a bit. Becker does not seem to see any point in having an economic sociology, since there are already economists who analyze economic phenomena. At best, Becker seems willing to grant that since sociologists are more sensitive to the effects of social change, they can be of help in a few special areas, such as the study of preferences. Coleman disagrees with Becker on this point; and, in his opinion, it is quite natural that there should be an economic sociology: "There is an old aphorism that war is too important to be left to the generals. Well, economics is too important to be left to the economists." Mancur Olson's attitude toward economic sociology is a combination of Coleman's and Becker's ideas. On the one hand, he encourages sociologists to analyze economic topics. Yet, it is clear that he expects them to come up with about the same answers as the economists.

The economists also have different opinions about what parts of the economy the sociologists should work on. To Albert O. Hirschman, economists have narrowed down so radically what they consider worth studying that vast areas are simply left by default to sociologists and other social scientists. Kenneth Arrow sees the whole thing in a different way. To him, "the economic system" is embedded in a "social system," and there are basically three ways in which the two systems are connected: through "the element of communication," through "shared social norms," and through "the institutions for enforcement." In Arrow's opinion, it is also clear that even if economists and sociologists may study the same economic reality, they ask very different questions. Economists are, for example, interested in what determines prices. Sociologists are not; and if they were, they would have to introduce "straight economic elements" into their analysis. It is also clear from Arrow's argument on this point that he identifies economic sociology with institutionalism of the old type, that is, with a thoroughly nonanalytical way of doing social science where one is mostly interested in historical details. Economic sociology, however, does not look like Arrow's portrait of institutionalism and never has. From the very beginning of economic sociology, a conscious effort has been made to find a mediating position between the historians' nonanalytical type of analysis and the neoclassical thinkers' nonhistorical type of analysis. This was the position of Weber and Parsons yesterday and it is the position of White and Granovetter today.

Arrow is more to the point when he argues that economic sociology does not ask the same questions as economics. Or at least this is true for what Granovetter calls the "old economic sociology," by which he basically means the works of the industrial sociologists and the structural-functionalists in the 1950s. The "new economic sociology," of which Granovetter is a proponent, is much less respectful of economic theory and tries explicitly to address the same type of questions as the economists do. The reason for doing this, it can be added, is a strong belief that neoclassical economics has failed to make sense of many important economic problems.

The person who laid the foundation for the "new economic sociology" was Harrison White through his work in the late 1960s and the 1970s. In his interview, he describes how he began by working on social mobility and internal labor markets, only to later make the startling discovery that *"there does not exist a neoclassical theory of the market."* What does exist is a theory of exchange. And this theory is of no help when one wants to model concrete production markets, something that White was to attempt in the 1970s. Another interest of White's during this period was networks, and he soon succeeded in getting some of his students to work on this topic. Several of these students, including Mark Granovetter and Michael Schwartz, were later to combine networks and economics.

According to Granovetter, it is exactly the "embeddedness" of economic action in various social networks that should constitute the focus of the new economic sociology. In his vision, the economic actions of individuals as well as large economic patterns are significantly affected by social networks. Granovetter is of course aware that sociological approaches other than network analysis have been used by the "new economic sociologists." He still maintains, however, that there is a certain affinity between the network approach and the other approaches, such as neo-Marxist sociology and historical sociology, in the sense that they all realize that economic actions are fundamentally influenced by the social context in which they take place.

Granovetter's own empirical work in economic sociology has primarily been in the area of labor markets, where he has studied how networks of friends and acquaintances influence people's chances of getting a job. It is also clear from the answers of several other people that labor markets constitute a very good topic for sociologists to study. According to Stinch-combe, labor market sociology is today among the most sophisticated areas of sociology. And Sørensen, who outlines his own interesting research in this area, emphasizes that the work on labor markets that many economists do is very sociological in nature. As a matter of fact, there is not much point in making a distinction between sociologists and economists in this area: "In some sense we sociologists are actually neo-institutionalists. Or the neo-institutionalists are sociologists, whichever way you want it." In addition, not only the neo-institutionalists feel a need for a sociological approach to these questions. It is equally true for people like Akerlof and Solow, who work in the tradition of mainstream economics. Indeed, Akerlof considers his efficiency wage theory "to be the first explicitly sociological model [of unemployment]" (Akerlof and Yellen 1986, 8). And when it comes to unemployment, Solow has described himself as a "frustrated seeker after sociological help."

Another area that seems well suited for economic sociology is international economic relations. Daniel Bell and Neil Smelser particularly stress this belief. The latter points out that the nation state is no longer a suitable unit of analysis; in his view, we now live in a "world system." Also, Bell is interested in the changes that are occurring in the international economy, but he sees the whole situation in a somewhat different manner. Bell believes the industrial production is becoming more local; trade is becoming more continental; and capital and currency markets are becoming more international. And, the old fashioned nation state is caught in the middle of all these contradictory changes.

Bell also emphasizes the importance of doing comparative research in economic sociology. In the interview, he compares the growth of capitalism in Europe to that in Japan, and he points out that in the former, a break with traditions had to occur in order to get capitalism going, while the latter has drawn its strength precisely from the traditions. Stinchcombe also underlines the usefulness of doing comparative research, for example, in order to confront the more static views of mainstream economics.

As to the future of economic sociology, it can be noted that some first steps on the road to institutionalization have been taken. The Center for Economy and Society at the University of California at Santa Barbara held its first annual seminar in May 1988. Some departments of sociology have also developed somewhat of a tradition of educating economic sociologists. This is especially true for the University of New York at Stony Brook, where many students have graduated with expertise in economic sociology under the guidance of Mark Granovetter and Michael Schwartz. In recent years, George Washington University has developed the Socio-Economic Project, run and founded by Amitai Etzioni. Its results include a series of conferences, many articles, and a book by Etzioni entitled *The Moral Dimension: Toward A New Economics*. Many sociologists would probably agree with James Coleman when he says that "there ought to be an economic sociology just like there is a political sociology." Indeed, Coleman is seconded by Stinchcombe on this point, who says that today it is widely recognized that economic sociology is "very exciting stuff and that any reputable sociology department ought to have economic sociology."

The future also looks promising if one looks at the intellectual side of the "new economic sociology." According to Granovetter, there are plenty of economic topics that sociologists have never tried their hand at and that can probably be analyzed from a sociological perspective with interesting results. Economic sociologists, he says, have already produced whole series of good work. Granovetter is also optimistic about possible breakthroughs in economic sociology: "the whoppers are coming somewhere down the road."

Transaction Cost Economics and PSA Economics

Transaction cost economics and what Akerlof calls "psycho- socio- and anthropo-economics" (here referred to as PSA economics) represent two other challenges to the traditional division of labor between economics and sociology. Transaction cost economics came into its own in the 1970s through the work of Oliver Williamson. It is sometimes seen as part of economic imperialism, and it is true that Williamson often relies on standard economic theory. It is, however, also true that Williamson comes out of the tradition of behavioral economics at Carnegie Tech and that he draws more on ideas like bounded rationality than on hard-core neoclassical economics. It should also be noted that Williamson basically sees transaction cost economics as situated at the junction of law, economics, and organization—in other words, at the boundary between economics and what in a loose sense can be called the social realm.

This social realm also includes sociology, and Williamson is especially interested in promoting a dialogue between economics and sociology. The two areas in sociology of greatest interest to Williamson are networks and what he calls "process considerations." In Williamson's mind, sociology has paid much more attention to process considerations than has economics. Two examples of process considerations, which are important to transaction cost economics, are sunk costs and the fact that small firms can perform certain transactions that large firms are unable to do.

But it is clear that just as there is a certain affinity between transaction cost economics and sociology, there are also some important differences. Williamson, for example, is not willing to accept the sociological notion of "power" (which dates all the way back to Marx and Weber) but insists that it must be operationalized. Williamson also displays more faith in the fact that the existing economic institutions offer efficient solutions to various problems than most sociologists would.

Williamson is optimistic about the future of transaction cost economics and feels that there exist several promising topics to examine. He specifically mentions incomplete contracting, business strategy, and process considerations. At Berkeley, where Williamson moved in 1988, his approach will be anchored in a new field in the economics department called The Economics of Institutions. This field is geared to economics students and to business school students. The link to the business school community, which behavioral economics has had from the start, will therefore also continue in Williamson's case.

PSA economics, as Akerlof has developed it, represents in some sense the very opposite of economic imperialism. "What I want to do," Akerlof says, "is always the opposite of what Becker does. I want to explain why the economy is *not* working; what interesting thing you need to bring in, so you do *not* get market clearing with discrimination; and so on." So if Becker wants to export economics into sociology, Akerlof wants to import sociology (and the other social sciences) into economics. PSA economics is indeed built on the insight that economic theory by itself cannot explain some of the key problems in modern life; it needs the help of sociology and the other social sciences.

According to Akerlof, his approach is not suitable for all economic topics. But it is definitely applicable to what he considers to be the two most important topics, namely, unemployment and third world poverty. During the years after 1984, when PSA economics was launched through the publication of *An Economic Theorist's Book of Tales*, Akerlof feels that his way of doing economics has done "pretty well." PSA economics has especially had an impact on macroeconomics through Akerlof's efficiency wage theory and near rationality models. In general, Akerlof feels that his work has helped to revive Keynesian economics and that it has had an impact on studies of finance, like those by Richard Thaler and Robert Shiller.

Akerlof is a subtle thinker and he is clearly loath to put together standard instructions for how to do PSA economics. In principle, it is a question of putting economics and the other social sciences together, but he emphasizes that in each case there also has to be an interesting idea involved. To just add "a" and "b" will only give you "a+b," he warns. This means that PSA economics is difficult to duplicate and not easy to teach to students. The latter task is further hindered by the fact that the students need to know economics as well as some other social science; and such students are difficult to find at the graduate level. The impression one gets from Akerlof is that it is more through his ideas that he wants to exert influence than through an institutional buildup.

Whether the programs of transaction cost economics and PSA economics will succeed is hard to judge. It is obvious, however, that the other three approaches discussed in this book—economic imperialism, rational choice sociology, and economic sociology—are all fairly large enterprises with a substantial amount of institutional structure to them. Transaction cost economics and PSA economics have both attracted their followers, but the number is perhaps smaller. This, of course, is no judgement on the quality of the ideas involved.

Social Rationality

When the issue of introducing rationality into sociology was raised in the interviews, the concept of rationality was discussed from a variety of different perspectives. Although the opinions of the economists vary quite a bit, they all agree that it is necessary to use rationality. Once this is realized, however, one can introduce "departures from rationality" (Schelling), try to complement the economic analysis with insights from the other social sciences (Akerlof), and so on. Amartya Sen also raises the question of "social rationality." According to Sen, there exists a link between rationality and society; rationality has an "inescapably social component." By this he means first of all that the identity of the individual is influenced by the groups of which he or she is a member. To Sen, "social rationality" pertains primarily to the individual and his or her links to the rest of the community. Akerlof, on the other hand, seems more willing to entertain the notion that whole groups of people can be more or less rational. In his example of the farm crisis, he hints that while certain groups may maximize in certain situations, others may not.

When asked about rationality, the sociologists immediately zeroed in on its social dimension. Daniel Bell points out that the concept of rationality is connected to social values and that these are always culturally shaped. To Stinchcombe, the essential quality about rationality is that it is a social phenomenon and not an individual one. Organizations can be rational but not individuals. The latter have no natural inclination to be rational, and they also lack the resources that an organization can bring to bear on its decisions. According to Smelser, however, it is not only a question of varying *degrees* of rationality; there can also exist different *kinds* of rationality. There is "communal rationality," "economic rationality," and so on. A question that is also discussed in one of the interviews is concerned with gender differences and rationality: is male culture, for example, more rational than female culture? The answer, we learn from Jon Elster, is "no."

It is not easy to summarize the differences between economists and sociologists on the question of rationality. Becker says that it is primarily a question of *confidence*; economists are more confident about the usefulness of rationality than sociologists. This may well be true, but there are also some important theoretical differences involved. The main one, in Stinchcombe's formulation (1986a, 5), is that while rationality is an *assumption* for the economists, it is a *variable* for the sociologists. This basically means that the sociologist will in each situation try to establish the exact form and degree of the rationality involved. The economist, on the other hand, will only do this as an exception.

It is evident that most of the serious theoretical work on the issue of "social rationality" still remains to be done. Some of the key questions that need to be discussed involve the relationship of rationality to *values*; its relationship to *personal identity*; and its relationship to *group behavior*. These all sound like ideal issues for sociologists to work on, but judging from the interviews it looks as if the economists are way ahead.

Final Remarks

It can be said that the interviews give much support to the idea that the present division of labor between economics and sociology is now coming to an end. Exactly how the new border will be redrawn is not clear. However, the following three tendencies will have to be taken into account:

1. Economists are increasingly working on topics that by tradition are seen as "sociological";
2. Sociologists are increasingly working on the same problems as the economists, that is, on traditionally "economic" topics;
3. New mixtures of economics and sociology are increasingly appearing.

It is difficult to predict the end result of this situation. A certain euphoria is common when things start to change—everything suddenly seems possible!—but it is not likely that economics will take over sociology (or the opposite). Both neoclassical economics and traditional sociology have so much going for them that they cannot be seriously challenged by the other science. In addition, both economics and sociology are professions with thousands of members, and it would take an earthquake to move these colossuses more than a few inches. Even if everyone agreed that a science was stone dead, it would be almost impossible to put it to rest. What is most likely to happen is that the border area between economics and sociology will increasingly come to life, and during the next few years it will be a hothouse for various experiments and interesting mutations between economics and sociology. The number of approaches will probably multiply, but the two cores are likely to remain untouched.

Time will sort out which of the approaches discussed in this book will be successful in the long run. During the next few years, some of them will probably lose whatever vitality they have today, while others will seem just as insightful if not more so. This is usually what happens in intellectual life; ideas change as the world changes. But there are also some thoughts that are more resistant to the changes of the day because they have a very rare and uncommon quality. These are the thoughts that will survive long after the current border dispute between economics and sociology has been settled. So, to close this book, I look to Amartya Sen, who is of the opinion that economics and sociology are not so dissimilar after all: "Indeed, both subjects are about human life in society. Economics is ultimately not about commodities, but about the lives that human beings can lead. These lives include making commodities as well as using them, but they are not the same as commodity production, exchange and consumption. The interest in the world of commodities is a derivative one, and the ultimate concern has to be with the lives we can or cannot lead."

References

Akerlof, George A. 1984a. *An Economic Theorist's Book of Tales.* Cambridge: Cambridge University Press.

Akerlof, George A., and Janet L. Yellen, eds. 1986. *Efficiency Wage Models of the Labor Market.* Cambridge: Cambridge University Press.

Becker, Gary. 1976. "The Economic Approach to Human Behavior." In *The Economic Approach to Human Behavior,* 3–14. Chicago: University of Chicago Press.

Coleman, James S. 1964b. *Introduction to Mathematical Sociology.* New York: Free Press.

———. 1973. *The Mathematics of Collective Action.* Chicago: Aldine Publishing Company.

———. 1974. *Power and the Structure of Society.* New York: W. W. Norton.

———. 1982. *The Asymmetric Society.* Syracuse, N.Y.: Syracuse University Press.

Etzioni, Amitai. 1988. *The Moral Dimension: Toward A New Economics.* New York: Free Press.

Leijonhufvud, Axel. 1973. "Life among the Econ." *Western Economic Journal* 11 (September):327–37.

Myrdal, Gunnar. 1953b. "The Relation between Social Theory and Social Policy." *British Journal of Sociology* 4:210–42.

Parsons, Talcott, and Neil J. Smelser. 1956. *Economy and Society: A Study in the Integration of Economic and Social Theory.* New York: Free Press.

Samuelson, Paul A. 1951. "Schumpeter as a Teacher and Theorist." In *Schumpeter, Social Scientist*, edited by S. E. Harris, 48–53. Cambridge: Harvard University Press.

Schelling, Thomas C. 1978. *Micromotives and Macrobehavior.* New York: W. W. Norton.

Stinchcombe, Arthur L. 1986a. "Rationality and Social Structure: An Introduction." In *Stratification and Organization*, 1–29. Cambridge: Cambridge University Press.

Glossary of Names

THE FOLLOWING represents a selection of the names mentioned in the interviews. Various standard bibliographical works have been used, especially Mark Blaug, ed., *Who's Who in Economics* (1986).

Alchian, Armen A. (1914–). Economist at the University of California at Los Angeles who has made contributions to such topics as evolution, property rights, and inflation. Author of "Uncertainty, Evolution and Economic Theory" (1950).

Allport, Gordon W. (1897–1967). Psychologist at Harvard University who has developed a theory of personality and contributed to the study of prejudice. Author of *Personality* (1937), and *The Nature of Prejudice* (1954).

Althusser, Louis (1918–). French Marxist philosopher whose popularity was at its height during the 1960s. Major works include *For Marx* (1965), and *Reading Capital* (1965).

Aron, Raymond (1905–1983). French philosopher, sociologist, and political commentator. Major works on contemporary politics, industrial society, and various philosophical topics. Works include *Eighteen Lectures on Industrial Society* (1961), and *Peace and War* (1962).

Arthur, W. Brian (1945–). Irish-born economist at Stanford University. Contributions to demography using rigorous, mathematical methods. Author of *Mathematical Modelling at IIASA* (1982).

Barnard, Chester I. (1886–1961). A businessman with extensive academic interests. Author of a classic in organization theory, *The Functions of the Executive* (1938).

Barro, Robert J. (1944–). Economist at the University of Rochester. Key participant in "new classical macroeconomics." Major works on rational expectations, business cycles, and monetary policy.

Barry, Brian (1936–). British-born philosophy educator at the University of Chicago. Interests include political theory, rational choice, and philosophy of law. Author of *Sociologists, Economists and Democracy* (1970) and coeditor of *Rational Man and Irrational Society* (1982).

Barth, Fredrik (1928–). Norwegian social anthropologist who has helped to modify the structural-functional paradigm. Major works include *Political Leadership among Swat Pathans* (1959), and *Models of Social Organization* (1966).

Bauer, Raymond A. Key figure in the social indicator movement. Major work is *Social Indicators* (1968). Bauer was born in 1916.

Baumol, William (1922–). Economist at Princeton University. Major contributions to such areas as welfare economics, unbalanced growth, and the behavior of firms. Works include the textbook *Economic Theory and Operations Research* (1961), and the coauthored *Contestable Markets and the Theory of Industry Structure* (1982).

Bendix, Reinhard (1916–). German-born sociologist at the University of California at Berkeley. Major works include *Work and Authority in Industry* (1956), and *Max Weber: An Intellectual Portrait* (1960).

Benedict, Ruth (1887–1948). U.S. anthropologist and originator of the so-called configurational approach to culture. Her most famous works include *Patterns of Culture* (1934), and *The Chrysanthemum and the Sword* (1946).

Bentham, Jeremy (1748–1832). British philosopher, reformist, and advocate of utilitarianism. His disciples included such economists as David Ricardo and John Stuart Mill. Author of *An Introduction to the Principles of Morals and Legislation* (1780).

Bergson, Abram (1914–). Economist at Harvard University who early made an important contribution to welfare economics and who later became a leading expert on the Soviet economy.

Bishop, Robert L. (1916–). Economist at MIT with microeconomics as his specialty. Principal contributions to demand theory, consumer's surplus, and various problems involving monopoly and microequilibrium.

Blumer, Herbert. Sociologist with major interest in participant observation and symbolic interaction. Works include *Symbolic Interactionism* (1969). Born in 1900, Blumer died in the early 1980s.

Boas, Franz (1858–1942). German-born anthropologist at Columbia University who helped to found modern anthropology. Works include *The Mind of Primitive Man* (1911), and *Race, Language and Culture* (1940).

Boring, Edwin G. (1886–1968). Psychologist at Harvard University with interests in experimental psychology and the history of psychology. Author of *A History of Experimental Psychology* (1929).

Boulding, Kenneth E. (1910–). British-born economist in the United States who has helped to synthesize neoclassical economics and Keynesian economics. Contributions to a wide range of topics, including evolutionary economics and normative economics. Works include *The Re-*

construction of Economics (1950), and *A Preface to Grants Economics* (1981).

Buchanan, James M. (1919–). Economist at George Mason University who is the founder of public choice theory. Works include (together with Gordon Tullock) *The Calculus of Consent* (1962). Received the Nobel Prize in 1986.

Bücher, Karl (1847–1930). German economist and historian. Principal contribution to the analysis of the economic development of Europe. Works include *Industrial Evolution* (1893).

Burawoy, Michael. British sociologist active in the United States. Principal contributions to industrial sociology and Marxist sociology. Author of *Manufacturing Consent* (1979), and *The Politics of Production* (1985).

Burt, Ronald S. Sociologist at Columbia University with major research interests in networks, markets, and quantitative methods. Author of *Corporate Profits and Cooptation* (1983).

Chamberlin, Edward (1899–1967). Economist at Harvard University whose major contribution was his theory of monopolistic competition. This theory was first presented in his doctoral dissertation from 1927 and later in *The Theory of Monopolistic Competition* (1933).

Chandler, Alfred D., Jr. (1918–). Business historian at Harvard Business School whose major interest has been the historical evolution of American firms. Author of *Strategy and Structure* (1962), and *The Visible Hand* (1978).

Clark, John Bates (1847–1938). Economist at Columbia University and an important member of the older generation of American economists. Principal contribution to marginal productivity theory. Author of such works as *The Distribution of Wealth* (1899), and *Essentials of Economic Theory* (1907).

Coase, Ronald H. (1910–). British-born economist at the University of Chicago Law School who has pioneered transaction cost economics and the application of economics to law. His most well-known works are "The Nature of the Firm" (1937), and "The Problem of Social Cost" (1960).

Coon, Carlton (1904–1981). Anthropologist who worked first at Harvard University and later at the University of Pennsylvania. Contributions to cultural and physical anthropology and archaeology. Works include *The Story of Man* (1954), and *The Hunting Peoples* (1971).

Coser, Lewis (1913–). Sociologist presently at Boston College. Major contribution to sociological theory, especially conflict theory. Works include *The Functions of Social Conflict* (1956), and *Men of Ideas* (1965).

Crozier, Michel (1922–). French sociologist and social critic. Principal contributions to the sociology of organizations. Author of *The Bureaucratic Phenomenon* (1964), and coauthor of *The Crisis of Democracy* (1975).

Cyert, Richard M. (1921–). Economist at Carnegie-Mellon University with research interest in economic organization, including oligopoly and simulation studies. Coauthor of *A Behavioral Theory of the Firm* (1963), which was written with James G. March.

David, Paul A. (1935–). Economic historian at Stanford whose principal contribution has been to further the development of quantitative economic history. Among major fields of interest are slavery, and technical, long-term growth. Works include the coauthored *Reckoning with Slavery* (1976).

Debreu, Gerard (1921–). French-born economist at the University of California at Berkeley. Major contributions to mathematical economics, including a famous paper from 1954 on generel equilibrium theory, coauthored with Kenneth Arrow. Received the Nobel Prize in 1983.

Deutsch, Karl W. (1912–). Political scientist at Harvard University who was born in Czechoslovakia. Author of many works on international relations and the nature of political science, including *The Nerves of Government* (1963).

Dewey, John (1859–1952). Philosopher, educational theorist, and key participant in the pragmatist movement. Works include *Democracy and Education* (1916), and *Reconstruction in Philosophy* (1920).

Dobb, Maurice (1900–1976). British economist at Cambridge University. Major contribution to Marxist economics. Works include *Studies in the Development of Capitalism* (1946).

Downs, Anthony (1930–). Economist at Brookings. Principal contribution consists of having pioneered the use of the economic approach to political problems through *An Economic Theory of Democracy* (1957). Other research interests include urban development and racial segregation.

Duesenberry, James S. (1918–). Economist at Harvard University whose major field of interest is monetary theory. Early in his career, Duesenberry was interested in economic sociology and also wrote the famous *Income, Saving and the Theory of Consumer Behavior* (1949).

Duncan, Otis Dudley (1921–). U.S. sociologist at the University of California at Santa Barbara. Principal contributions to methodology. Coauthor together with Peter Blau of *The American Occupational Structure* (1967).

Dunlop, John (1914–). Labor economist at Harvard University and former United States Secretary of Labor (1975–1976). Principal contributions to such areas as labor markets, trade unions, and industrial relations. Dunlop has coauthored *Industrialism and Industrial Man* (1960) and is the editor of the *Wertheim Publications in Industrial Relations.*

Durkheim, Emile (1858–1917). French sociologist and one of the founders of modern sociology. Pioneer in such areas as the sociology of religion, the sociology of education, and sociology of morality. Works include *The Rules of Sociological Method* (1895), and *Suicide* (1897).

Eastman, Max (1883–1969). American activist and writer. Editor of *The Masses* in the 1910s, and author of various books on socialism.

Eatwell, John. British economist of the Cambridge School who has collaborated with Joan Robinson in writing the unorthodox *Introduction to Modern Economics* (1973). Coeditor of *The New Palgrave Dictionary of Modern Economics* (1987).

Eccles, Robert G. Sociologist at the Harvard Business School. Main contributions to the transfer cost problem and the study of commercial banking.

Eckstein, Otto (1926–1984). German-born economist at Harvard University. First worked in public finance but most known for his econometric models for forecasting policy analysis. Works include *Core Inflation* (1981).

Edgeworth, Francis Y. (1845–1926). British economist and author of *Mathematical Psychics* (1881). Principal contributions to mathematical economics and to statistics.

Etzioni, Amitai (1929–). German-born sociologist at George Washington University with interests in policy analysis, organizations, and socioeconomics. Works include *The Active Society* (1968), and *The Moral Dimension: Towards A New Economics* (1988).

Fellner, William John (1905–1983). Hungarian-born economist who spent much of his professional life at Berkeley and at Yale University. Contributions to macroeconomics and oligopoly theory.

Finley, Sir Moses I. (1912–). British historian at Cambridge University whose specialty is the social history of Ancient Greece. Among his works are *The Ancient Economy* (1973), and *Economy and Society in Ancient Greece* (1981).

Fiorina, Morris P. Political scientist at Harvard University. Major research interests include U.S. Congress and elections. Author of *Retrospective Voting in American National Elections* (1981).

Firth, Raymond (1901–). Anthropologist born in New Zealand and active in England. Major contributions to anthropology in general and economic anthropology. Works include *We, The Tikopia* (1936).

Freeman, Richard B. (1945–). Labor economist at Harvard University. Major works include *What Do Unions Do?* (1984), coauthored with James Medoff.

Friedman, Benjamin J. (1944–). Economist at Harvard University whose major interest is the understanding of how financial markets work. Books include *Economic Stabilization Policy* (1975), and *The Changing Role of Debt and Equity in Financing U.S. Capital Formation* (1982).

Friedman, Milton (1912–). Economist and key figure in the Chicago School of Economics. Most known for his theory of monetarism, the essay "The Methodology of Positive Economics" (1953), and his defense of the free enterprise system. Received the Nobel Prize in 1976.

Geertz, Clifford (1926–). Social and cultural anthropologist at the Institute for Advanced Study in Princeton. Advocate of an interpretative approach in anthropology and author of various studies of Java, Bali, and Morocco. Works include *Peddlers and Princes* (1963), and *The Interpretation of Cultures* (1973).

Ginzberg, Eli (1911–). Economist and educator at Columbia University. Author of a multitude of books on various topics, including urban economics, health care economics, blacks in the economy, and women in the economy.

Goffman, Erving (1922–1982). Social psychologist and sociologist whose major interest was the structure of social interaction. Works include *The Presentation of Self in Everyday Society* (1959), and *Asylums* (1961).

Gordon, Robert J. (1940–). Economist whose principal contribution is to the study of inflation and the measurement of durable goods. Works include the anthology *Milton Friedman's Monetary Framework* (1974).

Haberler, Gottfried (1900–). Austrian-born economist who after a career at Harvard University is presently at the American Enterprise Institute. Major contribution to the theory of international trade. Works include *The Theory of International Trade* (1936).

Habermas, Jürgen (1929–). German social theorist and foremost contemporary representative of the Frankfurt School of "critical theory." Major works include *Knowledge and Human Interest* (1968), and *The Theory of Communicative Action* (1981).

Hahn, Frank H. (1925–). German-born economist at Cambridge University. Major contributions to mathematical economics, especially the theory of general equilibrium. Coauthor of *General Competitive Analysis* (1971).

Hansen, Alvin (1887–1975). Economist at Harvard University and chief propagator of Keynes's ideas in the United States. Contributions, e.g., to the theory of the multiplier. Works include *Business Cycle Theory* (1927), and *A Guide to Keynes* (1953).

Harrod, Sir Roy (1900–1978). British economist known for his work on economic growth ("Harrod-Domar Growth Theory"), and the standard work *Life of John Maynard Keynes* (1951).

Hart, H.L.A. (1907–). British jurist and philosopher who has spent most of his career at Oxford University. Works include *The Concept of Law*, and *Law, Liberty and Morality* (1963).

von Hayek, Friedrich A. (1899–). Member of the Austrian School of Economics, who has made contributions to the philosophy of economics, capital theory, and the theory of prices. Works include *The Road to Serfdom* (1944). Received the Nobel Prize in 1974.

Hechter, Michael (1943–). Sociologist at the University of Arizona. Major interest in rational choice sociology. Works include *Principles of Group Solidarity* (1987).

Hicks, Sir John (1904–). British economist who has made contributions to many branches of economics, especially general equilibrium theory and welfare economics. Received the Nobel Prize in 1972. Works include *Theory of Wages* (1932).

Hirshleifer, Jack (1925–). Economist at the University of California at Los Angeles. Principal contributions to the theories of optimal investment decisions and equilibrium in speculative markets. Also interested in expanding the economic approach to new areas.

Homans, George C. (1910–1989). Sociologist at Harvard University and one of the founders of exchange theory in sociology. Major work is *The Human Group* (1950).

Hotelling, Harold (1895–1973). Economist at Columbia University and the University of North Carolina who pioneered mathematical economics and statistical theory. Contributions to many areas, including location theory, demand theory, and taxation.

Howell, James E. (1928–). Economist at Stanford. Coauthor or author of such works as *Higher Education for Business* (1959), *Mathematical Analysis for Business Decisions* (1971), and *European Economics—East and West* (1967).

Hughes, Everett C. Sociologist and well-known member of the Chicago School in Sociology. Principal contribution to the sociology of professions. Works include *The Sociological Eye* (1971). Born in 1897, Hughes died in the early 1980s.

Husserl, Edmund (1859–1938). German-Austrian philosopher and one of the founders of phenomenology. Author of *Logical Investigations* (1900–1901).

Hyppolite, Jean (1907–). French philosopher whose studies on Hegel constitute his major contribution. Author of *Genesis and Structure of Hegel's Phenomenology of Spirit* (1946).

Iannaccone, Laurence R. Economist at Santa Clara University. Main research interests center on rational choice models of nonmarket behavior, especially religious participation and habit formation.

Janowitz, Morris A. (1919–). Sociologist at the University of Chicago. Major contributions to the sociology of the military and the history of sociological theory. Author of *The Professional Soldier* (1960).

Kahneman, Daniel. Psychologist at the University of California at Berkeley. Principal contribution to the analysis of the limitations on rational decision making in works coauthored with Amos Tversky, e.g., "The Framing of Decisions and the Psychology of Choice" (1981).

Kaysen, Carl (1920–). Economist at MIT where he is director for the program entitled Science, Technology and Society. Major interests in market power, business institutions, and education. Coauthor of *The American Business Creed* (1956).

Kerr, Clark (1911–). Labor economist and former president of the University of California at Berkeley. Contributions to the theory of labor markets and the theory of industrial society. Works include the coauthored *Industrialism and Industrial Man* (1960).

Keynes, John Maynard (1883–1946). British economist who reshaped twentieth-century economic theory through *The General Theory of Employment, Interest and Money* (1936).

Kindleberger, Charles P. (1910–). Economist at MIT who has written on international economics, financial crisis, and the history of economics. Works include *International Economics* (1953), and *Manias, Panics and Crashes* (1978).

Kluckhohn, Clyde (1905–1960). Anthropologist at Harvard University with interest in the concept of culture and in Navajo ethnography. Author of *Navajo Witchcraft* (1940), and *Mirror for Man* (1949).

Knight, Frank H. (1885–1972). Economist and social philosopher at the University of Chicago who was to play a major role in the clarification and development of neoclassical theory. His major work is *Risk, Uncertainty and Profit* (1921).

Koopmans, Tjalling C. (1910–1984). Dutch-born economist who spent much of his career at Yale University. Most known for his applications of mathematical statistics to economics. Received the Nobel Prize in 1975 for contribution to the theory of optimum allocation of resources.

Kuznets, Simon (1901–1985). Russian-born economist at Harvard University whose main interest was the historical and quantitative study of economic change. Major contributions to the study of business cycles, economic growth, and income accounting. Received the Nobel Prize in 1971.

Landes, David S. (1924–). Economic historian at Harvard University with special interest in European history. Works include *Bankers and Paschas* (1958), and *The Unbound Prometheus* (1969).

Laumann, Edward O. Chicago-based and Harvard-educated sociologist with broad interests, which include networks, organizations, and urban sociology. Coauthor of *Networks of Collective Action* (1976), and *Chicago Lawyers* (1983).

Lazarsfeld, Paul F. (1901–1976). Austrian-born sociologist who spent much of his career at the Bureau of Applied Social Research at Columbia University. Principal contribution consists of having pioneered empirical social research. Works include the coauthored *Die Arbeitslosen von Marienthal* (1933), and *The People's Choice* (1948).

Lefebvre, Georges (1874–1959). French historian whose field of specialization was the French revolution. Major works include *The Great Fear of 1789* (1932), and *The Coming of the French Revolution, 1789* (1939).

Leibenstein, Harvey (1922–). Economist at Harvard University who is most known for his theory of X-efficiency. Principal contributions to the theory of the firm and to the microeconomics of human fertility. Works include *Beyond Economic Man* (1976), and *General X-efficiency Theory and Economic Development* (1978).

Leontief, Wassily (1906–). Russian-born economist who has spent much of his career at Harvard University. His principal contribution is the input-output analysis. Received the Nobel Prize in 1973.

Lerner, Abba P. (1903–1982). Russian-born economist who has made contributions to international trade, Keynesian economics, and welfare economics. Works include *The Economics of Control* (1944), and *Selected Economic Writings of Abba P. Lerner* (1983).

Levy, Marion (1918–). Sociologist at Princeton University. Major contribution to functionalist theory in sociology, especially through *The Structure of Society* (1952).

Lewis, H. Gregg (1914–). Economist who has spent much of his professional life at the University of Chicago. Principal contribution to neoclassical labor economics on union-nonunion wage differentials.

Lewis, W. Arthur (1915–). Economist born in the West Indies who has made major contributions to the theory of economic development. Author of *The Theory of Economic Growth* (1955). Received the Nobel Prize in 1979.

Lindenberg, Siegwart M. (1941–). Harvard-educated Dutch sociologist with major research interest in rational choice. Presently at the University of Groningen in Holland.

Lipset, Seymour Martin (1922–). Sociologist at Stanford University whose interests include political sociology, stratification, and the sociology of education. Among his well-known works are the coauthored *Union Democracy* (1956), and *Political Man* (1960).

Lucas, Robert E., Jr. (1937–). Economist at the University of Chicago. Major contribution to the theory of rational expectations and a key figure in "new classical economics." Works include *Studies in Business-Cycle Theory* (1981), and the coedited *Rational Expectations and Econometric Practice* (1981).

Maine, Sir Henry Sumner (1822–1888). British legal scholar and historian. In *Ancient Law* (1861), Maine introduced the famous distinction of primitive societies mainly based on "status" as opposed to complex societies mainly based on "contract."

Malthus, Thomas (1766–1834). British clergyman and economist whose major contribution consists of the theory of population as developed in *An Essay on The Principle of Population* (1798).

Mannheim, Karl (1893–1947). German-Hungarian sociologist who has contributed to the sociology of knowledge (*Wissenssoziologie*). Major works include *Ideology and Utopia* (1929), and *Man and Society in an Age of Reconstruction* (1940).

Mansfield, Edwin (1930–). Economist at the University of Pennsylvania. Principal contributions to the economics of technical change, industrial organization, and the theory of the firm. Works include the textbook *Economics* (1974).

March, James G. (1928–). Interdisciplinary social scientist at Stanford University. Major contributions to organization theory and behavioral economics. Works include the coauthored *Organizations* (1955), and *A Behavioral Theory of the Firm* (1963).

Marglin, Stephen A. Economist at Harvard University. Principal contribution to Marxist economics. Works include "What Do Bosses Do?" (1974), and *Growth, Distribution and Prices* (1984).

Margolis, Julius (1920–). Economist at the University of California at Irvine, whose work has mainly been focused on government behavior in economic matters. Author of *The Analysis of Public Output* (1977).

Marshall, Alfred (1842–1924). British economist and one of the founders of modern economics. Most well-known work is *Principles of Economics* (1890).

Maxwell, James Clerk (1831–1879). British scientist who has contributed to several fields in classical physics, especially to thermodynamics and statistical physics.

Mead, George Herbert (1863–1931). Social philosopher, social psychologist, and key figure in the pragmatist movement. Mead's influence on certain parts of sociology has been great, especially on symbolic interactionism.

Mead, Margaret (1901–1978). Anthropologist and educator in whose works on gender, sex, and childrearing the concept of culture is especially emphasized. Her most famous work is *Coming of Age in Samoa* (1928).

Meltzer, Allan H. (1928–). Economist at Carnegie-Mellon University who has made principal contributions to the theory of money, economic policy, and theories of the size and growth of government.

Menger, Carl (1840–1921). Austrian economist and co-discoverer together with Jevons and Walras of marginal utility theory. Works include *Principles of Economics* (1871).

Merton, Robert (1910–). Sociologist at Columbia University who has played a key role in sociology since World War II. Major contributions to sociological theory and the sociology of science. Works include *Social Theory and Social Structure* (1968), and *Sociology of Science* (1973).

Mill, John Stuart (1806–1873). One of the great nineteenth-century British economists who has also made contributions to other fields, such as philosophy and political science. Work include *Principles of Political Economy* (1848), and *Utilitarianism* (1861).

Mincer, Jacob (1922–). Polish-born economist at Columbia University who pioneered the human capital approach and who has also made contributions to the economics of labor mobility and economic demography. Works include *Schooling, Experience and Earnings* (1974).

Mitchell, Wesley Clair (1874–1948). Economist with interest in institutional economics who helped to develop empirical research in the United States. His works include *Business Cycles* (1913).

Modigliani, Franco (1918–). Italian-born economist at MIT who is most known for having pioneered the life-cycle hypothesis of saving. Received the Nobel Prize in 1985.

Morishima, Michio (1923–). Japanese-born economist at the London School of Economics. Principal contribution to equilibrium theory and to Marxian economics. Works include *Marx's Economics* (1973).

Moynihan, Daniel Patrick (1927–). U.S. senator and educator. Interests in areas such as the family, urban affairs, and ethnicity. Coauthor of, e.g., *Beyond the Melting Pot* (1963), and *Maximum Feasible Misunderstanding* (1969).

Murray, Henry A. Clinical psychologist at Harvard University who developed a theory of personality. His major work is *Explorations in Personality* (1938). Murray was born in 1893.

Myrdal, Gunnar (1898–1987). Swedish economist and member of the Stockholm School. Myrdal was first a mainstream theorist and then an institutionalist. Author of *An American Dilemma* (1944), and *Asian Drama* (1968). Received the Nobel Prize in 1974.

Papandreou, Andreas George (1919–). Greek economist and since 1981 Prime Minister of Greece. While in the United States, he spent much time at the University of California at Berkeley. Author of *A Strategy for Greek Economic Development* (1962), and *Fundamentals of Model Construction in Macroeconomics* (1962).

Pareto, Vilfredo (1848–1923). Italian economist and sociologist. Principal contributions to mathematical economics, welfare economics, and sociology. His works include *Manual of Political Economy* (1906), and *Trattato di Sociologia Generale* (1916).

Parsons, Talcott (1902–1979). Sociologist at Harvard University who dominated sociology in the 1950s with his structural-functional approach. Author of *The Structure of Social Action* (1937), and *The Social System* (1951).

Pesch, Heinrich (1854–1926). German Catholic economist who emphasized the moral basis of economics and developed "Christian solidarism."

Pigou, Arthur Cecil (1877–1959). British economist and leading figure in Cambridge economics. Pigou pioneered welfare economics, e.g., in *Wealth and Welfare* (1912).

Piore, Michael (1940–). Economist at MIT who is most known for his contribution (together with P. B. Doeringer) to the theory of dual labor markets. Interests also in migration and industrial policy.

Pizzorno, Alessandro. Italian sociologist who has spent much of his career at Harvard University. Main interest in political sociology. Works include the anthology *Political Sociology* (1971).

Polanyi, Karl (1886–1964). Hungarian-Austrian born interdisciplinary social scientist who is most known for his contributions to economic anthropology. Major works include *The Great Transformation* (1944), and the anthology *Trade and Markets in the Early Empires* (1957).

Porter, Michael (1947–). Economist at the Harvard Business School. Main interest in the reorganization of firms to improve their performance. Works include *Competetive Strategy* (1980), and *Competetive Advantage* (1985).

Posner, Richard A. (1939–). Legal scholar at the University of Chicago Law School who is presently a judge. Principal contributions to the economic analysis of law. Major works include *Economic Analysis of Law* (1973), and *The Economics of Justice* (1981).

Radner, Roy (1927–). Economist who has spent most of his career at the University of California at Berkeley. Contributions to the theory of decision making, investment strategies, and higher education.

Rainwater, Lee (1928–). Sociologist at Harvard University. Main research interests include social welfare and the study of poverty. Author of *Behind Ghetto Walls* (1970).

Rawls, John (1921–). Moral philosopher at Harvard University. Major work is *A Theory of Justice* (1971).

Riesman, David (1909–). Sociologist at Harvard University with major interests in social psychology, the sociology of law, and the sociology of education. Author of *The Lonely Crowd* (1950).

Robinson, Joan (1903–1983). British economist who belonged to the modern Cambridge School. Principal contributions to economic theory and Marxist economics. Works include *Economics of Imperfect Competition* (1933), and *An Essay on Marxian Economics* (1942).

Rosen, Sherwin. Economist at the University of Chicago. Main research interest in labor economics and industrial organization.

Sabel, Charles F. Social scientist at MIT. Major research interest is technology and society. Author of *Works and Politics* (1982), and coauthor of *The Second Industrial Divide* (1984).

Samuelson, Paul A. (1915–). Economist at MIT and one of the most prominent economists of the twentieth century. Major contributions to most of the principal areas of economics, including welfare economics, mathematical economics, and foreign trade. Received the Nobel Prize in 1970.

Scheler, Max (1874–1928). German philosopher and sociologist who is one of the key figures in the phenomenological movement. Author of works such as *Ressentiment* (1912).

Schultz, Theodor W. (1902–). Economist at the University of Chicago who pioneered the human capital approach. Contributions also to economic growth and agricultural economics. Received the Nobel Prize in 1979.

Schumpeter, Joseph A. (1883–1950). Austrian-Hungarian born economist who spent most of his career at Harvard University. Principal contributions to the theories of economic change, entrepreneurship, and business cycles. Works include *The Theory of Economic Development* (1911), and *History of Economic Analysis* (posthumously published).

Schutz, Alfred (1899–1959). Austrian-born sociologist and social philosopher who is one of the key figures in the phenomenological movement. Author of works such as *The Phenomenology of the Social World* (1932).

Selznick, Philip. Sociologist at the University of California at Berkeley with major interest in the sociology of organization. Works include *TVA and the Grassroots* (1949), and *The Organizational Weapon* (1952). Selznick was born in 1919.

Shapley, Lloyd S. (1923–). Mathematician at the Rand Graduate Institute for Policy Studies. Author of various works on game theory, including the anthology *Advances in Game Theory* (1964).

Shepsle, Kenneth A. Political scientist at Harvard University with interst in the U.S. Congress and its system of committees. Works include *The Giant Jigsaw Puzzle* (1978).

Sherif, Muzafer. Turkish-born social psychologist. Works include *The Psychology of Social Norms* (1936). Sherif was born in 1906.

Shiller, Robert J. (1946–). Economist at Yale University. Principal contributions to empirical macroeconomics and finance. Works include "Do Stock Prices Move Too Fast to be Justified by Subsequent Changes in Dividends?" (1981).

Shils, Edward (1911–). Sociologist at the University of Chicago. Principal contributions to sociological theory in general, the study of Max Weber, and the concept of periphery. Author of *Center and Periphery* (1975).

Shubik, Martin (1926–). Economist at Yale University. Principal contribution to game theory. Works include *Game Theory in the Social Sciences* (1982).

Simmel, Georg (1858–1918). German sociologist and philosopher. Major contributions to formal sociology. Works include *The Philosophy of Money* (1907), and *Soziologie* (1908).

Simon, Herbert (1916–). Interdisciplinary scientist at Carnegie-Mellon University who has made contributions to economics, organization theory, psychology, and artificial intelligence. Works include *Administrative Behavior* (1947), and *Models of Man* (1957). Received the Nobel Prize in 1978.

Simons, Henry (1899–1946). Economist who is considered one of the founders of the Chicago School. Major interests in the free enterprise system and taxation.

Smith, Adam (1723–1790). British economist who is considered the father of economics through *The Wealth of Nations* (1776). Also the author of *The Theory of Moral Sentiments* (1759).

Smithies, Arthur (1907–1981). Australian-born economist who spent much of his career at Harvard University. Major interests included macroeconomics and the U.S. budgetary process.

Sombart, Werner (1863–1941). Flamboyant German economic historian and member of the Youngest Historical School. Author of *Der Moderne Kapitalismus* (1902, 1916–1927).

Spence, Michael A. (1943–). Economist at Harvard University most known for his work in the area of market structure and performance. Author of *Market Signaling* (1974).

Spencer, Herbert (1820–1903). Leading British intellectual in the nineteenth century who was interested, among other things, in sociology. His works include *The Study of Sociology* (1873), and *The Man versus the State* (1884).

Sraffa, Piero (1898–1983). Italian economist who spent his professional life at Cambridge University. Major contributions include the editing of Ricardo's work and *The Production of Commodities by Means of Commodities* (1960).

Stigler, George J. (1911–). Economist at the University of Chicago who has made major contributions to the economics of information, industrial organization, and economic theory in general. Received the Nobel Prize in 1982.

Stiglitz, Joseph E. (1943–). Economist at Princeton University. Major interest in the role of imperfect information in the competitive process.

Sutton, Francis X. (1917–). Sociologist and student of Parsons who later worked for the Ford Foundation. Coauthor of *The American Business Creed* (1956).

Svalastoga, Kaare (1914–). Norwegian-born and U.S.-educated sociologist who spent most of his career at the University of Copenhagen. Main interest in stratification. Author of *Prestige, Class and Mobility* (1959).

Sweezy, Paul (1910–). Leading Marxist economist and author of *The Theory of Capitalist Development* (1942) and, together with Paul A. Baran, *Monopoly Capital* (1966).

Tobin, James (1918–). Economist at Yale University and a major Keynesian economist. Contributions to Keynesian macro-models, growth theory, and other areas. Received the Nobel Prize in 1981.

de Tocqueville, Alexis (1805–1859). Nineteenth century intellectual claimed today by political science as well as sociology. Author of *Democracy in America* (1835, 1840).

Tullock, Gordon (1922–). Economist at George Mason University who has helped to pioneer the use of the economic approach to political topics. Coauthor of *The Calculus of Consent* (1962).

Turner, Donald F. (1921–). Lawyer and professor of law who has spent most of his career at the Harvard Law School. Turner was in charge of the antitrust division at the U.S. Department of Justice during the period 1965 to 1968.

Tversky, Amos. Psychologist at Stanford University. Principal contribution to the analysis of the limitations on rational decision making in works coauthored with Daniel Kahneman, e.g., "The Framing of Decisions and the Psychology of Choice" (1981).

Veblen, Thorstein (1857–1929). Economist and sociologist who helped to pioneer the institutionalist approach. Works include *The Theory of the Leisure Class* (1899), and *The Theory of Business Enterprise* (1904).

Vickrey, William (1914–). Canadian-born economist at Columbia University. Principal contributions to taxation, marginal cost pricing, and public choice theory. Works include *Agenda for Progressive Taxation* (1949), and *Microstatics* (1964).

Walras, Léon M.-E. (1834–1910). French-born economist who was active in Switzerland and who became one of the cofounders of marginal utility theory. Also the first to produce a general equilibrium model.

Weber, Max (1864–1920). German sociologist and one of the founders of modern sociology. Pioneered historical sociology, political sociology, and the sociology of religion. Author of such works as *The Protestant Ethic and The Spirit of Capitalism* (1904–1905), and *Economy and Society* (posthumously published).

Welsh, Finis R. (1938–). Economist at University of California at Los Angeles. Contributions to the study of the relationship between income and schooling, race differences in income, and patterns of lifetime earnings.

Wilson, James Q. Educator at Harvard University with major research interests in such areas as urban affairs and crime. Works include the co-authored *Crime and Human Nature* (1985).

Wilson, William Julius (1935–). One of the foremost sociological experts on race relations in the United States. Author of *The Declining Significance of Race* (1978), and *The Truly Disadvantaged* (1987).

Zeckhauser, Richard J. (1940–). Economist at the Kennedy School of Government at Harvard University. Principal contributions to policy analysis, agency theory, and population studies.

Index